# TRAUMATIZING THEORY

# CONTEMPORARY THEORY SERIES

Series Editor: Frances L. Restuccia,
Professor of English, Boston College

# TRAUMATIZING THEORY

## THE CULTURAL POLITICS OF AFFECT IN AND BEYOND PSYCHOANALYSIS

---

EDITED BY

## KARYN BALL

OTHER

Other Press
*New York*

Permission to reprint the following is gratefully acknowledged:

Chapter 7: "The Unbridgeable Distance to the Self: Sarah Kofman's Revision of Philosophy." Permission from *Die Philosophin* for English translation rights, Volume 15 (1997): 24–44.
Chapter 9: "Politics in the Age of Sex: Clinton, Leadership, and Love." Permission from the University of Minnesota Press to reprint *Cultural Critique* 46, pp. 241–271.
Chapter 10: "The Subject of True Feeling: Pain, Privacy, and Politics." Permission from the University of Michigan Press to reprint *Cultural Pluralism, Identity Politics, and the Law*, pp. 48–84.
Chapter 11: "Trauma Envy." Permission from the University of Minnesota Press to reprint *Cultural Critique* 46, pp. 272–297.

Production Editor: Mira S. Park
This book was set in 11 pt. Berkeley by Alpha Graphics in Pittsfield, NH.

10 9 8 7 6 5 4 3 2 1

Library of Congress Cataloging-in-Publication Data

Traumatizing theory : the cultural politics of affect in and beyond psychoanalysis / edited by Karyn Ball ; with an introduction by Karyn Ball.
    p. cm.
  Includes bibliographical references and index
  ISBN-13: 978-1-59051-249-4
  ISBN-10: 1-59051-249-9
  1. Psychoanalysis. 2. Psychic trauma. 3. Psychoanalysis and culture.
I. Ball, Karyn.
  RC504.T73 2007
  616.89'17—dc22
                                             2006012508

# Contents

# *Preface*

Other Press is extremely pleased to offer Karyn Ball's lucid, substantive, and serious collection, *Traumatizing Theory: The Cultural Politics of Affect In and Beyond Psychoanalysis*. A page-turner for anyone even remotely drawn to the subject of trauma, *Traumatizing Theory* contains eleven smart treatments of a wide variety of topics—from Deleuze's film theory, to Gerhard Richter, to the quagmire of adoption, to President Clinton as totemic Leader. This is a heterogeneous text in the best sense; there is no single agenda (psychoanalysis itself gets a little beaten up) but rather an energetic, fresh, and profound examination of everything under the black sun.

*Traumatizing Theory* is unmistakably on the cutting edge. The editor and the distinguished writers of her collection move trauma theory into a new postmodern phase. Grounded in history, this multifaceted study embraces philosophers such as Kierkegaard, Nietzsche, Heidegger, and Levinas as well as theorists such as Derrida, Foucault, Lyotard, and Deleuze. *Traumatizing Theory* is also politically savvy as well as, at times, poignantly personal; its theoretical sophistication by no means precludes an acute sensitivity to its delicate subject matter. Keenly aware of the tension between language and pain as well as the insidious trap of investment in the moral capital of trauma that anyone publishing on the topic is apt to fall into, this volume penetrates some of the most excruciating forms of human suffering, partly in an effort to demystify it by transforming its fragile traumatic affects into signification without losing contact with its semiotic traces.

Karyn Ball's collection demonstrates that the Contemporary Theory Series at Other Press is by no means solely dedicated to Lacanian studies. *Traumatizing Theory* epitomizes exactly what this series wants: new theoretical work with crucial practical implications, books that stretch the boundaries of theory as they are currently surveyed and expose the necessary imbrication of theory with the world in which we live our quotidian lives. This series does mean to offer a dwelling place for rich psychoanalytic work, even as it welcomes all theory being produced currently in, for example, feminist, queer, and other political arenas; film studies; or aesthetics. We want to cast an intricately woven but wide net.

*Frances L. Restuccia*
Contemporary Theory Series Editor

# Acknowledgments

The editor would like to acknowledge the gracious support of Dr. Jo-Ann Wallace, formerly Chair of the Department of English and Film Studies, and Dr. Harvey Krahn, formerly Associate Dean of the Faculty of Arts at the University of Alberta, who generously provided the funding for the translation of Astrid Deuber-Mankowsky's essay. I am also very grateful to Angela Facundo for her extensive help with the preparation of the manuscript, and to Jochen Schulte-Sasse, who encouraged me to pursue this project when I had abandoned hope. I dedicate this book to him.

# Contributors

**Karyn Ball** is an Associate Professor specializing in critical and literary theory in the Department of English and Film Studies at the University of Alberta in Edmonton. She edited a special issue of *Cultural Critique* on "Trauma and its Cultural Aftereffects" (46, 2000) and a special issue of *Parallax* (36, 2005) devoted to the concept of "Visceral Reason." Her article "Paranoia in the Age of the World Picture: The Global 'Limits of Enlightenment'" appeared in *Cultural Critique* (61, 2005) and an essay entitled "The Longing for the Material" was published in *differences* (17.1, 2006). Her book, *Disciplining the Holocaust*, will be published by SUNY Press. She is currently working on a second book, *The Entropics of Discourse: Climates of Loss in Contemporary Criticism*, focusing on the vicissitudes of politicized agendas in cultural studies.

**Bettina Bergo** teaches philosophy at the Université de Montreal. She is the author of *Levinas Between Ethics and Politics* and has translated numerous works by Levinas and others. Bergo recently published "Freud's Debt to Philosophy" in Jennifer Radden, ed.,

*Philosophy of Psychiatry: A Companion* (Oxford University Press, 2004); her "'Roulez! Il n'y a rien à voir': Seeing White in Phenomenology and Psychoanalysis" will appear in George Yancy, ed., *Philosophers on Seeing White* (Routledge, forthcoming). She is currently working on a history of anxiety in nineteenth-century philosophy and psychology.

**Lauren Berlant** is Professor of English at the University of Chicago. Author of *The Anatomy of National Fantasy* (1991) and *The Queen of America Goes to Washington City* (1997), she has also edited many books, including *Intimacy* (2001) and *Compassion* (2004). The article that appears in this volume comes from a forthcoming book, *Cruel Optimism*.

**Dominick Bonfiglio** is a freelance translator and a graduate student in Philosophy at the Humboldt-Universität in Berlin.

**Drucilla Cornell** is Professor of Political Science, Women's Studies, and Comparative Literature at Rutgers University. Prior to beginning her life as an academic, Cornell was a union organizer for a number of years. She has written numerous articles on contemporary continental thought, critical theory, grassroots political and legal mobilization, jurisprudence, women's literature, feminism, aesthetics, psychoanalysis, and political philosophy that have appeared in *Critical Inquiry*, *Constellations*, *Signs*, *Hypatia*, *Differences*, *Philosophia Africana*, *Philosophy and Social Criticism*, *International Journal of Philosophy*, *Cultural Critique*, *Cornell Law Review*, *Cardozo Law Review*, *Harvard Law Review*, and *Yale Law Review*. She is part of a published philosophical exchange with Seyla Benhabib, Judith Butler, and Nancy Fraser entitled *Feminist Contentions* (1995). Her work has been translated into French, German, Japanese, Serbo-Croatian, Portuguese, and Spanish. She has also published several books including *Beyond Accommodation: Ethical Feminism, Deconstruction and the Law* (1991, new edition 1999), *The Imaginary Domain: Abortion, Por-*

nography, and Sexual Harrassment (1995), *Just Cause: Freedom, Identity, and Rights* (2000), and, most recently, *Defending Ideals: War, Democracy, and Political Struggles* (2004).

**Astrid Deuber-Mankowsky** is currently Professor of Media Studies at the Ruhr University Bochum. Before her appointment in Bochum, Deuber-Mankowsky taught at the Institute for Cultural Studies at the Humboldt University in Berlin, where she helped to establish the Humboldt University's Gender Studies Program. Deuber-Mankowsky is also a co-founder and editor of *Die Philosophin*, a German language journal devoted to feminist theory and philosophy. *Der frühe Walter Benjamin und Hermann Cohen. Jüdische Werte, Kritische Philosophie, vergängliche Erfahrung* (Vorwerk 8 Verlag, 2000) was awarded the Humboldt University prize for best dissertation. Translations of her writings include "Walter Benjamin's 'Theological-Political Fragment' as a Response to Ernst Bloch's 'Spirit of Utopia'" (*Leo Baeck Institute Year Book* XLVII 2002) and "Woman. The Most Precious Loot in the 'Triumph of Allegory': Gender Relations in Walter Benjamin's Passagen-Werk." *Lara Croft: Cyber Heroine* was translated by Dominick Bonfiglio and published by the University of Minnesota Press in 2005.

**Ole Gram** works in the College of Liberal Arts at the University of Minnesota and has taught at Miami University in Ohio and the University of Minnesota. His article "Left Hook: Brecht, Boxing, and Committed Art" appeared in *XCP—Cross Cultural Poetics* 9 (2001). His "Escape Artists: Germany, Fortress Europe, and the Situationist Rescripting of Travel" is forthcoming in a special issue of *Cultural Critique* 65 (2007) on "Cultures of Finance."

**Eric Kligerman** is an Assistant Professor of German and Slavic Studies at the University of Florida, Gainesville. He has published articles on Daniel Libeskind and Anselm Kiefer. His book *Sites of the Uncanny: Paul Celan and the Visual Arts* will be published in Spring 2007 with Walter de Gruyter Press.

**Juliet Flower MacCannell** is Professor Emerita of Comparative Literature at the University of California Irvine, and has been honored with visiting graduate and distinguished professorships at U. C. Berkeley, Stanford University, and the University of Nevada, Reno. She is the author of several books, including most recently *The Hysteric's Guide to the Future Female Subject* and *The Regime of the Brother: After the Patriarchy*, which both explore the themes of leadership, love, and traumatic seduction. Her current research includes further reflections on the nature of leadership under capitalism, and the peculiar intersections among architecture, film, psychoanalysis, and politics. She has recently published essays on Badiou, J. H. Miller, Rousseau, Freud, Lacan, and Cixous, *Cape Fear*, "Jouissance," and Las Vegas.

**John Mowitt** is a Professor of Cultural Studies and Comparative Literature at the University of Minnesota in the Twin Cities. He was honored as a Scholar of the College, 2000–2003 and was appointed to the School of Social Sciences at the Institute for Advanced Study in Princeton for the academic year 2004–2005. He publishes widely in the areas of cultural studies, critical theory, film, music, and postcolonial studies. He is the author of *Text: The Genealogy of an Antidisciplinary Object* and *Percussion: Drumming, Beating, Striking*, published by Duke University Press in 1992 and 2002, respectively. His latest book is *Re-takes: Postcoloniality and Foreign Film Languages* (University of Minnesota Press, 2004).

**Sara Murphy** currently teaches literary and cultural theory at New York University's Gallatin School for Individualized Study. She is working on a project concerned with the construction of consent in rape law, literature, and psychoanalysis.

**Dorothea Olkowski** is the former Chair of Philosophy and the former Director of Women's Studies at the University of Colorado, Colorado Springs, as well as the author of *Gilles Deleuze and the Ruin of Representation* (1999). She is also the author of *The Universal (In the realm of the sensible)* (Edinburgh and

Columbia University Presses, 2007) and co-editor of *Feminist Interpretations of Merleau-Ponty* (Penn State Press, 2006).

**Susannah Radstone** is Reader in the School of Social Sciences, Media and Cultural Studies at the University of East London. Her essays on cultural theory, psychoanalysis, and memory studies, and on contemporary film and literature have appeared in *Screen, Signs, Cultural Values,* and *Paragraph*. Recent editorial projects include *Contested Pasts: The Politics of Memory and Regimes of Memory* (edited with Katharine Hodgkin, 2003) and *Memory and Methodology* (Berg, 2000). She is currently completing a monograph, *On Memory and Confession: The Sexual Politics of Time*, to be published by Routledge.

# Introduction:
# Traumatizing Psychoanalysis*

KARYN BALL

Since its incipient moments in Freud's first encounters with hypnosis, psychoanalysis has confronted one obstacle after another as its father sought to bestow upon it not only the legitimacy of a science, but the medical value of a cure. Yet as it evolved from Freud's rethinking of Jean-Martin Charcot's observations about hypnosis into a hand-tapping "talking cure," the budding discourse could not shed all of its mystical residues. The suspicion with which it was greeted would only be exceeded by the intensity with which it was reviled not only in its own time, but also thereafter as it made its way overseas. American psychiatry reduced Freudian psychoanalysis to an anachronistic biologism or, in the hands of its Calibans, the American ego-psychologists, into another narrative of progress: a magical summons to a real self that would transcend the shadows of neurotic

*I gratefully acknowledge the work of Angela Facundo, who carefully proofread several drafts of this introduction and provided summaries of the respective contributions that I consulted and occasionally drew upon in the course of my discussion.

anxiety, sexual repression, and a bad (suffocating or distant) mommy. Beyond the Oedipus complex, castration anxiety, guilt, and sexual repression, popular culture did not make much of other, arguably more crucial features of Freudian psychoanalysis: its emphasis on the metapsychology of the drives and the "work" of translation between the latent and the manifest content of dreams that decodes logics of censorship and desire. Though some of its elements were popularized by surrealism as well as film, television, and the confessional circuits of pseudo-existential group therapy venues such as EST in California, its most radical, ambiguous, and far-reaching implications remained, as it were, repressed.

Conventional wisdom among its defenders is that it is the psychoanalytic emphasis on the unconscious and the auto-erotic source of the drives that is most disturbing to laypeople, who are either too puritan, positivistic, or complacent to take it seriously. As Patricia Gherovici notes, Freud himself argued that "the revelations of psychoanalysis inflict a narcissistic wound similar to the one that Copernicus or Darwin produced."[1] She chooses to avoid a "psychoanalytic Catch-22" whereby the opposition to psychoanalysis is assumed to validate its concept of resistance. In exploring this concept, Gherovici observes that when the American disciples of Freud crystallized psychoanalysis into an analysis of resistances, they capitulated to a false dichotomy between the ego and the unconscious. Of course, to convert psychoanalysis into an "optimistic adaptative technique" for dissolving resistances is, as she argues, to dissolve psychoanalysis itself.[2] Many forms of resistance (if not all of them) could be said to stem from the unconscious ego and unconscious narcissism as such. This point in part spurs the Lacanian denunciation of the American revision of Freud, but it does not respond to one of Michel Foucault's most trenchant critiques of the psychoanalytic notion of the unconscious. While Freud's "discovery" of the unconscious presumably unsettles the idealization of a unified, present, and intentional identity, from a

---

1. Gherovici 2000, p. 96.
2. Ibid., p. 97.

post-metaphysical standpoint, it also reinscribes the category of consciousness, albeit by negation.

John Forrester argues that as "Foucault turned away from the archaeology of concepts to the genealogy of practices, so psycho-analysis became less a subversive principle than a propitiously typical, because purged and purified, element in the apparatus of knowledge-power that emerged in the nineteenth century to be-come dominant in the welfare states of the twentieth."[3] Indeed, Foucault's first volume of *The History of Sexuality* calls attention to the ways in which psychoanalysis reproduces a disciplinary will-to-power/knowledge. The question for Foucault is whether the sexual repression that assumes the status of a fulcrum concept for Freudian psychoanalysis is "truly an established historical fact." He asks: "Did the critical discourse that addresses itself to repres-sion come to act as a roadblock to a power mechanism that had operated unchallenged up to that point, or is it not in fact part of the same historical network as the thing it denounces (and doubt-less misrepresents) by calling it 'repression'?"[4] From a Foucauldian standpoint, psychoanalytic praxis reinscribes the repressive hypoth-esis as an epidemiological configuration: if the analysand is able to undo the buried knot of sexual repression brought on by societal censorship and guilt, to disinter the originary trauma that sealed a neurotic fate, then enlightened transformation will follow. Foucault's critique of the repressive hypothesis thus reverses the Enlightenment valuation of reason as a venue of progressive awareness. In his famous introduction to *The History of Sexuality*, Foucault is, once again, re-hearsing a critical repudiation of this narrative of progress that psy-choanalysis reinvents in the same move with which it installs the dark secret that must come into the light. It is as if Foucault were saying that for all its claims to secular authority, to granting intelli-

---

3. Forrester 1997, p. 205. Forrester adds, "Foucault's projected six-volume history of sexuality was conceived of as an archaeology of psychoanalysis, ask-ing how it had become possible for us, we Freudians, to say *this*, to act in *this* way" (p. 205).

4. Foucault 1990, p. 10.

gibility to the irrational behaviors that were formerly attributed to demonic possession or ignored altogether, psychoanalysis is still not secular enough: it has not forsaken the esoteric rituals of the dark-robed priests who claim a hermeneutical omnipotence in relation to the true meaning of the sacred texts and the texts of sin as it were. The psychoanalytic session revises the age-old technology of the confession to elicit symptoms from its subjects. After the priests sought to control their congregations with references to Satan, fire, and brimstone, Freud breathed new life into a confessional legacy by medicalizing the "demons" unleashed by the societal regulation of sexual instincts. Despite its scientific and secular purview, the psychoanalytic session might exorcize neurosis through frank talk in the same way that confession would extract the sin from the man.

Yet as John Rajchman (1985) and Christopher Lane (2001) observe, Foucault was never so absolute in his evaluations of psychoanalysis. Rajchman and Lane remind us that in *Madness and Civilization*, Foucault acknowledges his debt to Lacan's *Rome Discourse* of 1953 for rethinking psychosis as a "language without discourse."[5] Foucault also appreciated Freud, as Lane notes, for going beyond positivism by constituting the basis for "a dialogue with unreason."[6] Foucault more generally affirmed the critical value of psychoanalysis for radically transforming and subtending individual psychology.

In other moments, the Nietzschean skepticism that pervades Foucault's theory of disciplinary power pushes him overboard in his zeal to follow through on a post-Cartesian disarticulation of an ego-psychological fetishism of consciousness. Moreover, Foucault's Nietzschean commitments interfere with his post-Lacanian agenda to uncouple ethics from the drives[7] because he cannot finesse the pitfalls that arise from his efforts to think subjectification without a theory of the latent erotic valence of aggression. Nietzsche

---

5. Lane cites John Rajchman's *Michel Foucault: The Freedom of Philosophy*, p. 20 (Lane 2001, p. 312).

6. Lane cites Foucault, *Madness and Civilization: A History of Insanity in the Age of Unreason*, p. 198 (Lane 2001, p. 314).

7. I am borrowing Lane's phrasing in his characterization of Foucault's critical agenda of 1983 (Lane 2001, p. 330).

understands the will to power as a primal instinct to dominate, which he connects with freedom, creativity, and life itself. Bad conscience is the perversion of this instinct once it is internalized, repressed, and inverted into what Freud in 1924 delineated as the moral form of masochism.[8] Though Foucault eschews the celebration of individual will in Nietzsche's characterizations of the "will to power," a Nietzschean disgust with bad conscience remains ingrained in Foucault's diffusion of power and agency among the productive, contingent, and "microphysical" discursive relations that categorize and regulate subjects.

It is the instinctual valence of Nietzsche's definition of the will to power and bad conscience that vexes Foucault's effort to separate himself from the psychoanalytic emphasis on the drives. Nietzsche's "Second Essay" from *On the Genealogy of Morals* anticipates the Freud of *Civilization and Its Discontents*, who posits a subject traversed by guilt and aggression. As Judith Butler underscores in *The Psychic Life of Power*, this subject's narcissistic desire for love makes it susceptible to super-egoic self-surveillance and regulation (how else to ensure the other's acceptance?).[9] The "civilized" subject's inevitable failure to live up to the idealized expectations it has internalized as conscience or to vouchsafe unconditional absolute approval perpetuates more aggression against those who notice lapses of self-regulation and thereby provoke guilt.[10] Tak-

---

8. In Nietzsche's (1969) words, "This *instinct for freedom* forcibly made latent—we have seen it already—this instinct for freedom pushed back and repressed, incarcerated within and finally able to discharge and vent itself only on itself: that, and that alone, is what the *bad conscience* is in its beginnings" (Section 17, p. 87). See Freud's (2001) "The Economic Problem of Masochism."

9. See Butler 1997 and especially Chapters 2 and 3, "Circuits of Bad Conscience: Nietzsche and Freud" and "Subjection, Resistance, Resignification: Between Freud and Foucault," pp. 62–82 and 83–105.

10. In "'Conscience Doth Make Subjects of Us All'" (*The Psychic Life of Power*, pp. 106–131), Butler (1997) problematizes Louis Althusser's "recoiling" figuration of subjection and internalization that the concept of interpellation presumes:

Conscience cannot be conceptualized as a self-restriction, if that relation is construed as a pregiven reflexivity, a turning back upon itself

ing Butler's lead, if one were to summon the Freud of *Civilization and Its Discontents* to challenge the Foucault of *Discipline and Punish*, the following questions come to the fore: What is the Panoptical subject's desire? And how should we conceptualize the transgressive pleasure that surges up against a regulatory gaze when a repressed and exacerbated will to dominate is let loose on the road, in the workplace, or against those we claim to love?

When I revisit the theory of subjectification in *Discipline and Punish*, I find myself agreeing that power is relational, that visibility reinforces and economizes surveillance, and that subjects caught in the gaslight of the disciplinary gaze will internalize their own regulation rather than risk punishment or ostracism. I am also prepared to admit that such a disciplinary matrix might reproduce itself noncognitively and in the absence of conscious will. I am less able to accept that a subject absorbs and enacts the microphysics of power without an imaginary or affective cathexis that mitigates psychic dissonance.

This is to argue that there is something dissatisfying about Foucault's efforts in *Discipline and Punish* to rethink subjectification beyond consciousness, the libidinal economy, and repression. In Butler's words, this standpoint "presumes the efficacy of the symbolic demand, its performative capacity to constitute the subject whom it names."[11] To my mind, such a theoretical reduction to the symbolic paradoxically underwrites the importance of the psychoanalytic theses on sadomasochism. These theses comprise Foucault's own critical "unconscious"[12] by virtue of the resonances

---

performed by a ready-made subject. Instead, it designates a kind of turning back—a reflexivity—which constitutes the condition of possibility for the subject to form. Reflexivity is constituted through this moment of conscience, this turning back upon oneself, which is simultaneous with a turning toward the law. This self-restriction does not internalize an external law: the model of internalization takes for granted that an "internal" and "external" have already been formed. [114–115]

11. Butler 1997, p. 97.

12. Butler's epigraph to the chapter "Subjection, Resistance, Resignification: Between Freud and Foucault" is a citation from "Rituals of Exclusion,"

that could not have altogether eluded him between Nietzsche's excoriation of bad conscience and Freud's attention to the vicious cycle of death-driven aggression and guilt that belies the discontents of civilization.

Butler observes that Foucault engages with this problem to some extent when he suggests, in *The History of Sexuality*, that subjects take pleasure in their self-surveillance and discipline. I would add that this revision of bad conscience in Nietzsche's sense would appear to render disciplinary modernity sado-masochistic at its core: subjects are always authoritarian in their heart of hearts since they come to enjoy obedience and even take pleasure in the specter of their own well-deserved punishment; they also enjoy scenes of another's punishment (and will crave this prospect if the other seems to partake in more than his or her fair share of animal enjoyment).[13] There is, nonetheless, an *affective layer* to Nietzsche's description of bad conscience that Foucault throws out with the bathwater of the Freudian and Lacanian emphasis on the drives. This layer is missing or, perhaps more aptly, latent in Foucault's theory of subjectification.

---

an interview in which Foucault (1996) acknowledges: "My problem is essentially the definition of the implicit systems in which we find ourselves prisoners; what I would like to grasp is the system of limits and exclusion which we practice without knowing it; I would like to make the cultural unconscious apparent" (p. 73; Butler, p. 82). Butler subsequently notes that "the question of a suppressed psychoanalysis in Foucault" is raised by Foucault himself in his reference to a "cultural unconscious." For Butler, this question might be articulated as

> the problem of locating or accounting for resistance. Where does resistance to or in disciplinary subject formation take place? Does the reduction of the psychoanalytically rich notion of the psyche to that of the imprisoning soul eliminate the possibility of resistance to normalization and to subject formation, a resistance that emerges precisely from the incommensurability between psyche and subject? How would we understand such resistance, and would such an understanding entail a critical rethinking of psychoanalysis along the way? [p. 87]

13. In this connection, see Wendy Brown's (2001) "The Desire to be Punished: Freud's 'A Child is being Beaten,'" in *Politics Out of History* pp. 45–61, and her forthcoming book, *Regulating Aversion: Tolerance in the Age of Identity and Empire.*

Forrester, Rajchman, Lane, and Butler open up the value of psychoanalysis "after" Foucault to reflect on the reciprocal determinations among subject formation, power, and desire. In some measure, dwelling on the inconsistencies in Foucault's postmetaphysical dialogue with psychoanalysis frees us from the less interesting issue of whether it is a science or an art.[14] We might see it instead as a discourse about *economies of affect*—a discourse whose history is fraught with the politics of its changing reception and which cautions us, as Charles Shepherdson incisively observes, against considering the domains of nature and culture "as absolute points of reference."[15]

The legacy of psychoanalysis after Foucault informs the current institutional preoccupation with the social and political dynamics of affect. What the essays in this volume hold in common is their impetus to explore the coalescence of the personal, cultural, social, and political registers of affect not only in the realm of events, but also in the arena of theory itself. In different ways, each takes up the question of how attempts to represent and transmit trauma, mourning, and melancholy between and among generations are inseparable from the ongoing contestation about the authority of any framework of representation (including theory). Many of the contributors to this volume reevaluate psychoanalytic concepts in order to theorize the dynamics of affective investiture between the private and public realms. How does psychoanalysis enable us to conceptualize the circulation and vicissitudes of various kinds of affect that alternatively link and divide the private and public domains? How does psychoanalysis as a discourse of subject forma-

---

14. In his evaluation of the "Freud Wars" inside and in response to psychoanalysis, Forrester (1997) asks us to consider what "changes in our general categories are required by recognizing that psychoanalysis is both an art *and* a science?" What happens to these categories once we recognize that psychoanalysis "has produced in the analyst a cultural figure whose work is aesthetic as much as it is investigative . . . and has made available to the patient the opportunity to render his or her life a work of art, a narrative of chance and destiny as well as a thriller, whether psychological or otherwise"? (p. 5).

15. Shepherdson 2001, p. 7.

tion, desire, pleasure, and the traumatic secret disarticulate and/ or "territorialize" (to borrow Deleuze and Guattari's vocabulary) the presumed boundary between the individual and the collective? Perhaps more importantly, what are the limits of psychoanalysis as a framework that allows us to broach and to answer these questions? Do certain objects of socio-cultural analysis expose and thereby "wound" its ideology or call for new frameworks?

To respond to these questions, this volume will begin with the premise that psychoanalysis needs, initially, to be remembered as a "traumatizing theory" in its own right. Not only does it seek to take the "passions" seriously in a way that goes beyond the complacent myths of different generations who alternately identify them as dangerous, excessive, or honorable. Freud's perspective also exposes the modes in which modern society is burdened by its own presumed enlightenment insofar as it restricts the expression of feeling, pleasure, and desire, thereby feeding a human propensity for self-destruction and violence. From this standpoint, psychoanalysis is "traumatic" because it forces us to confront our instinctual residues in order to avoid becoming more bestial still.

Bettina Bergo offers us a historical perspective on the milieu in which Freud first introduced his conceptualization of hysteria. As Bergo acknowledges, once he identifies examples of so-called "male hysterics," Freud psychologizes a condition that was previously assumed to be anatomically specific to women. By displacing it from its "proper" origin in the woman's womb to a trauma- and anxiety-based causality, Freud disarticulates its gender specificity and thereby universalizes the condition of hysteria. This move scandalized the medical community of Freud's time. Patriarchal practitioners presumed that such anxiety was exclusively the effect of feminine hysteria, which allowed them to pathologize women as the weaker and instrinsically irrational sex. According to Freud, everyone can be and, indeed, is subject to such potentially pathological anxiety, which requires mechanisms to control it either through sublimation or release.

Bergo's treatment of the relationship between hysteria and anxiety is genealogical. It emphasizes how the ever fluctuating cultural meanings of these conditions both in Freud's time and in the history of ideas provided the backdrop in which he could destabilize essentialist concepts of femininity and otherness in general. An anti-Semitic milieu naturally strengthened the suspicion with which he was held as a Jewish researcher and intensified the disturbing impact of his ideas about male hysteria when he announced them in Paris. In Bergo's words, "an 'other,' Freud, was holding a mirror up to a society in whose eyes he was largely a 'guest.'" Bergo hereby highlights the significance of anti-Semitism in cultivating the liberal and universalist elements in Freud's work, which, despite its debt to Darwin, attenuated biologistic and racial hierarchies that naturalized social and political ones along with the gendered logic that shaped scientific and cultural discourses concerning the passions.

Bergo's essay foregrounds the value of Freud's challenge to the philosophical doctrine that insisted upon rational autonomy: the power of individual reason to master the passions. Her contribution is part of a larger project on discourses of the passions across the disciplines as well as the intersections between psychoanalysis and philosophy. The article is also devoted to the concept of anxiety between Kierkegaard and Heidegger in anticipation of Lévinas's reflections on an ethical subjectivity that is constituted intersubjectively in the other's approach. In contrast to Heidegger, Lévinas embraces the ethical dimension of anxiety as a reflection of responsibility for the vulnerable other.

Like Bergo, Dorothea Olkowski and Sara Murphy are also interested in exploring the relationship between anxiety and vulnerability in their respective considerations of the implications of Freud's ambivalent legacy for feminism and trauma theory. Olkowski begins "Catastrophe" with the story of a young woman who survived a rape, yet remains fearful and even agoraphobic in its aftermath. Alienating responses to her generalized fear hysterize this sense of vulnerability, thereby rendering it "irrational" on a psychic level and unintelligible on a social level. Olkowski juxtaposes this incident with one of Freud's famous cases: his study of

Katharina who claims to have witnessed her uncle's sexual relations with her cousin. Freud reads this scenario as a screen memory for Katharina's repressed seduction by her own father. What is provocative about this juxtaposition is how it highlights the misogynist residues in Freud's case studies. Such residues counteract the potentially universalist disposition of his rethinking of neurotic anxiety, which draws from his examination of hysteria. In this manner, Olkowski implicitly calls on us to reconsider Freud's suppression of the seduction hypothesis in which he broadened the implications of his female patients' allusions to incest by foregrounding their status as fantasies.

Though she begins with an account of the alienating aftermath of sexual violation for a young woman, Olkowski is not invested in resurrecting a conventional feminist critique of Freud. Her intervention targets the very metaphysics that overdetermines Freud's account of the relationship between the organic and individual dimensions of the psyche in the *Project for a Scientific Psychology*. This metaphysics leads him to represent the psychic apparatus as a closed system. Olkowski implies that this representation is reflected in an equally arbitrary assumption about the closure of the ego, which must face off against a barrage of stimuli from within and without.

In the *Project*, the Freudian subject is systemically governed by the aim of neutralizing "unpleasure" defined as excitations that disrupt the smooth running of the psyche. The problem with this model is that life processes cease to function if the ultimate goal of psychical mastery through quiescence is ever attained. Olkowski rightly interrogates this model by proposing that "the exigencies of life" that threaten stability are nonetheless essential to it; they cannot be used as a categorical prescription to define the "uncontrollable" woman's body. Olkowski insists upon the possibility for life in an open system that incessantly breaks down homogeneity.

This critique positions Olkowski to assert a less mechanistic *topos* of the psyche through Henri Bergson's concept of an open whole. This *topos* subtends the dichotomy between rationality, common sense, and the inhibition of stimuli on the one hand, and the "catastrophic" and "traumatic" loss of endogenous equilibrium on the other, which, in Freud's framework, quantitatively overwhelms rather than qualitatively transforms perception and memory. In questioning this dichotomy, Olkowski also challenges the gendered logic entailed by a "science" that polarizes pleasure and unpleasure. Mastery through repetition, stability, uniformity, sublimation—all of these forms serve the narcissistic investment in a closed system, presumably for the purposes of survival.

The originality of Olkowski's critical engagement with *The Project* comes to the fore in the style with which she relentlessly lays bare the economic and mechanistic presuppositions that ultimately restrict the Freudian subject. Olkowski does not adopt a typical distance or separation from Freud's work. Instead, she ironically ventriloquizes Freud to emphasize the ambiguities and contradictions implicit in his analysis of excitation within the nervous system and its resulting qualitative characteristics, pleasure and unpleasure. Her "channeling" of Freud "traumatizes" psychoanalysis itself by exposing its limits from the inside.

While Olkowski subtends the metaphysics of Freud's model of a psychophysical system that is vulnerable because it is closed, Murphy problematizes the gendering of vulnerability in the context of rape prevention pedagogy. In "Traumatizing Feminism: Prevention Discourse and the Subject of Sexual Violence," Murphy returns to the history of Freud's work with women patients in the 1890s. She notes that, in Freudian psychoanalysis, a "form of sexual violence provides the occasion for the groundwork of the classic psychoanalytic moment." Freud initially attributed the symptoms evinced by his female analysands to instances of sexual abuse. Yet by the late 1890s, as reflected in his exchange with Wilhelm Fliess, Freud withdraws from this understanding of the origin of the neurotic symptom when he abandons the "seduction hypothesis" for a theory of fantasy. Murphy observes that, in part, the feminist repudiation of Freud stemmed from his apparent elision of the traumatic reality of women's lives, which was displaced and trivialized by his theory of fantasy.[16] In her reevaluation of this development in Freud's thinking, Murphy's argument coincides with Bergo's in their recognition that, "after the abandonment of the seduction hypothesis, the hysteric became one way—*in extremis*—of discussing what for Freud was a basic structure of subjectivity."

Moving beyond the issue of whether incestuous seductions are real or fantasized, Murphy explores the ways in which the construction of harm that underlies the psychiatric paradigm hystericizes rape victims individually and collectively before and after the crime. Murphy acknowledges that while Freud's turn toward fantasy led to anti-Freudianism among feminists, rape-prevention discourse reinstaurates its materiality by reanimating the stereotype of the hysterical woman. This reanimation constructs the rape victim as an eternally vulnerable subject who must remain vigilant against the imminent prospect of violence against her in order to prevent it. Through her analysis of the prevention video *Campus Rape*, Murphy exposes how the pedagogical ethos and format of feminist anti-violence discourse deals with rape as a social problem, yet targets women's subjectivity and agency rather than rape itself; this discourse consequently risks perpetuating stereotypes of female identity as a weak version of the liberal individual whose freedom is bound up with his self-mastery in the face of internal and external onslaughts. In their concentration on victim subjectivity, preventative videos and other materials paradoxically link freedom and agency to acceptable codes of behavior that ultimately regulate the victim. The presumed efficacy of this regulation therefore pivots on women's acceptance of their vulnerability. As Murphy ironically notes, this feminist "recovery" of agency for women through consciousness-raising spurs the evolution of the stereotype of hypersexualized women into passive exchange objects between "lawless men" and "masculine institutions"

---

16. In *The Freud Wars*, John Forrester (1997) attributes some of this suspicion to feminists of the late 1970s who, in his characterization, turned from rape to child abuse "as their new crusade." For such "crusaders," "Freud and all the institutions of psychoanalysis became deeply suspect for having highlighted fantasy and desire, rather than brute reality and sexual exploitation" (p. 3).

of law. This discourse affects political paralysis, as Wendy Brown has argued, by virtue of its tendency to entrench identification in a monolithic amalgamation of individuals suffering from distinct events into a single object of inquiry.[17] Such suffering becomes ideologically necessary so long as the discourse striving for its eradication remains invested in the moral capital of traumatic pathos and empathetic identification with the victims.

Murphy draws on Mark Seltzer's notion of "wound culture" to problematize the boundaries between the discrete liberal individual who can be personally traumatized and a culture in which the ideology of individualism is merely the currency for alienation and anomie.[18] It is the blurring of these boundaries that impels a longing to recover a fully saturated meaning from viscera, which retain the power to puncture a reifying fog of spectacle. This longing is evinced in a scopophiliac fascination with the blood and guts spilled in accidents or the more figurative innards of others let loose through confession. Murphy's work has led her to this issue by virtue of the ways in which rape-prevention pedagogy relies on testimony from victims who make the sacrifice of revisiting their traumas on record in the interests of teaching women how they might avoid the same fate. The guarantee of a "safe and respectful space" for such testimony inadvertently compels raped women to fit into a confessional mold, which serves to affirm the efficacy and authority of the pedagogical materials. In exchange for a public recognition of her feelings, the victim willingly officiates the "mistake" she presumably committed in not properly internalizing her prescribed vulnerability prior to her violation. Despite their feminist ethos, these materials thus subjectify women as proto-victims who, after violence, must accept *responsibility* for their vulnerability. This subjectification functions to contain the radical openness of the aftermath of "catastrophe," as Olkowski has conceptualized

---

17. See Brown, *States of Injury: Power and Freedom in Late Modernity* (1995) and *Politics Out of History* (2001).

18. Seltzer 1998.

it, by implanting it within a closed redemptive economy that forces the confessing woman and her audience to admit the specificity of her risk *avant la lettre*. Only in this way might she retrieve her agency as a liberal individual who takes responsibility for her own needs (and pays any debts to society that accrue when she fails).

Bergo and Murphy read Freud as moving away from the hystericization of woman via the symptom and toward a hystericization of the symptom as a signifier of the vexed formation of the subject. This reading underscores the shifting status of repression in the psychoanalytic account of trauma. The issue is whether traumatic aftereffects should be conceived in terms of latency and belatedness, or "deferred action," in keeping with Freud's early formulations of neurotic development. This account assumes that an initial sexually loaded event is not actually experienced or known by a child and that it remains latent until a subsequent crisis or resonant event reactivates it in later years. In this formulation, the traumatic symptom is, as Murphy suggests, "formed through deferred action, that is to say, that memory revises and rearranges in accord with new information and new stages of development." Murphy adds, "It is this revision that is central to the production of symptoms, as the subject attempts to repress the new knowledge of old experience."

There are different ways of reading belatedness within Freud's work as well as its revision by subsequent trauma theorists. In *Beyond the Pleasure Principle*, Freud remarks the odd character of dreams occurring in traumatic neuroses that repeatedly bring the patient back into the situation of his accident. For Freud, the main point at stake here is that traumatic repetition appears to contradict his thesis from the *Traumdeutung* to the effect that dreams enact the fulfillment of repressed wishes. The veterans' compulsory return to painful scenes spurs Freud's reflections about a primal destructive urge "beyond the pleasure principle" that goads the psyche to neutralize tensions—to strive toward the excitation-free existence of inorganic matter and, thus, "to die in its own way." If *Beyond the Pleasure Principle* eventuates in this radical metaphysics of the death drive, then it is because Freud can only recuperate the thesis on wish fulfillment by translating it into a theory of primary masochism.

Cathy Caruth interprets Freud's observations in *Beyond the Pleasure Principle* about World War I veterans' nightmares as indicating the "surprising *literality* and nonsymbolic nature of traumatic dreams and flashbacks, which resist the cure to the extent that they remain, precisely, literal."[19] Without referring to Bergson, it is almost as if Caruth adopts a Proustian notion of involuntary (pure) memory, which is suddenly summoned into the present by a chance encounter with a Madeleine:

> It is this literality and its insistent return which thus constitutes trauma and points toward its enigmatic core: the delay or incompletion in knowing, or even in seeing, an overwhelming occurrence that then remains, in its insistent return, absolutely *true* to the event. It is indeed this truth of traumatic experience that forms the center of its pathology or symptoms; it is not a pathology, that is, of falsehood or displacement of meaning, but of history itself. If PTSD must be understood as a pathological symptom, then it is not so much a symptom of the unconscious, as it is a symptom of history. The traumatized, we might say, carry an impossible history within them, or they become themselves the symptom of a history that they cannot entirely possess.[20]

Ruth Leys and Dominick LaCapra have castigated Caruth for this model of traumatic belatedness, which according to LaCapra, conflates trauma and history. LaCapra wants to safeguard the distinction between "ontological," or "structural," trauma that he associates with the psychoanalytic account of neurosis, and what he calls "historical" trauma to refer to specific events and their consequences. For LaCapra, this distinction reflects different orders of reality: structural trauma is rooted in a subject's sense of "lack" that results from an inability to master his or her signification either for him- or herself or others. It is the absence of this mastery,

---

19. Caruth 1995, p. 5.
20. Ibid.

then, that becomes the negative pivot of the subject's neurotic constitution. Historical trauma, in contrast, is triggered by an actual loss rather than an unconscious absence.[21]

LaCapra's distinction between ontological and historical trauma on the one hand and absence and loss on the other is meant to ensure our recognition of the materiality of traumatic history in part to respect the painful realities of genocide and bereavement. Yet historical materiality, which LaCapra emphasizes on ethical grounds, is not literality in Caruth's sense. Caruth is interested in the experience of epistemological disjuncture signaled by the literality of traumatic memories. In contrast, LaCapra's respect for historical actuality does not hinge on a notion of "pure" memory that, by definition, has not been distorted or informed by any interpretative perspective. Indeed, his standpoint stipulates that memories and interpretations are mediated by ethnic, national, disciplinary, and/or transferential identifications that should be acknowledged in any genuinely critical reflection about the past.

Leys sees Caruth's reading of repression as a "radical reconfiguration of psychoanalysis in which the traumatic nightmare is defined as an 'unclaimed experience'—as a literal, nonsymbolic, and nonrepresentational *memory* of the traumatic event."[22] Leys argues that this conceptualization of latency is etiological in its implication that the traumatic event resembles an infectious disease "in which an 'incubation period' or period of delay intervenes between the initial infection and the subsequent appearance of the symptoms, than to Freud's concept of *Nachträglichkeit*."[23] This model tends to construct trauma as an external "foreign body" rather than acknowledging the ways in which trauma may be internal and, indeed, constitutive of subjectivity. It is for this reason that Leys accuses Caruth of "linear determinism, or direct action, of the past on the present."[24]

---

21. LaCapra 2001.
22. Leys 2000, p. 272. Leys's emphasis.
23. Ibid., pp. 271.
24. Ibid., p. 271.

The question that LaCapra's and Leys's respective critiques of Caruth raises is whether a notion of literality is logically necessary or morally desirable to found a recognition of the materiality of an event and its affective consequences. Leys, for her part, is right to point out that Caruth has radically reconfigured the Freudian perspective by ascribing literality to a trauma that returns in dreams. Freud's account treats the symptom as a material sign of the psychic reality of a current experience regardless of whether the past trauma to which it relates is "literal," or wholly or partly fantasized. In comparison, Caruth's formulation of latency suggests a need to affirm the materiality of a traumatic memory by removing it from the realm of fantasy. It is a materiality that remains, somehow, hermetically sealed and also, seemingly, unrepresentable (to the extent that memory as a mode of symbolization draws on fantasy). In a sense, then, this materiality can only be known by its negation.

For Leys, this standpoint aligns Caruth with a tradition of speaking about trauma, and the Holocaust in particular, as a sublime episode insofar as the magnitude and the intensity of the suffering it convenes transcends our ability to comprehend it in a single intuition. The assumption here is that our conceptual categories, and indeed, our language, are insufficient to do justice to so much pain and irredeemable loss. Yet it is notable that this rhetoric of unrepresentability is qualified by one of its inaugurators, Jean François Lyotard, when he proclaims historical judgment impossible in the absence of a single genre for determining its rules and aims, but nevertheless acknowledges its necessity: one must judge anyway. In *The Differend*, Lyotard guides us toward a recognition of the circumstances that differentiate and defer the signification of experience and memory and that trouble the empirical foundations of demonstration in the instance of historical testimony.[25] What is more, this *différance* also derails notions of experience as ontological property. The problem that Lyotard's position raises for Caruth is whether anyone can ever "claim" a "literal" experience. Lyotard's negative-aesthetic solution is elegant if not alto-

---

25. Lyotard 1988.

gether satisfying as a means of moving beyond empirical and ontological models of experience: we "feel" rather than "know" that an injustice has taken place that has been left in abeyance because of the silences that mark its wake. The question is therefore worth reiterating: How do we account for the materiality of this affect that Lyotard understands as a sign of a catastrophe over and against the determinism that Leys associates with Caruth's literalism?

One of the lessons I draw from Murphy concerns the problematic deployment of rape testimony, which moves dangerously close to the disciplinary technology of confession as Foucault understands it. In "Social Bonds and Psychical Order: Testimonies," Susannah Radstone explores a complexity not often acknowledged in Holocaust and trauma studies when she reintroduces the specificity of testimony within a confessional culture. Testimony, for Radstone, is a practice that aims to bear witness to the suffering of others and therefore cannot simply be elided with the technology of confession. Radstone observes that what she refers to as "Manichean" testimony dominates the genre at the expense of testimony about an ethical "gray zone," a term she borrows from Primo Levi to emphasize the ways in which "'one is never in another's place.'" Manicheanism insists on the unequivocal positions of victim and perpetrator. It calls for testimony that reproduces these identifications and thereby allows its hearers to retain their sense of "Holocaust piety," as Gillian Rose terms it: to identify solely with the innocent victims and to refuse potential complicity or identification with the perpetrators. This perspective encourages self-righteous responses to survivor testimony that serve to separate its hearers morally from prisoners forced to help with the cremation and cleanup following mass gassings in the death camps. In Radstone's reading, Levi enjoins us to see these extreme situations as limit cases that should unsettle our assumptions about what human beings are capable of as victims and perpetrators.

Radstone's distinction between the "Manichean" and "gray zone" modalities of testimony is valuable for the insight it brings to bear on the social and moral conflicts that determine our responses to testimony. First, this distinction illuminates how testimony of the Manichean order might incorporate the disciplinary valence of confession. Manichean testimony reproduces subjectification in Foucault's sense to the extent that it reveals the subject's desire to regulate itself even in the realm of the sympathetic imagination, which draws on fantasy.[26] In identifying with the victim, the hearer of such testimony imaginatively occupies and enjoys morally acceptable positions. Second, Radstone also speculates on the social conditions that foment the predominance of this mode of testimony over a gray zone form that enjoins questions about our complicity, at the very least on the level of fantasy, with the perpetrators' mentality.

Radstone sees the turn toward Manichean testimony and confession as a hypostatization of self-censure that registers "a one-sided struggle to resuscitate the superego in the absence of appropriate ideational objects. Its emphatic foregrounding of the dividedness of the inner world—its marking out of a *growing* distance between its protagonist and its self-censuring narrator marks out, too, the beginnings of a breakdown in relations between the ego and the superego." Her thesis is that the superego that commands such self-regulation has arisen in relation to certain recent historical developments emerging in the nineteenth century (according to Raymond Williams) that undermine a sense of community and also render the relationship with authority more diffuse. This diffusion makes it more difficult for subjects to internalize authority, to fantasize a resolution to their anger and resistance against it and its aggression; the absence of internalized personal authority therefore infringes on imaginary venues for working through the alienation and hostility that subjects feel in response to an antagonist they cannot locate.

In speculating on the relationship between the psychic and social conditions in which testimony is received, Radstone extends

---

26. For a more in-depth consideration of the implications of Radstone's essay and the sadomasochistic dimension of the sympathetic imagination, see my "Unspeakable Differences, Obscene Pleasures: The Holocaust as an Object of Desire" (Ball 2003).

the parameters of an inquiry into how to conceptualize affective phenomena as effects of both sociohistorical developments and the relations that reproduce their status in the current context. This standpoint has implications for the way I would like to read Caruth in light of and despite of her critics. I have already mentioned that Leys has criticized Caruth for adopting the position that the experience of history always remains "unclaimed" at an epistemological level as it transpires. To claim this experience requires that witnessing subjects allow themselves to be traumatized by its belated return. In Leys's view, this position converts all subjects of history into its witnesses who might inherit the traumas of others like an epidemic. On another level, Caruth is raising a more profound question about the knowability of any present as it takes place.

Caruth herself seems to bypass this question when she identifies PTDS as a "symptom of history" rather than a symptom of the unconscious. This distinction actually moves her closer to LaCapra's position than his critique of her allows. It also circumvents the potential relationship between history and the unconscious, to which Caruth's own readings of Freud's *Moses and Monotheism* attest.[27] The cultural politics that inform the writing of theory as reflected in the circumstances that surrounded Freud's divided writing of *Moses and Monotheism*, his departure from Vienna to avoid deportation and murder by the Nazis, destabilize this text's concerns. Here the prospect of literal memory is evacuated by the figurative and rhetorical dimensions of theory as well as by the unconscious content of its own form. Such forms may be treated as a sociohistorical and symptomatic materialization of the affective responses to the events and circumstances that inspire and coerce its inception. Psychoanalysis humbles our desire to attribute too much conscious intention to any art, literature, or theory, yet the recognition that not all elements in a work are intentional does not undermine our power to treat them as material to its meaning.

---

27. Caruth 1996.

This lesson might spur us to revisit the relationship between form as a sociohistorical effect and the unconscious as a repository for the traces of unprocessed and potentially traumatic experience. How might we think about form both as a product of history and as a response to or deflection of the affective "excess" of catastrophic events without any recourse to a theory of consciousness or to the unconscious as its supplement?

Olkowski implicitly raises this question when she evokes the Bergsonian concept of an open whole to counter Freud's reliance on the model of a closed thermodynamic system. In "Traumatic Concepts: Latency and Crisis in Deleuze's Evolutionary Theory of Cinema," I explore Deleuze's use of Bergson's *Creative Evolution* and *Matter and Memory* to consider the prospect of bearing witness to traumatic history through cinematic form, which he represents as a mode of thought. In seeking to move beyond psychoanalytic treatments of film, which focus on plot and character as surfaces that belie oedipal and otherwise repressed sexual conflicts, Deleuze reads the history of cinema as working through the differences between the "ancient" and "modern" standpoints on the relationship between space and time. While early cinema subordinated time to an idealized and immobile space, in part due to its reliance on the still-standing camera, post–World War II cinema increasingly converted time into an independent variable in keeping with Deleuze's definition (via Bergson) of the modern or "natural" standpoint. At this juncture, cinema no longer depends on the movement-image, which clearly connects perception and action. Instead, we increasingly see a cinema of the time-image, which enables an experience of the virtual whole of time to arise in tension-filled "intervals" wherein action is no longer anchored to perception or does not take place.

Nevertheless, to the extent that this evolutionary stage remains "latent" within early cinema, it would be difficult to say whether Deleuze's heuristic allows him completely to elude a psychoanalytic configuration of trauma. For it is, as Deleuze indicates, the traumas of World War II that exposed the failure to judge on time (to intervene against genocide), thereby placing the perception-action circuit in crisis and precipitating the proliferation of the time-image as a sign that cinematic thought has evolved. The historical traumas of World War II, the death camps, and Hiroshima are hereby presented by Deleuze as an unthought in Maurice Blanchot's sense: they cannot be "known" in the present; the magnitude of the injustice that was left in abeyance can only be indicated belatedly in the films of Hitchcock for example, which enunciate the passivity of the spectators in forcing us to witness violent crimes at close range. Here, the spectator is prevented from assuming a pious identification with victims that Radstone associates with Manichean constructions of testimony. Rather the viewer is implicated as a voyeur by the camera in the perpetration of the crime and in the lag between its perception and the action that might bring the perpetrators to justice.

Whether or not we are persuaded by his narrative of evolution and crisis, Deleuze does offer another philosophical model for reflecting on the ways in which a socio-cultural phenomenon attests to the history that led up to it as well as the conditions of its development. In addition, Deleuze's focus on *auteur* cinema positions him to foreground the potential of cinematic form to serve as an artistic medium of testimony. Because of its status as art, cinema can therefore be understood as absorbing, refracting, and acting out the return of repressed history on the level of its form. Eric Kligerman's contribution to this volume explores the ambivalence of this potential in the work of Gerhard Richter.

In "The Phantom Effect: The Return of the Dead in Gerhard Richter's *October 18, 1977 Cycle*," Kligerman reflects on the cultural politics of Holocaust memory in Germany. Kligerman begins by commenting on the reception of Richter's *October* series in the context of the Museum of Modern Art (MOMA) show at the Neue National Gallerie in the summer of 2004. What is odd about this reception, as Kligerman notes, is that while Richter himself saw this 1988 series as conveying a "theme of provocation," discussions about its homecoming deflected the political and traumatic implications of the fifteen paintings placed in a crypt-like space at the end of the exhibit. Kligerman's analysis of the series draws on

Freud's definition of screen memories as well as Abraham and Torok's concept of transgenerational haunting in order to explore the historical implications of Richter's use of the blurring technique in the *October 18, 1977 Cycle*. This technique reanimates an affective connection with the Holocaust through memories of the German Autumn of 1977 and the officially proclaimed "suicides" of key first-generation RAF members Andreas Baader, Gudrun Ensslin, and Jan Carl Raspe in the Stammheim prison. According to Kligerman's reading of Freud, screen memories form "out of a process of displacement and condensation" that allows them to substitute for "significant childhood impressions that are repressed." An essential component of the screen memory is its apparent irrelevance, which belies the interference of some other disturbing factor; it therefore surprises us that we have them at all. Kligerman argues that Richter turns the structure of screen memories into a technique that precipitates precisely this uncanny sense of surprise, an effect that reverses and counteracts inherited repression between generations. This technique serves to reanimate "affectively diminished memory by requiring the spectator to connect imprints concealed behind the blurring." Richter's blurring technique thereby compels the viewer to take an active role in forging associations between two traumatic memories. Hence as Kligerman suggests, "In his *October* series, Richter confronts the spectator with a palimpsest of two moments of censored memory: the memory of the Holocaust that Richter tried but failed to paint in 1964 and its screen memory via the *October* paintings," which are based on the photographs of the RAF taken by the police and displayed in the *Stern* magazine. Spectators are provoked to build an affective bridge to the mass murders and to a mourning that never effectively took place among the World War II generations of non-Jewish Germans, but that transgenerationally haunts their children (including the RAF) coming of age in the 1960s and 1970s as an inherited trace of their parents' traumatic shame. In this respect, then, the muted reception of the *October* series in the context of the 2004 MOMA exhibit in Berlin raises questions about the power of art to overcome the repression of World War II atrocities that are encrypted in melancholic fixations among the war and postwar generations. A related question is whether a more direct identification with traumatic history can transcend melancholic paralysis.

Kligerman's essay highlights a vacillation between melancholy and mourning in works that reflect on the Holocaust in particular and traumatic history in general. Such vacillation also surfaces in Sarah Kofman's concept of philosophy and her autobiographical writings. Deuber-Mankowsky's essay celebrates Kofman's defamiliarization of the concept of philosophy that detaches it from metaphysical binaries and insists upon its inextricable bond to life, desire, and the uncanny. According to Kofman, philosophy is a result of its author's traumatic experience, a situation that leaves philosophy in a state of flux as it becomes conditioned by personal and collective history. Kofman differentiates herself from Jean-Jacques Rousseau, whose philosophy represses an "original ambivalence" that occurs at birth, in which man presumably loses his strength by gaining mortality, life remains bound to death, and undecidability permeates all thinking. Rousseau carries this repression out by instilling a binary logic in his writing between the masculine and the feminine that doubly denigrates and splits off the feminine as the uncanny embodiment of a dangerous alterity. This denigration allows him to disavow the feminine as an external threat, which he can nonetheless master through philosophy. Kofman's self-negation through a "writing without power" is a reproof against Rousseau who "not only censures the feminine, but splits away the uncanny from the self into the foreign and exiles it to the external." Kofman, in contrast, appropriates and redeems alterity from a misogynist binary. In a Nietzschian spirit, Kofman strives toward freeing philosophy from a narcissism that employs such binaries to confirm the identity of the One, writing instead to redeem the heterogeneity of the relations between philosophy and life as a new ethical unity.

According to Deuber-Mankowsky, Kofman's critique of Rousseau and others including Immanuel Kant, Auguste Comte, Friedrich Nietzsche, and Sigmund Freud demonstrates a method of reading that reorients texts to discover the "utterly uncanny" effects of life:

"the way that life not only threatens the subject in its integrity, but subverts it and pulls it out of joint." In this vein, as Deuber-Mankowsky notes, Kofman's engagement with Freud seeks to free his psychoanalysis from a metaphysics of consciousness/unconsciousness, primary/secondary, dark/light, and masculine/feminine. This engagement serves as a departure point for her own effort to rediscover the "repressed desire for life in metaphysical texts." She thereby provides a model for recovering the materiality of affect in and as philosophy that goes beyond psychoanalysis. Kofman models this method in her own autobiographical writings, *Smothered Words* and *Rue Ordener, Rue Labat*, which reveal "the overlapping of the absolute of the private with the absolute of history." She thereby connects the personal trauma that revolves around her father's deportation to Auschwitz from Paris on July 16, 1942 with the collective traumatic history of the twentieth century. Though these writings explore an ambivalent childhood lived between the anti-Semitic French woman who adopted her during the war and the Yiddish-speaking Jewish mother who wanted to reclaim her daughter against the latter's wishes, Kofman's writing is an act of reparation that refuses to dichotomize these mothers as "good" or "bad" as a means of self-purification. It is a writing, as Deuber-Mankowsky reads it, that turns against itself and against repression in relentlessly exposing the adult Kofman's melancholy alongside the child Kofman's pathetic, desperate, and selfish desire for happiness in the face of a father's murder and a mother's love; it is therefore a testimony that refuses a Manichean solace, which could be derived from images of a heroicized and/or martyred child self.

Deuber-Mankowsky's analysis of Kofman enunciates the ways in which narration serves to articulate a yearning for wholeness that is, at once, ontological and historical. In Kofman's case, her desire to reanimate an authentic love for the biological mother, whom she felt she had betrayed, transpired in the intersecting memories of her father's deportation and the culturally alienating situation she learned to embrace for the purpose of survival. Yet these traumatic circumstances cannot completely represent the shame that surrounds her subsequent rejection of her biological mother. This shame disrupts authorial complacency and "suffocates" the power of her own language to convey a loss, which is no longer only personal and historical, but also profoundly moral.

It is Kofman's apparent yearning to find a narrative that could express this ambivalent loss, which blurs the boundary between mourning and melancholy as Freud delineated it in his 1917 essay. Once again, Freud in that essay differentiates between the actual losses that define bereavement and the unconscious loss or absence that impels melancholy as a narcissistic sadness without cause; however, Freud's own commitment to the importance of fantasy undermines his distinction to the extent that real losses may also come to serve as the focus of a melancholic attitude; reciprocally, it may be possible to mourn an absence if it is rendered conscious and relative in a social setting.

In "Transnational Adoption: The Ethics and Politics of New Family Stories," Drucilla Cornell problematizes Freud's distinction between mourning and melancholia in her exploration of the narratives that adoptive parents and their children create that defy the exclusionary, hierarchical, and heteronormative conventions of kinship. In Kofman's spirit, Cornell's essay also undoes the false binary between philosophy and life when she opens up her own story as the adoptive mother of a daughter from Paraguay. Her personal story eloquently broaches the heterogeneity of a collective and global history to foreground what Cornell, citing Gayatri Spivak, calls the "enabling violation" that made her adoption of Sarita possible.

Cornell acknowledges the economic inequalities, which separate countries in the global North and the global South that leave many children in serious poverty:

> These inequalities are created and sustained by the very countries that allow some of us the resources to adopt in the first place. Thus, what can be enabling for certain children—parents who adopt them and, in many cases, enable them to stay alive— is inseparable from the violation perpetuated through systematic inequalities. . . . Being part of the scene of adoption forces

us to acknowledge the great extent to which the postcolonial predicament is about the continuing legitimation of inequalities between the global North and global South.

In light of this predicament, Cornell cites Theodor W. Adorno's question as to whether "'a wrong life can be lived rightly.'" Her response is that "most of us try to live life rightly, making judgments of right and wrong because we have no choice but to make them." She avoids a Manichean fantasy that allows adopting parents simply to see themselves as saviors, thereby choosing bravely to enter the gray zones that haunt various scenes of adoption, including those that do not cross racial, ethnic, and national boundaries.

Cornell's analysis contests the personal or legal protocols that prevent children from knowing about their biological parents. The sealing of records perpetuates the adopted child's melancholy over the loss of its birth parent, which, in Cornell's words, "becomes the loss of its own ego due to the ambivalence that underlies the child's relationship to its adoptive parents." In reminding us that our responses to expressions of mourning and melancholy have consequences for others' abilities to come to term with pasts that continue to shape their presents, Cornell's focus on adoptive children also reveals the limits of Freud's 1917 distinction. Cornell cites Melanie Klein's view that the melancholic needs to proceed to the work of mourning that will allow her to re-instate the lost loved object along with the loved internal objects, which she feels she has lost. Only then can she transcend the depressive state that results both in her inability to internalize good objects and in a cathectic forfeiture of the image of a "good" mother, an image, which might be constructively linked to the actual mother who cares for her. It would seem, then, that adopted children may also be prone to Manichean constructions of "good" and "bad" parents that reinforce a desire for narratives that reconnect them to their origins and promise a sense of unity for the "unfettered" self.

Cornell's essay returns to the "enabling violation" with which she began to challenge the injustice of the closed system of adoption that disables adopting parents from recognizing the social and economic hardships that pressure mothers to give up their children. Cornell for her part argues for a work of reparation among adopting parents who mourn for a justice that was suspended by the conditions that propelled adoption in the first place. This work transpires in their respect for the needs of adopted children to narrate themselves in ways that interconnect with but also diverge from their parents' own narratives.

On the nether side of what Cornell has called the mourning for justice is the instrumentalization of trauma in the public sphere. The essays by Juliet Flower MacCannell, Lauren Berlant, and John Mowitt that are reprinted here depict various reified deployments of traumatic affect that foreclose and/or manage its politics.[28]

In "Politics in the Age of Sex: Clinton, Leadership, and Love," MacCannell turns to Freud's *Group Psychology and the Analysis of the Ego* to consider the Republican attempt to impeach Clinton and thereby conserve a coercive leadership structure that demands sexual repression from the "Leader" and the "horde" alike. MacCannell suggests that this Leader is "only a disguised version of the ego, for the only thing the ego ever loves without ambivalence (and with such strong and lasting attachment) is itself." However, under the shadow of a superego cast by the castration complex, "the Leader's 'paternalistic' protection is questioned while a new version of the old 'father' tightens its obscene grip." This is why, as Lacan recognized, the extimate superego hidden in the ego at the center of Freud's group "vitiates as much as it forges the social link."

MacCannell reads Nixon's humiliating resignation as a prior trauma that motivates Republicans' *ressentiment* against Clinton as a Democrat who, in their eyes, threatens to unleash the dangerous rivalry of the primal horde through his liberal *jouissance* and indiscreet sexual escapades. In her words, "Bill Clinton was being made to pay for Nixon's traumatic unmasking of the 'truth' of group life when it is rooted in the ego." The Republicans by this account

---

28. See my discussions of these essays in an introduction to a special issue of *Cultural Critique* on "Trauma as a Cultural Aftereffect," entitled "Trauma and Its Institutional Destinies" (Ball 2000).

remain committed to a primitive model of governance based on a superegoic identification with the totemic Leader, who maintains a unity among the group on the conditions that they are persecuted equally and that they fear him equally.

MacCannell speculates that public support for Clinton's presidency in the face of his impeachment may indicate readiness for a more democratic paradigm, a prospect that Freud himself belittled. This democratic model stipulates a group dynamic that not only allows the Leader to share his love (among various women, with his intelligent wife, with minorities), but would also permit him to be sexual without demonizing "it" as an obscene root of social being that must remain veiled lest it threaten to open a path of return for the primal father. MacCannell's analysis thereby serves to locate the boundaries of Freudian group psychology, which, for historical reasons, had difficulty extrapolating the potential for "sexually enlightened" governance beyond authoritarianism and primitive rivalries.

MacCannell's essay is valuable for its illumination of the relationship between democratic subject formation and the presumed privacy of sexuality. The essay thus provides a strategic bridge to Berlant's work here and elsewhere on the ways in which a politics of traumatic affect informs the signification of "private" versus "public" sex and democratic citizenship.[29] In "The Subject of True Feeling: Pain, Privacy, and Politics," Berlant examines the deployment of images of suffering that reinforces a "normative/utopian image of the U.S. citizen who remains unmarked, framed, and protected by the private trajectory of his life project." This "sentimental politics" officiates a reified mourning for those who have been excluded by the American Dream—the exploited worker; the starving, diseased child; or, for anti-abortion activists, the innocent unborn. As Berlant observes, such mourning fosters an idea of emancipation that shores up the perfection—the moral and ontological unity—of beautiful souls who can maintain a contemplative distance vis-à-vis the pain of others, no matter their proximity; it

---

29. See Berlant and Warner 1998 and Berlant 1997.

is, in Berlant's words, an "act of social deathmaking" insofar as it "ghosts" the realities of the subjects it cloaks in affect even when it is for a good cause. Sentimental politics fosters the rhetoric of a utopian promise that difference, including socio-economic inequities, can be sutured through empathetic identification; the problem is, as Berlant argues, that such rhetoric actually maintains the hegemony of national identity while occulting intercultural antagonism and cleavage.

Berlant's examination of anti-abortion rhetoric and various court cases concerning privacy rights, sexual privacy in particular, reveals sentimental politics as a contestation between two models of citizenship that serves, ultimately, to promote one of them: the "classic" model stipulates a citizen whose value is secured as a "cell of national identity" that establishes juridically protected personhood for abstract, that is, unmarked individuals; the "traumatic" model, in contrast, emerged from labor, feminist, and anti-racist struggles in the nineteenth century. It imagines the nation as peopled by "suffering citizens and noncitizens whose structural exclusion from the utopian-American dreamscape exposes the state's claim of legitimacy and virtue to an acid wash of truth telling that makes hegemonic disavowal virtually impossible, at certain moments of painful intensity." Berlant's intervention demonstrates how the "traumatic" model leads to various confusions. This model elides the difference between what a person is and what she becomes through social negation; it falsely posits an "origin" of structural violence and inspires a "dubious optimism" about law and other institutional venues of inequality as cures for the very harms they enable; the traumatic model also sets up a scarred and exhausted image of the marginalized that may serve as a foil for the healthy, homogeneous, national metaculture; lastly, in over-identifying the eradication of pain with the achievement of justice, this model equates pleasure with freedom while fallaciously assuming that changes in feeling on a collective scale amount to social transformation.

Berlant's critique of sentimental politics is indebted to Wendy Brown's 1995 analysis in *States of Injury* of the ways in which liberationist agendas are burdened by their "wounded attachments" to liberalism. Liberal ideology tends to conflate notions of individual freedom with privacy and thereby undercuts the efficacy of the tactics that are supposed to redeem oppressed groups from public disenfranchisement. In this respect, Berlant's extension of Brown's thesis resonates with Mowitt's argument that the traumatic model of citizenship also yields a certain degree of "moral capital" to the extent that "we" beautiful souls become invested in images of suffering. It is presumably a recognition of this suffering that confirms our concern for justice. In "Trauma Envy," Mowitt considers the implications of this paralyzing attachment as the implicit locus of trauma studies and identity politics. The failure in both instances to fulfill a liberationist agenda stems from their tendency to deploy liberal modes of empathy to displace the political with the ethical. One unforeseen consequence of this displacement is that it promotes *ressentiment* among conservative and reactionary groups, such as the men's movement, against feminists and "others" who have "stolen" the former's enjoyment by claiming a higher moral ground. It is this *ressentiment* that Mowitt calls "trauma envy."

Though his formulation of this term retains its link to Nietzsche's *On the Genealogy of Morals*, Mowitt complicates it by enunciating the cultural politics of psychoanalytic debates in the middle of the twentieth century, which culminate in Melanie Klein's revision of Freud's definition of *Penisneid* from the *Three Essays on the Theory of Sexuality*. In Mowitt's reading, Klein employs Karen Horney's claims about "masculine civilization" to recast Helene Deutsch's "trauma of castration" as "an echo of the more primordial trauma of nursing and ultimately weaning." Mowitt suggests that Klein's prioritization of the breast at the expense of the penis is not simply accidental since it indicates an attempt to finesse a certain analytical misogyny. Klein is, in effect, highlighting the value *attributed* to the breast as the source of the elusive "good feed." The victim of all of this is, of course, the one who feels deprived of the "good" breast and comes to envy those who are perceived as enjoying greater access. What is striking about Mowitt's reading of Klein here is his observation that the guilt attending "good feed breast envy" is made the responsibility of another. He thereby elucidates the dynamics of trauma envy among cultural conservatives and the men's movement: their greed for the moral capital appropriated by the raced, sexed, and gendered other translates into "envy" for the good feed. To portray the injustice of this deprivation and seek compensation, they must ultimately make recourse to the traumatic model of citizenship as Berlant has characterized it. This model founds their efforts to disavow guilt for their greed by projecting it onto the "tenured radicals" whose multiculturalist curriculum destroys the utopian promise of a unified culture proffered by the Great Books of Western Civilization. As we have seen, conservatives in the 1990s also blamed single welfare mothers, who necessarily embody the "bad" breast as a gift that also takes.

Mowitt's critique is not limited to the cultural conservatives. He also exposes the trauma envy that motivates Slavoj Žižek's "Multiculturalism, or the Logic of Multinational Capitalism."[30] Žižek posits the Real as a traumatic "impenetrable kernel resisting symbolization" that has no ontological consistency, yet constitutes the subject. Mowitt observes that this topos "transcendentalizes" trauma by rendering the Real pivotal to all modes of subject formation. As a result, actual trauma is "ghosted," to borrow once again from Berlant, to the extent that it has become the extimate property of everyone and, thus, of no one in particular. In a word, Žižek gives us a kind of "traumatic socialism" with all the failures that such a system of property distribution entails. Equality is reduced to the dystopic thesis that we are all created in such a way that no one has access to the good feed and that we might as well give up this fantasy and share the poverty. Ultimately, however, Mowitt raises a crucial issue that Berlant's critique of sentimental politics underscores: To what extent do we not only make trauma essential to morality, but also cast morality as the remedy to trauma? How shall we divest the moral capital of trauma itself, to

---

30. Žižek 1997.

wean ourselves from a paralytic politics that never inaugurates the conditions for genuine transformation? It is my hope that this volume will be read as part of an ongoing effort to respond to this question.

## REFERENCES

Ball, K. (2000). Trauma and its institutional destinies. *Cultural Critique* 46:1–44.

———— (2003). "Unspeakable differences, obscene pleasures: the Holocaust as an object of desire." *Women in German Yearbook* 19:20–49.

Berlant, L. (1997). *The Queen of America Goes to Washington City: Essays on Sex and Citizenship*. NC: Duke University Press.

Berlant, L., and Warner, M. (1998). Sex in public. *Critical Inquiry* 24(2): 547–566.

Brown, W. (1995). *States of Injury: Power and Freedom in Late Modernity*. Princeton, NJ: Princeton University Press.

———— (2001). *Politics Out of History*. Princeton, NJ: Princeton University Press.

Butler, J. (1997). *The Psychic Life of Power: Theories in Subjection*. Stanford, CA: Stanford University Press.

Caruth, C. (1996). Unclaimed experience: trauma and the possibility of history (Freud, *Moses and Monotheism*) and traumatic departures: survival and history in Freud (*Beyond the Pleasure Principle, Moses and Monotheism*), In *Unclaimed Experience: Trauma, Narrative, and History*, pp. 10–24 and 57–72. Baltimore, MD: Johns Hopkins University Press, 1996.

Caruth, C., ed. (1995). Trauma and experience: introduction, In *Trauma: Explorations in Memory*, pp. 3–12. Baltimore, MD: Johns Hopkins University Press.

Forrester, J. (1997). *Dispatches from the Freud Wars: Psychoanalysis and Its Passions*. Cambridge, MA: Harvard University Press.

Foucault, M. (1967). *Madness and Civilization: A History of Insanity in the Age of Unreason*, trans. R. Howard. London: Tavistock.

———— (1990). *The History of Sexuality: An Introduction*, volume 1, trans. R. Hurley. New York: Vintage.

———— (1996). Rituals of exclusion. In *Foucault Live: Collected Interviews,*

*1961–81*, trans. L. Hochroth and J. Johnston, ed. S. Lotringer, pp. 68–73. New York: Semiotext(e).

Freud, S. (2001). The economic problem of masochism. *The Standard Edition of the Complete Psychological Works of Sigmund Freud*, Vol. 19, trans. and ed. J. Strachey, pp. 159–170. New York: Vintage.

Gherovici, P. (2001). Psychoanalysis: resistible and irresistible. In *Lacan in America*, ed. J.-M. Rabaté, pp. 93–105. New York: Other Press.

LaCapra, D. (2001). Trauma, absence, loss. In *Writing History, Writing Trauma*, pp. 43–85. Baltimore, MD: Johns Hopkins University Press.

Lane, C. (2001). The experience of the outside: Foucault and psychoanalysis. In *Lacan in America*, ed. J.-M. Rabaté, pp. 309–348. New York: Other Press.

Leys, R. (2000). *Trauma: A Genealogy*. Chicago: University of Chicago Press.

Lyotard, J.-F. (1988). *The Differend: Phrases in Dispute*, trans. G. Van Den Abbeele. Minneapolis: University of Minnesota Press.

Nietzsche, F. (1969). Second essay: "guilt," "bad conscience," and the like. In *On the Genealogy of Morals and Ecce Homo*, trans. W. Kaufmann, pp. 57–96. New York: Vintage.

Rabaté, J.-M., ed. (2000). *Lacan in America*. New York: Other Press.

Rajchman, J. (1985). *Michel Foucault: The Freedom of Philosophy*. New York: Columbia University Press.

Seltzer, M. (1998). *Serial Killers: Death and Life in America's Wound Culture*. New York and London: Routledge.

Shepherdson, C. (2000). *Vital Signs: Nature, Culture, and Psychoanalysis*. New York: Routledge.

Žižek, S. (1997). Multiculturalism, or, the logic of multinational capitalism. *New Left Review* 225 (September–October):28–51.

# Conflicting Logics of the Passions: The Strange Career of Hysteria and Anxiety in the Nineteenth Century

BETTINA BERGO

## INTRODUCTION. VIENNA 1886: FREUD'S REPORT ON HYSTERIA IN MEN

On October 15, 1886, upon his return from the Salpêtrière Clinic of Dr. Jean-Martin Charcot in Paris, a young *Dozent* in neuropathology named Sigmund Freud presented his findings to his colleagues at the Viennese Society of Physicians. His findings were not controversial, at least they had not been so in France. Dr. Charcot had documented a number of cases of male hysteria, and Freud now proceeded to a discussion of their symptoms and to Charcot's etiology. Before he could develop his claims, his audience erupted in scandal. The idea of male hysteria "was incredible," they argued. According to Freud, "One of them, an old surgeon, actually broke out with the exclamation: 'But, my dear sir, how can you talk such nonsense? *Husteron* (sic) means the uterus. So how can a man be hysterical?'" As Freud noted years later, his surgeon colleague—who went unnamed but may have been Freud's teacher, Theodor Meynert—not only perpetuated the myth of the wandering womb, which led to hysteria when it traveled up the body and got "lodged in the throat";[1] the unnamed surgeon did not even know that the Greek source was the feminine *he hustera, not* the neuter *tò husteron.* In other words, the cranky physician hardly knew his own Greek. It took a young "outsider" to rectify both a misunderstood malady and the classical education of his colleague.

Sander Gilman reports this story in a penetrating essay on the cultural creation of what he calls "the Jewish Psyche." This is part of his larger work on the nineteenth-century European cultural imaginary, and the ways in which this imaginary conceived of Jews and women. As it happens, the movement of ideas about emotions, passions, and psychiatric disorders coming out of France toward Germany and Austria parallels in part the rise of urban Jewish populations in Berlin and Vienna[2] and the emergence of a new, "scientific" anti-Semitism in German-speaking cultural institutions.[3] This is of great importance here because, in the *fin-de-siècle* bourgeois society, the notions of cultural decadence—already voiced by philosophers like Friedrich Nietzsche, Joseph Arthur comte de Gobineau, Max Nordau, Otto Weininger—had flowed together with the "social" Darwinism of Herbert Spencer and Ernst Haeckel. Though not yet ideology per se, Spencerist "cosmic" evolutionism extended Darwin's ideas to cultural and racial groups, legitimated the notion of a hierarchy of collective unconsciouses, each one

---

1. Gilman 1991, p. 60. This is the famous "globus hystericus" or first theory of the origin of hysteria. I discuss the model of the human body that accounted for its plausibility when I turn to Dianne Sadoff's history of anxiety below.

2. See Lindemann 2000, p. 53. Lindemann writes, ". . . from the mid-eighteenth century until the eve of the Holocaust, the Jewish population increased faster than the non-Jewish population. There was also a more rapid move of Jews than non-Jews into urban areas, especially capital cities." Again: ". . . a large proportion of the Jews of Vienna by the time Hitler lived there (1908–13) had abandoned the most visible signs of their Jewishness. . . . *Their numerical rise was particularly striking: from 6,000 in 1860 to 175,000 in 1910, an increase of around thirty times within two generations.* Budapest, the other capital of the Dual Monarchy, experienced an even more precipitous increase in the same years, resulting in a Jewish percentage of 23 percent by 1914, compared to Vienna's 9 percent" (Ibid., p. 57).

3. Gilman 1991, p. 61.

conditioned by their "fitness for survival."[4] As the student of French fascism, Zeev Sternhell put it,

> applied to society, Darwin's hypotheses no longer constitute a scientific theory, but become a philosophy, virtually a religion. . . . These new theories completely reject the traditional, mechanistic conception of man, which argues that behavior is commanded by rational choice.[5]

In this toxic confluence of ideas, aspects of character, body traits, intelligence, and dispositions that denoted an ineptitude for survival, were attributed to women, and liberally to other "others," preeminently the recently expanded Jewish urban populations of Berlin and Vienna. Gilman writes:

> Freud's understanding as against the understanding of his time was that hysteria did not manifest itself as a disease of the "womb," but of the imagination. This did not absolve the female from being the group most at risk, however; for the idea of a pathological human imagination structurally replaced the image of the floating womb as the central etiology of hysteria. What was removed from the category of hysteria as Freud brought it back to Vienna was its insistence on another group, the Jews, which replaced the woman as essentially at risk.[6]

---

4. See Sternhell 1978, p. 146ff. See his Chapter III, "Déterminisme, nationalisme, racisme," whose conclusions—notably the one that held that the French mistook nationality, culture, and social-Darwinian "populations" for *races* organized according to a vertical hierarchy—are borne out by Renan, who attempted to clarify these terms.

5. Ibid., p. 147. Sternhell adds, shortly thereafter, that "The discovery of the unconscious at the end of the century contributes a complementary, even cardinal, dimension to the anti-rationalist and antidemocratic impetus. In this domain, the work of Gustave Le Bon enjoyed a success almost unequalled to this day. His *Psychological Laws of the Evolution of Peoples*, first published in 1894, goes into its fourteenth edition in 1914, and his best known work, *Crowd Psychology*, which dates from 1895, goes into its 31st edition in 1925, and its 45th one in 1963. Translated into sixteen languages, LeBon's work . . . is one of the *greatest scientific successes of all times* . . ." (p. 148, my translation).

6. Gilman 1991, p. 61. See his Chapter III, "The Jewish Psyche: Freud, Dora, and the Idea of the Hysteric."

## "CONCEPTUAL CONTAGION" AND THE SCANDAL
## OF A MASCULINE PATHOLOGICAL IMAGINATION

The replacement Gilman notes here was anything but complete. Such replacements, from women to Jews, from women to Africans, women to other "Others," *cannot* be complete in fact because of the very grammar by which symbolic abjections—whether in psychiatry, medicine, or literature—rely upon a binary structure that appears to be determined by conceptual clusters including the positive and the negative, the active or virile and the passive or effeminate, the healthy and the degenerate.

Gilman has done extensive work on the conflation of Jewishness and femininity in *fin-de-siècle* Europe. I dwell on it here for two reasons. The first concerns social imaginaries: there is a striking *symbolic contagion* to nineteenth-century ideas on "femininity," with its associations of weak passions, anxiety, fragile bodies, sexual continence, *or* sexual promiscuity.[7] In the literary and popular imaginaries, this symbolic contagion spreads to other "others," and "sticks": in turn, the "others" become anxious, duplicitous, and *otherwise* intelligent, that is, possessed of a different logic.[8] Thus,

---

7. Ibid., pp. 38–59, 145. Gilman writes, "The very analysis of the nature of the Jewish body, *in the broader culture or within the culture of medicine*, has always been linked to establishing the difference (and dangerousness) of the Jew. This *scientific vision* of parallel and unequal 'races' is part of the polygenetic argument about the definition of 'race' within the *scientific culture of the eighteenth century*. In the nineteenth century, it is more strongly linked to the idea that some 'races' are *inherently weaker, 'degenerate,' more at risk* for certain types of disease than others. In the world of nineteenth-century medicine, this difference becomes labeled as the 'pathological' or 'pathogenic' qualities of the *Jewish body*" (p. 39; my emphasis). Many of these qualities are adapted from the vision of the pathogenic qualities of the female body that, itself, is functionally and necessarily pathologized—if only because it goes through phases of toxicity around menstruation and menopause.

8. As Gilman notes, in his Chapter V, "The Jewish Genius: Freud and the Jewishness of the Creative" (pp. 128–149). This different logic is tied to the binary classification of creativity and neurosis. Freud struggled against this binary and the identification of Jews with madness and sexual degeneracy. The Italian criminal anthropologist, Cesare Lombroso, contributed to this binary with his work *Genius and Madness* (1864). He wrote, "This fatal privilege [of a combined

in the 1880s, the French historian Renan pronounced that "the term Jew . . . denotes a special way of thinking and feeling."[9] Another case in point is found in the tragic work of the Jewish classicist, Otto Weininger. This was *Sex and Character*, published in 1903 and celebrated in its time.[10] Its thesis: European culture was decaying;

---

madness and creativity] has not attracted the attention of the leaders of that anti-Semitic movement which is one of the shames of contemporary Germany. They would be less irritated at the success of this race if they had thought of all the sorrows that are the price of it, even in our epoch; for if the tragedies of the past were more bloody (sic), the victims are not now less unhappy . . . and because of it deprived them even of the consolation of being able . . . to contribute to the most noble among the *selections of species*" (cited by Gilman, p. 131, my italics). Note even here, in a work dating from eight years after Darwin's *Origin of Species* (1856), the pseudo-Darwinian concept of "selections of species" and "race."

9. Renan also remarked in his Sorbonne lecture "What Is a Nation?" delivered March 11, 1882, that the great mistake of the present was to confound a race with a nation. He writes, "In our day, we commit a still graver error: we confuse races with nations, and we attribute to ethnographic, or rather linguistic groups a sovereignty analogous to that of authentically existing peoples. Let us attempt to come to some precision about these difficult questions, in which the slightest confusion about the meaning of terms, at the source of our reasoning, can ultimately produce the bleakest errors. What we are about to do is delicate; it is almost vivisection. We are going to treat living beings the way one ordinarily treats the dead. We will apply utter coldness, the most absolute impartiality" [Bergo's translation]. Despite his "cold" reasoning, Renan defined the nation as a "soul" and a group that suffered together as well as having conquered together. The nation was a united domain under a dynasty (the traditional definition), but he was skeptical about the notion of race, and blamed ethnography for its overuse; it had no right to appear in nineteenth-century European politics because there were no pure European races: "As we historians understand it, race is thus something that is *made and unmade*. The study of race is capital for the scholar, concerned with the history of humanity. It has no applications in politics. The instinctual consciousness that presided over the creation of the map of Europe *did not take any account of race*, and the first nations of Europe are essentially nations of mixed blood" [Bergo's translation] he wrote. If race was not absolutely determining, Renan maintained in an earlier work that it had shaped the identity of Jews. See Renan's *The Life of Jesus* (1869). Cf. Lindemann 2000, pp. 43, 129.

10. Gilman (1991) puts it succinctly: "What [Weininger's] *Sex and Character* did was to restate in a scientific, i.e., biological context, Arthur Schopenhauer's views on women and simply *extend the category of the feminine to the Jew*" (p. 133). Note here the enduring normativity of the pessimistic philosophy of will of Schopenhauer; note, too, that what is preserved of his thought, here, is

its degeneracy was manifest in its growing effeminacy. The redemption of culture could only take place through the liberation of "woman" from herself, that is, through the cessation of "man's" sexual use of "woman." However radical, the ideas about different others and cultural degeneration promulgated by these authors are anything but unique at this time. Indeed, some of the most powerful ideas to be found in late nineteenth-century European writings were rooted in the rhetoric of a pathologized femininity capable of spreading more or less like a disease. Thus Freud's announcement that he had seen and worked with male hysterics in Paris entailed a double scandal: the possibility of a pathological *masculine* imagination, and the fact that an "other," Freud, was holding a mirror to a society in whose eyes he was largely a "guest."

The second reason for examining Gilman is this: to be a psychiatrist or neurologist in Vienna at this time, and to be Jewish, brought up the question of legitimacy by virtue of the same conceptual contagion just mentioned. Gilman shows that "Jews did different science"—were supposed to have a different "gaze" in the nineteenth-century academy. In Freud's case, this worked like a gauntlet waiting to be taken up. Thus, after the disaster of October 15, he produced before his colleagues, on November 26, a case of a Viennese male hysteric: Herr August P. In so doing, Freud began explicitly to *psychologize* the condition of hysteria, moving it from the body to a trauma- and anxiety-based causality.

We can only speculate whether, at a different time in history, the presentation of a male hysteric would have elicited much more than passing curiosity. But in doing so when he did, Freud held up a mirror to Viennese society that reflected its own cultural anxieties over demographic change, ideological tensions, and a rising women's movement. More important still, Freud drove a nail into

---

largely his gynophobia, which becomes in a more popular work like that of Weininger, a different sort of classificatory device. Schopenhauer, though ignored today, also influenced Freud. For an explicit reference to Schopenhauer, see "Formulations Regarding the Two Principles in Mental Functioning (1911)," in Freud (1966)2:213–226, and *Beyond the Pleasure Principle* (1920), in Freud (1966)18:1–64.

a coffin he scarcely imagined he was touching: the essentialist conception of masculine versus feminine passions and disorders. That conception is the philosophical point I will be tracing. I will return to it shortly. For now, let us look at the evolution of hysteria as an idea. When Freud returned to the University[11] with a male hysteric then in his care, one might suppose he was insisting vainly on a battle that he would win only later on: the psychologization of what was hitherto a physiological (noxious humors in the female body) or religious disorder (possession). He was modifying a category already in semantic flux. That a neurological disorder proper to women by virtue of their degenerate bodies could be detected in men called for a rethinking of the meaning of hysteria. As Gilman reminds us, hysteria went from being a disease of the body to being a disease of the imagination—of course, this was imagination *combined* with memory and repression.

## A CHRONOLOGY OF HYSTERIA ETIOLOGY
## FROM THE ENLIGHTENMENT

Dianne Sadoff has traced the evolution of hysteria systematically.[12] Hysteria passes through three stages, she argues, before Freud learns about it at the Salpêtrière Hospital in Paris. When medicine conceived the body anatomically, hysteria was a disease of the womb in a body whose organs were like islands on a map—or indeed, like ships, floating north and south, capable of influencing each other by proximity.[13] This "uterine theory" was present through the Enlightenment, along with enduring suspicions about demonic possession of certain women. As concern with disease focused more on the physiology of the body, hysteria was a disease of imbalanced

---

11. See "Pre-Psycho-Analytic Publications and Unpublished Drafts," in Freud (1966)1:24, notably, "Beobachtung einer hochgradigen hemianästhesie bei einem hysterischen Manne" [Observation of a Severe Case of Hemi-Anaesthesia in a Hysterical Man"].

12. See Sadoff 1998, pp. 59–71.

13. Ibid., p. 71.

animal spirits and seething humors—all in a body now conceived as a container.[14] With advances in neurology and reflex theory, hysteria had its third avatar and became a disease of the nervous system. The womb was said to be connected by nerves and veins to every other bodily organ in a woman: it easily influenced any and every other organ in that body.

Writing in the mid-nineteenth century, the British neurologist Thomas Laycock insisted that this curious female "wiring" accounted for women's "feminine virtues" and passions. Among these, Laycock included "compassion, kindness, piety, honesty, sincerity, constancy." But the connections between womb and organs also accounted for women's faults, including "religious enthusiasm, erotomania, nymphomania, monomania, rage, jealousy, craftiness, and cunning."[15] The uterus had become, in the neurological age, the primary seat of reflex action in women. Sadoff concludes, "When irritated . . . uterus or ovaries relayed reflex irritation to other parts of the body, causing attacks, convulsions, insensibilities, and paralyses."[16] Note, at each point in this evolution—which follows no clear linear succession—female reproductive organs are *eo ipso* the primary entity or force in hysterical etiology. No surprise, then, that Freud's Viennese teachers would identify female virtue, passions, and vices with the uterus—whether it floated, or released humors, or radiated neural irritations. Only when a significant part of the pathological field could be shifted from physiology to psychology could there be a properly masculine hysteria. That shift began in France with Pinel, Esquirol, and finally Charcot. In the shift itself, which involved changes in the symbolic meaning of male and female bodies, sexuality was implicated early on.[17]

---

14. Ibid., p. 59.
15. Ibid., p. 68.
16. Ibid., p. 66.
17. And Janet, who was Charcot's other illustrious student. The literature on the emergence of a moral (Pinel) and psycho-physiological reading of disorders like hysteria is considerable. For recent, interesting work by French psychiatrists reading little-explored, archival material and disputing the Foucauldian thesis that post-French Revolutionary medicine "silenced" madness's voice, see Swain 1977 and Gauchet and Swain 1997.

Freud's teacher, Charcot, had insisted upon two things in hysteria. First, the disease was a *single physiological* reality; although he referred to its symptoms as "stigmata,"[18] thereby mythologizing them, Charcot developed a precise taxonomy of the four phases and lesser types of hysteria. But Charcot insisted nonetheless on the duplicity of the hysteric in inventing his *or* her symptoms. When all was said and done, Charcot suspected that sexual dysfunction, or frustration, lay at the root of hysteria. Freud reports that Charcot whispered gleefully at a dinner party to a gynecologist friend, "but in these cases it is always a genital thing, always!"—"toujours la chose génitale, toujours."[19]

## FREUD'S "PSYCHOLOGIZATION" OF HYSTERIA AND THE ENLARGEMENT OF THE CONCEPT OF SEXUALITY

Freud liberated hysteria from Charcot's narrow conception of sexuality and duplicity. He pushed the disease further toward a psychological meaning, rather than a mythico-physiological one. Freud would argue that hysteria was a disease of trauma and "reminiscence," not of sexual frustration tangled in the duplicity of the "other."[20] Herr August, Freud's male hysteric, suffered from the predictable anaesthesias, paralyses, and fainting spells, but for Freud, these were set off by traumatic events in August's life. Trauma and anxiety hereby became the new core of hysteria's etiology. As Freud wrote in 1886, while still a neuro-pathologist,

> When, on October 15th, I had the honour of claiming your attention to a short report on Charcot's recent work in the field

---

18. Charcot is quoted as saying, privately, that one should always expect "*la chose génitale*"—genital, or sexual, matters—to be at work in the etiology of female hysteria. This may also be related to the work he pursued on demonic possession in art—a study that contributed to his categorization of hysterical "phases." See Charcot and Richer 1984.

19. Sadoff 1998, p. 58.

20. See Freud, "Pre-Psycho-Analytic Publications," p. 24.

of male hysteria, I was challenged by my respected teacher, Hofrat Professor Meynert, to present before the society some cases in which the somatic indications of hysteria—the "hysterical stigmata" by which Charcot characterizes this neurosis—could be observed . . . I am meeting this challenge to-day . . . as far as the clinical material at my disposal permits . . .[21]

We should note that the senior physicians of the General Hospital of Vienna had refused to allow Freud to use their material after his October report—so profound was the resistance to his work, and to him as well.

But Freud continued: "I am meeting this challenge to-day—insufficiently, it is true—by presenting before you an hysterical man, who exhibits the symptom of hemi-anaesthesia to what may almost be described as the highest degree."[22]

What caused the hemi-anaesthesia and, as Freud notes afterward, Herr August's convulsions? Freud described his patient's impoverished family background, his parents, and his siblings. Then he added a catalyzing traumatic incident. Three years earlier, "his brother threatened to stab him and ran at him with a knife."[23] This incident was followed by a "fresh agitation": a woman accused Herr August of theft.[24] As a result of repeated psychological traumas,

[i]n accordance with a hysterical hemi-anæsthesia, our patient exhibits, both spontaneously and on pressure, painful areas on what is otherwise the insensitive side of his body—what are known as "hysterogenic zones," though in this case their connection with the provoking of attacks is not marked.

Having pointed out the hysterogenic zones, Freud changed his language and tone:

21. Ibid., pp. 24–25.
22. Ibid., p. 25.
23. Ibid., p. 26.
24. Ibid.

the trigeminal nerve, whose terminal branches . . . are sensitive
to pressure, is the seat of a hysterogenic zone; also a narrow area
in the left medial cervical fossa . . . as well as the left spermatic
cord [is] very sensitive to pain, and this zone is continued along
the course of the spermatic cord into the abdominal cavity to the
area which in women is so often the site of "ovaralgia."[25]

In Freud's November talk, we note the dual presence of a psychological and a physiological explanation for hysteria. It was 1886
and Freud had not yet developed his psychoanalysis. Nevertheless,
the psychological account included an extended exploration of family
background, coupled with traumatic and anxiety-producing inci-
dents. Indeed, in Freud, the physiological explanation seems the
more mythic component, the component still largely influenced by
Charcot. It included locating the hysterical "stigmata" and hysterogenic zones on the body, and finding a physiological seat in the nervous system and around the reproductive organs. Hence there is a
"hysterogenic zone," and Herr August feels pain around the spermatic cord, which is also, and usually, the "site for 'ovaralgia,'" or
the hysterical affliction of the ovaries.[26] The hysterical man's body
becomes the analogue of the pathological female body.

---

25. Ibid., pp. 30–31.
26. We should nevertheless keep in mind that Freud added a precious insight into his own diverging views on hysteria in a brief essay entitled "Hysteria," first published in 1888 in the *Handwörterbuch der gesamten Medizin* (Vol. 1,
ed. A. Villaret, Stuttgart, pp. 886–892), and reprinted in Freud (1966)1: 37–58.
There, he wrote, "The name 'hysteria' originates from the earliest times of medicine and is a precipitate of the prejudice, overcome only in our own days [!], which
links neuroses with diseases of the female sexual apparatus" (p. 41). There, he
added, already demonstrating a potential skepticism about the Cartesian psycho-
physiological parallelism that was part of Charcot's diagnostic suppositions, but
which Freud would challenge explicitly by 1912, "Hysteria is based wholly and
entirely on physiological modifications of the nervous system and its essence
should be expressed in a formula which took account of the conditions of excit-
ability in the different parts of the nervous system. A *physio-pathological formula
of this kind has not yet, however, been discovered*; we must be content meanwhile
to define the neurosis in a purely nosographical fashion by the totality of symptoms occurring in it . . . without any consideration of the closer connection between these phenomena" (Ibid).

Later, through their collaborative practice, Freud and Breuer would expand the psychological explanation with emphasis on an impossible remembrance: they coined the expression "the hysteric suffers from reminiscence," meaning not a wistful reconstruction of some past time, but something akin to being haunted by a memory that will no longer take shape. Hysteria is "the precipitate of a reminiscence," Freud added in the 1910s, now combining chemistry and literature in his new metaphor for the disease.[27] Reminiscence thus proves to be more than the fruit of a diseased imagination, as Gilman has held. Rather it signals the existence of a "something" that is in some sense a memory as well as the activity (or influence) of an unconscious censoring function.[28] When censored, the memory is lost to consciousness, somatized, and it may return as a sign or symptom "disguised" on its return because it originated in events too distressing for the psyche to reckon with them. In the repression of traumatic memories, the Freudian unconscious is born, of course, and with the unconscious comes the confirmation of the Romantics' pessimistic idea that humans are incapable of exerting sustained control over their passions.[29] Freud's

---

27. See "Introductory Lectures on Psychoanalysis: The General Theory of Neurosis (1916–1917)—Lecture XXV, Anxiety," in Freud (1966)16:241–477. Cited by Lucille B. Ritvo 1990, p. 180.

28. Of this censoring function, Freud wrote in 1912, "[We] learn that the unconscious idea is excluded from consciousness *by living forces*, [these] oppose themselves to its reception, while they do not object to other ideas, the preconscious ones" (p. 27).

29. Freud wrote in the Spencerian-Darwinian language that would long be his own, that the overflow of excitations within the neuro-psychic system constitutes the "prototype . . . of *psychical repression*" ("The Interpretation of Dreams [continued]," in Freud [1966]5:600), cited by Ritvo 1990, p. 187. He added, in his "History of the Psycho-Analytic Movement," that "the theory of repression . . . is the corner stone on which the whole structure of psycho-analysis rests" (Freud [1966]14:16).

What had been interpreted as the even flow of conscious mental life, integrating emotions and reason into itself, and unfolding like a discursive narrative with a clear before and after, now becomes broken into fragments or at least bifurcated into the accessible events and the inaccessible events of the life of the (conscious and unconscious) mind. For Freud, the unconscious is the difficult but unifying force of the breaks or hiatuses of mental life, like forgetfulness and slips of the tongue.

dynamic forces of unconscious, preconscious, and conscious mentality mean—if one avoids hypostatizing them—that consciousness can experience itself as passive in itself. Consciousness can experience itself as subjected to forces that it may attempt to represent verbally, or through the images of dreams, but that are fundamentally independent of consciousness itself.[30]

## THE "THIRD COPERNICAN REVOLUTION" AND THE MUTATION OF THE PASSIONS

This loss of control was a last gasp of the heritage of philosophical autonomy. And, as we know from Michel Foucault's *History of Sexuality*, the "talking cure" replaced the religious confession. But it also replaced philosophical schemes for the "education" of the passions into virtues. From the Stoic ideal of *apatheia*, or implacable mind, to Kant's Categorical Imperative, the philosophical compass always pointed toward rational autonomy and the cultivation of a good will. It was argued that rationality could guide the passions into an enduring, peaceable coexistence and, thereby, procure responsible freedom for men. If this could not be so, then the "psychological" promise of the Enlightenment was undermined — and with it, its social optimism as well. It is no accident that Freud would speak of his work on unconscious guilt and anxiety as bringing about a third "Copernican Revolution" after Copernicus and Darwin.[31] This third revolution dislodged humans from their last (psychological) position of power: the power of reason both to master and guide passions toward virtue.

---

30. See below, note 79, for a brief discussion of Judith Butler's "Freudian" (and Lacanian) thesis of the emergence of subjectivity through a certain subjection in *The Psychic Life of Power: Theories in Subjection* (Stanford, CA: Stanford University Press, 1977).

31. See "A Difficulty in the Path of Psycho-Analysis" (1917) in Freud (1966)17:135–144, where Freud identifies psychoanalysis as the third "death blow" to man's narcissism. Also cited by Ritvo 1990, p. 22ff.

## MEYNERT'S (LATE) CONFESSION

The "episode" of the male hysteric has an end we know well; namely, the burgeoning of psychoanalysis and the new conceptual basis for reading bodies and discourses that psychoanalysis gave us. But the episode has a lesser, more ironic ending as well. This second ending illustrates the conceptual contagion I spoke of earlier. Freud's once revered teacher of neuro-psychiatry, Theodor Meynert, whose work and personality influenced the young Freud, "while [he] was still a student,"[32] first spearheaded the embittered attack on him on October 15, 1886—only to make him a late-coming deathbed confession, years later. "You know," sighed Meynert, "I was always one of the clearest cases of male hysteria." Freud transcribed the confession in 1900 in his *Interpretation of Dreams*.[33]

## WHY STUDY HYSTERIA? OR HYSTERIA'S RELATIONSHIP TO THE HISTORY OF ANXIETY: A GENDERED LOGIC OF THE PASSIONS

This story is longer, in actuality. To complete it, we would have to follow Freud's progressive abandonment of his *neurotica*—an abandonment begun around the publication of the "Dora Case" (of *"petite hystérie"*). This was occasioned by two other turns in his thought. First, Freud's abandonment of his neurophysiologic model of perception, memory, and consciousness, which reserved a particular place for anxiety, hysteria, and physical pain in the *Project*

---

32. "An Autobiographical Study," in Freud (1966)20:10. Cited by Ritvo 1990, Chapter 12, "The *Expression of the Emotions, Psychiatrie*, and *Studies on Hysteria*," pp. 170–171. Note that, following his presentation on male hysteria, Freud was excluded from Meynert's laboratory. He writes, "'I found myself forced into the Opposition. As I was soon afterwards excluded from the laboratory of cerebral anatomy,' of which Meynert was the chief, and 'for terms on end had nowhere to deliver my lectures, I withdrew from academic life'" (Ibid., p. 15, cited by Ritvo 1990, p. 171).

33. Cited by Ritvo 1990, p. 170.

*for a Scientific Psychology* (1895). Second, the dissolution of his distinction between "realistic anxiety" and "fantasmatic anxiety" produced an internal fragmentation of the category of hysteria, which passed from traumatogenic causation to infantile fantasy and narcissistic conflict ("Little Hans," 1909), supplemented later by the conflicted identifications Freud discussed when he considered the "shell shock" trauma of soldiers returning from the front in World War I.

The present vignette presents an episode in a history that caps off those confluent strains of nineteenth-century thought, which combined *la grande anatomo-physiologie*[34] with its "irritable" nervous system and homeostatic economy with atelic conception of human essences structured by conflicting figures of inherited degeneration and the composite images of ethnicities (Galton). Into the mix came Ernst Haeckel's para-Darwinist theory of recapitulation (i.e., ontogeny reproduces phylogeny) that psychoanalysis replayed as psychological and psycho-social development.[35] In the present "heuristic fiction," anxiety is *the* passion that leads to neurosis.[36] And anxiety figures in all of us along a continuum of social

---

34. See Michel Foucault, *Le pouvoir psychiatrique: Cours au Collège de France (1973–1974)* (Paris: Éditions du Seuil, 2003).

35. Ever governed by the Renaissance notion of the "scala naturae," "recapitulation" argued that embryonic development passed through every stage of living beings, from fish to amphibians to mammals and ending with man. A difficulty arose, however: What was the gendered nature and meaning of the human embryo? Given that the incipience of "maleness" amounted to a nearly revolutionary event in the development of the embryo, should the pre-sexuate embryo be understood to be asexuate—a kind of universal model—or essentially effeminate? The debate unfolded, unsurprisingly, according to conceptions of femininity (with phenomena of inherited fragility, even degeneracy) and in light of socio-political anxieties fueled by feminist, motherhood, and socialist movements. For one discussion of sexuation, development, and the surprising "identity" of Jews, see Sander Gilman, *The Case of Sigmund Freud: Medicine and Identity at the Fin de Siècle* (Baltimore, MD: Johns Hopkins University Press, 1993), pp. 95–100.

36. Charcot insisted on the unity and the reality of hysteria as *one* illness with multiple forms. In so doing, and before Freud and Breuer, Charcot tied sexual dysfunction and even the experience of sexual violence to the etiology of nervous diseases. I will not go into Freud's complex classification of hysterias here,

and existential malaise, on one side, and psychosis on the other. The "Age of Anxiety": How is it that the triumph of narcissistic wounds—inflicted successively by Kant, Darwin, and Freud—could inaugurate reactive mechanisms of control such that subjects were now constituted and governed not on the basis of sovereignty, but on determinations of inherited degeneracy and taxonomies of very idiosyncratic disorders? Foucault's 1973–1974 *Collège de France* lectures have shown how the hysterical subject of Charcot's Salpêtrière emerged through a relationship of co-constitution, wherein the experimental neurologist became plenipotentiary physician[37] once provided with a legitimate psychological *patient type*, the epilepto-hysteric. That is: without a stable grammar of measurable symptoms, without a distinct hysterical *subject*, the psychiatric clinician had neither object nor title. It was Freud who noted the price paid for the construction of a preeminent psychiatric object: hysteria proved to be a disorder so plastic and amorphous that Charcot's work had to be recommenced, starting with a review of the simplest types and the most common symptoms. He jotted that down in his "Dora" report and, predictably, never ventured it, because by 1905 Freud had doubts about the univocity of hysteria as a psychiatric illness.

---

except in relation to anxiety. That will give us our transition to the question of the structure of this book. In a 1910 essay called "'Wild' Psychoanalysis," an expression denoting the sort of para-analysis many Viennese physicians were toying with, Freud distinguished between the emotion called anxiety, anxiety neurosis, and anxiety hysteria. These differences are clear enough: anxiety is a feeling or "combination of certain feelings in the pleasure–unpleasure series"— but a feeling, whether it is unpleasant or not, whether it has an object or not—a feeling is not neurosis. "Anxiety neurosis," like neurasthenia, has a bodily etiology and is tied to sexuality. "Anxiety hysteria" is also characterized by a bodily factor, notably the life, or sexual, drive, *libido*, which follows a typical physiological mechanics of building up and awaiting discharge through activity. However, in building up, the force or drive encounters a developed resistance to it, which creates a conflict difficult to overcome. The distinction between anxiety neurosis and anxiety hysteria lies in the gravity of the psychological conflict between drives and their mental "processing." And this conflict contributes to a reactive process of holding down, or turning away from certain ideas and feelings: repression. See Peter Gay 1989, pp. 351–356. Also see note 33.

37. See Michel Foucault, *Le pouvoir psychiatrique*, Op. cit.

A comparable scenario emerged with the popularization of Darwinian evolution. However marginal the teleology factor in evolutionary theory, however surreptitious the Lamarckian question of adaptation's role in his evolutionary theory,[38] complexification remained the fundamental principle. Even though the great predecessor Buffon could speak about regression within species, eighteenth-century naturalists were not preoccupied with a global notion of degeneracy. Degeneracy arises with the confrontation of Goethean science, Romanticism and more cosmologically oriented Darwinisms (Haeckel, Spencer). It is as though, confronted with the reality of working-class misery and torn between Lamarckian adaptation and natural selection, nineteenth-century speculation could not avoid a negative narcissism that asked: How can we be the outcome of millennia of complexification? In the attempt to develop a typology of those groups most prone to inherited regression and psycho-physiological degeneracy, a racial and gendered logic provided the little-remarked backdrop. The case of the hysterical man illustrates the cultural and philosophical supposition that the significant passions followed gender matrices (strong–weak, autonomous–heteronomous). This was so taken for granted that philosophers rarely wrote about it. One who did so, however, undertook to prove that all living beings were *materially* bisexuate. Such

---

38. In his *Expression of the Emotions in Man and Animals*, Darwin grappled mightily with the question of habits, adaptation, and the transmission of habitual characteristics. He revisits Charles Bell's theory that the raising of eyes in a posture of devotion is "an action neither taught nor acquired" (p. 217). He wonders whether "our children acquire their knowledge of expression solely by experience . . ." (p. 353). He reckons that some "gradually acquired . . . movements of expression" could "likewise have become instinctive" (Ibid). He holds adaptability and natural selection together in a struggle against polygenesis and its racialist suprematism (p. 355). He argues that "good spirits" are expressed in a way common to "all the races of man," and yet, the development of smiling and laughter is "a gradual acquirement" (p. 210). Affectivity and passions, their expression and aptitude for decoding confound univocal arguments about natural selection with questions of habits and their origin, and the (Lamarckian) transmission of habitual, adaptive behavior. In 1872, Darwin is thus less Darwinian than he was in 1858 see Darwin, *The Expression of the Emotions in Man and Animals*, 3rd edition (New York: Oxford University Press, 1998).

bisexuation required extensive analysis of the ideal masculine and feminine types. Otto Weininger unfolded his *"Prinzipielle Unter-suchung"* ("foundational investigation," 1903), in which the ideal masculine was equated with plenitude—better, with "presence" in the metaphysical sense, while the ideal feminine was equated with negativity, or metaphysical absence.[39] Between these two ideal points came all factical persons—with certain regularities distributed across different "races," notably that of the Jews whom Weininger claimed to vindicate, before contemporary anti-Semitic stereotypes, by recourse to male-female essentialism and to the question of *"sexuelle Zwischenformen"* [sexual intermediary forms]: Jews, he maintained, are traditionally closer to "the feminine" pole—not unlike the Chinese.[40] Beyond a bathic tale of a failed marriage between Nietz-

39. In a move that anticipated Freud (because written between 1900 and 1902) and Lacan, Weininger explored the "unbegriffliche Natur des Weibes, aus dem Mangel des Ich zur erklären" [unconceptualizable nature of the female explained through the lack of an ego]; see *Geschlecht und Charakter: Eine prinzipielle Untersuchung* (Vienna and Leipzig: Wilhelm Braumüller, 1903, 1921, 22nd ed.), Chapter 9, "Masculine and Feminine Psychology" ["Männliche und weibliche Psychologie"], pp. 232–272.

40. See Weininger, Chapter 13, "Das Judentum" [Judeity or Jewishness], in *Loc. cit.*, pp. 399–441. The phenomenon of saying aloud what so many intellectuals discussed only in the parlor-rooms is so obvious here that Weininger merits quoting at length: "These objections could go farther, however, and reach a point whose ignorance of the [present] theory would be a reproach to it. That is, there are peoples and races [*Völkerschaften und Rassen*], wherein men [*Männern*], though they should in no way be designated as sexual intermediary-forms [*sexuelle Zwischenformen*], so rarely approximate the idea of manliness [*Männlichkeit*] . . . that the principles, indeed the entire foundations [*die ganzen Fundamente*] on which the present work rests, could thereby be forcefully shaken. What should we make, for example, of the Chinese, with their feminine [*weiblichen*] lack of needs [*Bedürfnislosigkeit*] and their lack of any striving? One finds oneself obliged to believe, here, in the greater femininity of an entire people. . . . But how does it stand [*wie verhält sich dann*] with Negroes? Among Negroes, there has not been perhaps a single genius; and morally, they stand, generally, almost so low that in America one has begun publicly to fear one has committed an imprudent prank. . . . Thus, if the principle of sexual intermediate-forms has any prospects for becoming meaningful as a racial anthropology [*Rassenanthropologie bedeutsam zu werden*], then it must be admitted that, up to now, the deductions have referred to the Aryan man and woman. . . .

scheanism and Kantian morality, followed by his much publicized suicide, Weininger's work typified unspoken—or unpublicized— prejudices of the nineteenth century. The investigation, whose main title was *"Geschlecht und Charakter"* [Sex and Character], combined biology and zoology with a vulgarized Nietzschean ideal of self-overcoming, and a categorical imperative against instrumentalizing other human beings—which Weininger applied primarily to sexual intercourse. *Sex and Character* wanted to be a defense of femininity and Jewishness—notably against harsher misogynies and full-blown racist stereotypes. Reading it as an original polemic, Karl Kraus, the remarkable editor of *Die Fackel*, defended it. After Weininger's death in 1903, the work sold off the shelves. It influenced authors from Wittgenstein to D. H. Lawrence and James Joyce. As the intellectual coal mine canary of the *Belle Époque*, Weininger spread the anxious racial anthropologies of the parlor-room across pages and pages of middle-brow reading material, bolstering it with the ongoing debates in embryology, physiology, and zoology.

The connection between Freud, Fliess, and Weininger is notorious. The theory of bisexuation was supposed to have been passed to Weininger indirectly through a patient of Freud's

---

"Judaism, which I have chosen for an object of discussion above all because . . . it is the toughest and most feared adversary of the perspectives developed here . . . Judaism [*das Judentum*] appears anthropologically to possess, in common with the two above-mentioned races, i.e., with Negroes as with Mongolians [*Mongolen*], a certain kinship [*verwandtschaft*]" (pp. 400–401). From there, Weininger argues, ostensibly against anti-Semitism, that the latter amounts to a deep-seated reaction of men, whatever their ethnicity, to the Jew *within them!* Fundamentally, however, the "problem" of Jews—which may or may not be that of "Negroes and Mongols" (this, he never clarifies)—is that "der echte Jude hat wie das Weib kein Ich und darum keinen Eigenwert" [the authentic Jew has no ego and thereby no personal conviction of worth] (p. 408). How to prove such a thing? In several ways, among which Weininger employs the *a posteriori* claim: "Jews like to stick together like women, but they have no real interactions with each other as autonomous, mutually separated essences [*voneinander geschiedene Wesen*], under the sign of a supra-individual Idea" (p. 408).

(Hermann Swoboda).[41] Wilhelm Fliess accused Freud of communicating his core insight without crediting him for it, which led to the breakup of Freud's first long-term intellectual *liaison*.[42] Despite the rupture between them, and despite the more hallucinatory theories of Fliess (e.g., the developmental correlation between the nasal mucosa and female genitalia), Freud never dropped his allegiance to a weak notion of bisexuation, which would pass from biological to symbolical after 1902—not to mention a certain conception of female *and* male metabolic periodicity. But theories of factical bisexuation proceeded on the postulations of unchanging essences, nature, or fundamental makeup, whether these were related to something like Kant's notion of "intelligible character" or a new avatar of the *ewige Weiblichkeit*.

If the passions characterized as pathological in Kant's *Anthropology* bore the stamp of a gender and racial-cultural specificity (e.g., his North American savages and their "passion" of patience), Charcot and Freud's anxiety hysteria opened pathology to a trauma-based etiology, only to have it collapse back again into more gender-specific categories.[43] But the redoubling was never complete. After 1905, Freud grew dismissive of hysteria; it was as though he had been largely deceived: "The observation [the "Dora" case] that I am sketching here seems . . . not to merit publication. '*Petite hystérie*' with the

---

41. Not that Fliess and Freud were the only ones to discuss this. Magnus Hirschfeld coined the notion of sexual "Zwischenstufen"—*intermediaries*. A physician himself, he published from 1899 through 1923 the *Jahrbuch für sexuelle Zwischenstufen* and may well be credited with creating the first movement for homosexual rights.

42. The Freud–Fliess letters (all from Freud) depict a powerful, somewhat eroticized friendship. For discussion of this see S. Gilman, *The Case of Sigmund Freud*, Op. cit., pp. 101–104.

43. For Charcot, this is largely because the consistently histrionic patients at the Salpêtrière, those most apt to be *mise en scène* and to furnish predictable, complete four-stage "*crises*," were women. One such patient, "Augustine," was the object of prodigious photographic recording. See G. Didi-Huberman, *The Invention of Hysteria: Charcot and the Photographic Iconography of the Salpêtrière* (Cambridge, MA: MIT Press, 2004). Also see Foucault, *Le pouvoir psychiatrique*, Op. cit.

most banal somatic and psychic symptoms. . . . Certainly, observations of a more interesting and better done quality on hysterics have been published . . . I would only remark that all the accumulations of the strange and astonishing phenomena that come about in hysteria have *not helped us* progress much in the comprehension of this illness, which remains ever enigmatic. What we need is precisely to throw light on the simplest and most frequent cases, and their typical symptoms"(Freud 1997, p. 14, emphasis added). This implied that Charcot's enterprise, whose rethinking Freud was calling for, had not so much failed as become intractable or worse, irrelevant—a "Dark Continent" in the psychoanalytic project.

The flight from hysteria was rooted in three things: the protean transformations of hysterical symptoms, the explosion of suspected cases, and the impossibility of drawing a line between the ordinary feminine *bourgeois* condition and pathological extensions of it. Freud was motivated by another difficulty, however: the slippery mimetics of transference and countertransference. Whatever he may have said about Dora, her precipitate departure after three months was a firm response to his then triumphalist directiveness in the treatment, which was related to Freud's obsession with the infantile preconditions of her father fixation, and his determination to link hysteria with a *strictly* sexual etiology. If these goals did not free him to make hysteria once again a purely feminine disorder, they certainly moved him toward the old association: femininity-sexual duplicity. The characteristically mimetic quality of hysterical interaction passed between the patient and the therapist himself.

We know from Juliet Mitchell's work that Freud never wrote up his male hysterics.[44] The case he related to Fliess, and with which he identified, is illustrative. Herr P. suffered from intense agoraphobia. He avoided social gatherings generally because he was invariably given to violent blushing in the company of women. He related that his blushing in such gatherings was the result of fantasies of

---

44. Juliet Mitchell, *Mad Men and Medusas: Reclaiming Hysteria* (New York: Basic Books, 2001).

sexual possession.[45] Freud admitted to Fliess that he could understand P.'s dilemma. Thus what I have been calling the gendered logic haunted both diagnosis and treatment. In so doing, it inaugurated a contagion mechanism, whereby male patients and their therapists found themselves in symbolic positions analogous to the conditions and disorders of "effemination"—despite the masculine fantasies that could be found on both sides.

With the development of the oedipal schema, hysteria returned to the "phantasmatics" of castration and cleaved to states of abjection, whether transient or enduring. This proved impressively out of touch with the findings recorded about shell-shocked veterans after World War I. It is as though the "matricial" function of gender in the attribution of psychiatric disorders necessitated the preservation of invisible but heuristic types. Such a preservation also served the ideal of nineteenth-century philosophical pedagogies, like Fichte's and Herbart's.[46] Therein, it was a matter of an education for freedom and virtue, in which strong passions could not be effectively paired with reason to produce virtues. Likewise, Freud's disappointing therapeutic results with hysterics ruled out a simple cure for anxiety hysteria and found him increasingly defensive about the "talking cure" when it confronted disorders of feminine sexuality. By mid career, in any case, anxiety was neither

---

45. Not so unlike the story of the "Rat Man," whose early sexual initiation (age five) took the form of asking nannies to let him pass under their skirts. The fear he developed, that his sexual exploits would bring some harm to his father, resulted in obsessive rituals to keep him from his sexual drives. What must be emphasized here is that hysteria, phobia, and obsession are all transformations of the *Triebe*, the drives. In this sense, they are interrelated the way variations on a physiological disorder are related.

46. Johann Friedrich Herbart (1776–1841) published a celebrated *Lehrbuch zur Psychologie* in 1816 (Leipzig: August Wilhelm Unzer). It established the grounds of his *Allgemeine Pädagogik aus dem Zweck der Erziehung abgeleitet* (Göttingen: Röwer, 1806) [*General Pedagogy Derived from the Goal of Upbringing*]. J. G. Fichte's (1762–1814) pedagogy was based on a reading of Kant that privileged practical reason in the self-realizing acts whose context is a (national) community, cf. *Reden an die deutsche Nation* [Discourses to the German nation], 1806.

a disorder worthy of interest nor a mere sign of repression. Examined in the metapsychology, anxiety proved to displace the Ego itself in the genesis of the second psychic topography with its id, emergent ego, and introjected superego.[47] How did this happen? As we know, between 1893 and 1895, what Freud called "anxiety neurosis" resembled hysteria and accompanied it. Both were linked to buildups of sexual tension that the psyche could not manage. These erupted as symptoms and that way, were usually discharged. By the turn of the century, Freud connects anxiety decisively with repression. It shows up when repression, which binds our psychic energy to a different feeling or idea, breaks down. The breakdown of repression is frequent in neurosis because what was repressed was a sensuous excess, something "too much" for the psyche, and this "too much" returns to be discharged otherwise. But in returning, it attaches itself to a new idea and so projects outside itself the meaning of the anxiety that it itself created.

Of course, if this is right, and anxiety is the passion caused by a nonconscious refusal of an excessive drive, sensation, or idea—that is, by repression—then the psyche can thrust something "down" as it were, making it nonpsychic, and creating a bodily symptom. Yet the same symptom is rarely enough to keep the nonpsychic or physical excitation from returning to discharge itself. The relationship between the psychic, or the psychological, and the physical thus becomes circular. How then do we distinguish between the anxiety (or any other strong passion) caused by a real, external event, and the anxiety caused by a recollected, or even imagined, internal event? In tracing the origin of anxiety, Freud found himself

---

47. See Samuel Weber's excellent remarks on this in his chapter "Metapsychology Set Apart," in *The Legend of Freud*, pp. 67–98. As he puts it, ". . . what Freud is describing is nothing less than the manner in which the ego constitutes itself by setting itself apart from the indifferentiation of the primary process. If the latter can be said to consist in the incessant alteration of ever-different cathexes . . . anxiety entails the alteration of that alterity through a process of repetition that organizes space and time in terms of a dyadic opposition: that of inner/outer and past/future. In so organizing space and time, anxiety situates the ego as the dividing line between the two opposing poles" (p. 91).

in a debate around "original" or "birth anxiety." This first real, physically induced anxiety would arise at the time of our physical separation from the mother's body. This was his colleague Otto Rank's position—and before him Freud had also held it. But in 1926, when he returned to the idea of an original traumatic cause, and an original passion of anxiety, Freud realized something important that Rank had misunderstood. If neurotic anxiety repeats an event that happened to us "objectively" at birth, and if the neurotic repeats it over and over, displacing the cause of the anxiety each time the neurotic repeats it, then what is the original content that first caused the anxiety? Rank supposed it was some perceptual content, something perceived at birth by the neonate. In his *Inhibitions, Symptoms and Anxiety*, Freud (1926) responded as follows: "In the act of birth there is an objective danger to life. We know what this means in reality. But psychologically speaking this tells us nothing. The danger of birth has yet no psychical content."[48]

If the passion, even the neurosis, of anxiety originates at birth, only to be replayed and transformed time after time, we must admit that when it arose first, it did so in a mind that could not yet say "I." The newborn has no ego, if Freud is right, for the ego gradually develops thanks to perception and interaction with the outside world. In other words, our selfhood, our so-called ego, solidifies as it establishes the meaning of what is inside and outside us. It constructs itself by setting itself increasingly apart from the confusion of inner passions, which Freud called our "primary process." So the self, or the subject, creates itself there, precisely where it is able to identify causes of its own feeling of helplessness. That is, in the mnemic trace. No self would ever emerge if anxiety engulfed us completely with each of its repetitions, and again: the first anxiety, the birth anxiety, had no "us," no "me" to engulf. Thus, each time we experience anxiety, whether real or imagined, having the

---

48. Freud, "Inhibitions, Symptoms and Anxiety" in *The Standard Edition*, Vol. XX (1925–1926), James Strachey and Anna Freud, eds. (London: The Hogarth Press, 1959), p. 135.

experience means that we identify a danger, and in so doing displace the first "event" of anxiety anew.

The question I am asking is this: If anxiety lies on the line between the psychic and the bodily; if anxiety is "there" before there is a "there" or a "me" at all, then shouldn't we ask whether this is not true for other strong passions that are rooted in, or reduced to anxiety? The eventuality of such a situation would have posed serious difficulties to Freud's theory of affects and passions, by definition conscious affairs, even though certain higher-level affects like guilt could be unconscious when accompanying an idea that was repressed. Anxiety thus remained the "sovereign" passion in the second topography.

## ANXIETY AND THE CIRCLE OF SUBJECTIVITY IN NINETEENTH-CENTURY EXISTENTIALISM

Freud's second topography (id, ego, and superego) encompasses the first (primary, secondary processes). But by mid-career, one passion clearly precedes both the perceptual consciousness (pcs system) and cognition: anxiety. It is thus not misguided to say that anxiety comes to precede agency; indeed, anxiety precedes the passive-active dichotomy. Within nineteenth-century mechanism, anxiety could function simultaneously as sensation and as what Freud's erstwhile mentor, Josef Breuer, called "idea-affects." This was because the source of sensation and idea-affects was found by dividing all excitations into endogenous and exogenous ones, then reducing these to a constant that represented the change from rest to motion (Freud called this $Q_\eta$ in his *Project*, which was contemporary with the *Studies on Hysteria*). Absent a materialist reduction, the distinction between affectivity and sensibility was more complicated, given the psychodynamics of affectivity and its "higher functions." Remarkable here is that, in the second topography, the epiphenomenal Ego floats on a metaphoric sea of affects, whose emergence in repetition is the precondition both for subjectivity itself and for pathologies besetting the subject. Anxiety, thus doubly rooted in physiological systems and intersubjectivity, was there before "I" was there, while the *repetition* of anxiety sets the ego apart as it sets it in a situation of helplessness, which the ego must try to explain to itself. By 1926, Freud's theory of anxiety discerned something like a hermeneutic circularity between anxiety and ego formation, which undermined any static notion of a ground that the tradition would have called a *sub-iectum*.

In tracing the etiology of anxiety back prior to the instance (the ego) supposed to recognize it, Freud struck up against the irreducible reciprocity of anxiety and the emergence of the protective layer called self or Ego. In so doing, however, he repeated a discovery made fifty years earlier by Kierkegaard. The latter uncovered the circle of anxiety when he explored the fact of humans as beings able-to-do, in lieu of the idealists' anthropological opposition between freedom and necessity. Kierkegaard's *Concept of Anxiety* (1844) likewise set mood and passion prior to conceptual determinations like self-positing freedom or mechanistic determination. Anticipating thinkers from Heidegger and Scheler, to Levinas and Kristeva, Kierkegaard unfolded a precognitive "understanding" that was objectless, atelic, and had a preeminently practical corollary: it opened to narcissistic neurosis (for Kierkegaard "inclosing reserve") or again, to an ethical openness uncharacteristic of the philosophical inquiries of his time, much less of the aforementioned pedagogical projects. The remarkable extension of anxiety by Heidegger, despite his debt to Paul's messianic awaiting (and its anxious projective anticipation of the "return"), unfolds similarly through our being overcome by anxiety, which reveals the nothingness of world and self. For Heidegger as for Kierkegaard, anxiety (originates in and) dissolves our attachments to objects. When Heidegger considered how we are brought before ourselves, in the uncanny [*unheimlich*] experience of anxiety, he diverged from Kierkegaard who had insisted that anxiety opened a path to the possibility of faith (keeping in mind that faith, for Kierkegaard, was aporetic and as nigh-to-impossible as grasping death was, for Heidegger). For Heidegger, borrowing massively from Kierkegaard, anxiety evinces the possibility of nothingness; it raises

the question, Why is there anything at all? Because of its volatiliz-
ing power, anxiety breaks ties, sets "us" apart from circumstances
and things. What is thereby "revealed" differs according to the
enterprise of thinking (psychoanalysis, existentialism). The point
is simply this: the young Heidegger's work was parasitic upon
Kierkegaard, who first explored the passion of anxiety and the circle
of an indeterminate subject and its equally underdetermined "possibilities," which insist in us, affectively, prior to cognition of freedom and necessity. Now, Heidegger's work leads us in a direction
different from Kierkegaard, toward a question about the ground of
all beings. Indeed, the question of Being in Heidegger set fears about
the self-destruction of Western philosophy—not to mention Oswald
Spengler's "*Untergang*" ["decline"] of European civilization—on an
entirely different, *metaphysical*, footing. But this dual borrowing and
transposition would not have been possible without reflection on
anxiety as *degré zéro* of sensibility and passions. We should keep
in mind that Kant's transcendental philosophy, which critics like
Solomon Maimon argued had definitively separated lived experience
from the formal preconditions of perception and understanding, had
provided considerable motivation to the neo-Kantian turn toward
psychologies (both empirical and speculative, when psychologizing
Kant's categories), not to mention the emergence of psychoanalysis.[49]
Kant's transcendentalism, which barely survived Hegelian, Schopen-
hauerian, and Nietzschean attacks on it, was restored, on a phenom-
enological footing, when Heidegger established a difference of levels
between things in the world and their condition of possibility, known
in his early work as the "ontological difference." Unlike Kant, however, with the ontological difference came an unanticipated function
for passions like anxiety—they revealed questions that the understanding betrayed through reification. Nevertheless, passions like
anxiety also had to be enlisted in service of Heidegger's "resolute"
(virile?) approach to mortality. The Kierkegaardian opening to faith

---

49. See Paul-Laurent Assoun's (1976) discussion of the influence of Kant,
but above all Schopenhauer's reading of Kant, on Freud, in *Freud, la philosophie
et les philosophes*, Part II, Chapters 3 and 4, pp. 159–203.

was, as it were, sublimated thanks to the imaginary that underlay a Catholic, existentialist resistance to neo-Kantianism.[50]

## HOW ANXIETY BECOMES *THE* PASSION
## FOR PHILOSOPHY

The OED tells us that "anxiety" comes into English in the sixteenth century as a synonym for woes and unease. It appears to have required over a century to be mentioned in nosologies, along with heart disease.[51] The physio-spiritual ambiguity of the concept accompanies its history. The Latin *anxietas* denotes a permanent (pathological) condition, while *angor* is a transient passion. More corporeal, the verb *angere* means physically "to choke." Some historians have argued that *anxietas* spread in the Roman Empire along with the rise of Stoicism and Christian sects.[52] As its roots suggest, anxiety is neither just emotion nor passion, neither just corporeal discomfiture nor spiritual malaise. It is arguably passion's *point de départ*.[53] Certainly, the philosophical origins and interpretations of anxiety are central to nineteenth-century culture and science. For even in the nineteenth century, intellectuals not only read philoso-

---

50. For a pithy analysis of Heidegger's roots in a marginalized, Catholic opposition to the German universities of his time, and his relation in this to Carl Schmitt, see J. Taubes, *En divergeant accord: À propos de Carl Schmitt*, ed. E. Stimilli and P. Ivernel (Paris: Rivages, 2003).

51. Cf. Lovell's *History of Animals and Minerals* (1661) on "the paine and anxiety of the ventricle" in *OED* 1989. Any assimilation of anxiety and desire, or solicitous feeling, does not take place until 1769, when it appears alongside a political concern and desire "for the general welfare."

52. Dodds 1965. For the argument that Christianity merely arrived on an already deeply "anxious" scene, in which the *bacchanalia* were in decline by virtue of the dynamic relationship among orphic sexuality, fragile potency, and mortality, see classicist Pascal Quignard's *Le sexe et l'effroi* (Paris: Gallimard, 1996).

53. When anxiety is faint, it can take the form of apprehension or excitation, something pleasant or unpleasant; either way, it lacks a clear object. When anxiety is intense, it staggers us and is clearly part of what the eighteenth century called "melancholia," which regroups anxiety and depression.

phers, they debated them. Philippe Pinel's revolutionary books, which launched the field, in France, of mental hygiene and therapy by distinguishing between retardation and forms of madness, were entitled respectively: *A Philosophical Nosography or the Method of Applied Analysis* (1798) and the *Medico-Philosophical Treatise on Mental Illness or Manias* (1801).[54] In both these cases, "philosophical" meant neither metaphysics nor empiricism. The adjective referred to the inferences about mind that Pinel drew from his observations.

In the twentieth century, despite his disavowals, Freud was in dialogue with philosophy.[55] He sought to set himself explicitly apart from Cartesian mind–body parallelism (cf. his 1915 essay "The Unconscious"), and from Schopenhauer and Nietzsche's conceptions of the will. However, by Freud's time, late Idealism was looking more like a compendium of errors committed against the dynamic conceptions of the embodied psyche—at least to the natural sciences.[56] The psyche had largely become an object of science. Predictably, this appropriation was every bit as problematical, since the contemporary neurology had barely escaped the tutelage of materialist anatomo-physiology rooted in Pierre Magendie's hydraulics metaphor and

---

54. Pinel 1798. Then, Pinel, *Traité médico-philosophique de la maladie mentale ou la manie*, 1801, 1809.

55. This is especially clear in his correspondence with E. Silberstein (1870s) and with Wilhelm Fliess (1880s through 1901). In both of these collections of letters, two things are clear: Franz Brentano's philosophical psychology influenced Freud, especially by way of its dynamic conception of consciousness and intentionality; second, Freud was indeed building a system designed to bridge the speculative and the empirical (clinical). He once asked Paul Häberlin whether the unconscious should not be considered the best instantiation of Kant's Ding-an-sich. Häberlin laughed and informed Freud that the two notions were situated on entirely different levels of discourse. This is reported by Ludwig Binswanger, *Sigmund Freud: Reminiscences of a Friendship*, trans. N. Guterman (New York: Grune & Stratton, 1957).

56. The question of gender was not well handled by philosophy: Schopenhauer's work, to note but one example, abounds in misogyny. But a curious thing happens in 1844, when Søren Kierkegaard writes the first book entirely dedicated to anxiety: the question of what women are, what their spirits are like, also arises in relation to their greater experience of anxiety and spirituality.

F.-J.-V. Broussais's neural irritation model. Indeed, the topographi-
cal model of brain function localization, pioneered by the British
neurologist John Hughlings Jackson (1835–1911),[57] ironically resuscitated a principle dear to phrenology. Hughlings Jackson urged,
in the 1880s, that since rationality was the latest development in
the evolution of intelligence, it must reside in the most recently
evolved cortical area, the frontal lobes. Few would argue today that
there is a single cerebral seat for rationality. But nineteenth-century
neuropsychiatry was rife with these adaptations of Darwinism and
with phreno-localization theories. Given the awkwardness of the
emergent sciences, and their wayward ambitions for Darwin's use
(not to mention a real vassalage to metaphors drawn from discov-
eries about electrical currents)—given all that, why *did* philosophy lose its critical value for knowledge of the mind?[58]

## KANT'S "DESTRUCTION" OF RATIONAL PSYCHOLOGY:
## THE IMPOSSIBILITY OF A "SOUL-SUBSTANCE"

An answer to this question would require the recapitulation of, at
least, Hegelian, neo-Kantian, and Nietzschean conceptions of the
psyche. In each one of these, the notion of the soul is different.
Nevertheless, we can use our heuristic "fiction" to highlight salient
moments in the parting of ways between philosophy and psychiatry. I am calling this a fiction because, here, it is a "mythos" or
emplotment of fragments that are, themselves, true. As we know,
in his *Critique of Pure Reason* (1781), Kant showed that it was logically inconsistent to talk about a *substance* that is *spiritual* and takes
up no space. Since Descartes, a "substance" meant something real,
an entity observable *or* deducible—whether spatial, cogitating, or
causal. In fifty pages, Kant demolished the philosophical basis for

---

57. Hughlings Jackson's (1835–1911) application of a Darwinian conception of evolution to the genesis of the brain and nervous system influenced Freud's
work.

58. Stanley Finger, *Origins of Neuroscience: A History of Exploration into
Brain Function*, pp. 271ff.

the deduction of a mind-substance.[59] Lay people might believe in a psyche or a soul, but its philosophical underpinnings, the claim that the soul was a *res* or substance, and had an existence of deducible necessity —this much disappeared with Kant. Consequently, outside certain questions of aesthetics, which addressed those emotions apt to point reason toward its supra-sensible vocation, "rational psychology" no longer had a proper object. According to Kant, the true domain for psychology was not philosophy, but science. Psychology should thus become the empirical observation of behavior.[60] As a result, the meaning of the passions fell into a certain chaos. Descartes and others had assumed that passions were attributes of the soul, or movements of the *res cogitans*.[61] Without a soul as substrate, however, what interest could the attributes that were the passions hold for philosophy?

Kant argued that sensations of "like" and "dislike" accompanied aesthetic ideas *inter alia*, and these, whether they arose in music or in poetry, could stand in the place of a category like "the whole," denoting an "unspeakable wealth of thought." Affects of awe and fear also pointed reason toward its supra-sensuous vocation. Before the sublime, we feel amazement, admiration, enthusiasm. But in such cases, we are concerned with more than everyday affects because the experience of the dynamic sublime entails "a straining of our forces by ideas that impart to the mind a momentum whose effects are mightier . . . than are those of an impulse produced by presentations of sense."[62] In those affects accompanying

---

59. See Kant 1781.

60. See Strasser 1957.

61. Descartes, *Traité des passions*, written in French like the *Discourse on the Method*, is known to English-speaking readers as the *Passions of the Soul*. It did not appear until 1649, when it was published in Amsterdam and only later in Paris.

62. Immanuel Kant, *Critique of Judgment*, trans. W. S. Pluhar (Indianapolis, IN: Hackett, 1987), p. 132; Akademie page 272. Kant is speaking specifically of enthusiasm, here, though a mind that is "without affects" while "vigorously pursu[ing] its immutable principles is sublime, and sublime in a far superior way," he adds, ever scrupulous in regard to the role of the passions in the transcendental project.

the sublime, reason discovers something like an unstructured regulative ideal that announces to it its capacity to pursue the moral good. Outside this calling, affects may be treated within "pragmatic anthropology." But the interest of philosophical anthropology lies outside the transcendental project. In his lectures on *Anthropology from a Pragmatic Point of View* (1780), we find Kant discussing emotions and passions from a psychological and practical perspective. He praises, there again, the Stoics' ideal of self-possession, (*phlegma in significatu bono, apatheia*[63]), and insists that, psychologically speaking, emotions and passions are akin to disorders whose specific difference lies in their duration.[64]

## KANT AND A GENDERED LOGIC OF THE PASSIONS

In characterizing passions and emotions as impediments to clear-headed rationality, Kant was presenting an ancient and widespread perspective on the passions, for which our highest virtue lay in rational self-possession. Kant's anthropological discussion of the passions is guided by their value for virtue and health: "Passions are divided into those of natural inclination (innate passions) and those arising from the culture of mankind (acquired passions). Passions of the first kind are the inclinations of freedom and sex; both are linked with emotion. Those of the second kind are ambition, lust of power, and avarice, qualities . . . linked . . . with the persistence of a maxim meant for a certain purpose."[65] In short, acquired passions are tied to the will to social gain.

---

63. See Kant 1780, §754, p. 156. These are Kant's lectures prior to, and during, his 'critical' period, which began around 1780.

64. "Emotion [Kant (1780) argued] is surprise through sensation, whereby the composure of mind (*animus sui compos*) is suspended. Emotion . . . is precipitate, . . . [it] grows to a degree of feeling which makes reflection impossible (it is thoughtless). . . . Emotion is like an intoxicant which can be slept off; passion is to be regarded as an insanity which broods over an idea that is imbedding itself deeper and deeper. . . . Passion . . . no man wishes for himself. Who wants to have himself put in chains when he can be free?" (§74, p. 157).

65. Ibid., p. 175.

For Kant, innate passions could be grouped largely according to their presence in one or the other sex, because of the different reproductive roles of the two sexes.[66] As he points out, "Civilization does not establish these feminine characteristics, it only causes them to develop and become recognizable. . . . Feminine traits are called weaknesses . . . but reasonable persons see very well that those traits are . . . the tools for the management of men."[67]

Kant's distinction between innate and acquired passions floats somewhat, as does his distinction between emotion and passion, but in a few instances, he is explicit: "Passion surrenders [freedom and self-control], and finds pleasure and satisfaction in a servile disposition."[68] Moreover, unlike men, with their "passion for freedom" and their capacity for courage,[69] women exhibit passions like anxiety and fear that lead, in the best of cases, to patience: "Patience is . . . not courage. Patience is a *feminine* virtue because it does not muster the strength for opposition; it only hopes to make sorrows (suffering) bearable through habit."[70] In the same discussion, Kant adds that "the Indians in America" exhibit a similar passion to patience. They "throw away their weapons when they are encircled and . . . let themselves be slain quietly."[71] The pairing of the exotic and the feminine proceeds according to a logic of passions that escape direct service to reason or prove uncooperative with it for the sake of freedom. To be an "other," for Kant, entails missing a chance at rational freedom—by virtue of the acculturated body in women's case, or because of ethnic culture, in that of "Indians."

Kant was expressing one of two basic, contemporary outlooks on emotions and passions. The first outlook came from Romanticism,

---

66. See his §87, his "The Character of the Sexes," p. 216ff, and his "On the Character of the Species," p. 237.

67. Kant 1780, p. 217.

68. Ibid., p. 174.

69. Ibid., pp. 175ff, 162.

70. Ibid., p. 162. Emphasis added.

71. Ibid., p. 162.

which held that passion was the source of heroic gestures.[72] The second outlook saw passions and emotions impinging on rationality and the ability to act freely in a moral way. In both cases, a loose logic of nature, culture and gender, and ethnicity structured the possible distribution of passions and virtues. If patience was a feminine virtue, it was because patience was tied to a passivity that was willed but not rational. According to Kant, "[Passions] must take root gradually and even be able to coexist with reason. One can . . . easily see that passions do the greatest harm to freedom . . . passion is an illness which abhors all medication. One labels passion with the word *mania* [for that reason] . . ."[73] Even the passions that coexist with reason are often too far from it to be reliable. Anxiety, fear, patience, but also hatred and ambition may coexist with reason, only to undermine it later. They prey more readily on women than men, since Kant had already argued that "the word 'fool' applied to a woman does not have the same harsh meaning as the word 'fool' applied to a man . . ."[74]

## FROM KANT TO KIERKEGAARD, AND BEYOND: PHILOSOPHY MOVES FROM THE "SOUL" TO PASSIONS AS A DIFFERENT KIND OF "KNOWING"

As philosophy and psychology pursued their divorce, a series of factors thrust philosophy toward a concern with the meaning of

---

72. In what is a multifarious and sometimes contradictory "tradition," which precedes romanticism, the "passioni violentissime" are responsible for the first human speech, according to Vico. The "ruling passion" is at the root of the principle of individuation for Pope. For Mandeville, passions are to morality what physics is to movement. Hume argues that reason bathes in passions, rather than being interrupted by them. But it is in German-speaking literature that passions get tied to the notion of genius. J. F. Abel, Schiller's teacher, praised the passions as the source of "those courageous acts and . . . great ideas that cause the astonishment and admiration of each century." Herder, Fichte, and even Hegel, speculatively, follow suit. For a concise history of the concept of "emotion," "passion," *Affekt*, and *Leidenschaft*, see Hengelbrock and Lanz 1980. "Examen historique du concept de passion," *Nouvelle Revue de psychanalyse: La Passion* 21, (Spring 1980): 77–91.

73. Kant 1780, p. 172.

74. Ibid., p. 107.

embodied historical existence. These included directly the meta-
morphosis of Kant's transcendental categories into a psychologistic
concern with mental functions, the rise of the social sciences, and,
arguably, the polarizations of Hegelianism. Behind this, however,
lay the hundred-year-long debate[75] about the "transmutation" or
evolution of animals, and the age of the earth, a plethora of "Darwinisms," the prestige and mutability of materialism in science, and
advances in technology that led to the use of electricity as a diagnostic tool and a means of studying emotions.[76] The Romantics'
inquiry—What does it mean for humans to be creatures whose
behavior is governed by drives?—found a place in nineteenth-
century psychology and neuroscience. Of course, it was no nov-
elty for philosophy to allow science a role in the construction of
explanatory systems. What was new was philosophy's hermeneutic pursuit of facticity and finiteness, whose surprising counterpoint
in natural science was the search for the material grounds, the location, and the operation of psychic life. It would appear that the age
of philosophical systems ended in an age of new beginnings (repeated
beginnings): Husserl's repeated search for an apodictic ground
for his phenomenology and Heidegger's return to the new (pre-
Socratic) beginning, and then to the "other," German and poetic,
beginning of the question of Being and its obfuscation. All this is
to recall that the purpose of my *mythos* is to argue that philosophers, above all existentialist philosophers, took up anew a kind
of questioning in which the passions were not disorders or thin
forms of judgments, but expanded possible approaches to meaning.
This proved inevitable, as formalism in philosophy came under

---

75. See Buffon's *Histoire naturelle*, in 36 volumes, published from 1749,
and Darwin's *Origin of Species* (1856). Buffon was a vitalist who believed that
species were fixed, but that a law of continuity (from Leibniz) governed nature
such that species distinctions could not be made categorically because all of being
was interrelated.

76. Above all, Faraday's 1832 demonstration that the electricity induced
by a magnet, voltaic electricity produced by a battery, and static electricity were
all the same, argued for a unitary notion of force in physical bodies, against the
older Leibnizian arguments for a quantifiable, mathematizable force, and a "life
force" coming from bodies that were, themselves, active forces.

attack and as psychology proceeded to interpret and classify the passions by itself. By the mid-nineteenth century, passions like anxiety had become a different kind of object for philosophy. In many cases, this implied parallel tracks for philosophy and psychology, with occasional points of intersection between them. Thus, Husserl's transcendental ego *is* a psychological ego, albeit viewed from a different perspective. Psychoanalysis—absent questions of invalidation—is a *hermeneutics of the psyche, related through narrative fragments and an interpretive grammar inflected by the various currents of analysis.*[77]

## CONCLUDING REMARKS

A study of anxiety in psychology and philosophy should develop along three lines of inquiry.[78] First, anxiety is "psychologically" (and metabolically) prior to rational or cognitive subjectivity. Its description gives us an approach to ourselves as subjects that emerge at the site of accumulated mnemic traces, themselves the product of interaction with the world and others. Anxiety's origin lies prior to, and outside of, the ego conceived as a protective pellicle between "inside" and "outside." Pathological anxiety comes to be through a series of retroactivating repetitions such that, each time we are seized by the passion of anxiety, it points back to a precursory threat or trauma, whose initial onset predated the self. In anxiety, we "understand" something outside our available memories, something difficult to express in narrative or conceptual forms.

---

77. No need to say that many have ventured this argument, from Paul Ricoeur (1977) through Paul-Laurent Assoun (1976, 1980), Jacques Lacan (1978), and most recently, Richard Boothby (2001). Samuel Weber (2000), though without intending to make the Freud-hermeneute case, presupposes it and treats Freud's problematics, like that of anxiety, as problems with a philosophical underpinning. See also Didier Anzieu (1986).

78. I illuminate this relationship by pairing certain philosophers: Kierkegaard and Nietzsche, Darwin and Herbert Spencer; Freud and Otto Weininger in light of the latter's claim about the "feminization" and "Judaicization" of European culture.

Anxiety invites us to ask whether there is not a sensuous bodily intelligence governed by its own logic much the way that dreams have an internal logic not far removed from pathologies like hysteria.

Anxiety has to do with sexuality and psychoanalysis' metaphysics of "the drives." Foucault showed us that sexuality is an over-determined concept, but it may be that most concepts with political and philosophical weight are *surdéterminés*. Of course, anxiety also has to do with meanings of lived time and memory for body and mind. This is to argue that a subject becomes possible, as Judith Butler put it, only through the complex foldings entailed in "sub-jection."[79] A subject evolves through transformative dependencies upon others, which, if they begin in affective modes, evolve into recurrent moods and optics.

Second, anxiety is the first of the emotions-passions. For Freud, it comes to precede any pleasure–unpleasure continuum, as well as the distinction and dissociation of drives between "life" and "death," though it accompanies the expression of both. As a kind of vibrating excitation, lacking an object, anxiety blurs the distinction between physical sensations and those more psychical feelings that Husserl called intentional because they were always on the verge of becoming thought. Itself over-determined, anxiety denotes an affective continuum[80] bridging corporeal and psychic life.[81] It should be studied in that way.

---

79. See J. Butler, *The Psychic Life of Power: Theories in Subjection*, Op. cit.

80. For a discussion of the meaning Freud attributes to sexuality, as against the everyday physician's definition of it, see Freud, "'Wild' Psychoanalysis," in *The Freud Reader* (Gay 1989), pp. 351–356. Thus: "We use the term 'sexuality' in the same comprehensive sense as that in which the German language uses the word *lieben* ('to love'). We have long known, too, that mental absence of satisfaction with all its consequences can exist where there is no lack of normal sexual intercourse; and as therapists we always bear in mind that the unsatisfied sexual trends (whose substitutive satisfactions in the form of nervous symptoms we combat) can often find only very inadequate outlet in coitus and other sexual acts" (p. 353). Also see note 22 *supra*. This is one of the essays that, between 1910 and 1915, combats naïveté in science and in philosophy with a special vehemence. The object here is scientific misrepresentations of psychoanalysis.

81. Philosophy has thus learned at least that the subject is not unitary, but split; it recognizes that agency is not simple, but over-determined, reactive,

Finally, anxiety arises as social contagion and creation. It is part of a circle of normativity: anxiety structures (nonconscious) self-perception as much as it describes states of mind present and known to us. Anxiety has proven a fecund concept—by which to regroup individual disorders and the malaise of ages, the *Belle Époque* and the post-World War II period—but it has "infected" us the way repertories of symptoms in diagnostic manuals leave us pondering our well-being. That anxiety should accompany and promote abjection is unsurprising. It was long associated with passivity and the "effeminate" passions of Jews and exotic peoples. These passions in turn were superposed to the infantile passions and applied to those groups *not* identified with feminine characteristics. Thus, the regal yet infantile *Sénégalais*, sent to head up the front in World War I; or again, the Malagasy who revolts against his putative white "ancestor-replacement."[82] It has been argued that Freud's investigations offered him but a microcosm of the Viennese *bourgeoisie* and, therefore, that Freud's theories mirror rather limited cultural spheres (the ambient anti-Semitic Catholic culture and a German-speaking Jewish culture). Certainly, these two "worlds" responded to him out of their particular anxieties: "It is *you* who are these things" or "You, Jews, who do this sort of science." But, as Meynert's hushed confession to Freud suggests, repressed cultural anxiety was destined to a cyclical return out of which we have yet to step.[83]

---

repetitive, and that intentionality shades off into degrees of semi-consciousness, including the "ecstasies" of senses, daydreaming, and types of sleep. It has argued, further, that the mind–body dualism is neither dual nor monistic, but an irreducible symbiosis.

82. For the analysis of the supposed oedipal fantasies of the Malagasy see O. Mannoni, *Prospero and Caliban: The Psychology of Colonization*, trans. P. Powesland (Ann Arbor, MI: University of Michigan Press, 1990, first published in French in 1947). For discussions of the "infantile" Sénégalais in Western imagery, see Paul S. Landau's work in *Images and Empires: Visuality in Colonial and Post-colonial Africa*, ed. Landau and Kaspin, pp. 233–251. (Berkeley, CA: University of California Press, 2002).

83. Julia Kristeva's (1976) insight from her essay "Women's Time" is helpful here. Anxiety tells us that humans need to "provide [themselves]," she writes, "with a *representation* (animal, female, male, parental, etc.) in place of what con-

## REFERENCES

Anzieu, D. (1986). *Freud's Self-Analysis*, trans. P. Graham. Madison, CT: International Universities Press.

Assoun, P.-L. (1976). *Freud, la philosophie et les philosophes*. Paris: Presses Unversitaires de France, 2005.

———— (1980). *Freud et Nietzsche*. Paris: PUF. Also, trans. R. Collier. London and New York: Athlone, 2000.

Boothby, R. (2001). *Freud as Philosopher: Metapsychology after Lacan*. New York: Routledge.

Butler, J. (1993). *Bodies That Matter: On the Discursive Limits of "Sex."* New York: Routledge.

———— (1997). *The Psychic Life of Power*. Stanford, CA: Stanford University Press.

Charcot, J.-M., and Richer, P. (1984). *Les Démoniaques dans l'Art: Suivi de la Foi qui Guérit*. Paris: Macula.

Dodds, E. R. (1965). *Pagan and Christian in an Age of Anxiety: Some Aspects of Religious Experience from Marcus Aurelius to Constantine*. Cambridge: Cambridge University Press.

Finger, S. (1994). *Origins of Neuroscience: A History of Exploration into Brain Function*. New York: Oxford University Press.

Freud, S. (1912). The unconscious in psycho-analysis. In *Sigmund Freud Collected Papers*, Vol. IV, trans. J. Riviere. London: Hogarth, 1949.

———— (1966). *The Standard Edition of the Complete Psychological Works of Sigmund Freud*, 24 vols, trans. and ed. J. Strachey and A. Freud. London: Hogarth.

———— (1997). *Dora: An Analysis of a Case of Hysteria*. New York: Touchstone.

Gauchet, M., and Swain, G. (1997). *Le vrai Charcot: Les chemins imprévus de l'inconscient*. Paris: Calmann-Lévy.

Gay, P., ed. (1989). *The Freud Reader*. New York: W.W. Norton.

---

stitutes us as such, in other words, [in the figurative site from which comes language and] symbolization" (Ibid., p. 393). For Kristeva this is a psychic imperative. And it concerns how we create a "we" together, as we also build an "I" or a "me." What *kind* of representation we need is a different matter. It is our choice, and the choice of cultures. The challenge is to create practices by which we can set representations in the metaphoric place where our activity of symbol making originates: in the passionate hiatus whence we begin to speak.

Gilman, S. (1991). *The Jew's Body*. New York: Routledge, Chapman and Hall.

Hengelbrock, J., and Lanz, J. (1980). Examen historique du concept de passion. *Nouvelle Revue de psychanalyse: La Passion* 21 (Spring):77–91. German edition from the *Historisches Wörterbuch der Philosophie*, Dir. J. Ritter (Darmstadt: Wissenschaftliche Buchgesellschaft, 1971).

Kant, I. (1780). *Anthropology from a Pragmatic Point of View*, trans. V. L. Dowdell, ed. H. Rudnick. Carbondale and Edwardsville, IL: Southern Illinois University Press, 1978.

———— (1781). "Transcendental dialectic: the paralogisms of pure reason. In *Critique of Pure Reason*, trans. N. K. Smith, pp. 328–383. New York: St. Martin's Press, 1965.

Kierkegaard, S. (1848). *The Concept of Anxiety: A Simple Psychologically Orienting Deliberation on the Dogmatic Issue of Hereditary Sin*, trans. and ed. R. Thomte and A. B. Anderson. Princeton, NJ: Princeton University Press, 1980.

Kristeva, J. (1976). *New Maladies of the Soul*, trans. R. Guberman. New York: Columbia University Press, 1995.

Lacan, J. (1978). *The Four Fundamental Concepts of Psychoanalysis*, trans. A. Sheridan. New York: W.W. Norton.

Lindemann, A. (2000). *Anti-Semitism before the Holocaust*. Essex: Longman Press, Division of Pearson Educative Ltd.

Pinel, P. (1798). *Nosographie philosophique, ou, La Méthode de l'analyse appliquée à la médecine*. Paris: Richard, Caille et Ravier, An 7.

Ricoeur, P. (1977). *Freud and Philosophy: An Essay on Interpretation*, trans. D. Savage. New Haven, CT: Yale University Press.

Ritvo, L. B. (1990). *Darwin's Influence on Freud: A Tale of Two Sciences*. New Haven, CT: Yale University Press.

Sadoff, D. F. (1998). *Sciences of the Flesh: Representing Body and Subject in Psychoanalysis*. Stanford, CA: Stanford University Press.

Sternhell, Z. (1978). *La Droite révolutionnaire 1885–1914. Les Origines françaises du fascisme*. Paris: Seuil.

Strasser, S. (1957). Kant and the origin of modern trialism. In *The Soul in Metaphysical and Empirical Psychology*. Pittsburgh, PA: Duquesne Studies Philosophical Series 7, pp. 35–39; Louvain: Editions E. Nauwelaerts, pp. 58–69.

Swain, G. (1977). *Le Sujet de la folie: Naissance de la psychiatrie (Précédé de 'De Pinel à Freud' par Marcel Gauchet)*. Paris: Calmann-Lévy, 1997.

Weber, S. (2000). *The Legend of Freud*. Stanford, CA: Stanford University Press. Expanded Edition.

# 2

# Catastrophe

Dorothea Olkowski

Presented with the theory that the United States has become a culture of fear cultivated by dominant classes to maintain political and economic control, a student demurs. "Oh," she exclaims, "It's not that. I used not to be afraid of anything, I was fearless, but since I was held up and robbed by a man with a gun and nearly kidnapped, I have changed." Not only was the student mugged, but there was a fumbled attempt at abduction, with a possible threat as well of sexual assault and even murder. Moreover, she insinuated that she did not resist the robbery, but she did resist the attempted abduction with its implicit sexual violation, in spite of the lethal weapon threatening her. Her insinuation rests, in part, on the conclusion that "Now I am afraid of *everything*; my boyfriend thinks I'm crazy because I'm even afraid of the neighbors." Her story manifests itself as an unmistakable objection grounded in personal experience that appears to undermine the cogency as well as the unilateral nature of any claims for cultural or political influences on perception and emotion. But her statement, so personal and individual on its surface, may merely mask another claim, one that is far more pervasive. "I" was not fearful, but now, due to an individual incident, now "I" am terrified. In fact, I am not just afraid of the person who robbed me but of everyone, and this is because I am innocent, completely faultless in this and all matters of crime and sex, but because of this event "I" am no longer secure, no longer a member of a consistent and constant world, a stable world. Inevitably, "I" am irrevocably altered, "I" must be (to protect myself from those who might blame me) ubiquitously afraid; I fear everything, and even the boyfriend (who may have some faults for which I am not responsible) does not comprehend the depth of my fear (in case you think that living with a boyfriend is not the act of a virtuous young woman).

This experience and the retelling of this fear-inspiring incident have a certain impact and are meant to reinforce a specific point of view. Any "I" subject to such an assault would begin to feel fear; something prescribed is at work, cultivating this fear. The suggestion that social and cultural factors influence a set of beliefs and behaviors is easily dismissed; cultural contingency remains simply that and nothing more. In this explanation, the powers and role of the "I" have been magnified, deepened, and in the light of the circumstances that have given rise to it, glamorized not only by society, but also of necessity by the victim herself in order to remain above reproach. What can be more magnificent than an unwitting victim who survives her assault? What can be more heroic, in the grips of a catastrophe, than to resist abduction or sexual aggression and to escape, traumatized, apprehensive, defiled, but able somehow to go on with one's life? And, given this "I," already central to all of "our" collective beliefs, values, actions, and thoughts, this "I" enduring and carrying on at the heart of the harrowing incident, its value is secured as all the efforts of our greatest minds reinforce this position. Indeed, the structure of this traumatic incident and its aftermath evokes another.

> One day two years ago some gentlemen had climbed the mountain and asked for something to eat. My aunt wasn't at home, and Franziska, who always did the cooking, was nowhere to be found either. We

looked everywhere, and at last Alois, the little boy, my cousin, said: "Why Franziska must be in Father's room!" And we both laughed but we weren't thinking anything bad. Then we went to my uncle's room but found it locked. That seemed strange to me. Then Alois said: "There is a window in the passage where you can look into the room." We went into the passage; but Alois wouldn't go to the window and said he was afraid. So I said: I'll go. I'm not a bit afraid.[1]

Now, Katharina is periodically afraid of everything. Her nerves are bad, she is often out of breath, suffocating. Something presses on her eyes, her head feels heavy, she hears dreadful buzzing and feels something crushing her chest. Her throat squeezes together, her head hammers and she is frightened, so frightened that she thinks she will die, and in the long moments of these events, she fears going anywhere, thinking that someone, some unspeakable person might be standing behind her ready to grab her while in front of her, she sees an awful face.

As it turns out, the artless and ingenuous girl reported her experience to her aunt and repercussions followed. Disagreeable scenes, open talk in front of the girl and her cousin revealing sexual secrets and anger, a pregnant young woman, divorce, finally a move away from the scene to another town. For the girl, the incident was linked to memories of the uncle's repeated attempted molestation of herself and memories of his coverups of his sexual liaisons with Franziska, her own cousin. Later, the analyst admits that the uncle is really the father and the aunt, the mother of the fearful girl. The mother, it appears, responds much less to the attempted molestations of the girl than to the affair with the servant. The girl expresses ignorance of her father's sexual intentions toward herself. Like the student, she is vague about exactly what happened. "Mere suspicion of sexual relations calls up the affect of anxiety in virginal individuals."[2] Her fear? A result of her "moral and physical disgust" as she "confesses" to the analyst that she had "felt her uncle's

---

1. Breuer and Freud 1956, "Case 4, Katharina," pp. 127–128. This case is reported solely by Freud.
2. Ibid., p. 134. This case is reported solely by Freud.

body" next to hers, though she refuses to reveal which part of the body she had felt.[3] In this case, however, we have no heroic victim. The enraged uncle-father tells Katharina that she is at fault for speaking up and he threatens to do her harm. The mother, who receives the confidences of the girl regarding her father's attempts on her, decides to keep this information in reserve in case the father causes trouble in court.

Fearfulness, this case history avers, is neither contingent nor cultural. It is a question of the interactions between life and death instincts [drives]. It is ignorance on the part of the ego, lack of reason and common sense in sexual matters insofar as the ignorance of a presexual girl is declared to be not that far removed from conscious rejection of sex by a fully sexual adult woman, a woman like Anna O.[4] Regardless of her marked intelligence and powerful intellect, Fräulein Anna O., at the age of 21, is still described in sexual terms: "the element of sexuality was astonishingly undeveloped in her."[5] This, apparently, because the woman had never been in love. Indeed, when and where would such a young woman have met a man with whom she could fall in love? She had been forced by circumstances, by familial conformity to local standards of behavior for women, to spend her time caring for a sick and dying parent rather than attending university, her preferred objective. Her reported infatuation with her analyst may or may not have occurred, but certainly his repeated visits and conversation may well have been the only intelligent contact Anna O. was able to claim from the confinement of her tedious life.[6] Repeatedly protesting that his

---

3. Ibid., p. 131.

4. Ibid., p. 134. The view of women as both sexually timid and a tease is expressed in many of Freudian texts. This contradiction is fed by the idea that hysterical symptoms are the expression of secret and repressed wishes, intimacies, and secrets whose revelation Freud's hysterical patients are not eager to betray. Freud viewed his duties to science—to still suffering patients—as superseding his duties to any one individual. Eventually, nearly all the names in the case histories were made public. See Freud 1963.

5. Ibid., p. 21. Of course, it has been suggested that Breuer wanted to exonerate himself from any wrongdoing in the case.

6. Ibid., p. 41 nt. 1. These are Breuer's own reflections.

patient was totally innocent in matters of sex, the analyst reports only that Anna would confide in him and only in him, that he habitually paid her daily visits for treatment, and that after absences on his part, her condition noticeably deteriorates. In Anna's life, years of morphine addiction and an increasingly complex symptomology with or without sexual overtones may have been a small price to pay for the quotidian pleasure of some intelligent company with its attendant relief from the daily drudgery and dread precipitated by endless hours, days, and months of caring for the sick.[7] Indeed, from the doctor's standpoint, which is implicit in his analysis of the patient, the prohibition on pleasure is exactly what we have come to expect, not from our civilization in its efforts to thwart Eros, but from our own egos. There exists, we are cautioned, "a *tendency to keep intracerebral excitation constant.*"[8] In a state of constancy, the organism is ready to work; in a state of expectation, efficiency is impaired yet uniformity remains unbroken. The organism is in a state of "incitement," the urge to make use of the increased energy in a functional manner until a state of true "excitement" is attained. In this case, anything can happen; discharge can be violent or pathological, like an electrical short circuit. There is a failure here, a failure of what has been described as "good sense," that is, of equilibrium. It prevents the uniform distribution of intracerebral excitation and permits an "abnormal expression of emotion," due either to the high level of intracerebral excitation that fails to be leveled down through ideational or motor activity, or to a weakening of resistance on the part of the nervous system.[9] Not surprisingly, the sexual instinct is the name given to the most powerful source of persisting increases of excitation—therefore of

---

7. Borch-Jacobsen 1996.

8. Breuer and Freud 1956, p. 197. The first law of thermodynamics states simply that "energy is conserved," when energy is defined as "the capacity to do work." The physicist Kelvin concluded around 1851 that all phenomena could be explained in terms of the transformation of energy *without* allusions to underlying models. See Atkins 1984, pp. 8–9.

9. Breuer and Freud 1956, pp. 198–205. For "good sense" as equilibrium see Deleuze 1968, pp. 288–293, or 1994, pp. 223–227.

neurosis. The fault lies with the uneven distribution of excitation throughout the nervous system, disturbing ideas, impairing perception, blinding creatures to danger, and intensifying male aggression—at least until there is sexual discharge. Animals, men, and neurotics all experience this *endogenous* heightening of excitation originating in the "sexual glands" and continuing, a nonuniform distribution of increased excitation, until discharged. Failure to reestablish uniformity, by whatever means possible, can be and usually is traumatic.[10]

Given the psychological, philosophical, and scientific obsession with human happiness, at least in the West, the boundaries between the "I" or ego and the world seem to have become the primary focus of our concern and interest. Uncertain boundary lines between ego and world or ego and others, in most cases, are the very definition of psychological pathology. They are said to be catastrophic, plunging the ego into a cauldron of neurotic behaviors in an effort to reestablish some sort of control over its own drives as well as intrusions and exclusions coming from others. "Any experience which calls up distressing affects—such as those of fright, anxiety, shame or physical pain—may operate as a trauma of this [psychical] kind," whether there is a single provocative experience or a group of them.[11] Projections of one's own ideas onto others or onto objects or the inability to claim as one's own ideas, feelings, or perceptions that have been attributed to one's particular ego are cause for concern, since "normally, there is nothing of which we are more certain than the feeling of our self, our own ego."[12] Individual responses to violations of this boundary, however, although apparently circumstantial ("I was held up at gunpoint and now I am terrified") are taken to be grounded in something more determined, something a *priori* rather than contingent, something neuropsychologically structured, something pervasive rather than

---

10. Breuer and Freud 1956, pp. 200, 201.
11. Ibid., p. 6.
12. Freud 1961, p. 12. "This ego appears to us as something autonomous and unitary, marked off distinctly from everything else."

localized. The infant, of course, makes no such distinction between herself and the world, but very soon it appears to the adult observer that because the infant's own body is always present to herself, she learns to distinguish between herself and things that do come and go, the bodies of others. But the key determinants in making a distinction between self and others, between oneself and the external world, are internal ones—not so much the perceived and verifiable comings and goings of persons and objects as the arrival and departure of pleasure and pain. The little self, the budding ego tries, we are assured, to escape from anything that is a source of irritation, irritation that invariably is experienced as unpleasure. Driven by the never-ending pursuit of physical and mental balance, an equilibrium that would impede breakdown and disorder, the pursuit of pleasure in its most limited form, the avoidance of pain, is the ultimate imperative.[13]

Yet closer inspection reveals that pleasure and pain do not necessarily yield the difference between what is internal and what is external, what belongs to the self and what belongs to the world, what is necessary and what is contingent, insofar as not all pleasure arises from within and not all pain from without. It is obvious that with respect to the external world, there are many terrors to guard against. To some extent, nature remains a frightening force—earthquakes, tornadoes, floods, famine, disease, freezing conditions, excessive heat all continue to threaten. Even in the contemporary era, no one is exempt from natural disaster. This is compounded, for humans, by the fact of their mortality, a fate that cannot be comprehended and generally fails to be acknowledged except by those in great pain, but that seems to correspond to a generalized notion of individual breakdown and dissipation. The experience of one's own body, its limitations and inadequacies, may also at least frighten those who pay attention. Most prevalent, however, are thought to be the sufferings brought on by society, by our fellow human beings, sufferings that range from the great to the small:

---

13. Ibid., p. 14. The separation of the ego from pain contributes in a large degree to its isolation.

from war, poverty, oppressive governments, and families to excessive and diverse cruelties and insults, panics and shames. Here size and spread are insignificant since the latter, the small sufferings, can ruin a life as easily as worldwide traumas. It is a question of what Henri Bergson would call the "intensity" of suffering and the specific nature of its connection to and enhancement by other aspects of one's body and one's life.[14] Such terrors have been collectively called, perhaps inappropriately, the reality principle—inappropriately, insofar as "reality testing" is a function of the ego, and what the use of the term implies is that, for this theoretical stance, fear is internal and ego-driven, regardless of the stimulus.

In the process of psychic formation, the id is modified by the direct influence of the external world that it does not yet know or perceive as external. Moreover, the ego is described as a "projection of a surface," and so would seem to contain, perhaps in holographic fashion, all the information buried in the depths of the id. The ego, representing reason and common sense, seeks to control the passions through those means.[15] Thus reason and common sense become synonymous with reality. The purpose of the reality principle seems to be, as much and as far as possible, to make the experience of pleasure unattainable or at least ambiguous, since both from without and from within, we believe that we are threatened with disintegration and harm by objects and events that may be sources of happiness but equally or eventually turn into sources of torment. Hence pleasure, far from being a "principle" guaranteed by neurophysiological structures or physical laws, is something far more ambiguous. By definition and in practice, it might as well be called the no-pleasure pleasure principle. Defined as the

14. See Henri Bergson 1959, p. 47. Originally published in French in *Bergson Oeuvres* (Paris: Presses Universitaires de France, 1959), 34. I have provided an extended account of such a heterogeneous or intensive event in Olkowski 1999, pp. 125–129.

15. Freud 1960, pp. 15–16. In these passages, reason and common sense appear to be indigenous to the ego, as if acting as the border guard between id and world automatically generates them. It is unclear here what comes from the id and what from the world.

momentary and swift satisfaction of needs and desires that have been unsatisfied and burgeoning, it is clear that this notion of pleasure involves something limited and inexorably fleeting, vanishing as suddenly as it appears, overtaken by psychic forces far more powerful and pervasive. Happiness is never a positive emotion in its own place, but is most often characterized as the pleasure of escape, escape from suffering and unpleasure.[16]

To where do we escape? Sexual satisfaction makes its mark as the principle option on the "positive" side of the equation, the side taken up by Eros that functions to preserve life where preservation means unifying disparate energies, focusing on the goal of organizing them. But contrary to all expectations, the erotic impulse inexorably emerges as a negative, an irritation, bringing not harmony and unity but agitation and breakdown. "Aside from reproduction sex is . . . part of a natural tendency to mix things up, to randomize, to lose discrete identity due to the tendency of material systems to reach more probable states."[17] Erotic agitation implies loss of identity, destabilization, and contingency, disorder and deterioration. For human beings, it implies a loss of awareness, often unwelcome, commensurate with the suspension of reason and common sense, particularly when we understand such satisfaction as the sudden fulfillment of needs (the argument is that satisfaction is preferably sudden, a qualification that largely restricts pleasure to males) that have been dammed up to a high degree—a term insinuating that pleasure is no more than the release of tension. Acute gratification in the form of release implies the suspension of reason and common sense, the loss of order, a general degradation of one's being. By contrast, small-scale deterioration and disorder are much less disruptive of the state of constancy that we take to be central to our universal disposition but the very antithesis of acute, preferably sudden, enjoyment. Once agitated, we

---

16. Freud 1961, pp. 23–24. These substitutes are posited as indispensable for *everyone*.

17. Margulis and Sagan 1997, p. 19. The second law of thermodynamics states that the distribution of energy changes in an irreversible manner.

become aware of the potential for loss. Our choice is clear, either eliminate the agitation or eliminate its sources. So-called desexualization calls for replacing these myriad disequilibriums with something else, something that is also destructive but in a manner seemingly commensurate with the order of the universe.

Fearing loss of identity, of potency, of particularity, we emphasize the importance of maintaining and reproducing ourselves in the midst of the material and energetic flows that stimulate and alter us repeatedly and without our consent. We retreat, literally, into our skins, claiming ourselves to be free beings to the extent to which we can separate ourselves from all other creatures, those of our own species as well as those of other species. Rationally and common-sensibly, we assume that the offspring we generate, the emotions we allow ourselves to feel, the actions we take, the words we speak and write are acts of free beings, effects of our distinct, personal, and individual bodies and minds. This relative constancy, this calmly rational behavior, allows us the fantasy that our moments of pleasure, our "happiness" in the form of a sudden satisfaction of needs is in service to something else, something characterized by disequilibrium and disorder. A certain determinism takes over, reminding us that having arisen out of matter and energy, we will return to that state, that the little ego is simply an element of an idealized, stable world.[18] And psychologically, everything we "do" reinforces this situation. If we choose sublimation, it is because it appears to render our state constant; we believe it gives us a mechanism for avoiding physical and psychical disorder, decreasing our turmoil and confusion. Sublimation in all its forms is simply another word for equilibrium, and we are ingenious and prolifically inventive in creating ever new modes of detour even when their effect is to render our daily lives deplorable and insignificant. The alternatives here are so profuse as to constitute an almanac of misery.

We begin by attempting to influence our own organism. We may hide ourselves away to limit interaction with any other forces

---

18. Prigogine 1997, p. 26.

or beings. We may turn to intoxication; alcohol and drugs are greatly underappreciated in the economics of the libido for providing an "anti-pleasure pleasure" that necessitates no association with other beings and for allowing an escape from reality, from reason and common sense. Intoxication expends energy that otherwise might be dissipated in sudden, presumably pleasurable sexual encounters that, if promiscuous, are judged to be overwhelmingly and decisively destructive to our own being and counter to the presumed order of the universe. We may also "kill off" the instincts, which is to say, any nonrational and noncommon-sensible awareness. Meditation, yoga, scholarly retreat all return us to a state of equilibrium and relieve us of the pressure arising from the persistence of the exigencies of life: hunger, respiration, sex. Intellectual or aesthetic satisfactions, in particular, divert attention from uncompromising demands threatening us with extreme disorder. The more formal these efforts, the better, since messy materialization risks returning the poet or visual artist, along with the writer, philosopher, and scientist, back to the torment of disequilibrium, an irrational defiance of the laws of nature that, we believe, must be obeyed whether or not they are commanded. Yet even among those few with the talent or interest in pursuing the path of the intellectual or the artist, few are recognized for their contributions, and even ordinary tribulations may interfere with one's life's work, driving some further inward on a path of social, cosmic, or religious delusion.

If independence from the external world is never assured, then neither is it recommended as a secure site for fleeing the push-pull of dissipation and uniformity. In spite of the variety of means of evasion of this push-pull, most follow a route that is clearly less demanding and dependent on circumstances, the route of giving in to nature, to the constancy principle, and simply doing what seems most "natural," devoting our lives to reality. Much of America, it would appear, has chosen this route on which the controlling figure of good sense reigns supreme and the "I" is at the height of its potency, inhibiting any influences that threaten stability. This course is clear, its requirements replete with compensation. Limit ourselves to an existence of mind-numbing uniformity, whose rewards include all the accoutrements of consumer life that cloud any awareness of the implications of an augmented body mass and attenuated mental acuity or physical activity that accompany the slow slide into oblivion. "If a man thinks himself happy merely to have escaped unhappiness or to have survived his suffering, and if in general the task of avoiding suffering pushes that of obtaining pleasure into the background, [r]eflection shows that the accomplishment of this task can be attempted along very different paths; and all these paths have been recommended by the various schools of worldly wisdom and put into practice by men."[19] Meanwhile, all around us, animate creatures, from the most rudimentary living matter to the most complex, are continuously making use of the capacity to metabolize, trapping sunlight and elements for movement and action: carbon, hydrogen, oxygen, sulfur, nitrogen, phosphorus. Colonies of microbes, themselves evolving from bacteria, once fused, shared bodies and "in a process reminiscent of both sex and infection, penetrated and began living in larger cells," promiscuously at first, but in the long run, habituated and relatively stable.[20] Everywhere, along with the general principle of disorder and deterioration, there appears to coexist an inexplicable tendency toward auto-poeisis and renewal. In spite of our occasional awareness of the influence of flows of energy and matter, the openness of systems, both living and nonliving, and the influence of a multitude of events in the universe, we persist in the narrative of our autonomy and self-production. We have developed an entire vocabulary and complex theories that map out the extent of this production, theories intimately connected to ideas about value. Happiness has become individualized in a generic sort of way. We think that it is a question of the economics of the individual's libido. How much psychical and emotional energy do we, each of us individually, have to spare and what is its orientation? The fail-

---

19. Freud 1961, p. 26. This long list of sublimations is inspired by Chapter II.

20. Margulis and Sagan 1997, pp. 22–24.

ure to achieve happiness, along with fear, anxiety, physical and psychical pain, like that of the mugged student, is assumed to correspond to something *a priori* and universal for her sex. That is, with respect to happiness, male human beings in particular are singled out as closed systems, if not radically isolated ones. The *a priori* erotic "man" privileges so-called emotional relations; the self-sufficient narcissist appropriately turns to mental satisfactions; the aim-oriented achiever tests his strength against the world. But each of these types becomes that type in relation only to his own internal influences, the manner in which his ego achieves equilibrium, avoiding pain but also avoiding pleasure by finding substitute satisfactions. Women, on the other hand, presumably make up the majority of those who cannot or do not transform and rearrange their libidinal components and have no hope of nonsexual satisfactions relating to the external world. Neurosis will be more common here. Thus a young woman who has been assaulted may expect to feel fear not only of her attacker, but also of a vast array of unrelated persons or situations. In the same circumstances, a young man unable to redirect his libido will likely turn to chronic intoxication or complete randomization, that is, psychosis.[21]

What force is at work determining these outcomes, judging them to be inevitable? Are they inexorably prescribed? What about the plausible thesis that "all of us dwell in a pervasive, if neglected cosmic context. . . . The softness of sundown and the cover of night predispose cyclical sexual beings to bring forth music, dancing, and revelry. . . . The theme of living matter internalizing, with increasing variation, the cyclicity of its cosmic surroundings applies also to the rhythm of sexual love as a permutation of the primordial music of the universe."[22] Cosmic rays and solar radiation constantly enter the earth's biosphere, and life is assembled by converting this

---

21. Freud 1961, 33–36, 59. "Psychoanalysis has scarcely anything to say about beauty either. All that seems certain is its derivation from the field of sexual feeling" (p. 33).

22. Margulis and Sagan 1997, p. 27. This view goes against the idea that any living thing is an isolated structure.

energy from the sun. Local order is achieved in a process in which dissipating energy flows through structures, yet something is always left behind. Disturbingly, what is left behind is an even greater disorder. Urine, feces, sweat, pollution, garbage, and carbon dioxide are all examples of the "inevitable messes made by human life"; perhaps we would be wise to add to this list neurosis, psychosis, and chronic intoxication.[23] Or, is this simply a view of life in the shadow of Plato and Parmenides, whose hypotheses that motion is not real and change an illusion continually emerge and reemerge as the millennialist victors in philosophical, psychological, and scientific debates, debates about ultimate reality and first principles? Meanwhile, amidst the detritus and the mess, individual and massed earthly organisms are open, open to the material and energy flows and to the pleasures accommodating these flows: "thrusting, coming, sneezing, drinking, eating, defecating, urinating, sunbathing, sweating," which, along with seeing and hearing, are all made possible by open orifices and open streams, the influence of energy and material flows, the influence of myriad events spinning toward us from the stars and planets, the clouds and rain, cities bustling with citizens, those with whom each one of us has daily exchanges.[24] And although the earth is identified as a closed system, closed mostly to external material flows, the universe itself may well be part of an open system. Nothing dictates that the universe is closed or isolated, nothing except a system of beliefs and values associated with our ideas about happiness and the ideology according to which any disruption of constancy, of repetition and homogeneity, that is, any catastrophe, is glamorized as part of an inevitable spiral toward death.

Reflections of this ideology may also be found, not surprisingly, in various attempts at developing a "psychology that shall be a natural science: that is, to represent psychical processes as quantitatively determinate states of specifiable material particles,"

---

23. Ibid., pp. 38–39. This would at least make mental life an expression of the universe in which it arises.

24. Ibid., pp. 32–33.

with particular attention to the questions of what distinguishes activity from rest, and the role of material particles.[25] Given the general clinical observation that there are excessively intense ideas associated with states of hysteria and obsession, what other conclusion was possible than that of a disorder with respect to the quantity of energy in the central nervous system? The principal theorem postulated is that the nervous system tends to divest itself of quantities of energy and to be predisposed toward immobility, which is to say uniformity, homogeneity, constancy, regularity, even torpor. In fact, this discharge, via the muscles, is the primary function of the nervous system such that inertia or constancy is not "upset" by the flight from any stimulus but remains proportional to the quantity of energy. Inertia is perturbed, however, by another set of factors, factors that are identified as purely internal, as arising not in relation to energy and material flows coming from outside, but rather, as purely "endogenous" stimuli, coming from the inside and only from the inside and demanding to be "discharged."[26] Cells demand satisfaction. Hunger, respiration, sexuality are all forms of upsetting demands, demands that pull the nervous system away from its inertial contentment and force some action upon it. Why? Why after all should the perfectly uniform nervous system be forced to upset its regularity, its repetitive and redundant operations? The answer is simple—life. Life's "exigencies," as if turning the word into a qualifier, would reduce what it qualifies to an anomaly, a set of contingent factors that refuse to follow the general theorem but that nevertheless may be minimized if not discounted; as if life and its demands were purely internal and unrelated to external energy and material flows. What matters here is expressed in the second theorem, that the ultimate elements of the nervous system are neurones (ultimate material units of the nervous system) capable of receiving and discharging excitations, quantities of energy.

---

25. Freud (1966)1:295.

26. Ibid., pp. 296–297. "With an [increasing] complexity of the interior [of the organism], the nervous system receives stimuli from the somatic element itself—endogenous stimuli—which have equally to be discharged."

One set of neurones receives and adequately discharges stimuli from outside. Another receives and discharges what are described as excitations of a purely internal, endogenous origin; equalization without, equalization within. The perceptual system, although subject to the violent motions of powerful masses that transmit their motion, nonetheless manages a remarkably rapid discharge of this motion, with the result that there can be little if any disruption of the system's processes coming from without. The internal system is totally out of contact with the external world and is impermeable; that is, its neurones resist discharge and so construct some sort of memory. Internal stimuli are posited as being of a comparatively small order of magnitude, presumably, since there is no place for them to go; a truly powerful or violent motion would simply rip the body apart. The one exception to this rule is pain. Defined as the irruption of a large quantity of energy in the *internal* nervous system, pain is an unmitigated failure of the internal dimension of the nervous system to play its designated role, to maintain inertia; thus panic ensues. When pain arises, it arises in the internal system, leaving behind permanent markers "as though there had been a stroke of lightening."[27] Such a determination leads to the inevitable conclusion that pain *is* internal and, in the internal system, pain can be *catastrophic*. The avoidance of unpleasure coincides with the avoidance of any significant increase in the quantity of energy, whereas pleasure is nothing more than an effect of the discharge of this excessive energy. Typically, the increase of energy attending these events forces an increased discharge; when this event is marked, it corresponds to what is called memory, and the necessity of releasing energy from such an event is obvious.[28]

Under certain conditions, endogenous stimuli accumulate, increasing in quantity so as to overcome all resistance and imper-

---

27. Ibid., p. 307. This also begins to make it clearer as to why there is no positive pleasure.

28. Ibid., p. 322. The failure or inability to release energy would end in a fabulous explosion, so the likelihood of a purely internal system begins to diminish.

meability, at least temporarily. The first path to discharge is taken to be strictly internal, characterized by screaming, crying, vascular innervation, panic, and the expression of emotion in general. Perhaps it is internal because in no way does this lessen the endogenous stimuli. Here, only external intervention will suffice: feeding, cuddling, cooing, soothing, bringing forth calm in a manner the internal system cannot. The poor, miserable creature's eventual awareness of this calm and of the external sources responsible for it arises from sensations that are the work of a third set of neurones whose energy comes strictly from the internal system but whose quantity of energy is so low that it registers not as quantity, but as a qualitative characteristic—periodicity or temporality—which becomes quality, which is to say, consciousness.[29] It is this latter qualitative, periodic, or temporal characteristic of physical processes alone that affects the internal system of neurones and mediates between the internal and external system neurones on its way to becoming *conscious* and being discharged in motion without any trace of memory. Nonetheless, the manner in which any qualitative factors might influence neurones remains obscure, and the precise relation of qualitative factors to external, quantitative motion is similarly clouded.

In the connections of the purely mechanical, meaning physical nature of these processes, something nearly inexplicable is at work; some organization has formed in the internal nervous system that interferes with the mechanism of the flow of its processes and takes over for the mechanical processes under conditions characterized by pain or the avoidance of pain. This interference is evidenced in the "observation" that any hostile mnemic "image" is regularly abandoned by its energy cathexis as soon as possible. This organization, this interference, is the ego, *a totality of the internal nervous system's cathexes, at a given time*, in which there is a permanent component rather than a changing one. We must keep in mind the claim that the primary function of the nervous system is inertial; its role is to bring the quantity of energy to zero. The

---

29. Ibid., pp. 316–318 and 311–313; see also nt. 2, p. 313.

development of an ego, on the other hand, counteracts this function; it arises as an effect of the need to maintain a store of energy sufficient to meet the demand for a specific action, an action initially brought on by the so-called exigencies of life: hunger, respiration, sex.[30] Hunger, respiration, sex, not primary functions, merely exigencies, urgencies, necessities, crises. In this conception, the ego's principle purpose is clear—inhibition. Ego is, then, a network of neurones inhibiting the course of a quantity of energy. Previously impermeable neurones are altered by the passage of an internal excitation: hunger, respiration, sex. This modifies them and they become capable of conducting new excitations from one to another; they gain memory.[31] Different pathways between neurones represent different memories; the magnitude of an impression and the frequency of repetition of the impression determine which neurones will be connected, which pathways will be taken, which memories will determine the orientation of energy. Strongly affected neurones, side by side, orient the energy. When energy enters the system from outside, it gains entrance because the neurones have already been made permeable by their own inner exigencies. This outside energy is then forced onto a pathway that presumably spares the nervous system the release of unpleasure, pathways already traced by the excitatory process and its number of repetitions, pathways already "facilitated" by the exigencies hunger, respiration, sex. Inhibition serves the primary function of constancy through the ego, and the ego serves the primary function of constancy through inhibition, keeping the neurones from releasing energy when there is no perception but only a memory, and also, redirecting hostile memory images so as not to release unpleasure. The stronger the unpleasure, the stronger the inhibition, but this simply means that if the energy of the excitatory process is stronger and the number

---

30. Ibid., pp. 323, 297. So it appears that the ego, a totality at a given time, could in principle alter, and thus it might be illusory to determine that ego boundaries are stable.

31. Ibid., pp. 323, 300. Translated into the terms of mechanistic physics: connection between neurones depends on the quantity of energy passing through the neurone in an excitatory process and on its number of repetitions.

of repetitions is greater, the threat of releasing unpleasure is also greater. Unpleasure is not a single event but a process, a life and death struggle, a fight to the end between excitation and inhibition that inhibition, the name of the ego, must win.

What then of the so-called catastrophic event, the traumatic scene? What to make of Anna O.'s cries, "tormenting, tormenting," and Frau Emmy von N.'s exclamations, "Keep still—Don't say anything—Don't touch me," and Miss Lucy R.'s olfactory disturbances, Katharina's vision of the awful face, and Fräulein Elisabeth von R.'s incapacity to walk or stand?[32] What then of the heroic ego, panicked and paralyzed but persisting, willing to go on? Will, after all, is defined as simply the impulsion that sustains psychical activity. Translated into the terms of mechanistic physics: connection between neurones depends on the quantity of energy passing through the neurone in an excitatory process, and on its number of repetitions.[33] Internal neuronal resistance is restored after the ego carries out its function and the energy current is inhibited. The restoration of resistance is proportional to the amount of energy that has just passed through, but constant among all neurones is the threshold of resistance. In this manner, when neurones are subject to invading external energy, they can and must fall back on their own internally produced energy paths, uniform throughout, to sustain themselves. But this implies that the path of survival, that is, the path of will and the path of destruction are essentially the same; the path of conduction that connects neurones, the internally originating impulsion that sustains all psychical activity, also opens the door to its destruction. And it is life itself, its exigencies, urgencies, necessities, crises—hunger, respiration, sex— that are also death.

On the most radical level, certain categories of activities in life— food, drink, sex, intellectual and artistic creativity—are presented as arising as an effect of the inhibitions practiced by the ego when

---

32. Breuer and Freud 1956, pp. 25, 49, 119, 126, 152. These are the symptoms Freud and Breuer comment on.
33. Freud 1966, p. 317.

there is a disjunct between neurones representing wished-for objects and neurones representing external objects. Their noncoincidence becomes the impetus for judgment: differentiating wished-for images from perception; associating one image with another similar one; dissecting perceptual complexes as analogous to memory images, such that judgment and cognition are deemed to be one and the same. Then, the aim and end of all thought processes is declared to be uniformity, defined as "bring[ing] about a state of identity, the conveying of a cathexis of a [quantity of energy] emanating from outside, into a neurone cathected from the ego."[34] Imperfect coincidence results in unpleasure, requiring that a third neurone intervene to allow an association between what is wished for and what is perceived. Such association, it is implied, is the foundation of all cognition. Coincidence between wish and perception ends thought and brings about action where action is simply the effect of constancy between neurones! No wonder the women depicted in the case histories published by the founders of psychoanalysis could be considered its coauthors but were excluded from participation in the educational and intellectual milieu. Their ideas were taken from them, transformed into narration, then renarrated within the framework of sexual disequilibrium. Because they were labeled hysterics, by definition, the noncoincidence of their wishes and their perceptions is nearly absolute. Because their *a priori* egos are given as highly inhibited, because they experience little coincidence between wish and perception, they are, in this account, highly susceptible to associative thinking, that is, to cognition period. Emmy von. N. could be credited for developing the idea that the patient needs to tell her complete story her own way without constant interruptions; Elisabeth von R. for the concept of free association as well as for the idea that patients need to work through symptoms over and over; Lucy R. for the idea that every symptom has a meaning, none is arbitrary or absurd, and for insisting on the idea of free association as well as dispensing with hypnotism in favor of concentration; and even Katharina seems to have implicitly understood the necessity of talk-

---

34. Ibid., p. 332.

ing about disturbing sexual experiences, particularly the attempted molestations by her own father.[35] With the exception of Katharina, who is represented as a simple mountain girl with a distinct dialect and whose ego inhibitions may seem to be subject to skepticism by the analyst (who states that even as a child, she must have possessed far more sexual knowledge than she admits to), each of the women is described as having a strong intellect. Anna O. is markedly intelligent, with an astonishingly quick grasp of things and penetrating intuition, influenced only by arguments, never by mere assertions; Emmy von N. speaks with perfect coherence and reveals an unusual degree of education and intelligence; Lucy R., an English governess who describes herself as a poor woman in service to a rich man, appears to speak with maturity and insight; Elisabeth von R. is described as good-looking and unusually intelligent.[36] But in the end, it is the analysts, not the women, mere female patients labeled "hysterics," who are fully credited with these ideas. Does it matter that the ideas of traumatized hysterics and neurotics are disclaimed as the inescapable effect of an aim-inhibited ego whose organization and functioning are *a priori* givens? Is this why ordinary (not yet neurotic) women "soon come into opposition to civilization and display their retarding and restraining influence. . . . [thus] The work of civilization has become increasingly the business of men, it confronts them with ever more difficult tasks and compels them to carry out instinctual sublimations of which women are little capable"?[37]

Are we spiraling between the nineteenth century and the twenty-first, between classical and nonequilibrium thermodynamics, between Eros and Thanatos, between the majority of women who cannot sublimate and women who are intelligent only as long as they suffer from neurosis, between the *a priori* ego and an ego open to all the influences of matter and energy in the universe? "Classical

---

35. Gay 1989, p. 78. Lacking refinement, Katharina is generally assumed to lack intelligence as well.

36. Breuer and Freud 1956, pp. 21, 49, 117, 171. Notably, Breuer pays more attention to the woman's intelligence than does Freud.

37. Freud 1961, p. 59. The women are therefore intelligent only insofar as they are neurotic and lacking in intelligence insofar as they are sexualized.

thermodynamics studies structures of decreasing complexity—machines that lose the capacity for work—whereas nonequilibrium thermodynamics studies entities, including living beings, which increase their complexity and gain a capacity for work."[38] The debate between closed and open systems is a manifestation of the conflicts between these two types of thermodynamics. Classical dynamics postulates and studies systems (like that of the "Scientific Psychology"), which are closed if not isolated; shut off from material flows, the systems break down. Nonequilibrium dynamics postulates and studies systems that are open to material flows and energy. If the psyche is a closed system, its limited material and energy flows must be redirected. Sexual activity is taken to be dispersal, whereas its inhibition allows at least for constancy. Not surprisingly, this perspective is forced to the conclusion that the psychophysiological forces operating for every human individual manifest a duality, if not a contradiction: one orientation toward serving her own purposes and one in which she is an involuntary link in a chain.

The necessity of this thesis goes hand in hand with our ideas about the ego and its role in life. Disturbances of the ego are taken to be catastrophic. The female student's mugging, the sexually blind Katharina's avoidance of her father's attempts to molest her are external factors, cultural and social, perhaps even economically contingent factors, but psychologically they have been interpreted in absolute terms that exclude contingency. The neurotic response is a given, especially among women who are declared to be averse to sexuality yet who are also said to be among the more beautiful and attractive representatives of their sex.[39] If hunger, respiration, sex are the exigencies of life, the exigencies that first penetrate and make accessible an insular nervous system cut off from the world, then they do not open the individual to the world, but instead contribute to her dissipation. If these exigencies are turned back, associated with other energy flows, accommodated by other indirect means, dissipation lessens but psychopathology runs rampant.

---

38. Margulis and Sagan 1997, p. 32.
39. Freud 1989, p. 561.

After all, most of the women in the case histories report problems with the most basic aspects of life. They refuse to eat or drink, they cannot breathe, they separate themselves from their parents or children or spouses. Men, it appears, deliberately sacrifice themselves for the sake of society. Women, according to this way of thinking, want to be loved without loss. If their egos inhibit this loss, it is because they function mechanically, according to the rules of a closed system. Treatment for their neuroses must focus on this. If men sacrifice themselves for civilization, then so too must women. They must cease wishing and begin to sublimate.

But if the psyche, the world, and the cosmos are not closed systems, if there is the possibility that they are open to vast material and energy flows, then something else may be conceived. Trauma itself would demand reconceptualization. Anna O. possessed a powerful intellect, poetic and imaginative gifts. She was forced to lead an extremely monotonous life in a puritanical family with no intellectual stimulation. Later in life, Anna O.—Bertha Pappenheim—became both an advocate for feminist causes and a social worker. The other women appear to be no less capable. Judging only by her symptoms, her fascination with gruesome stories about animals, her horrifying dreams in which chairs and tables turn into snakes or a monstrous vulture tears at her or wild animals leap over her, as well as her apparent ability to remain critical of her analyst even while under hypnosis, Emmy von N. appears to be a brilliant if beleaguered woman who chose not to remarry and broke off all relations with her daughters in order not to lose the wealth they would have inherited from their father. These traumatic hysterias are not the problem; they are the inadequate and painful solutions. The goal of analysis is to return patients to "normal" life, yet in these cases and perhaps in every case, this means return to a cycle of repetition and monotony, to a constant state in which women may learn to sacrifice themselves for the sake of civilization. No wonder the student embraces the alternative of living in fear as a heroic victim who may reenact her fright and claim the attentions of her boyfriend, which she otherwise might not be able to attain. This clarifies why some of the neurotics "recovered" and some did not. It has everything to do with the contingencies of their lives and much less to do with the *a priori* functions of the ego.

This is why in an open system, catastrophe is characterized by discontinuity, the singular leap from one system to another in the proximity of conflict regions, regions of instability characterized by breaks, falls, disruptions. Before Freud, Jean Charcot noted that his neurotic patients improved markedly when moved away from their families, and the patients that were the focus of the case histories often fared better on their own, without family ties. This evidence might call for greater attention to open systems. How open remains to be determined. A completely random system is perhaps too radical as a solution, yet surely, if freedom means anything, we might try at least to differentiate between the illusions of autonomy and the creation of something new. We might try to pay attention to the material and energy flows of open systems, a disruptive and disturbing awareness for which we have few words, few ideas, and few images. In general, we imagine that awareness of the influences of one's own sensibilities is to be avoided at all costs. Rather than turning our attention to these myriad and heterogeneous sensibilities, we heap them together, giving them a single name; we call them sexual drives or erotic instincts simply because we have no other way to make sense of what is happening to us when our sensibilities are influenced by other beings, other elements. But if trauma is not to be reduced to a gender stereotype, and pleasure is not to be limited to the distribution of equilibrium, then perhaps we are long overdue for rethinking the structure not only of our psyche and our civilization, but its place in scales both larger and smaller, those of energy and material flows as well as those of open systems.

## REFERENCES

Atkins, P. W. (1984). *The Second Law*. New York: Scientific American Books.

Bergson, H. (1959). *Time and Free Will: An Essay on the Immediate Data of Consciousness*, trans. F. L. Pogson. New York: Macmillian.

Borch-Jacobsen, M. (1996). *Remembering Anna O. A Century of Mystification*, trans. K. Olson and X. Callahan. New York: Routledge.

Breuer, J., and Freud, S. (1956). *Studies on Hysteria*, trans. J. Strachey and A. Strachey. London: Hogarth.

Deleuze, G. (1968). *Différence et répétition*. Paris: Presses Universitaires de France. [Trans.: *Difference and Repetition*, trans. P. Patton. New York: Columbia University Press, 1994.]

Freud, S. (1960). *The Ego and the Id*, trans. J. Riviere, rev. J. Strachey. New York: W.W. Norton.

———— (1961). *Civilization and Its Discontents*, trans. J. Strachey. New York: W.W. Norton.

———— (1963). Dora—an analysis of a case of hysteria." In *Collected Papers*, Vol. 10, ed. P. Rieff. New York: Collier.

———— (1966). Project for a scientific psychology. In *The Standard Edition of the Complete Psychological Works of Sigmund Freud*, Vol. 1, trans. J. Strachey, pp. 281–397. London: Hogarth.

———— (1989). On narcissism: an introduction. In *The Freud Reader*, ed. P. Gay. New York: W.W. Norton.

Gay, P., ed. (1989). *The Freud Reader*. New York: W.W. Norton.

Margulis, L., and Sagan, D. (1997). *What Is Sex?* New York: Simon & Schuster.

Olkowski, D. (1999). *Gilles Deleuze and the Ruin of Representation*. Berkeley: University of California Press.

Prigogine, I. (1997). *The End of Certainty: Time, Chaos, and the New Laws of Nature*. New York: Free Press.

# 3

# Traumatizing Feminism: Prevention Discourse and the Subject of Sexual Violence

SARA MURPHY

## I

In cultural representations, rape tends to concentrate with stunning efficacy cultural anxieties concerned with the sexual difference, the relations between minds and bodies, persons and spaces, agency and desire. Rape has functioned as an enduring and flexible trope, a nearly empty signifier through which meanings proliferate. Polysemantic as it is, rape, as Frances Ferguson once noted, "is remarkable for focusing attention on mental states and their apprehension."[1] This is most evident in the law of rape, for while inquiry into intention and desire plays a role in the adjudication of many different kinds of crimes, in none but rape do mental states receive such intense scrutiny; in no crime but rape do mental states play such a central role in the very act of defining whether or not a crime has taken place.[2] Yet this focus on mental states is famously

---

1. Frances Ferguson 1997, p. 88.
2. For two among many discussions on the problematic status of criminal intent in rape proceedings, see Gans 1996 and Archard 1999.

subject to a marked asymmetry: "... The focus of rape law and practice has been on the victim's mental state and behavior."[3] If the apparent physiological similarity between an act of rape and an act of consensual sexual intercourse can be credited for this focus, that apparent similarity also accounts for the fact that in a case of rape, it is the victim's mental state, more so than that of the alleged perpetrator's, that is frequently under scrutiny. But if rape law has historically been a particularly virulent site for interrogation into the status of the female body in its proposed relation to the female mind, rape has functioned more broadly as a privileged locus for interrogation into female desire.

In this essay, I want to attend to a particular aspect of rape as a locus upon which cultural anxieties are played out: the nexus between rape and trauma. If rape concentrates attention on mental states, recent discourse has tended to displace the juridical interest in mental states prior to or during the act of violence in favor of concern with postrape mental states, articulated in terms of trauma. "Rape trauma syndrome" was introduced by feminist clinicians who sought to demonstrate that victims of sexual assault suffered a suite of symptoms that could be likened to those presented by war veterans and others who were subject to extreme violence, with the aim of helping individual women as well as making manifest harms that had been erased or rendered invisible by pervasive cultural myths.[4] There is no doubt that a broader understanding of the traumatic impact of sexual violence upon women has been in many ways salutary. Where the broader politi-

---

3. Burgess-Jackson 1999, p. 21.

4. Burgess and Holmstrom 1974. Burgess and Holmstrom conducted a study of women treated in a Boston hospital after having been sexually assaulted; their argument is that a similar pattern of symptoms as those seen in war veterans and other victims of extraordinary violence afflicted women who had been sexually assaulted. This article is one of, if not the first to formally insist upon a category of posttraumatic stress syndrome specific to survivors of sexual assault. It was not until six years later, in the third edition of the *Diagnostic and Statistical Manual* that posttraumatic stress was admitted as an official diagnosis. For a more recent discussion of traumatic stress and women from the standpoint of a feminist psychotherapist, see L. Brown 1995.

cal context that once framed such clinical interventions has receded, however, the effect has been one of "the establishment of contemporary feminism as a victim's services squad."[5] When the most prominent social manifestation of feminist antiviolence work has to do with clinical interventions, there is the risk of a covert reiteration of the intent focus upon women's mental states, detaching sexual violence from the wider context of gender oppression while inscribing it within isolated subjectivities.

I want to trace some of the effects of a seepage from the clinic into broader public discourse, that is, a predominant representation of the harm of rape as psychic damage to individual women. One approach to examining these effects involves an understanding of the harm attributed to rape that underlines the psychiatric paradigm while apparently displacing the political means for contemporary feminism. But we might also reframe the question so as to suggest that what appears as a displacement in fact involves a mapping of the psychiatric onto the social and political. Popular representations of rape and particularly of rape victims call upon us to revisit trauma theory in order to distinguish the ways in which the traumatic has come to define subject positions in discourse and to discern what is at stake in what might be termed the cultural labor of the traumatic. That is to say, when confronted with these particular inscriptions of the harm of rape, we might need to ask—to put it colloquially—whose trauma is it anyway?

Sexual violence and the traumatic have historically been linked together, albeit in curious ways. It is a linkage marked by breaches, absences, and displacements. A form of sexual violence provides the occasion for the groundwork of the classic psychoanalytic account of trauma, and for that reason it is worth dwelling on for a moment. In the early 1890s, Freud hypothesized that the symptoms he saw in his predominantly female analysands were rooted in instances of child sexual abuse. Freud theorized that the instance of "seduction" in childhood was originally experienced passively;

---

5. McCaughey 1997, p. 17. See also Matthews 1994 and Bevacqua 2000, especially pp. 66–69.

the putatively asexual child could not understand what was happening to her and therefore this experience alone did not constitute a trauma. A later experience, apparently innocent and occurring after sexual maturity, would then trigger a memory of the first event, providing it with a context that it could not originally have. In this early formulation, several crucial aspects of the psychoanalytic theory of trauma were in place, notably that the traumatic symptom is formed through deferred action, that is to say, that memory revises and rearranges in accord with new information and new stages of development. It is this revision that is central to the production of symptoms, as the subject attempts to repress the new knowledge of old experience.[6]

By the late 1890s, as is well known, Freud had come to revise significant aspects of his original theory of seduction and the etiology of the hysterical symptom. Writing to his friend Fliess, Freud confessed, "I no longer believe in my *neurotica*."[7] But the case was more complex; he had come, for a variety of clinical reasons, to believe that the stories of childhood sexual abuse that his hysterical patients told him had more the status of fantasy than reality.[8] A good portion of the structure outlined by the theory remained; but one effect of the shift in Freud's thinking at this point was the

---

6. See in particular Freud (1896)3:191–222, for a sum-up of Freud's views on the role seduction played in the creation of hysterical neurosis. In the text of a paper given by Freud at the Viennese Society for Psychiatry and Neurology, Freud concludes by acknowledging he expects his findings to be met with "contradiction and disbelief."

7. Freud (1897)1:259–260.

8. In the above-cited letter to Wilhelm Fliess, Freud offers four sets of reasons for abandoning the seduction hypothesis. First, he notes that he has not succeeded in bringing any analysis of a hysterical patient to a successful conclusion; second, he worries that his hypothesis requires that sexual perversity in fathers, "not excluding my own," had to be extremely widespread in order for it to be the key factor in hysterical illness; third, "there are no indications of reality in the unconscious, so that one cannot distinguish between truth and fiction that is cathected with affect." Fourth, he argues that the unconscious has proven to be in very large measure inaccessible to the conscious mind, such that accurate recall of profoundly repressed instances of abuse in early childhood is unlikely.

introduction of a notion of a psychic reality functioning with a fair degree of independence from empirical reality. The scene of actual seduction or abuse was no longer a central moment in the aetiology of the hysterical symptom. In his repudiation of the seduction hypothesis, Freud had, importantly, come to believe that there was such a thing as infantile sexuality and that therefore the hysteric's own infantile wishes and desires could play a role in her plight.

Particularly in the later twentieth century, the "seduction hypothesis" and Freud's repudiation of it became a locus for controversy and played a considerable role in feminism's anti-Freudianism.[9] Among other things, Freud was accused of falsifying his clinical data in a way that reinforced cultural and juridical stereotypes of women's hypersexualization and their lack of truthfulness, especially in cases of sexual assault.[10] At the same time, however, Freud never denied that sexual abuse exists and that it may well play a role in the formation of neuroses.[11] It is perhaps more precise to say that the theory he was then building could not effectively account for that role; the theory took a different turn.[12] The hysterical woman is no longer afflicted solely or necessarily by the failed repression of the memory of an actual event of abuse; after the abandonment of the seduction hypothesis, the hysteric became one way—in extremis—of discussing what for Freud was a basic structure of subjectivity. Insofar as one exists in time and in relation to exteriority, one is "traumatizable." Laplanche and Pontalis note that the crucial question posed by the seduction phantasy is "whether it is . . . the transposed expression of a fundamental datum . . . the fact that the child's sexuality is entirely organized by something which comes to it, as it were, from the outside. . . . Viewed from this angle, seductions really experienced as well as

---

9. See, for instance, Susan Brownmiller's (1975) discussion of the seduction hypothesis, pp. 305–306 and *passim*; Herman 2000.

10. See particularly Masson 1985.

11. Freud 1953–1973.

12. This argument is nicely made by Gerald Izenberg (1991).

seduction phantasies become nothing more than the concrete expression of this basic fact."[13]

Viewed from a slightly different angle, this description begs the question of the particularity of sexual assault as a signifier for "that which comes to the subject from the outside." If the theory of trauma is hinged upon the transformation of the real event into a complex psychic reality, it does nonetheless seem overdetermined that the paradigm for that real event should be sexual assault—indeed, it does seem as if the psychoanalytic theory of trauma can only find its bearings at the cost of the reality of rape, of its transformation into a powerful metaphor for human permeability and vulnerability.

As Ruth Leys and Juliet Mitchell have pointed out recently in rather different contexts, the history of the theory of trauma is itself subject to a gendering in the early twentieth century.[14] In the gendering of the theory of trauma, sexual assault as a metaphor for such vulnerability disappears. Mitchell charts this process in terms of the disappearance of the nosological category of male hysteria into "war neuroses" in the period between the world wars. Sketching the situation at early mid-century, Mitchell argues that "an interest in male hysteria developed as a very wide-ranging concern with the conditions of human birth and the psychic results of the very earliest relationship with the mother, a very early Oedipal or pre-Oedipal relationship, whereas interest in female hysteria slipped into a preoccupation with female sexuality and the construction of femininity."[15] As rape had disappeared as a potential cause for the hysterical symptom, hysteria itself disappeared into an inquiry into femininity, normal and pathological.

Or so it seems. On another reading, we might say that sexual violence, in some form, never quite leaves the scene. The metaphorical force of seduction phantasy is displaced into the language

---

13. Laplanche and Pontalis 1973, p. 407. The broad implications of this revision of the seduction-phantasy are central to Laplanche's later theoretical work. See Laplanche 1999, particularly Chapters 6 and 7.

14. Leys 2000, especially Chapters 1 and 3. Mitchell 2000.

15. Mitchell 2000, p. 159.

of an excessive openness to the other—mimesis, masquerade, maso-chism, absence—that is said, in the classic descriptions, to charac-terize pathological femininity. In the work of Helene Deutsch in particular it resurfaces; for Deutsch, a certain measure of masoch-ism is a necessity for appropriate femininity, and she goes so far as to say that rape fantasies can be a central characteristic of both the normal and the pathological.[16] Thus, even if a trace of actual sexual violence remains in these psychoanalytic formulations, it lurks there as a phantom, a specter haunting theorizations of femininity.

While this trajectory, admittedly synopsized here, demon-strates to us one way in which material reality can become institu-tionalized as characteristics of psychic life, it also suggests that the figural power of sexual violence to articulate sexual difference with human vulnerability does not necessarily weaken, but rather shifts shape and emphasis, precisely insofar as it works that articulation. And in this way, trauma, understood most basically as a breach that occurs as the result of a premature exposure to exteriority, always occurring before the subject can be ready for it, sustains its links with sexualized violence.

If trauma in one way is originary and inescapable, it also is understood in terms of the effects of an extraordinary event, an impact coming from outside the subject, which can only be inte-grated at the cost of the integrity of the subject itself. While psy-choanalytic discourse suggests to us that these two senses of the traumatic cannot be effectively disambiguated, more popular under-standings of trauma have privileged the latter. Yet some recent theo-rists have argued that the two notions should be theoretically separated. Kelly Oliver has insisted, for example, that this slipperiness

---

16. In *Against Our Will*, Susan Brownmiller (1975) spends a good deal of time on Deutsch's theories of female masochism, calling Deutsch "a traitor to her own sex" (p. 350). Deutsch 1944–1945, especially Vol. 1, Chapters 2, 6, and 7; Karen Horney took up the problem of female masochism and rape fantasies as well. In subtle and not-so-subtle disagreement with Deutsch, Horney attributed them to cultural factors. The question of a specific female masochism or, at the least, a particular passivity of disposition associated with femininity courses through discussions of femininity in the 1920s and 1930s. See Horney 1967.

of the concept risks normalizing the effects of violence; it makes the process of becoming a subject seem indifferentiable from experiences of oppression and violence.[17] Addressing this problem, Dominick LaCapra has elegantly argued in favor of a distinction between absence and loss, which he suggests may be mapped onto a distinction between structural and historical trauma: "One may argue that structural trauma is related to [even correlated with] transhistorical absence [absence of/at the origin] and appears in different ways in all societies and all lives. . . . Historical trauma is specific and not everyone is subject to it or entitled to the subject position associated with it."[18]

Yet in the case of sexual violence, precisely because it inscribes something transhistorical and associated with origins—sexual difference—at the same time as designating an actual and alarmingly common historical occurrence, the situation becomes especially clouded. Indeed, part of what I want to suggest here is that in recent cultural representations of rape, and particularly in a common representation of the rape victim as inevitably and normatively traumatized, the two understandings are, however covertly, articulated together, in a way that evokes hysteria or pathological femininity more than the psychoanalytic theory of trauma that was eventually and complexly derived from it.

Rape in the contemporary imagination has come to figure the traumatic itself, conveying a particular assemblage of anxieties about the status of the subject, sexual difference, and the law. However, it seems that in order to understand what is at stake in this particular association of rape and the traumatic, it is necessary to make a sequence of fine distinctions. If on the one hand, the construction of a female subject of violence, the attribution of whose traumatized state has migrated from what was apparently descriptive to something that seems to operate as normative, testi-

---

17. Kelly Oliver 2001, pp. 68–84. In this chapter, Oliver critiques "a normalization of trauma" she sees in contemporary theory, with particular focus on the work of Judith Butler on the one hand, and Dominick LaCapra and Eric Santner on the other.

18. LaCapra 2001, p. 78.

fies to the necessity of disambiguating two principle understandings of trauma, on the other hand these depictions insist, perhaps unwittingly, that rape presents a particular set of difficulties for their conceptual disentanglement.

Understood as an originary wounding, trauma is effected through a separation from the maternal body, a moment inextricable from the inscription of sexual difference. Rape can be understood as violent re-enactment of sexual difference upon the bodies of its victims, in a version that seeks to reduce those victims not to their own bodies but to a fantasized body of woman. Insofar as the theory of trauma can be understood as entailing a theory of sexual difference, we must acknowledge that it may not be useful or even possible to wholly disengage these two senses of the traumatic.

At least in certain mediatized representations, the figure of the rape victim-as-traumatized has more to do with what Mark Seltzer has termed our contemporary "wound culture" than the actual effects of sexual violence on any individual woman or group of women. In Seltzer's analysis, "wound culture" is a state of affairs in which the traditionally delineated boundaries between public and private, interior and exterior, body and machine, psyche and social collapse into one another, where any division of form and the ambiguity that it might seek to order and contain ceases to be meaningful.[19] If rape provides an enduring site for focusing attention on the possible disparities between the forms of bodily actions and the intelligibility of mental states, in so doing it has also registered distinctions between the public and the private, the sociality[20] of conduct and the privacy of desire.

---

19. Seltzer 1998, especially Chapter 10, "Wound Culture," pp. 253–291. LaCapra notes that it is when the two kinds of trauma he discerns—the historical and structural—are not practically and theoretically separated that something like Seltzer's wound culture emerges. See LaCapra 2001, p. 64.

20. In my use of the term "sociality," I am following Seltzer, whose employment of it I understand to be consonant with the definition provided in the *Oxford English Dictionary*, especially the definitions provided at 1(c) and 2: "Contrasted with *sociability*, social intercourse in its formal or conventional aspect"; and "the action or fact on the part of individuals of forming a society or associating together; the disposition, impulse or tendency to do this." Whereas *sociability*

Current popular discourse on rape is no less a privileged site for the working-through of such questions; but they are formulated considerably differently. In much popular discourse around rape, even that intended to prevent the occurrence of sex crime, bits and pieces of feminist jurisprudence, activism, and clinical intervention are marshaled in an often apparently incoherent way that might lead us to believe that what is at stake is not so much concern for prevention or a feminist politics, but rather that the figure of the rape victim, particularly insofar as she can be represented as a "torn and exposed individual," has become a principal figure of a sociality that can only be constituted as wound.[21]

## II

To frame this discussion in terms of cultural representations of rape and women, I want to sketch out a history of feminist antiviolence efforts. While these efforts, principally of feminism's "second wave," in many ways transformed the common understanding of sexual violence, they also reframed that violence in ways that have proven limiting as well as liberating. Moreover, I want to suggest that it is particularly the limiting aspects of feminist antiviolence rhetoric that have conditioned recent prevention discourse. Examined closely, prevention discourse reiterates many of the topoi of second-wave antiviolence rhetoric; but in the process, what might have been originally seen as descriptive has become normative to the extent that the understanding of rape as a political problem for feminist activists has come to be reinscribed as a social problem. If rape has come to figure for a sociality that cannot simply be seen as wounded,

---

denotes an attribute or characteristic of individuals or groups of individuals— and in the course of the eighteenth century, acquires additional specificity, designating an array of attitudes and behaviors—*sociality* evokes an abstract capacity of humans to engage in systems of common life, and in this sense, can be profitably compared to *society*, both terms describing that which is distinct from state apparatuses. See also in this connection Williams 1976.

21. Seltzer 1998, p. 253.

but is in some sense itself a wound, such a figuration is inextricable from the framing of rape as a social problem remediable, at least in part, through a variety of pedagogical techniques.

Given the work done in the 1960s and 1970s by feminist activists, legal scholars, and theorists toward politicizing rape, the transformation of rape into a social problem, best addressed through various institutional and therapeutic initiatives, testifies to the appropriation of feminist politics by mainstream liberalisms—but it is also suggestive of rape's susceptibility to cultural metaphor-making. Situating rape as an index of women's oppression, as Pamela Haag has pointed out, "second wave" feminists paid assiduous attention to the act itself, the way in which it was treated by the courts, the way in which victims were treated by society at large, and the role the threat of rape played, implicitly or explicitly, in the everyday lives of women, whether or not they were themselves victims.[22] Citing the program of the New York Radical Feminists, Haag notes that "[rape's] disappearance . . . would indicate that a substantial revolution has succeeded, but it would not constitute one."[23] But if groups like the Radical Feminists advocated forms of resistance to rape that extended from individual self-defense to political organizing,[24] feminist analyses of rape that emerged in the later 1970s

22. Haag 1996, p. 37.
23. Ibid., p. 38.
24. See Connell and Wilson 1974 and Medea and Thompson 1973. Haag (1996) astutely points out that early radical feminist antirape efforts were suspicious of or had given entirely up on the law: "[Medea] and others matched their continuum view of rape with a corresponding lack of enthusiasm for the law, an institution superfluous to the transformative work they assigned to particular kinds of mental and physical training" (p. 39). This is underlined in a particularly compelling way in a short film made in the early 1980s, "The Confrontation," in which a group of women, supporting a friend who has been raped, engage in what was at that time seen as one possible feminist response to rape: confronting the perpetrator in his workplace or another public location. It is made clear in the film that police reporting is not a viable option, in part because the victim is a working-class Latina who took a ride from a party from the perpetrator, a white, middle-class man. This "feminist training film" should be contrasted with the prevention video I focus on later in this essay. "The Confrontation," dir. A. Irving, written with J. Gellman (1983), dist. Women Make Movies.

and 1980s often repositioned sexual violence in subtle ways. From an index or barometer of unfinished feminist revolution, rape came to operate more as a large-scale metaphor for women's oppression.

Perhaps most famously, in *Against Our Will*, Susan Brownmiller argued that rape was a pervasive regulatory strategy for keeping women in their place: "From prehistoric times to the present, I believe, rape has played a critical function. It is nothing more or less than a conscious process of intimidation by which all men keep all women in a state of fear."[25] Nadia Burton has argued that the work of Brownmiller and others falls prey to a reductionist tendency, marking "sexual violence as the single site of women's oppression."[26] Such a monolithic conception of sexual violence occults the differences between and among women and between and among different forms of oppression. Rape becomes the normative experience that links women together, that identifies them as a group with shared concerns.

Burton has drawn attention to the ways in which feminist rhetoric, in its efforts to take apart commonly held views of violence against women, risked creating a "new and equally rigid discursive world."[27] One task of feminist theorists of rape in the 1970s and 1980s was to debunk calcified myths having to do with who was a likely rapist and who was a likely victim. While there is enor-

---

25. Brownmiller 1975, p. 5.

26. Burton 1998, p. 183. What should be underlined here is that while Brownmiller's extremely influential argument might be problematic insofar as it makes sexual violence the central site of oppression, at the same time her arguments about the regulative role of such violence (because it's sexual) find echoes in many contemporary feminist analyses, usually in the context of citations of Foucault's *History of Sexuality*, Vol. 1. Foucault, notoriously enough, was relatively blind to gender and his sole comments on rape, in a 1979 interview, involve an off-the-cuff advocacy of decriminalizing it, making it instead a civil offense and claiming that being raped was not substantially different from "being punched in the nose." At the same time, he offers a model of the ways in which sexuality becomes a site for the production and regulation of subjects; where he and Brownmiller differ is in their respective understandings of power, violence, and gender.

27. Ibid.

mous liberatory potential in the insights that rapists were not at all necessarily strangers and that any woman could become a victim of rape, no matter her age, race, profession, class, or mode of dress, antiviolence rhetoric seemed to underline women's vulnerability and their apparent incapacity to resist. The emphasis on women's inability to resist attackers was a calculated response; in both American law and in British common law, evidentiary requirements of immediate outcry and physical resistance made prosecution of rape cases enormously difficult, if not impossible, for women who had neither screamed, nor reported to the police immediately, nor emerged from an attack bruised, battered, or dead.[28] But if the goal of feminist antiviolence rhetoric was to challenge the ways in which women's behaviors and mental states were stipulated by law and society, it effected the replacement of those stipulations with a new set in which the woman, fear-frozen in mind, weak in body, threatened pervasively, has no way out of assault.

Feminist analyses of rape came directly and indirectly to shape the emergence of prevention discourse in the 1980s, as aspects of this new understanding of rape and its harms were buttressed by a number of studies[29] that offered empirical evidence of the prevalence of rape and other forms of sexualized violence, particularly among college-aged populations. Defined in new terms, rape came to be seen as a different kind of object of inquiry; no longer as readily contained in a narrative of dangerous men and loose women, it

---

28. "Rape," the English jurist Matthew Hale famously said, "is an accusation easily to be made and hard to be proved, and harder to be defended by the party accused, tho' never so innocent." Quoting Hale was for a very long time a common cautionary instruction to juries in rape cases. While the evidentiary demand of "hue and cry" was a holdover from British common law, the revision of the U.S. Modern Penal Code (1955–1962) defines "gross sexual imposition" when "a male . . . compels [a woman] to submit by any threat that would prevent resistance by a woman of ordinary resolution." Of course the question of who this "woman of ordinary resolution" is, exactly, remains a question, evoking as it does the pervasive nineteenth-century notion in U.S. and British jurisprudence that such a woman simply could not be raped. For a discussion of American jurisprudence on this issue, see Robertson (1998): 345–388.

29. See Warshaw 1988; Koss 1988.

came gradually to be understood as a social problem that was rooted in gender relations, communication, stereotypes of masculine and feminine sexuality. Understood in these terms, it was no longer a natural if unpleasant fact of life, but presumably a problem remediable through pedagogy. By the late 1980s, schools, universities, and other institutions had begun to develop ways of teaching students about rape, with the goal of decreasing its incidence.

As Martha McCaughey has pointed out, however, antirape efforts of this kind have had limited focus. One brand of it emphasizes masculinity, exploring male behaviors and assumptions that lead to sexual assault. McCaughey and Neil King have drily termed this "the dangerous men"[30] theory of rape prevention; the assumption underwriting these kinds of prevention materials is that by engaging men in reflection about their own assumptions about their physicality, masculinity, and their attitudes toward women, they can be dissuaded from sexual violence. But, as she argues, this method, "instead of [working] toward making male violence impossible," has a quite different effect: "men's power to coerce women physically becomes naturalized in the popular imagination."[31] This strategy is frequently underwritten by a notion that men are oblivious both to their own strength and power and to the harms done to women by rape. If only they could understand how harmful rape is, the argument goes, they would stop doing it. Scenarios demonstrating how injured and distraught women are by sexual assault, often incorporating first-person testimony, are recruited in this effort.

Where rape prevention discourse is motivated by liberal individual assumptions about the transformative powers of education, the tools of such education must include what Luc Boltanski, citing Hannah Arendt, terms "the politics of pity."[32] For Arendt, the politicization of pity entails an importation of social concerns into the political realm that in turn compromises any authentic poli-

---

30. McCaughey and King 1995.
31. McCaughey 1997, p. 16.
32. Boltanski 1999, pp. 3–19.

tics: ". . . Pity does not look upon both fortune and misfortune, the strong and the weak, with an equal eye; without the presence of misfortune, pity could not exist, and therefore has just as much vested interest in the existence of the unhappy as thirst for power has a vested interest in the existence of the weak. Moreover, by virtue of being a sentiment, pity can be enjoyed for its own sake and this will almost automatically lead to the glorification of its cause, which is the suffering of others."[33] Politicized pity, in other words, entrenches precisely the positions—fortunate and misfortunate—that it nominally sets out to unsettle.

This effect of politicized pity is exemplified by the implicit and explicit acknowledgments legible in antirape materials that education and pleading become insufficient mechanisms. In fact, there is usually considerable attention devoted to the legal consequences of rape. When antirape materials of this kind end with the tap of the policeman on the alleged perpetrator's door—as is the case in *Playing the Game*—heterosexual masculinity is being reiterated as precisely that which finds its richest and most effective articulation as a relation between men in which conscience can only be constituted through the threat of the law. Women, in this scenario, are reinscribed as exchange objects, at risk from lawless men and therefore in need of the protection of masculine institutions and agencies.

When, however, the possible or actual rape victim herself is the proposed audience for antirape discourse, something changes. Prevention advice directed to women is notable, as McCaughey and Sharon Marcus have observed, for the absence of encouragement to active, physical resistance.[34] Women are indeed encouraged to say "no" loudly and clearly; but beyond that, much antirape discourse, with its focus on "safe" conduct and practices, reiterates in negative a clichéd portrait of the rape victim whose behavior has in some sense precipitated or invited violence. Drawing women's attention to their own purported vulnerability, antirape discourse

---

33. Arendt 1963, p. 84.
34. McCaughey 1997; Marcus 1992.

of this sort not only reproduces and enforces a representation of femininity as by definition weak; it also prescribes standards of feminine conduct that not only would allegedly shield a natural weakness from harm, but also might serve as instruments for the distribution of culpability should a rape actually occur.

This can be read as a particular instance of what political theorist Wendy Brown has called "wounded attachments": the identification of a politically marginalized identity with the "wounds" that are the effects of that marginalization. Sharing Arendt's concern with the deployment of affect in the political sphere, Brown worries that in producing political identities based on damages inflicted by dominant groups, those marginalized risk fetishizing the wound as evidence of identity and thus reinforcing precisely that which should be the impetus for political change.[35] But in these instances, it is not so much the case that women themselves are assuming a "wounded" identity; rather, female audiences are being interpellated as misfortunate or at the very least highly vulnerable. A thin veneer of feminism quickly gives way to expose the underside of pity in Arendt's sense: the fortunate, even if educated by sentimental means, must have the misfortunate to pity. When examined in terms of their strategies of affect, sentiment, and wounds, antirape materials as a genre can be seen to take part in a broader trend that Lauren Berlant sees as having a specifically American genealogy and that she terms "national sentimentality, a liberal rhetoric of promise . . . which avows that a nation can best be built across fields of social difference through channels of affective identification and sympathy."[36] If antirape materials often seem more in the business of policing masculinity and femininity along the usual asymmetrical axes, one might also conjecture that, despite their roots in feminist antiviolence work, they have the more conservative agenda of healing the rifts between genders raised to the surface of the culture by feminist thought and praxis.

---

35. W. Brown 1998.
36. Berlant 2000, p. 44.

These materials also appear to align themselves with corporeality as it traditionally figures in liberal individualist thinking, in which the body is in some sense owned, or governed, by an abstract self or mind in the terms of property rights.[37] This is one condition of possibility shaping the bureaucratization and rationalization of feminist antiviolence efforts. If female victims of violence have, as Nancy Fraser argued, been increasingly "psychiatrized, addressed as victims with deep complicated selves,"[38] the self as an embodied existent, situated within matrixes of power relations, is elided.

What I want to suggest, however, is that in the social construction of the rape victim as traumatically impacted, rape comes to be the scene for the articulation of a crisis in the concept of the liberal individualist self. My example here will be a widely circulated video produced in the late 1980s by the Santa Barbara Rape Treatment Center for audiences of university students.[39] While it seems to deploy some of the techniques discussed above, this video presents a curious amalgamation of law, celebrity, and victim testimony that eventually displaces any attempts at prevention discourse altogether in favor of a discourse of wounds. That discourse finds its most direct avenue in the production of gendered subject positions, but here the power of rape to direct attention to female mental states is extended such that rape becomes a figure and index for a wound culture, a culture, in other words, that is haunted by the phantoms of a liberal individual, the plausibility of whose actual existence is in question.

*Campus Rape* is set on a University of California campus and focuses on the personal stories of four women who were raped

---

37. Rosalyn Diprose (1994) illuminates the ways in which feminist thought has often unwittingly carried with it liberal assumptions about mind/body relations. Alan Hyde (1997) has demonstrated through compelling readings of case law the ways in which the body is inscribed in law as subject to the mind as controlling agency, especially Chapters 3, 4, and 9. Ann Cahill (2001) has recently produced a very rich phenomenologically oriented discussion of how we can theorize rape as an embodied experience.

38. Fraser 1989, p. 187. See also Matthews 1994 and Bevacqua 2000.

39. *Campus Rape*, 1989, 21 minutes.

under various conditions during their student lives. The documentary style presents rape as an authentic social problem, afflicting real college women—unlike some other videos in the same genre that offer a scenario played out by actors. The representation of rape as an issue confronting both genders and potentially resolvable by improved communication between them is further underlined by the use of a male and a female "narrator," actors from the popular 1980s television show *LA Law*. The actors are not in character, but clearly are used for their recognizability and for their affiliation with a television series about law.[40] The actors explain the issues at hand, add further narrative detail and frame the stories of the women students, and in general offer editorial glosses on each story; their function is both pedagogical and in a certain sense, moral. The predominant editing technique used breaks each woman's story up, interspersing it with cuts back to the narrators who distill the major points in each woman's story, constituting broad themes among the diverse testimonies.

The documentary style and use of first-person testimonies are characteristics of a rape prevention pedagogy that Michael Gray and his colleagues have termed "personalized rape prevention."[41] Personalized rape prevention is directed at women students, supposing a female audience who resist feelings of vulnerability and are difficult to convince through the simple provision of statistics or other abstract information. Gray and his colleagues call for a rape prevention program that employs rhetoric inviting identification, with the goal of expanding "the perception of vulnerability and the intent to avoid risk-taking behaviors."[42] It is only with the deployment of a certain form of mimesis that the target audience can be persuaded: personalized rape prevention should demonstrate to students that "others just like them on their campus or in their town

---

40. It is perhaps worth noting that the female actor played a prosecutor and the male a divorce lawyer, thus adding an odd twist to the video's intersection of criminality and gender communication.

41. Gray et al. 1990.

42. Ibid., p. 217.

have been victimized."[43] Gray and his colleagues do not address specific media to be used in prevention programming of this kind, but the technology of video is particularly effective in inviting the sort of identification that they urge. Each young woman whose story is told in *Campus Rape* is photographed alone, telling her story to the camera; they are photographed in everyday locations and lighting, living rooms, what appear to be dormitory rooms, and in one case, outside on a campus bench. The effect is not of juridical testimony, but rather of the intimate sharing of confidences.

Each of these women has a horrifying story of violence to tell—some were raped by acquaintances, some by friends. This aspect of the video underlines the important point that rape is damaging no matter how or where it happens—as well as the point that many, many rapes are committed by persons familiar in some way to the victim. I will return to the idea that the telling of these stories and the mimetic identification sought by the video could have a preventative impact; for the moment, we might say, in bracketing the question of prevention, that there is a good to be derived simply from the telling of these stories. To bring an often-silenced crime out into the open is a task that feminism has long sought to accomplish; the women in the video can be understood to enact the bearing-witness imagined by Kelly Oliver in which "those othered can begin to repair damaged subjectivities by taking up a position of speaking subjects."[44] However, the formal aspects of the video, the production itself, work against such a project of bearing witness. Narratives of violence are subtly transformed into interrogations of female subjectivity; the video seems intent on dissolving each woman's individuality as their stories come to be represented through a hypostatized figure of the traumatized female—even when facts retailed by each woman seem to contradict such an inscription of trauma. This is underlined rather spectacularly at one juncture, when in a "guest" interview with the actress Kelly McGillis speaking out about the consequences of her own rape, McGillis's

---

43. Ibid., p. 218.
44. Oliver 2001, p. 7.

face fades into that of one of the four young women whose stories are the center of the video.

Each woman profiled in the video is photographed alone in what seem to be confined spaces; one seems positively trapped in the corner of a living room. Only one is shown outside and she is cloistered in a darkened grove of trees. They tell their stories directly to the camera; any presence of an interlocutor or interviewer is erased. In fact, with one interesting exception, any presence of a broader social world that these young women might inhabit—friends, family, current lives—is occulted. The interiors in which most of them are photographed are painstakingly neutral and anonymously institutional. The effect of such intense focus on these carefully edited testimonies is one of repetition; not only are these women isolated in their victimization, but their stories are fundamentally all alike. There is no mention of any impact that cultural or racial differences might have had on their experiences and the aftermath of these experiences. Each woman's story is set up to fit into a single template: nice girl, good family, off to college, and as one of the *L.A. Law* narrators puts it, "all these good feelings shattered."

In fact, the theme of shattering, understood as a breaking of emotional or psychic stability, pervades the video. What is highlighted in the testimonies is the postrape mental state of each woman —in some instances, a radical contrast between pre-violence and post-violence states is underlined. "Your ten minutes of pleasure took away two years of my life," one woman asserts, imaginarily addressing her rapist, summarizing a theme that recurs throughout; to wit, that what is principally at stake in instances of rape are the somewhat mysterious psychic scars left on individual subjectivities. While for the most part, the camera assiduously keeps a steady and uniform distance from each woman as she speaks, it zooms into a close-up on one woman just as she describes "terror in her heart" while discussing the aftermath of her rape—and then, once those words are pronounced, it rather awkwardly returns to its original focus.

Psychic scars of this kind are implicitly represented as not only the inevitable result of sexual assault; they take precedence over other kinds of scars. One of the women tells of being attacked while sleeping by a man who broke into her dormitory during a vacation period. She describes in vivid terms being beaten within an inch of her life, but the focus of her story remains on the rape as the central event in the assault. Rape, the message seems to be, is the worst thing that can happen to any woman; only sexual wounds can be at the source of psychic trauma; while other bodily injuries heal and vanish without a trace, the wounds of rape are necessarily as profound and long-lasting as they are invisible.

Fraser discusses the phenomenon by which feminist initiatives, intended to politicize crimes like rape and domestic battery by embedding them in a broader context of women's structural oppression, were bureaucratized and rationalized in the course of the 1980s. Fraser points out that one effect of increased state and federal funding for various woman-centered initiatives has been the transformation of political demands, made by women in solidarity on the grounds of shared experience of structural oppression, into needs and services.[45] Understood as a social problem, rather than as a political one, violence against women posits victims as individuals, but in a paradoxical sense. Thus from this video we receive an image of the rape victim as simultaneously the bearer of a deep and perhaps irrevocably damaged psychology and a statistic, infinitely reproducible. The paradigmatic victim, as constructed in *Campus Rape*, is knowable insofar as she knows no type; the practical and theoretical insight that rape crosses boundaries of age, race, ethnicity, and class has been converted into one about women's transcendent vulnerability.

Utterly individual and assimilable to a category: it is these two, only apparently contradictory, inscriptions that enable the techniques of mimetic identification in "personalized rape prevention." Collapsing a number of different instances and individuals into a general message of psychic pain produces a subject position that is designed to close the distance pity would entail. Each one of these women is presented as serious-minded, high-achieving, and determined, precisely the sort, we can speculate, that Gray and his

---

45. Fraser 1989, pp. 144–190.

colleagues imagine when they think of those female students who resist a notion of their vulnerability. The women featured in the video are, as narrator Susan Dey says at the beginning, "just normal students" who were "enjoying their college experience." Pity requires a distance if not a disparity in status or position between the one who pities and the unfortunate; but here the similarity between the proposed audience for the video and the women who are featured in it works against the instigation of pity. Instead, the video, with its strategies of close-up photography and emphasis on personal narratives in which postrape emotional states are emphasized, works to deplete any distance between victim, story, and audience.

There is very little about actual resistance in this prevention video—and what there is emphasizes that it is not very effective. In the women's stories, the narrative of the event itself is articulated with the emotional and psychic aftermath of the violence; their own efforts to discuss their resistance at the time of the assault or after, to permit them narrative or interpretive distance on the events in their lives, are either not mentioned or treated lightly. One woman, for instance, indicates that after her assault by a stranger she organized the other women in her dormitory around safety issues; but rather than dwelling on this courageous effort, the video portrays it as a sentimentalized healing ceremony. If the kind of prevention materials that address themselves to women and underscore women's vulnerability often seem to aim at behavioral changes that would, presumably, avert violence, this video is intriguing in the ways that it undermines the very strategies it proposes. The job of resuming each story and deriving a preventative message from it falls to the television actor narrators, Susan Dey and Corbin Bernsen. They never appear in the same space as the women telling their stories; in fact, they appear to exist in a parallel universe, wandering together across campus in the bright sunlight, stopping periodically, as the video cuts back to them, to punctuate a given woman's story. If the women's stories are presented in such a way as to demand from the viewer a mimetic identification, Dey and Bernsen are presented as the voices of authority, an older, wiser, but fairly hip heterosexual couple who understand the dangers confronting young college women and understand the necessity, at least in certain situations, of good inter-gender communication.

Yet communication between the genders doesn't seem to be the answer, even in cases where the victim knew her assailant. The cases of acquaintance rape represented here are not cases of misfires in a consensual sexual encounter, where "no" is somehow not said loudly enough or is interpreted to mean "yes." One student goes to work on math problems with a classmate; he proceeds to lock her in and rape her. Another starts the evening in a pleasant enough double date, only to find herself later on alone with a fellow who seems best described as a sexual predator. The advice proffered by the narrators not to drink excessively or to do drugs is peculiarly inappropriate in these cases; the scholarship student in biology doesn't seem to have gotten drunk while preparing for a math exam. Like the advice on alcohol and drugs, some of the other prevention tips offered are not in themselves irrelevant ones; at one point, after the woman who was badly beaten tells her story, Bernsen is shown in front of a dorm entry, instructing viewers not to jam doors open off-hours, certainly not a useless tip for managing safety in public spaces. But it is never clear that the stranger who assaulted this woman indeed gained entry to the building in this way, and the stories that come amplify the suggestion that the practice of maintaining locked doors in off-hours is not always entirely effective. One of the other women students was accosted by a man with a gun in a stairwell; it was mid-morning and presumably the dormitory doors were no longer locked for the night.

Rather than building an armature of prevention advice, the video actually implicitly works to undermine all the classic prevention strategies that are proffered to women by police, school administrators, and social workers. The net impression is that while these are reasonable cautions to take, they are frequently inadequate; coupled with the paucity of any narrative of personal or political resistance from the featured women themselves, the corollary emerges that for middle-class college-aged women, at least, public and private spaces collapse into a zone of acute unsafety. In the final segment of the video, one young woman concludes a speech about how important it is for victims to get help and speak to someone about what has happened to them by ruefully stating, "Talk is our only defense." The gleaming California sun belies the violence lurking in every imaginable corner; every man is not only potentially violent, but also potentially unstoppable. Susan Dey concludes the video's narration by these young women who chose to tell their stories in the hopes of raising awareness and preventing another woman from suffering as they have; this hope of prevention nevertheless rings hollow in such a context. Instead the message is one of female individuality in deep crisis: extraordinarily isolated and, despite high achievements and ambitions, menaced from all sides, telling their very real suffering into the empty eye of the camera.

If this video enacts the conflation of prevention and aftermath that characterizes much antirape discourse, it understands aftermath in emotional and psychological terms. While we are assured that rape is a very serious crime, there is very little in the video about legal outcomes for the women's experiences. This is especially striking, considering the gravity of the crimes each woman endured. Perhaps it is surprising, too, given the narrators' provenance, a television show about law. Susan Dey, in fact, played a prosecutor, perhaps provoking viewer expectations of an avenger, out to fight crime against women even in her off-hours. Such expectations are defeated; of course, they aren't real lawyers, the video seems to remind us, they only play them on TV. Therefore they do not in any political sense represent the law's authority. In terms of the rhetoric of this video, and the broader genre of prevention materials to which it belongs, however, this is not a trivial point. As I noted above, prevention materials—especially those directed at young men—often feature the law precisely in its power to disambiguate mental states through the interpretation of behavior and to enforce with its threat correct masculine conduct. Where communication between genders fails, the message to men goes, there is the law. If you don't believe that her "no" meant "no," the sheriff will be at your door.

In this video, however, where the proposed audience is female, the law is represented only obtusely, through the presence of out-of-character actors, known for their weekly portrayals of lawyers on television. If they appear to represent a locus of authority in their roles in the video, the very fact that their advice is so often weak and inadequate to the stories told seems to underline the incapacity of law to respond to the kinds of violence against women the video seeks to prevent. When it comes to rape, it suggests, the law can only operate as a mediatized fiction; the fact that our actor/lawyers do not exist in the same visual space as the young women victims emphasizes a particular kind of disjunction between the legal and the emotional. We could say that the law here is presented as a fiction, a construction with more or less of a bearing on the truth. But we can be more specific: it is precisely the law's capacity to stipulate mental states and associate them with particular sets of behaviors or social positions and conditions that is put into question, albeit implicitly, in this video. The sort of truth that law can posit is displaced; and if it at first glance seems that this kind of truth is displaced in favor of claims for a greater truth of the emotions, in a move that the history of the novel makes familiar to us, a rather different dynamic is suggested. A discursive struggle for the primacy of one over the other would generally be reliant upon a stable opposition developed between law's truth and individual emotional truth, but the significance of trauma is that the conditions of possibility for such an opposition have collapsed.

## III

*Campus Rape* seeks to draw its audience into a world, one vividly resembling the world in which that audience lives, where it is not so much a question, as it surely is in feminist jurisprudence on rape, of whether the law will believe one's claims, interpret one's conduct in a way that permits justice to be done with the least amount of damage to the victim. The law is simply shown to be irrelevant. Legal consequences of crime here are replaced by psychic consequences, or more precisely, it is suggested that psychic consequences exceed possible legal understandings and remedies, in a way that no legal reform could ever answer. In some sense, it is true that law—even with feminist reforms—is acutely limited in its capacity to apprehend, define, and respond to the psychic consequences of violence.[46] But *Campus Rape* is not a theoretical reflection on the vicissitudes of criminal or civil law; it is a video that supposedly aims at preventing sexual assault among college-age women. Not only, then, does this video imply that law is neither a deterrent nor a remedy for sexual assault; it transforms the interrogation of female mental states that has historically characterized rape proceedings into a rhetoric of trauma. The women's testimonies, represented and edited as they are, indeed tell stories of traumatic event and effect. But more importantly, the demand for mimetic identification made by the pedagogical techniques deployed here has the effect of giving the video a traumatic structure; inseparable from this traumatic structure is the manifestation of law as media spectacle, as an unenforceable fiction in the face of not only female suffering, but of female psyches.

There is a connection to be made between this traumatic structure and the ineffectivity of the video's prevention discourse. If law has relied upon its ability to stipulate mental states, especially in cases of rape, the historical period immediately preceding the production of this video, and other prevention materials directed at the same audiences, challenged its ability. Many of the central rape law reforms advocated by feminist lawyers and legal scholars focused specifically on the ways in which female mental states were stipulated in law, based upon bodily wounds, behaviors, language, profession, position, relation to the accused party. What *Campus*

---

46. We might chart here the trajectory from early radical feminist antiviolence efforts that explicitly argued that the law was at worst in some sense complicit with violence against women and at best had through its inadequacy forfeited any claim to represent women's interests to the feminist legalism of Catharine MacKinnon, who seeks a wholesale reform of the legal system to this representation that seems in a diffuse way a response to three decades of feminism. For a powerful analysis and response to MacKinnon as well as a larger argument about the limits of law for feminist politics, see Cornell 1995.

*Rape* registers, I would suggest, is the traumatic effect of the incapacity of law—and for that matter, institutions, such as colleges and universities—to stipulate female mental states based on conventionalized interpretations of behavior. If conduct that allegedly manifests particular mental states can no longer be effectively interpreted to do so, law and other institutions that model their practices upon legal ones have no ability, so it appears, to discern truth with any certainty. The juridical subject, ordered along axes of public/private, inside/out, reasonable/unreasonable, disintegrates.

If modern law has seen itself as the leading mediator of the relations between and among private individuals, thereby ensuring an operative sociality, rape, at least in popular discourses, has become an index of its inadequacy to do so. Particularly through the figure of the traumatized female subject, it marks the presence of a sociality constituted through wounds. For Mark Seltzer, the notion of "wound culture" is something rather different than other recent discussions of the relation of injured identities to the political, such as those of Wendy Brown and Lauren Berlant. In both of these writers' work, the structure analyzed has more to do with the "politics of pity," in which political change is called for on the grounds not of abstract principles of justice but rather an emotional appeal made to those in power by those in some way disadvantaged.[47] In what Seltzer calls "wound culture," however, it is the structure of the traumatic that shapes the relations between people.

"Public corporeal violence," he writes, "has become a way of keeping open the possibility of the shared social spaces of the public sphere itself."[48] At stake in the display of injured or traumatized states, in this analysis, is neither principally an imprecation for restitution nor the invitation to bear witness. In Seltzer's ironic updating of the Habermasian public sphere, the subject positions that would enable political or ethical engagement disappear, insofar as the governing force is one of mimesis; identities blur into

---

47. W. Brown 1995; Berlant 2000.
48. Seltzer 1998, p. 280.

one another and collapse; alterity cannot be imagined except as a version of self and vice versa.

In psychoanalytic theory, the concept of the trauma has a famously ambiguous, if nonetheless central, status. Does it, as the etymology of the term might suggest, describe an impact coming from outside the subject? Does it designate the impact of some force internal to the subject? Can it be said to be the founding moment of subjectivization, that which in some sense conditions the subject's psychic autonomy? Or does trauma designate the inherent fiction entailed in a conception of psychic autonomy? Trauma indeed appears as a "borderland concept,"[49] which marks and denies difference between body and mind—as its etymological root would imply—but between self and other. It is, as Seltzer notes, "a concept that leaks." Yet, this is arguably a productive leakage; only those who would want to make of psychoanalysis a normativizing and coherent apologia for bourgeois individualism would see such conceptual impurity as a flaw.

For Seltzer, trauma can be effectively redefined in terms of a "breakdown between the psychical and the bodily, between private and public registers . . . the problem that the trauma poses is a radical breakdown as to the determination of the subject, from within or without; the self-determined or the event-determined subject; the subject as cause or caused; the subject as the producer of representations or their product."[50] In this, Seltzer evokes and expands upon the role the concept has played, in ways occult and patent, in the figuring of the modern subject, from survivor of a train wreck in *Beyond the Pleasure Principle* to Benjamin's descrip-

---

49. "One might say of the trauma what Freud said of the instincts: the trauma 'appears to us as a borderland concept between the mental and the physical'" (Ibid., p. 259). This seems to be taking a bit less liberty than Seltzer here seems to think, especially if we recall the misleading English translation of the word *Trieb* as "instinct" rather than "drive" in the Strachey edition. It is precisely in the course of investigating trauma in *Beyond the Pleasure Principle* that Freud comes to theorize the death drive. That trauma bears quite closely on the drives and that both furthermore seem to position the subject in a borderland between mind and body, between self and other, is of central importance.

50. Ibid., p. 280.

tion of the shock experience characteristic of modern urban life. Whereas for Freud, and for Benjamin rereading Freud, the question is one of parrying shocks, of a consciousness produced in the management of shock experiences, Seltzer describes a situation in which effective management of the intrusion of stimuli has apparently become impossible.

"Wound culture" is one in which Freud's "protective shield" has given way. The literal fascination with broken bodies and shattered minds testifies, not to a parrying of shock through a reprojection of it onto objects that can purportedly transform and contain it, but to a mimeticism: what is inside is outside. Difference is collapsed. In the popular construction of the figure of the rape victim as normatively traumatized, however, that collapse is both enacted and contained. If that construction precisely figures for "the radical breakdown in the determination of the subject," it is because it can operate at once as the site of this mimetic fascination, and through its stabilization of an idea of sexual difference, contain cultural anxiety associated with such a breakdown.


## IV


While this reading of the complex of relations sustained in the cultural imaginary between rape and trauma invites us to think in different ways about representation and/of trauma, it seems to tell us very little about rape. It seems, at first glance, to leave rape "academia's untheorized and apparently untheorizable issue."[51] I want to suggest this is not entirely the case. By exploring the peculiar configurations of rape and trauma, genealogically as well as in terms of current cultural representation, we can clarify some of the conditions that have contributed to the current undertheorized status of rape in feminist and gender studies. As rape has fallen from its primacy in earlier feminist theory and praxis, particularly as it moved from being understood principally as a barometer to being

---

51. Mardorossian 2002, p. 743.

identified as a condition of female oppression, there has been simultaneously increased presence of sexual violence—and particularly of its victims—in a variety of discourses. But in prevention materials, as in television, film, and memoirs, the focus has most frequently been laid upon the aftermath of sexual violence, expressed as trauma. This seems itself to be an index of the "untheorizability" of rape; representing it almost entirely in terms of trauma, of wounds, seems to leave little room for thinking in other terms about gender, sex, and violence. Resituating trauma, however, in the terms offered by Seltzer's reading of psychoanalysis, permits us to trouble the association of rape and woundedness, by suggesting that there is more at stake in this association than a straightforwardly psychoanalytic understanding would permit.

As Rajeswari Sunder Rajan has put it, an "absolute distinction between 'real' rape and the 'representation' of rape breaks down in a situation where the literary text and feminist politics are engaged upon the same terrain and engage with each other through the dialectics of 'representation' and the 'real.'"[52] We can extend this to include other forms of representation in addition to literary texts, including and perhaps especially mediatized representations intended for various audiences. In the contemporary landscape, rape and trauma have come to be articulated together such that—in distinction to trauma being understood as one possible effect of violence—rape comes to be a figure for the traumatic, comprehended as a crisis in the subject's relations to exteriority, to agency, to causality. Insofar as this is the case, it marks a shift in the politics of representation described by Sunder Rajan as a "dialectics of representation and the real." Not only is there no *absolute* distinction between the two, as she notes, but representation and real are so deeply permeated with each other as to make incomprehensible a dialectical relationship that would permit rape as an object of inquiry and political action to be rendered in some sense distinct

---

52. Rajan 1993, p. 78.

from cultural representations that frame it as indistinguishable from broken female minds.

What we can say then is that contemporary depictions of rape are structured in terms of the traumatic; but the trauma at stake is not, in this sense, the trauma of rape as it might affect actual women. Instead, here trauma describes a current anxiety around the subject, which finds one of its privileged expressions in the figure of the rape victim. The rape victim functions as a vehicle for the depiction of violence in terms that efface embodied subjectivities in order to produce as normative particular mental states.

If it is through rape that a normativized state of trauma can be produced, this is at least partly because it is through the representation of rape that sexual difference is elaborated and contained. Rape is an act that articulates symbolic with literal violence, reinscribing upon the bodies of its victims the marks of a sexual difference that pretends to deny all enigma. If, to once again quote Seltzer, "the attribution of trauma, in any event, bends event-reference to self-reference, transferring interest from the event (real or posited) to the subject's (self-) representation,"[53] this does not simply signify the far reaches of the psychiatrization of female subjects of violence, nor does it only reiterate that "the unsupported word of the raped woman cannot represent rape,"[54] although both are certainly valid. As rape cedes the scene of representation in favor of the wounded subject, what is being reproduced is, in Wendy Brown's description, "a figure of woman wholly defined by sexual violation, wholly identified with sexual victimization."[55] But what is also at stake is that this figure of woman is deployed to contain a subject in crisis, for which stabilizing sexual difference would be—were it possible—tantamount to stabilizing self-difference.

---

53. Seltzer 1998, p. 265.
54. Rajan 1993, p. 75.
55. W. Brown 1995, p. 131.

## REFERENCES

Archard, D. (1999). The *Mens Rea* of rape: reasonableness and culpable mistakes. In *A Most Detestable Crime: New Philosophical Essays on Rape*, ed. K. Burgess-Jackson, pp. 213–229. Oxford and London: Oxford University Press.

Arendt, H. (1963). *On Revolution*. New York: Viking.

Berlant, L. (2000). The subject of true feeling: pain, privacy, politics. In *Cultural Studies and Political Theory*, ed. J. Dean, pp. 44–84. Ithaca and London: Cornell University Press.

Bevacqua, M. (2000). *Rape on the Public Agenda: Feminism and the Politics of Sexual Assault*. Boston: Northeastern University Press.

Boltanski, L. (1999). *Distant Suffering: Morality, Media, Politics*, trans. G. Burchell. Cambridge and New York: Cambridge University Press.

Brown, L. (1995). Not outside the range: a feminist perspective on psychic trauma. In *Trauma: Explorations in Memory*, ed. C. Caruth, pp. 101–111. Baltimore, MD: Johns Hopkins University Press.

Brown, W. (1995). *States of Injury*. Princeton, NJ: Princeton University Press.

——— (1998). *States of Injury*. New York: Routledge.

Brownmiller, S. (1975). *Against Her Will: Men, Women and Rape*. New York: Simon & Schuster.

Burgess, A. W., and Holmstrom, L. L. (1974). Rape trauma syndrome, *American Journal of Psychiatry* 131:981–986.

Burgess-Jackson, K. (1999). A history of rape law. In *A Most Detestable Crime: New Philosophical Essays on Rape*, ed. K. Burgess-Jackson. Oxford and London: Oxford University Press.

Burton, N. (1998). Resistance to prevention: reconsidering feminist antiviolence rhetoric. In *Violence Against Women: Philosophical Perspectives*, ed. S. French, W. Teays, and L. Purdy. Ithaca, NY: Cornell University Press.

Cahill, A. (2001). *Rethinking Rape*. Ithaca, NY: Cornell University Press.

*Campus Rape*. (1989). Santa Barbara, CA: Rape Treatment Center.

Connell, N., and Wilson, C., eds. (1974). *Rape: The First Sourcebook for Women*. New York: New American Library.

Cornell, D. (1995). *The Imaginary Domain*. New York: Routledge.

Deutsch, H. (1944–1945). *Psychology of Women*, 2 vols. New York: Grune & Stratton.

Diprose, R. (1994). *The Bodies of Women: Ethics, Embodiment and Sexual Difference*. New York: Routledge.

Ferguson, F. (1987). Rape and the rise of the novel. *Representations* 20 (Fall): 88–112.

Fraser, N. (1989). *Unruly Practices: Power, Discourse and Gender in Contemporary Social Theory*. Minneapolis: University of Minnesota Press.

Freud, S. (1896). The aetiology of hysteria. In *The Standard Edition of the Complete Psychological Works of Sigmund Freud*, Vol. III, trans. J. Strachey, pp. 187–222. London: Hogarth, 1953–1973.

——— (1897). Letter to Wilhelm Fliess, September 21, 1897 (Letter no. 69). In *The Standard Edition of the Complete Psychological Works of Sigmund Freud*, Vol. I, trans. J. Strachey, pp. 259–260. London: Hogarth, 1953–1973.

——— (1953–1973). Three essays on the theory of sexuality. In *The Standard Edition of the Complete Psychological Works of Sigmund Freud*, Vol. VII, trans. J. Strachey, pp. 123–243. London: Hogarth.

Gans, J. (1996). When should the jury be directed on the mental element of rape? *Criminal Law Journal* 20 (October): 247–266.

Gray, M., et al. (1990). The effectiveness of personalizing acquaintance rape prevention: programs on perception of vulnerability and on reducing risk-taking behavior. *Journal of College Student Development* 31:217–220.

Haag, P. (1996). Putting your body on the line: the question of violence, victims, and the legacies of second wave feminism. *Differences* 8(2): 23–67.

Herman, J. L. (2000). *Father–Daughter Incest*. Cambridge, MA: Harvard University Press.

Horney, K. (1967). The problem of feminine masochism. In *Feminine Psychology*, pp. 214–232. New York and London: W. W. Norton.

Hyde, A. (1997). *Bodies of Law*. Princeton, NJ: Princeton University Press.

Izenberg, G. (1991). Seduced and abandoned: the rise and fall of Freud's seduction theory. In *The Cambridge Companion to Freud*, ed. J. Neu, pp. 25–43. Cambridge and London: Cambridge University Press.

Koss, M. (1988). Hidden rape: sexual aggression and victimization in a national sample of students in higher education. In *Rape and Sexual Assault II*, ed. A. W. Burgess, pp. 3–25. New York: Garland.

LaCapra, D. (2001). *Writing History, Writing Trauma*. Baltimore, MD: Johns Hopkins University Press.

Laplanche, J. (1999). *Essays on Otherness*. New York: Routledge.

Laplanche, J., and Pontalis, J.-B. (1973). *The Language of Psychoanalysis*, trans. D. Nicholson-Smith. New York: W. W. Norton.

Leys, R. (2000). *Trauma: A Genealogy*. Chicago: University of Chicago Press.

Marcus, S. (1992). Fighting bodies, fighting words: a theory and politics of rape prevention. In *Feminists Theorize the Political*, ed. J. Butler and J. W. Scott, pp. 385–403. New York: Routledge.

Mardorossian, C. (2002). Toward a new feminist theory of rape. *Signs* 27(3):743–775.

Masson, J. M. (1985). *The Assault on Truth: Freud's Suppression of the Seduction Theory*. New York: Harper, 1992.

Matthews, N. (1994). *Confronting Rape: The Feminist Antirape Movement and the State*. New York: Routledge.

McCaughey, M. (1997). *Real Knockouts: The Physical Feminism of Women's Self-Defense*. New York: New York University Press.

McCaughey, M., and King, N. (1995). Rape education videos: presenting mean women instead of dangerous men. *Teaching Sociology* 23(4): 374–388.

Medea, A., and Thompson, K. (1973). *Against Rape: A Survival Manual for Women*. New York: Farrar Straus.

Mitchell, J. (2000). *Mad Men and Medusas: Reclaiming Hysteria*. New York: Basic Books.

Oliver, K. (2001). *Witnessing: Beyond Recognition*. Minneapolis: University of Minnesota Press.

Rajan, R. S. (1993). Life after rape. In *Real and Imagined Women: Gender, Culture, and Postcolonialism*. London and New York: Routledge.

Robertson, S. (1998). Signs, marks, and private parts: doctors, legal discourse, and evidence of rape in the United States, 1823–1930. *Journal of the History of Sexuality* 8(3):345–388.

Seltzer, M. (1998). *Serial Killers: Death and Life in America's Wound Culture*. New York and London: Routledge.

Warshaw, R. (1988). *I Never Called It Rape: The Ms. Report on Recognizing, Fighting, and Surviving Date and Acquaintance Rape*. New York: Harper & Row.

Williams, R. (1976). Society. In *Keywords: A Vocabulary of Culture and Society*, pp. 291–295. Oxford and New York: Oxford University Press, 1983.

# 4

# Social Bonds and Psychical Order: Testimonies

Susannah Radstone

> *I know that the murderers existed . . . and that to confuse them with their victims is a moral disease or an aesthetic affectation or a sinister sign of complicity; above all, it is a precious service rendered (intentionally or not) to the negators of truth.*[1]

> *[T]he time has come to explore the space which separates . . . the victims from the persecutors. . . . Only a schematic rhetoric can claim that that space is empty: it never is . . .*[2]

Until recently, Foucault's 1981 thesis concerning confession's dominance in contemporary Western society has remained influential. Literary histories[3] have described the immense transformative shifts undergone by confession from the religious confessions of St. Augustine to the contemporary confessions of, say, Philip Roth. Yet confession has nevertheless been treated as though its various historical manifestations share something in common: a retrospective acknowledgment, by the confessant, of his or her own guilt, sin,

---

1. Levi 1989, pp. 32–33.
2. Ibid., p. 25.
3. Axthelm 1967.

or wrongdoing. Even so, literary surveys of confession have argued for the specificity of a particular variant of the confessional mode that first became dominant within autobiographical writing during the mid- to late nineteenth century.[4] This modern confession emerged as the confessant began to seek absolution not from an outside power, but via an "inward turn."[5] Since then, whether in the self-revelatory writings of William Burroughs and Alexander Trocchi in the 1960s, or in the woman's confessional novel of the 1970s and 1980s and the more recent confessions of "new" men in the 1990s, confession's dominance appears unassailed.

On a Foucauldian reading, the modern confession constitutes a "technology of the self"—one of the "modes by which, in our culture . . . a human turns himself into a subject."[6] This account of the post-eighteenth-century western confession's increasingly inward turn, its growing dominance of the literary field, and its cultural instrumentality as a "technology of the self" needs to be set against an acknowledgment of the heterogeneous and differentiated field of confession. Confession does not now (if it ever did) constitute a homogeneous culture. Though contemporary confessions share some ground (self-scrutiny; self-implication), there are significant differences *between*, say, the confessional outpourings of Philip Roth's tortured eponymous alter ego, *Portnoy*, and the self-lacerations undergone by Mira, in Marilyn French's *The Women's Room*.[7] These differences matter. They suggest that confessional "culture" is a contested field to which a number of related but distinct modes may belong, albeit in some cases only partially.[8] Though Foucault's thesis acknowledged both the agonism of "technologies of the self"—that "where there is power, there is resistance"[9]—and

---

4. Axthelm 1967; Stelzig 1984.
5. Kahler 1973; Lasch 1979; Sennett 1977.
6. Foucault 1982, pp. 777–778.
7. Roth 1969; French 1978.
8. Radstone 1989.
9. Foucault 1981, p. 95.

that "there can exist different and even contradictory discourses within the same strategy,"[10] these claims can be overshadowed by the positing of an "age" or a "culture" of confession. Moreover, though the positing of the presence of contradictory discourses within the same strategy remains as a corrective against the positing of a homogeneous culture of confession, it *can* provide the pretext for the inclusion within a field, of texts or practices that may be more appropriately located elsewhere.

These qualifications are of particular significance to what follows. I will propose that confessions need now to be mapped alongside and in relation to testimonies. Like confessions, testimonies cannot be taken to constitute a unified or homogeneous "culture." Yet at least since the 1980s, the confessional injunction has been countermanded by an injunction not to self-scrutiny and self-implication, but to bear witness, rather, to the sufferings of others. In what follows, my aim is to distinguish between two currently discernable tendencies within testimonies: testimonies shaped by a Manichean vision and those that occupy the "gray zone." Below, I try to account for the dominance of the Manichean testimony over the testimony of the "gray zone."

The two *only apparently* contradictory epigraphs that head this essay are both taken from Primo Levi's last meditation upon his experiences of imprisonment inside Auschwitz concentration camp. Taken together, they mark out the space to be addressed in this essay, a space that I will describe, following Levi, as the "gray zone." This equivocal ethical space—a space "of half-tints and complexities"[11]—is a space trampled on by a Manichean "*desire* for simplification."[12] In the testimonies addressed below, this "gray zone" has become only attenuatedly available. In what follows, one possible explanation for the attenuation of an ethical "gray zone" within testimonies will be offered.

---

10. Ibid., p. 102.
11. Levi 1989, p. 22.
12. Ibid., p. 23.

The extraordinary impact of Shoshana Felman's and Dori Laub's seminal work *Testimony*[13] and of Cathy Caruth's[14] equally influential studies of trauma can be attributed in part to the recent ascendancy of Holocaust Studies, as well as to a theoretical consonance between their theoretical concerns with the transmission of the untransmittable, and the themes of postmodernist theory more generally. Yet though sufficient, this explanation of their canonicity does not adequately explain the fascination exerted by these studies, for the nerve that they have hit is vibrating far beyond the world of academia. A longer essay might trace the complex and polyvalent impact of the injunction to bear witness to testimony across film, literature, and also, perhaps popular television.[15] Such a survey might reveal that common to much of this, U.S. and British contemporary testimonial material is a Manichean certainty concerning the spaces occupied by and the distinctions between "good" and "bad."

Here, I can only focus on one testimonial domain—that of testimony's inflections of contemporary work in the humanities, where the Manichean tendency is, I propose, all too evident. The testimonial perspectives of Caruth, Felman and Laub, and their followers mobilize a dialogics of witnessing to testimonies of trauma —to the overwhelming and well-nigh unrepresentable experiences of *innocent* victimhood. As Levi has insisted, the necessity of remembering rather than obfuscating the *distinction* between "victims and murderers" is a burden history must never abnegate. Yet the position of witness is a complex one that can exceed an empathic identification with victimhood to include identifications with other positions available within any given scenario, including, especially, those of perpetration. If history is not to repeat itself, the

---

13. Felman and Laub 1992.

14. Caruth 1995, 1996.

15. Here, I have in mind T.V. shows such as *Ricki Lake*, in which guests speak out about wrongs done to them by errant partners and the like. These shows, which arguably straddle confession and testimony, are far too complex and multifaceted to be discussed here, but need to be included, I want to suggest, in any comprehensive mapping of the testimonial cultural field.

task of witnessing and remembering the sufferings of others ought not to be separated from the difficult acknowledgment of testimonial witnessing's darker side. In turning, now, to some contemporary academic treatments of testimonial witnessing, I will suggest an explanation for the marginality within this field of an ethical "gray zone."

## TESTIMONY'S BLIND SPOTS

Marianne Hirsch's essay "Projected Memory" appears in a recent collection[16] belonging to an important movement within the humanities. Inspired in part by Walter Benjamin, this movement seeks to redeem the forgotten sufferings and traumas of others and to interpret contemporary texts and practices as instances of testimonial witnessing. This academic "witnessing" understands the difficulties of its tasks in relation to the "unrepresentability" of the very sufferings that it seeks to redeem. Bearing witness to such testimonies demands, therefore, sophisticated dialogical interpretation in which the witnesser plays a key role. Whether this witnesser is understood as reader/listener/spectator or as a construct internal to testimonial texts or discourses, it is witnessing that enables testimony, though what is witnessed may be the sheer impossibility of representing that which struggles toward, but refuses representation. This is work of importance that demands respect. It seeks to keep faith with a variety of postmodernisms while also attempting the historical articulation of the past by "seiz[ing] hold of a memory as it flashes up at a moment of danger."[17] This movement struggles to exercise Benjamin's "*weak* Messianic power"[18] with which every generation is endowed—a power "to which the past has a claim."[19] But the memories flash up "at a moment of danger."

---

16. Hirsch 1999.
17. Benjamin 1968, p. 255.
18. Ibid., p. 254.
19. Ibid.

These witnessed testimonies belong to the context of their remembrance—a historical, cultural, and psychical context that mediates
memories at the point of their redemption. How, then, do the
mediations of our present historical, cultural, and psychical context bear upon the redemptive testimonial witnessing under discussion here? How, that is, do our present "dangers" shape the
testimonial theories and practices produced by this work? This is
the question I now want to explore.

Hirsch's essay, which concerns itself with the ethical aesthetics
of "postmemory," questions the canonical status of photographs
of child-victims for the following generation. Hirsch conceives of
postmemory as yet more disabling than first generation memory.
Moreover, Hirsch's postmemory permeates groups linked by
ethnicity and is not limited to survivors' children. Yet Hirsch's
opening epigraph comes from Binjamin Wilkomirski's infamously
*fictional* survivor "autobiography."[20] On my reading, this reference indicates that postmemory's reach may exceed generational
transmission predicated upon bonds of ethnicity or family to in-
flect a wider cultural domain than Hirsch acknowledges.

Hirsch's ethical aesthetics of postmemory borrows from Kaja
Silverman the term "heteropathic" identification[21] to describe a
memorial relation to the experience of others predicated upon both
identification and difference: "[H]eteropathic memory [feeling and
suffering with the other] means . . . the ability to say, 'It could have
been me; it was me, also,' and *at the same time,* 'but it was not me.' "[22]
Thus Hirsch's ethical aesthetic of postmemory seeks to witness the
particularity of its historical subjects without subjecting them to
forms of incorporative identification that strip them of their very
subjectivity. Yet heteropathic postmemory is put in jeopardy, ar-

---

20. Wilkomirski 1996.
21. Hirsch 1999, p. 9; Silverman 1996. Psychoanalysis distinguishes between "an identification that is heteropathic and centripetal where the subject
identifies his own self with the other, and an idiopathic and centrifugal variety
in which the subject identifies the other with himself" (Laplanche and Pontalis
1988, p. 206).
22. Hirsch 1999, p. 9; her emphasis.

gues Hirsch, by the ubiquitous presence of images of children, which have become *the* canonical and iconic representations through which the horrors of the Holocaust are "routinely" memorialized.

Hirsch explains the iconicity of Holocaust photographs of children by reference to their capacity to reveal the sheer sense-lessness and horror of the Third Reich's inclusion of even *children* within the category of threatening "other."[23] Though canonical images of children *can*, argues Hirsch, achieve a degree of hetero-pathy, in the complex, triangulated relations of looking that they invite, heteropathic potential is more commonly collapsed into identity.[24] Hirsch argues that the identification these images in-vite between the spectator's childhood self and the pictured child-witness is counterpointed, or even undercut, by the more knowing adult spectator's observance and by the inevitable acknowledgment that this "wasn't me." Yet these distancing potentials are *themselves* undercut by "the child's openness to identification" and by the present political climate's construction of "the child as an un-examined emblem of vulnerability and innocence." Thus, images of children are too easily open to "trivialization and stereotype,"[25] which empties them of their particularity, specificity, subjectivity. The spectatorial over-identification with a trivialized and univer-salized interpretation of "vulnerability" and "innocence" can be mitigated, argues Hirsch, by the production of viewing contexts that minimize the potential for such over-identification through strategies of distanciation and displacement that avoid over-identification while representing "all that cannot be—and perhaps should not be—worked through."[26]

Though the question of context is central to Hirsch's ethical aesthetics of the image, she deploys the term in relation to aesthetic strategies of montage and distanciation. Yet there is arguably another context that has given rise to *this* aesthetics—a context in which

---

23. Ibid., p. 10.
24. Ibid., p. 16.
25. Ibid.
26. Ibid., p. 22.

identification with innocent victimhood as well as the search for villains has become rampant.[27] This context can be more clearly grasped by identifying the path *not* taken by Hirsch: a path that is only limitedly available within the testimony work here under discussion.

Hirsch's essay opens with a quotation exemplary of "postmemory" from Jaroslaw Rymkiewicz's novel *The Final Station: Umschlagplaz*.[28] In this quotation, the narrator considers his response to a photograph, taken in the Warsaw ghetto, of soldiers aiming guns at a group of women, men, and children. The quoted passage begins by referring to the child in the foreground: "[t]he photograph everyone knows: a boy in a peaked cap and knee-length socks, his hands raised."[29] In what follows, however, the narrator's focus falls not on the child, but on the soldiers:

> To the right stand four Germans. . . . Two of their faces, three even in good reproductions, are clearly visible. I have pored over that photo for so long and so often that if I were now after 45 years to meet one of those Germans in the street I'd identify him instantly.[30]

In the quoted passage, the narrator goes on to discuss an imaginary conversation between his own boyhood self and the boy in the photograph's foreground, and it is *this* imaginary conversation that leads Hirsch to discuss the over-identificatory potential of iconic Holocaust images of children. But what of the narrator's comments concerning his obsessive relation to those German *soldiers*: "I have pored over that photo for so long and so often that if I were now after 45 years to meet one of those Germans in the street I'd identify him instantly"? What might this quotation suggest about the witnessing positions proffered by this photographic image? In Hirsch's essay, the focus falls entirely on the over-identifications that constitute the iconic fascination of Holocaust images of *children*.

---

27. Antze and Lambek 1996, p. xxvi.
28. Rymkiewicz 1994.
29. Rymkiewicz quoted in Hirsch 1999, p. 3.
30. Ibid.

In her quest for an ethical aesthetics, Hirsch advocates recontextualizations of such images that deploy broadly avant-gardist strategies to undercut over-identificatory impulses. But in this move, what is lost is the opportunity to explore further the *complex* and *multiple* identifications *this* image offers—identifications that are not excluded by an interpretive framework of testimonial witnessing and that include, but are certainly not limited to, an identification with the child. For even where bonds of ethnicity do arguably link the spectator/witness *to* the child, that child forms part of a *scenario* that includes also adult women, men of the ghetto, and, most troublingly, perhaps, those soldiers whose faces were so indelibly etched on *The Final Station*'s narrator's memory. Theories of testimonial witnessing insist on the relation between text and history/memory, at the expense of theories that emphasize fantasy and its scenes. But must one choose between a reading that foregrounds the spectator's *witnessing* of a child's suffering and a reading that addresses a range of potential identifications proffered by this scene, identifications that might move between the child, the men and women—and the soldiers, also? Rymkiewicz's narrator knew those soldiers' faces well enough to identify them after 45 years. But the capacity to identify (as in an identification lineup) does not exclude the possibility of identifying *with*. Indeed, in what follows, I want to suggest that scenarios that include the exercise of power and authority arguably prompt a particular identification *with* the wielder of that power, as well as with the object upon whom it is exercised. Yet though these complex webs of identification arguably constitute aspects of the "personal and public fantasy" of Hirsch's "projected memory" in Hirsch's essay, the soldiers, as well as *The Final Station*'s narrator's emphatic and obsessive relation to their images are rendered totally invisible. Why?

## THE PATH NOT TAKEN: SEEKING THE GRAY ZONE

Though Hirsch's essay explores a number of contextualizing strategies that might inhibit an over-identification with the victims of trauma, one strategy for the representation of Holocaust suffering remains unspoken, in this as in other "canonical" testimonial work. This strategy—a strategy that *has* been advocated but has remained marginal within writings on Holocaust representations, involves working *against* the grain of identifications with "pure" victimhood, not by deploying avant-gardist strategies of displacement and distanciation, but by undercutting the sense of an absolute distinction between "good" and "evil" and by proffering, or even foregrounding, potential identifications with perpetration as well as with victimhood. This is *not* to say that the writers I am advocating here propose that the distinctions *between* perpetration and victimhood should be blurred. Far from it. For to read that into this work would be to collapse the distinction between fantasy and reality. Identification expresses a perceived resemblance derived from a fantasy,[31] and it is the contention of the writers I mention below, that an art-work's ethical *value* lies in its capacity to move its spectator through fantasy identifications with perpetration as well as with victimhood. There is a presumptuousness—an omnipotence, even, at the heart of all identification—a presumptuousness that, as Primo Levi has shown us, can shade into self-righteousness. Levi remonstrates with those who condemn prisoners forced to work alongside the SS guards in the camp crematoria by claiming that "in your place I would not have lasted for a single day."[32] For Levi, "one is never in another's place. Each individual is so complex an object that there is no point in trying to foresee his behaviour, all the more so in extreme situations. . . ."[33] Heteropathic identification with perpetration as well as with victimhood—"it could have been me, but it wasn't me"—might mitigate this self-righteousness. It might mitigate (in some small measure) the historical repetition of atrocity by avoiding the Manicheanism and simplification that lie at the heart of Fascism itself. By reminding us of the *presumptuousness* of an identification with utter innocence, the work discussed below

---

31. Laplanche and Pontalis 1988, p. 206.
32. Levi 1989, p. 43.
33. Ibid.

holds faith with Levi, who argued that "ambiguity is ours, it is our second nature, we hybrids moulded from clay and spirit. . . ."[34]

In an essay explicitly informed by Levi's concept of "the gray zone," Gillian Rose takes exception to the routinized equation of the Holocaust with the unrepresentable and the ineffable. Terming such equations "Holocaust piety," Rose seeks out, in their place, representations that are less "*nice* about 'the ineffable.'"[35] Rose savagely attacks the film *Schindler's List* (Steven Spielberg, U.S., 1993),[36] which she compares unfavorably both with the original novel[37] and with the film *The Remains of the Day* (James Ivory, U.S., 1993). The novel *Schindler's Ark* draws comparisons between its eponymous hero, Schindler, and Goeth, the German commander with whom he negotiates, while the film *Remains of the Day* encourages spectatorial identification with a butler who finds himself complicit with Nazism. Rose's reading of the film *Schindler's List* argues that it, in contrast, "depends on the sentimentality of the ultimate predator" who need never acknowledge or identify herself with the predation of any victim since "she can destroy the whole cycle."[38] What Rose emphasizes here is the hidden *violence* that subtends identification solely with victimhood, since it is only from a position of absolute power that the predatory capacity of others can cease to be a point of identification. Thus, for Rose, Spielberg's *Schindler's List* avoids the difficult task enjoined on us by atrocity: that of working-through our fantasy identifications *with* perpetration, rather than only with victimhood.

Like Rose, Eric Santner[39] insists on the urgency of creating a culture in which moral ambiguities and identificatory equivocations can hold sway against the "certainties" of Manicheanism. But

---

34. Ibid., p. 50.
35. Rose 1998, p. 244.
36. For a much more favorable and compelling reading of the ethical aesthetics of *Schindler's List*, see Elsaesser 1996. For comprehensive coverage of debates on *Schindler's List*, see Loshitzky 1997.
37. Keneally 1982.
38. Rose 1998, p. 246.
39. Santner 1990.

I'm thinking, also, of the writings of Primo Levi and those of Jean Améry,[40] whose accounts of survivorhood testify to their profoundly difficult, though different relations to revenge and resentment. These writers imply a testimonial witnessing very different from that which Bryan Cheyette has called the "Manichean moral certainty of contemporary writers and filmmakers in relation to the Shoah."[41] This witnessing takes place, rather, in what I want to call, following Primo Levi, "the gray zone": a zone in which, quoting Cheyette on Levi again, one can begin to tell and listen to the story of "someone who understands, only too well, his own potential to dehumanize"[42] and in which what is remembered is, in Rose's phrase, our shared, "all too human"[43] condition. The availability of this gray zone varies from conjuncture to conjuncture. In the rest of this essay, I want to pursue the question of its contemporary marginality.

The confessional incitement to self-implication contrasts with testimony's witnessing of external events and the actions of an implicated and censured other. Up until very recently, it was still accepted that the West was dominated by the incitement to confess. Yet though confession still marks contemporary British and U.S. television and literature, testimony's ascendance cannot be ignored. *Both* confession *and* testimony emerge in societies that are struggling, to a greater or lesser extent, with similar problems: problems related to authority and social order that can best be understood from a psychosocial studies perspective.

## TESTIMONY AND AGGRESSION: *CIVILIZATION AND ITS DISCONTENTS*

Whether seen from a Foucauldian or from a Freudian perspective, confession, self-implication, and the production of conscience are

---

40. Améry 1980.
41. Cheyette 1998, p. 273.
42. Ibid., p. 280.
43. Rose 1998, p. 244.

construed in relation to the sustenance of social order and the orchestration of individuals into a larger unit. Neither Freud nor Foucault viewed civilization's constraints without ambivalence. For Freud, the costs of sustaining social order were understood in relation to inner psychical conflict. For Foucault, the costs of social order are understood in relation to the internalized ordering of subjectivity. Central to both Foucault's conception of order and Freud's view of civilization is a "self-regulating" citizen, whose subjection is related to his or her self-implication. This self-regulation through self-implication depends, in its turn, upon the presupposition of a mode of subjectivity constituted through both division and relatedness. The narrative that follows will map a relation between changes in the experience and structure of contemporary western social authority and these intrapsychical relations. Though in a longer essay, the Foucauldian analysis might be undertaken alongside the Freudian one, in what follows I will focus only on the Freudian argument.

In *Civilization and Its Discontents*, Freud explored the relations between social bonds and psychical order. In this examination of the struggle between individual and social aims, the focus falls upon those mechanisms implemented by a mature society so that its aims—the greater good of the many—might hold sway over the individual's drives. How, Freud asked, does the power of a community come to hold sway over the power, or "brute force," of the individual?[44] Freud's response described the psychosocial processes which give rise to *internalized* authority, in the shape of the superego. Freud's description of superego formation is centrally concerned with the small child's negotiation of complex and ambivalent feelings toward its first authority figure: for Freud, the father. The child depends upon and seeks love from the father, but also develops "a considerable amount of aggressiveness . . . against the authority which prevents him from having his first, but none the less his most important, satisfactions."[45] Freud describes the mechanisms the child deploys to find his way out of this "economically

---

44. Freud 1930, p. 284.
45. Ibid., p. 322.

difficult situation" in terms of identification and the splitting of the ego. Instead of attacking the father, the child

> takes the unattackable authority into himself. The authority now turns into his super-ego and enters into possession of all the aggressiveness which a child would have liked to exercise against it. The child's ego has to content itself with the unhappy role of the authority—the father—who has been thus degraded. Here, as so often, the (real) situation is reversed: "If I were the father and you were the child, I should treat you badly." The relationship between the super-ego and the ego is a return, distorted by a wish, of the real relationships between the ego, as yet undivided, and the external object.[46]

For Freud, then, the maintenance of social order hinges upon the availability of an identifiable and incorporable authority figure. Identification with this figure "expresses a resemblance . . . derived from a common element which is a fantasy"[47]: the common element is the power/aggressiveness that the father wields and that the child wishes to wield against him. The resultant division allows for some intrapsychical, rather than wholly other-oriented, venting of aggression. Thus, the attacks of the superego upon the ego come to substitute for the child's aggressive wishes toward the authority figure. For Freud, then, the maintenance of social order depends upon processes of identification and division that transform an *external* into an *internal* conflict. Social order comes to depend upon both the maintenance of *relations* between this newly divided mind and the capacity to tolerate inner conflict.

If social order rests, as Freud said it did, upon the dominance of intrapsychical over interpersonal conflict, what are we to make of that nineteenth-century moment of the confession's inward turn when the ordinarily "quiet," though painful, conflicts between the superego and the ego became the matter of so much writing? This was the period, in the West, of the birth of recognizably modern

---

46. Ibid.
47. Laplanche and Pontalis 1988, p. 206.

metropolitan life. It was in 1847–1848 that Raymond Williams saw the decisive emergence of "a new and major generation of English novelists, struggling to make sense of a crisis in experience as [t]he first industrial civilisation in the history of the world [came] to a critical and defining stage."[48] For Williams, "this is a period in which what it means to live in a community is more uncertain, more critical, more disturbing as a question put to societies and to persons than ever before in history."[49]

In the *modern*, nineteenth-century inward-turning confession, the confessant seeks out "what is hidden from himself."[50] The narrator is therefore split between a narrating superego and a narrated ego. The related dividedness of intrapsychical life that, in Freud's "mature" society, went about its business relatively "quietly" and below the surface becomes the explicit focus of attention. But how can the relationship between the ubiquity of the inward-turning modern confessional and the crisis of experience with which it is associated best be understood?

Williams's understanding of the crisis that emerged in the mid-nineteenth century foregrounds confused relations between individuals and communities. As this crisis deepened, so did the confession's inward turn. For Christopher Lasch, this inward turn signaled the emergence of a narcissistic culture lacking strong fathers. Notwithstanding its infamous misogyny, Lasch's *The Culture of Narcissism* (1979) shares with Williams's analysis an emphasis upon crises of authority—be that familial or political—in the formation of an inward confessional turn. But can the relations between the dominance of confession and confusions concerning authority be more precisely understood?

The substitution of the Kleinian or object-relations term "states" over the Freudian term "stages" emphasizes the provisional nature of psychical resolution. It replaces Freud's emphasis upon "achieved" stages, with an understanding of the unceasing and ongoing nature

---

48. Williams 1984, p. 9.
49. Ibid., pp. 11–12.
50. Foucault 1981, pp. 66–67.

of psychical labor prompted by the vicissitudes of experience. Freud's account of the *achievement* of superego formation emphasized the incorporation of a "split" father. An object-relations perspective foregrounds "states" over "stages," but it also foregrounds the inevitable mediation of psychical life by the social. If psychical life is understood in relation to both "states," and to "sociality," how might the historical vicissitudes of political and social authority bear upon psychosocial life? What dynamic might operate, that is, between psychical "states" and the confusions and diffusions of modern and postmodern authority?

From an object-relations perspective, aggressivity toward the "good enough" authority of Freud's "mature society" can be managed through ongoing acts of incorporative fantasy, so that aggressivity toward that authority comes to be contained, by transmutation into intrapsychical conflict. But in a society where authority is diffuse, incomprehensible, or even incoherent, aggressivity *toward* that authority is less easily managed, since that authority is harder to identify and thus less available for incorporative fantasy. In short, in the society described by Raymond Williams, identification with the aggressor, which arguably provided the original means through which aggression came to be *contained*, has become problematic. Perhaps the hyper self-censure of the inward-turning confession registers the struggle to sustain the burden of intrapsychical conflict, at a time when ego/superego relations can be less easily shorn up through incorporative fantasies linked to authority structures in the present. The hypostatization of self-censure represented by confession registers, perhaps, a one-sided struggle to resuscitate the superego in the absence of appropriate identificatory objects. Its emphatic foregrounding of the dividedness of the inner world— its marking out of a *growing* distance between its protagonist and its self-censuring narrator marks out, too, the beginnings of a breakdown in relations between the ego and the superego.[51] Perhaps

---

51. This hypothesis is borne out by Theodor Reik's (1961) finding that tension prompts the "retroactive transmutation of th[e] self-tormenting attitude. . . . In turning back, the instinct hitherto directed against the ego . . . drives towards eruption against an external object . . ." (p. 414).

Freud's fantasy of the mature society was written, indeed, at the very moment when this struggle was taking place.

My hypothesis concerning the psycho-politics of confession mobilized a contemporary object relations approach to psychosocial relations that revises Freud by suggesting a relation of ongoing mutual implication between the psychical and the social. I will now turn to consider the emergence of testimony. Ian Craib's object relations thesis concerns the relations between changes in authority, government, and communication, and an increasing inability to tolerate the inevitable inner conflicts of everyday psychical life. For Craib, the late twentieth-century West has seen a fragmentation of economic and social life and increasingly centralized and amorphous systems of surveillance and control. These developments are linked with identifiable fantasies: specifically omnipotent fantasies of organization and control bound by a common thread: an "absence of internalised personal authority."[52]

## TESTIMONIAL IDENTIFICATIONS, VICTIMHOOD, AND THE PROBLEM OF AGGRESSION

Craib associates overwhelming contemporary social systems with two defensive unconscious scenarios: *omnipotent* fantasies of organization and control and identifications with *victimhood*. The former defend against anxiety by mastering, in fantasy, that which seems unmasterable, while the latter represent a return to those infantile feelings of helplessness provoked by a social system that evokes the size and immense power attributed to parents by the child, while sustaining fantasies of perfection. Though this dominant scenario's combination of fantasies of power with fantasies of victimhood appears contradictory, common to both is the absence of or, better put, the denial and displacement of aggression: control and organization are linked with a self that has achieved total mastery and "evacuated" all "badness" or aggression from itself, while

---

52. Craib 1994, p. 109.

the victim displaces all aggression into that which it believes to be its victimizer. But though the projection and denial of aggressivity lie at the heart of the scenarios Craib describes, there are two areas of his thesis that remain sketchy. First, he underemphasizes the *aggressivity* tied to an identification with victimhood and, paradoxically, with the denial of aggression.[53] Second, Craib's remarks about the absence of "internal authority" and the consequent intolerability of inner conflict seem to suggest that it may be becoming harder to contain aggression through the mechanism of superego/ego relations. But he simply doesn't address the question of exactly if or how the contemporary psychosocial scene either revises or sustains this division.[54] This is the question to which I am now going to turn.

In discussing the modern, inward-turning confession, its compulsive hypostatization of self-censure arguably represented an attempt to resuscitate the inner world's capacity to contain aggressivity in the absence of social reinforcement, in the shape of adequately identifiable and incorporable authority figures. Craib's account describes the *further* diffusions and confusions of authority associated with postmodern social systems in which power is both more dispersed and yet more deeply penetrative and overwhelming than in the communities described either by Williams or by Lasch. My contention is that the ungraspability and the *un-*

---

53. Rose 1998, p. 246.

54. This is not to say that the divisions of the inner world collapse, but it is to say that more work needs to be undertaken on exactly how postmodern experience may be refiguring those divisions, and it is to contest the emphasis that has been placed on the role of the "internal witness" in the work of testimony: "the testimony is, therefore, the process by which the narrator (the survivor) reclaims his position as a witness: reconstitutes the internal 'thou,' and thus the possibility of a witness or a listener inside himself" (Felman and Laub 1992, p. 85). Such analyses of the inner dynamics of testimony seem to me to be shaped *by* testimonial culture in that their account of inner life stresses only the difficulties posed to the self by events, rather than those difficulties posed by difficult or even intolerable fantasies, often of revenge or aggressivity, fantasies that remain unacknowledged and unaddressed in testimonial theory's model of the survivor and the internal witness.

*identifiability* of contemporary authority exacerbate aggressivity while attenuating possibilities for identification. Under these circumstances, the transformation of aggression against an external authority into intrapsychic conflict becomes yet more deeply unmanageable and threatening than in the age of confession. This, I think, is a danger of our times. In these dangerous moments, memories flash up, but they are memories *shaped* by our present dangers, dangers that our testimonies and witnessings can either reinforce or mitigate.

## THE GRAY ZONE

Marianne Hirsch's analysis of the projective fantasies that shape the postmemorial reception of Holocaust images links the iconicity of images of childhood with the universalizing and homogenizing lure of fantasies of innocence and vulnerability. Yet Hirsch's quest for more ethical, that is, less universalizing and homogenizing forms of witnessing leads her to consider ways of recontextualizing such images of childhood, so that some testimony might be made to postmemory's imbrication with the particular, specific, and, to a degree, always unrepresentable sufferings of *others*.

Hirsch's advocacy of particular avant-gardist strategies of recontextualizing distanciation hinges on a comparison of two photographs that include images of child survivors. Hirsch chooses to compare the *Stroop Report* photograph, with which her essay opens, with a photograph that she believes achieves a degree of heteropathy, Lorie Novak's "Past Lives." This photograph of a composite projection onto a wall superimposes images of child Holocaust victims and a picture of Ethel Rosenberg, convicted and then executed for atomic espionage, upon a childhood image of the photographer pictured with her mother. Hirsch's reading of "Past Lives" foregrounds its reflexive *staging* of postmemory and its critical relation to the over-identificatory potential of images of child victims. It is through specific *distancing* devices of recontextualization, argues Hirsch, that over-identification of images of child victims with the spectator's childhood self—the "child witness"—can be avoided in the interests of heteropathic memory. For Hirsch, in "Past Lives," the layering of Ethel Rosenberg's face over images of child-victims and of the photographer herself "introduces a third term between the child victim and the child witness, and refocuses the attention onto the two adults in the text."[55] Yet Rosenberg's face surely offers not simply "distance" between spectator as child-witness and the images of child-victims, but a point of potential identification: identification with an image of Rosenberg described by Novak herself as "hauntingly maternal."[56] This is a potential point of identification made invisible, I want to suggest, by the context of canonical testimony. Yet it *remains* a point of identification proffered by the image—a point of identification with a maternal figure who, if the law is to be believed, betrayed her children and their nation. Though there is not space here to consider the complex questions of authority, identification, and sexual difference raised by "Past Lives," it is nevertheless important to acknowledge that the work attempts to stage feminine postmemory and to work through its burden *via* an *identification* with, rather than by distancing itself from, an image of perverse or "toxic" maternity.

Hirsch's discussion of Novak's "Past Lives" contrasts that image's arguable heteropathy with the photograph that forms the frontispiece to her own article. This first photograph—a photograph that has been much reproduced—is an archive photograph from the *Stroop Report* on the destruction of the Warsaw Ghetto. As Hirsch's opening extract from Jaroslaw Rymkiewicz's *The Final Station: Umschlagplatz* explains, this image is "the photograph everyone knows: a boy in a peaked cap and knee-length socks, his hands raised."[57] Certainly this *is* the photograph that everyone knows and its canonical status as an image of a *child-victim* rests, to some extent, on the cropping of this image prior to its various reproduc-

---

55. Hirsch 1999, p. 17.
56. Novak quoted in Hirsch 1999, p. 6.
57. Ibid., p. 3.

tions.[58] But in the version reproduced by Hirsch, "extraneous" material has not been cropped out. The boy is not separated out, that is, from *his* context. We see him accompanied by, though slightly apart from, a group of men, women, and children. And as the narrator of *The Final Station* emphasizes, behind them and slightly to the right "stand four Germans."[59] This is the version of the photograph that prompts Rymkiewicz's narrator to meditate upon *not only* the identification that he makes between that boy and his own boyhood self (the identification that Hirsch's analysis pursues), but also, as Hirsch's chosen extract makes plain, his fascination with the *soldiers*: "If I were now after 45 years to meet one of those Germans in the street I'd identify him instantly."[60] Earlier, I proposed that the remarks made by *The Final Station*'s narrator about the soldiers *as well as* his imaginary conversation with the boy in the photograph's foreground are suggestive of the complex web of identifications that are arguably constitutive of testimonial witnessing, and I asked why it might be that canonical testimonial theory, as exemplified by Hirsch's essay, limits itself to a discussion of the identificatory relation between witness and victim. What, that is, is the nature of a fascination that can etch those soldiers' faces deep into memory, and why does Hirsch pass over this passage?

There is, of course, a number of competing perspectives that can be drawn on to explain the fascination exerted by those soldiers. It might be proposed, for instance, that the etching of the solders' faces onto the narrator's memory exemplifies the "wounded attachment" characteristic of Nietzschian *ressentiment*, which "produces a site of revenge to displace the hurt."[61] *Ressentiment* does indeed offer an explanation for why those faces etch themselves in the memory: "if something is to stay in the memory, it must be

---

58. I am grateful to Peggy Phelan, who made this point after my original oral presentation of this paper at Lancaster University's *Testimonial Culture* conference.

59. Ibid.

60. Ibid.

61. Brown 1995, p. 68.

burned in. . . ."[62] Yet the passive version of memory it produces sheds no light on the processes by means of which the psyche actively mediates the images of which it is constituted. My revised reading of Freud's *Civilisation and Its Discontents* suggests, rather, that encounters with representatives of authority (*and* its perversion) will prompt secondary identifications modeled on that primary identification rooted in the child's *ambivalent* relation to its first authority figure—an ambivalence that finds no place in the Nietzschian schema and that Judith Butler's[63] bracketing of Freud with Nietzsche arguably underplays.

Contra Hirsch, and following but revising the Freud of *Civilisation and Its Discontents*, I am suggesting that the quoted passage from *The Final Station* is suggestive of the complex identifications in play in postmemorial testimonial scenarios. For the narrator's comments arguably point to the possibility that alongside an identification with the child victims runs an identification with the soldiers—a secondary identification that takes as its model that primary process by means of which the child negotiates ambivalence and which inaugurates conscience. But this terrifying authority is equivalent neither to the "good enough" authority assumed by Freud nor to the diffusions and pervasiveness of that postmodern authority identified by Craib. The authority struggled with here is perverse or "toxic" authority and the toxicity of this authority cannot be wholly incorporated. This toxic authority *demands* revenge. It is this demand, I want to suggest, that is suggested by the emphatic juxtapositioning of "after 45 years" and "I'd identify him instantly." As Nancy Wood has pointed out, this refusal of time's capacity to heal is characteristic of what Jean Améry termed "the victim's resentment"[64]:

> The victim's resentment, Améry declared, was in the first instance a "protest against the anti-moral natural process of heal-

---

62. Nietzsche quoted in Brown 1995, p. 68.
63. Butler 1997.
64. Wood 1998.

ing that time brings about . . . the resentment of the victim of
Nazism . . . was . . . locked by memories of the deed into a temporal order resistant to the forces of attenuation that remote-
ness through time otherwise effected.[65]

Toxic authority leaves its mark across time, but the mark it leaves,
I want to propose, is a mark etched upon a psyche struggling to
incorporate it on the model of a primary *ambivalence* that it catastrophically disappoints. The toxicity of Nazism and the diffusions
of postmodern authority are *not* equivalent. The authority of the
Third Reich was not hard to identify. But it was perverse. In such
circumstances, identification cannot (and should not) simply contain aggressivity through conversion into intrapsychic conflict. Yet
I want to insist that even the route *to* resistance passes *through* an
identification grounded in the child's ambivalence toward its first
authority figure and in a wish grounded in an unconsciously grasped
*resemblance*: the child's wish to exercise against that authority figure the aggressivity exercised against it. But Hirsch's reading is made
under the contemporary conditions, Craib's account of which I
described earlier, conditions in which the ungraspability of authority leads to the displacement and distortion of aggression, rather
than its incorporation through secondary identification. Craib identified two dominant displacements of aggression: an identification
with victimhood that denies its own aggressivity and fantasies of
innocent "goodness" in which aggression has no place. Under these
conditions, a postmemorial witnessing that embraces both an identification with the child victim and a more torturous identificatory
struggle with the soldiers cannot be countenanced. The soldiers
disappear. And what, then, of the men and women pictured alongside that child victim and those soldiers?

Though I have suggested that the constituency of postmemory
may exceed the ties of ethnic, familial, or group relation, Hirsch's
essay seeks to bear witness to a second-generation postmemory
forged through identifications grounded in those very relations.

---

65. Ibid., pp. 259–260.

Perhaps what is truly paradoxical about the effects of canonical testimonial work's constraints is not the removal of the soldiers from the scene of postmemorial identification, but the disappearance of the potential the *Stroop Report* photograph offers for identificatory fantasies linked with those men and women of the ghetto. These men and women's determination for revenge was forged, I want to insist, *through* processes that passed through identificatory travails with their tormentors—processes the traces of which emerge in *The Final Station*'s narrator's "even after 45 years . . . I'd identify him instantly."

The focus on victimhood and suffering exemplified by Hirsch's analyses can be linked to that essay's psychosocial context—a context within which identification with "pure" victimhood holds sway. The ethics of witnessing that follows from my essay and that I'm advocating takes a different form. We might return to the *Stroop Report* photograph and attempt to bear witness to the more complex, difficult, and equivocal identifications that together constitute its unrealized *potential*. What I'm suggesting, then, is that we struggle to read this image in the "gray zone," that is, in a zone in which neither "pure" victimhood nor "pure" perpetration holds sway. This would be a witnessing that works against the grain of canonical testimonial work. It is a witnessing made both urgent and difficult by the particular dangers of the times in which we live.

## ACKNOWLEDGMENTS

With thanks to Couze Venn, for last-minute advice.

## REFERENCES

Améry, J. (1980). *At the Mind's Limits: Contemplations by a Survivor on Auschwitz*. Bloomington: Indiana University Press.

Antze, P., and Lambek, M., eds. (1996). *Tense Past: Cultural Essays in Trauma and Memory*. New York and London: Routledge.

Axthelm, P. (1967). *The Modern Confessional Novel*. New Haven, CT: Yale University Press.

Bal, M., Crewe, J., and Spitzer, L., eds. (1999). *Acts of Memory: Cultural Recall in the Present*. Hanover and London: University Press of New England.

Benjamin, W. (1968). *Illuminations: Essays and Reflections*, trans. H. Arendt. New York: Schocken.

Brown, W. (1995). *States of Injury: Power and Freedom in Late Modernity*. Princeton, NJ: Princeton University Press.

Butler, J. (1997). *The Psychic Life of Power*. Stanford, CA: Stanford University Press.

Caruth, C., ed. (1995). *Trauma: Explorations in Memory*. Baltimore, MD: Johns Hopkins University Press.

———— (1996). *Unclaimed Experience: Trauma, Narrative, and History*. Baltimore, MD: Johns Hopkins University Press.

Cheyette, B. (1998). The ethical uncertainty of Primo Levi. In *Modernity, Culture and "the Jew,"* ed. B. Cheyette and L. Marcus, pp. 268–281. Oxford, UK: Polity.

Craib, I. (1994). *The Importance of Disappointment*. London: Routledge.

Elsaesser, T. (1996). Subject positions, speaking positions: from *Holocaust, Our Hitler,* and *Heimat* to *Shoah* and *Schindler's List*. In *The Persistence of History: Cinema, Television and the Modern Event*, ed. V. Sobchack, pp. 145–183. New York and London: Routledge.

Felman, S., and Laub, D. (1992). *Testimony: Crises of Witnessing in Literature, Psychoanalysis, and History*. New York and London: Routledge.

Foucault, M. (1981). *The History of Sexuality, Vol. 1: An Introduction*. Harmondsworth, UK: Penguin.

———— (1982). The subject and power. *Critical Inquiry* 8:777–797.

French, M. (1978). *The Women's Room*. London: Sphere.

Freud, S. (1930). *Civilisation and Its Discontents*. In *Pelican Freud Library, Vol 12*. Harmondsworth, UK: Penguin, 1985.

Hirsch, M. (1999). Projected memory: Holocaust photographs in personal and public fantasy. In *Acts of Memory: Cultural Recall in the Present*, ed. M. Bal, J. Crewe, and L. Spitzer, pp. 3–23. Hanover and London: University Press of New England.

Kahler, E. (1973). *The Inward Turn of Narrative*. Princeton, NJ: Princeton University Press.

Keneally, T. (1982). *Schindler's Ark*. London: Hodder and Stoughton.

Laplanche, J., and Pontalis, J.-B. (1988). *The Language of Psycho-Analysis*. London: Karnac.

Lasch, C. (1979). *The Culture of Narcissism*. New York and London: W. W. Norton.

Levi, P. (1989). *The Drowned and the Saved*. London: Abacus.

Loshitzky, Y. (1997). *Spielberg's Holocaust: Critical Perspectives on Schindler's List*. Bloomington: Indiana University Press.

Radstone, S. (1989). *The Women's Room: Women and the Confessional Mode*. Ph.D. thesis: Joint School of Literature and Film, Warwick University.

Reik, T. (1961). *The Compulsion to Confess: The Psychoanalysis of Crime and Punishment*. New York: Evergreen.

Rose, G. (1998). Beginnings of the day: fascism and representation. In *Modernity, Culture and "the Jew,"* ed. B. Cheyette and L. Marcus, pp. 242–256. Oxford, UK: Polity.

Rymkiewicz, J. M. (1994). *The Final Station: Umschlagplatz*, trans. N. Taylor. New York: Farrar, Straus and Giroux.

Santner, E. (1990). *Stranded Objects: Mourning, Memory and Film in Postwar Germany*. Ithaca, NY, and London: Cornell University Press.

Sennett, R. (1977). *The Fall of Public Man*. Cambridge, UK: Cambridge University Press.

Silverman, K. (1996). *The Threshold of the Visible World*. New York: Routledge.

Stelzig, E. L. (1984). Poetry and/or truth: an essay on the confessional imagination. *University of Toronto Quarterly* 54:17–37.

Wilkomirski, B. (1996). *Fragments: Memories of a Childhood, 1939–1948*, trans. C. B. Janeway. London: Picador.

Williams, R. (1984). *The English Novel from Dickens to Lawrence*. London: Hogarth.

Wood, N. (1998). The victim's resentments. In *Modernity, Culture and "the Jew,"* ed. by B. Cheyette and L. Marcus, pp. 257–267. Oxford: Polity.

# 5

# Traumatic Concepts: Latency and Crisis in Deleuze's Evolutionary Theory of Cinema

KARYN BALL

In *The Invention of Memory* (1988), Israel Rosenfield contests prevailing theories of memory as a localized and static entity, a storagehouse of fixed images that exist in trace form until an experience precipitates their reemergence in the present.[1] Working through the case studies assembled by Pierre Janet, Paul Broca, Sigmund Freud, Elizabeth Warrington, and Gerald Edelman, he traces a line of evidence that ultimately suggests that memory is neither fixed nor static. It is not a site of deep storage, but is rather an unpredetermined set of organizing, categorizing, and mapping processes that are contingently mobilized in varying contexts.

For readers of Henri Bergson such as Gilles Deleuze, Rosenfield's challenge to modular and localization theories of memory is not particularly radical. Bergson had already considered the extent to which the emergence of memory in consciousness is bound to movement as well as to time, to the body making contact with a world rather than to a resurgent unconscious content (*à la* Freud).

---

1. Rosenfield 1988.

In this respect, Bergson's theory of memory is less unilateral than Rosenfield's although preceding the latter's by a full century. Like Rosenfield, Bergson offers an alternative dynamic metaphor over and against storage metaphors of memory as a repository wherein fixed images might retain their essential contours and latent emotional charge throughout time. In *Matter and Memory*, memory undergoes an evolution whereby a virtual content becomes first a memory-image before it is actualized in response to the needs of the moment.[2] This theory of memory both confirms and counters Freud's economic understanding of the relation between the storage function of the unconscious and the sorting and absorbing powers of the perceptual-conscious system. For Freud, the transactions conducted between the perceptual-conscious and the unconscious comprise a closed economy. Within this economy, libidinally charged memory is experienced as a stimulus that triggers a regulative principle to maintain homeostasis. For Bergson, as well, the relations among perception, consciousness, and memory are dynamic, but they are not in any sense closed. The Bergsonian economy is, paradoxically, an "open totality," shaped by the perceptual-conscious and the contingencies of the body's movements in the world. This open totality appears in the intervals between movements, which indicate (without fixing) "the whole" as duration and spirit. Duration is, consequently, an immanence that cannot be localized, insofar as it emerges in the intersections and exchanges between the virtual and actual, between memory and action, space and time.

It is worth noting that despite their differences, Rosenfield, Freud, and Bergson each derive their theoretical projections about the structure of memory in part from the evidence provided by aphasic cases, which is to say, from the failures of linguistic memory suffered by patients who have undergone some form of trauma (though, of course, Freud's considerations of trauma are not restricted to aphasic patients). This derivation raises a question about how the peculiar dynamics of trauma might come to constitute the implicit foundation of a general theory of memory. Such a theory

---

2. Bergson 1991.

would have no independent status in its own right insofar as it has been defined in relation to the repressions, dissociations, and fixations that distinguish traumatic memory. In short, trauma is inversely installed in the history of memory theories.[3]

This traumatic installation goads post-psychoanalytic theories of subject formation that presumably aim to provide an alternative to the metaphysics of consciousness. When Michel Foucault constructs a scenario of self-surveying subjects whose bodies are imprisoned by their "souls," he distances himself from the Freudian model of consciousness for its complicity with disciplinary technologies that implant "sex" as a dangerous secret. In a similarly Nietzschean spirit, Deleuze and Guattari have excoriated psychoanalysis for its "Oedipal imperialism" and for its anthropocentric fetishism of human intention in its conscious and unconscious forms. In *A Thousand Plateaus: Capitalism and Schizophrenia*, Deleuze and Guattari (1987) propose post-humanist metaphors of reading and writing in order to create a new "semiotics of perception" that counteracts the hermeneutics of surface codes distorting hidden interiors or repressed depths. Deleuze's Bergsonism in the *Cinema* books can be read in keeping with this agenda as an attempt to go beyond psychoanalytic film theories that decode the unconscious and sexual motivations behind characters' actions as well as camera angles, movements, and cuts. Bergson's theses in *Matter and Memory* and *Creative Evolution* provide Deleuze with the theoretical conditions for pursuing an immanent reading of cinema that works through the traces of a psychoanalytic counter-inheritance.[4] This counter-inheritance is discernible in the motif of a latent, traumatic, yet potentially transformative "unthought" that drives Deleuze's narration of the evolutionary unfolding of cinematic "thought" before and after World War II. The narrative

---

3. I am borrowing Tom Cohen's (2005) phrasing here from *Hitchcock's Cryptonomies, Vol. II: War Machines* (p. xiii). See also *Hitchcock's Cryptonomies, Vol. I: Secret Agents*.

4. Deleuze 1989a: *Cinema 1: The Movement-Image* and 1989b: *Cinema 2: The Time-Image*.

climaxes in his delineation of the "crisis" of the *movement-image* leading to the emergence of the *time-image* in the postwar period. My argument is that this post-psychoanalytic reading of latency and crisis in cinematic thought symptomatically repeats and absolves a traumatic plot that eventuates in the return of an epistemological, historical, and political repressed.

It is in this respect that Deleuze's investment in the Bergsonian theory of an open whole might be situated within the context of a French thought that responds politically and morally to the traumas of the mid-twentieth century: the Holocaust, the revelations of Stalin's atrocities, the bombing of Hiroshima and Nagasaki, and the involvement of the French military in the torture of Algerians. This is a skeptical thought with a Nietzschean and post-Marxist disposition that finds totalitarian shadows lurking in "identitarian" or univocal systems of representation and particularly those presupposing the potential for recovering the ultimate ground of truth at the expense of difference, indeterminacy, and/or otherness. However, Deleuze's rejection of "totalizing" and foundationalist systems does not posit transcendence as a topological outside whence the rescue of resistance, excess, and incommensurability becomes possible. Instead, he revises the structuralist figure of the *interval* to emphasize non-intentionalist and value-neutral relations between image and matter, action and reaction. Citing Bergson, Deleuze writes that the interval is "only possible in so far as the plane of matter includes time"[5]; it is key to Deleuze's standpoint on the *immanence* of matter and relations drawing from Bergson's concept of the virtual whole as duration and becoming and, thus, as an affective thread of tension, potential, and transformation.[6] Giorgio

---

5. Deleuze 1989a, p. 61.

6. I am grateful to Peter Canning for this point. In Deleuze's reading of Bergson, the whole that is affected by the interval is open, hence constituting an open totality. In contrast, transcendence must posit a closed totality in order to construct an outside. As Canning puts it in "The Crack of Time and the Ideal Game" (1994), "Deleuze does not wallow in the finitude of 'castration' and 'transcendence,' because everything is becoming-idea, becoming-body, becoming-virtual, becoming-actual in a circuit without end or beginning, the new world-image of absolute immanence" (p. 81).

Agamben notes that Deleuze's immanence is a "pre-individual and absolutely impersonal zone beyond (or before) every idea of consciousness"; it is, in this respect, a post-humanist principle of indetermination between the inorganic and the organic, between the not-external outside and not-internal inside of every thought, and the unthought (in abeyance) of every plane as such.[7]

Keeping this definition of immanence in mind, my discussion retraces Deleuze's historical narrative of cinema punctuated by a crisis of the movement-image that leads to the predominance of the time-image in the post-World War II period. I will therefore be concerned with determining how the movement-image embodies the latent conditions for its eventual crisis and how this upheaval itself prefigures the traumatic upsurge of a virtual (repressed) time. This crisis is Deleuze's figure for the shocking impact of the genocide perpetrated by the Nazis on witnessing, judging, and memory. Ultimately, then, this traumatic configuration functions rhetorically for Deleuze as an epistemological, historical, and political unthought whose eruption hastens the birth of an increasingly modern cinematic thought.

## I. BERGSONIAN LATENCIES

In Chapters 1 and 4 of *Cinema 1*, Deleuze characterizes Bergson's work as a move to create philosophical concepts that would be consonant with the modern scientific perspective. Interestingly, this reformulation assumes its significance in light of Bergson's critique of the "cinematographic illusion" in *Creative Evolution* (1907). In that context, Bergson dismisses cinema as a culmination of the naïve "ancient perspective" that subordinates time to an idealized, immobile space.[8] For Bergson, this conception runs counter to "modern science," which is defined "pre-eminently by its aspiration to take time as an independent variable."[9] Early cinema is therefore

---

7. Agamben 1999, pp. 225, 228.
8. Deleuze 1989a, p. 3.
9. Bergson 1907, p. 355. Quoted by Deleuze 1989a, p. 4.

"an ambiguous ally" in the effort to formulate concepts befitting a modern scientific perspective because it reproduces the notion of misconceived movement by which "natural" perception itself proceeds. The "correct" or "modern" model in Bergson's view would consist instead of "a state of things which would constantly change, a flowing-matter in which no point of anchorage nor centre of reference would be assignable."[10] For movement to be conceived in a manner consistent with this perspective, it must not be recomposed in relation to privileged instants, positions, or poses; rather a transcendental concept must yield to a sensible analysis of "immanent material elements," that is, to an examination of mechanical succession as the defining principle of the relation between movement and "non-privileged" instants.[11]

The *Cinema* books represent Deleuze's attempt to read the history of auteur cinema as a "creative evolution" in Bergson's sense despite the latter's resistance to film as a new medium. Deleuze's trajectory for the development of cinematic thought foregrounds its agency in correcting the ancient perspective on movement and time. To this end, Deleuze will employ Bergson's theses from *Matter and Memory* (1896) to "prefigure the future and essence of the cinema" in the evolution of its "thought" from the ancient perspective toward a modern or immanent view of movement that relates it to "any-instant-whatever."[12] The problem is one of reconciling a "naïve" cinema that Bergson critiques with cinematic evolution as Deleuze via Bergson re-imagines it. This reconciliation takes shape in Deleuze's consideration of another of Bergson's theses from *Creative Evolution*: "things are never defined by their primitive state, but by the tendency *concealed* in this state."[13] In following through on the implications of this thesis, Deleuze maintains that Bergson was restricted in his reflections to a "primitive state" of cinema where "the image is in movement rather than being movement-

---

10. Deleuze 1989a, p. 57.
11. Ibid., p. 4.
12. Ibid., p. 3.
13. Ibid., p. 25. My emphasis.

image." He consequently could not anticipate cinema's later developments whereby a more advanced relation between movement and time appears.[14] This would be the cinema which, for Deleuze, "fully belongs to the modern conception of movement." Cinematic movement would, in this incarnation, permit a "continuity constructed at each instant, which now only allowed itself to be decomposed into its prominent immanent elements, instead of being related to prior forms which it was to embody."[15] In the course of Deleuze's analysis, this later development will be interpreted as confirming Bergson's theses from the first chapter of *Matter and Memory*. In that context, movement is understood as an expression of a change of duration or in the whole as such. Hence, if cinema "seems to be the last descendent of this lineage which Bergson traced," this is because it realizes the modern concept of movement in the course of its history.

Deleuze reads the principles proposed in *Creative Evolution* (1907) as a map of cinema's development.[16] Yet he will portray this development as a realization of Bergson's earlier theses and conclusions from *Matter and Memory* in 1896. In effect, Deleuze adopts the speculations of *Creative Evolution* to recuperate the relevance of a work by Bergson published just after the official birth of cinema in 1895 in the cinématographe of the Brothers Lumière. This recuperation provides Deleuze with a means to resolve an apparent contradiction between Bergson's critique of cinema and his prioritization of the modern perspective on movement and time. More significantly, it also positions Deleuze to introduce this resolution as an epistemological trajectory that cinema "thinks" over time. Cinema is hereby conceived as an evolving form of perception that will eventually realize its agency as the "organ for perfecting a new reality."[17] In short, by reading Bergson's critical view

---

14. Ibid., p. 24. It is worth noting that, in Deleuze's view, the modern scientific perspective is not impervious to the illusions that Bergson attributes to ancient philosophy.

15. Ibid., p. 7.

16. According to Deleuze's dating (see 1989a, pp. 1–2).

17. Ibid., pp. 7–8.

of cinema into the future and, as it were, against itself, Deleuze produces a genetic and evolutionary concept of cinema.

I have been suggesting that in its history as a concept, cinema is, for Deleuze, the actualization of the "virtualities" in Bergson's philosophy. This mode of figuration has a number of implications for Deleuze's thinking on the status of cinematic movement. Extrapolating from *Matter and Memory*, Deleuze will construct cinematic movement as the translation of a virtual memory into a selectively constituted concrete perception. As a subtractive actualization of memory, concrete perception overcomes the dualities between image and movement and between consciousness and matter. The history of cinema expresses this transformation on a macro level as a process of evolution that culminates in the emergence of "time as an independent variable" in the post-World War II period. The emergence of the time-image in postwar film is Deleuze's cinematographic figure for Bergson's concept of the open whole that is in duration and is, moreover, "duration itself, in so far as it does not stop changing."[18]

---

18. Ibid., p. 11. Helpful for an understanding of this evolution is Deleuze's detailed summary of the relation between movement and duration in view of its relevance to cinema:

> The organisation of matter makes possible the closed systems or the determinate sets of parts; and the deployment of space makes them necessary. But the point is that the sets are in space, and the whole, the wholes are in duration, are duration itself, in so far as it does not stop changing [. . . .] Thus, in a sense movement has two aspects: On the one hand, that which happens between objects or parts; on the other hand that which expresses the duration or the whole. The result is that duration, by changing qualitatively, is divided up in objects, and objects, by gaining depth, by losing their contours, are united in duration. We can therefore say that movement relates the objects of a closed system to open duration, and duration to the objects of the system which it forces to open up. Movement relates the objects between which it is established to the changing whole which it expresses and vice versa. Through movement the whole is divided up into objects, and objects are re-united in the whole, and indeed between the two "the whole" changes. We can consider the objects or parts of a set as *immobile sections*; but movement is established between these sections, and relates the objects or parts to the duration of a whole which changes, and thus

Deleuze observes that both the ancient and modern perspectives on movement share the mistaken assumption that the whole must be given or giveable in order to be meaningful. In Deleuze's reading of Bergson, the whole is "open" and is therefore not "giveable." This openness reflects its tendency "to change constantly, or to give rise to something new, in short, to endure."[19] Deleuze maintains that the whole represents "the register in which time is being inscribed." It is his indeterminate figure for a virtual memory that transpires in relations between objects and phenomena rather than as a property inhering in them.[20]

For Deleuze, both the ancient and scientific perspectives misconceive movement in failing to think the whole as virtual memory and relation. This "lapse of memory" underlies Deleuze's analysis of the link between movement and image. The movement-image is the cinematic enunciation of Bergson's definition of concrete perception as the "prejudiced, partial, subjective" product of a selective process that is geared toward a potential action. This process subtracts from the object that which does not interest the perceiver as a function of his or her needs.[21] These needs are partly informed by memory that determines the relevance of perceptual phenomena. Reciprocally, the demands of perception pressure the conversion of a virtual memory into memory-images, which attenuate the concrete perception of present phenomena through their resonance with the past.

---

expresses the changing of the whole in relation to the objects and is itself a *mobile section* of duration. Now we are equipped to understand the profound thesis of the first chapter of *Matter and Memory*: (1) there are not only instantaneous images, that is, immobile sections of movement; (2) there are movement-images which are mobile sections of duration; (3) there are, finally, time-images, that is, duration-images, change-images, relation-images, volume-images which are beyond movement itself. . . . [Ibid., p. 11]

This passage encapsulates Deleuze's evolution of "primitive" cinema distinguished by immobile sections of duration to "classical" pre-WWII cinema as marked by the shift toward mobile sections, to the postwar cinema of the time-image.

19. Ibid., p. 9.
20. Ibid., p. 10.
21. Ibid., pp. 63–64.

Following Bergson, Deleuze equates this virtual memory with the whole as the openness of relations among objects and phenomena. In "concrete perception," however, this whole is subordinated to a selection process that delineates privileged instants. This connection is significant because it delimits concrete perception as the privileging of certain aspects of perceptual phenomena and the corresponding negation of others. It thereby constitutes the ground of a movement that Deleuze identifies as "false." False movement frames closed sections at the expense of a realization of the relations affecting the whole or time; however, these provisional framings are only intelligible in relation to what they negate. The negated comprises a perceptual "elsewhere" that is relegated to a field outside of vision (the *out-of-field*). This is the case, even though the whole never disappears, but rests in the "thread" connecting the seen set of the framed image with the unseen set of the out-of-field:

> when we consider a framed image as a closed system, we can say that one aspect prevails over the other, depending on the nature of the "thread." The thicker the thread which links the seen set to other unseen sets the better the out-of-field fulfills its first function, which is the adding of space to space. But, when the thread is very fine, it is not content to reinforce the closure of the frame or to eliminate the relation with the outside. It certainly does not bring about a complete isolation of the relatively closed system, which would be impossible. But, the finer it is—the further duration descends into the system like a spider—the more effectively the out-of-field fulfills its other function which is that of introducing the transspatial and the spiritual into the system which is never perfectly closed.[22]

The out-of-field does not merely serve as an excluded space that produces the parameters of a closed segment. It also introduces a "spidery" transspatial, temporal, and spiritual dimension into a system that, as I have suggested, is not "giveable" because it is never completely closed. In Deleuze's Bergsonianism, the transspatial is

---

22. Ibid., p. 17.

interwoven with virtual memory, duration, and the spiritual. It exerts pressure on the boundaries of the visible field in instances when the thread linking the framed image to its out-of-frame supplement is very fine. In these instances, the thread fails to reinforce the closure of the frame or to eliminate its relation with the outside.

In practice, the out-of-field is the cinematographic site of the unseen that defines the "not outside outside" and the "not inside inside" of a visible closed section of movement. On a figurative level, the out-of-field may also testify to a "more disturbing presence, one which cannot even be said to exist, but rather to 'insist' or 'subsist,' a more radical Elsewhere, outside homogeneous space and time."[23] It is a symptomatic absent-presence that indicates the dynamism of the whole that has been subordinated to the discernibility of a closed section. Its "disturbing" impact derives from the pressure it exerts on the provisional closure of a visible field.

Deleuze's delineation of the out-of-field as a "dangerous supplement" sets up a precedent for a movement-image that embodies the conditions for its eventual crisis. As a troubling symptom of phenomenal excess bracketed out by the frame's subordination of the whole, the out-of-field that haunts the limits of the visible prefigures the upsurge of a traumatic unthought that unsettles the dominance of the movement-image and mobilizes cinematic thought to turn toward time.

To summarize, my analysis suggests that Bergson's definition of concrete perception provides the conceptual basis for Deleuze's formulation of the movement-image that dominates classical cinema. The movement-image evolves, in the course of Deleuze's narrative, into a cinematic inscription of concrete perception as the effect of a process of selection and subtraction. In this regard, movement-image cinema retains the traces of an ancient overcoding that negates the immanence of movement, memory, and time. Yet to the extent that the intelligibility of this image depends on the exclusion of an out-of-field, it defers a traumatic potential to shatter the cohesion of a visual field. This deferral foreshadows the

---

23. Ibid.

inaction and disavowal of bystanders during World War II who failed to be effective witnesses of genocide. It is therefore crucial to Deleuze's understanding of the crisis of the movement-image that spurs the rise of the time-image in postwar film. I will return to this point when I discuss Deleuze's analysis of Alfred Hitchcock, but first I will connect the cinematic epistemology that Deleuze develops through his reading of Bergson to its configuration as a historical evolution.

## II. FROM "ANCIENT" MOVEMENT TO "INDEPENDENT" TIME

On a narratological level, the movement-image functions as the conceptual protagonist of Deleuze's narrative about pre-World War II classical cinema. Before World War II, the cinema did not give us "an image to which movement is added." In Deleuze's words, it immediately gives us a movement-image as a mobile section of duration alternating between objective and subjective poles: what happens in the relations between sets or closed systems "which are defined by discernible objects or distinct parts" and that which expresses the duration or the whole, "a spiritual reality which constantly changes according to its own relations."[24] In its objective mode, the movement-image consists of total, diffuse universal variation, with no center. Its objective character derives from its relation to objects such that perception and matter become indistinguishable.

In its subjective mode, the movement-image is related to a specialized "living image" which Deleuze identifies as a *center of indetermination*. This center is formed "in the acentered universe of movement-images," which is to say, in the *interval* between action and reaction. As a so-called "living" image, the interval is distinct from *objective* images, which react "on all their facets and in all their parts." In contrast, a *subjective* image "only receives ac-

------

24. Ibid., p. 11.

tions on one facet or in certain parts and only executes reactions by and in other parts." It thereby functions to isolate certain images from "all those which compete and act together in the universe."[25]

The structure of the movement-image in its subjective perceptual mode consists of an action *framed* in relation to a center of indetermination. The "art" of framing demarcates the parts belonging to a set as a system that is only "relatively and artificially closed." This provisional closed system is an effect of a *cut* that produces the shot as "the determination of the movement to a whole." The shot establishes this movement between elements or parts of the set within a closed system.[26]

It is helpful to recall here that when Deleuze speaks of a set as a closed system, he is contrasting it to the whole. The whole is inextricably bound up with Bergson's concept of duration as the openness of "that which changes." It is on this basis, then, that Deleuze defines movement as a change in the whole, and thus as an articulation/contraction of duration. Nevertheless, the shot is never simply an expression of a relation to a set since it comprises movement in two facets "as inseparable as the inside and the outside, as the two sides of a coin." Deleuze states that movement "expresses a change of the whole, or a stage, an aspect of this change, a duration, or an articulation of duration."[27] "*It is*," as he emphasizes, "*the relationship between parts and it is the state [affection] of the whole.* On the one hand it modifies the respective positions of the parts of a set, which are like its sections [*coupes*], each one immobile in itself; on the other it is itself the mobile section of a whole whose change it expresses."[28]

*Montage* performs the cinematic operation whereby the movement-image is related to duration and thereby precipitates an indirect image of time. In *Cinema 1*, montage is presented as an

---

25. Ibid., p. 61.
26. Ibid., p. 18.
27. Ibid.
28. Ibid., p. 19.

operation that assembles the three "avatars" of the movement-image: *perception-*, *action-*, and *affection-images* (primarily delineated through long shots, medium shots, and close-ups respectively).[29] Each of these shots corresponds to one stage or aspect of Bergson's understanding of the process of selection, which relates memory, perception, and action. This categorization permits Deleuze to define action as the culmination of a subjective perspective that affects the subordination of the whole as an open and virtual memory contingently attenuated by perception and action.

The first avatar of the movement-image is the *perception-image* as a process of selection that takes place between the objective view commanded by the camera and the subjective view that organizes a center of indetermination. The second avatar of the movement-image is the *action-image* that consists of a reaction of this center as defined by the parameters of the perception-image. The action-image relates movement to "acts" in the same way that the perception-image relates movement to rigid and moving objects and bodies. The third avatar of the movement-image is the *affection-image* that occupies the interval between received and executed movement, between the virtual action of things and their actualization in a new state. The affection-image "surges in the centre of indetermination that is to say in the subject, between a perception which is troubling in certain respects and a hesitant action."[30] It is the image that connects perception- and action-images in the subject.

Of the three images, the affection-image is the most crucial to the shift that Deleuze traces from a classical prewar cinema wherein time is subordinated to movement to a modern cinema wherein movement is subordinated to time as an independent variable. First, the affection-image occupies without filling the interval between perception (virtual action received) and execution (reaction to the received virtual action). This interval represents the site whence the possible, the new, and also freedom might emerge. The location of the affection-image in the interval is therefore key to the

---

29. Ibid., p. 70.
30. Ibid., p. 65.

opening of the movement-image to time. Second, to the extent that it refracts the portion of external movements not captured in either objects of perception or acts of the subject, the affection-image relates movement to a power and/or quality. It transpires in the coincidence of subject and object and, reciprocally, in the aesthetic domain of spectator reception. Third, by virtue of its agency in establishing the relation between a received (virtual) and executed (actual) movement, the affection-image serves to translate perception into reaction; yet it is also the site where this movement ceases to be translation. Deleuze writes:

> it is not sufficent to think that perception—thanks to distance—retains or reflects what interests us by letting pass what is indifferent to us. There is inevitably a part of external movements that we "absorb," that we refract, and which does not transform itself into either objects of perception or acts of the subject; rather they mark the coincidence of the subject and the object in a pure quality. This is the final avatar of the movement-image: the *affection-image* [. . . .] This is the origin of Bergson's wonderful definition of affection as "a kind of motor tendency on a sensible nerve," that is, a motor effort on an immobilised receptive plate.
>
> There is therefore a relationship between affection and movement in general which might be expressed as follows: the movement of translation is not merely interrupted in its direct propagation by an interval which allocates on the one hand the received movement, and on the other the executed movement, and which might make them in a sense incommensurable. Between the two there is affection which re-establishes the relation. But, it is precisely in affection that the movement ceases to be that of translation in order to become movement of expression, that is to say quality, simple tendency stirring up an immobile element. . . .[31]

The close-up is the cinematic vehicle for what Deleuze refers to as "movement of expression" to describe an affective quality or

---

31. Ibid., pp. 65–66.

tendency which "stirs up" an "immobile element" and is "most frequently buried in the rest of the body."[32] The close-up provides a medium for the resurgence of this buried element as the corporeal trace of a repressed (virtual) time. Its arousal indicates the temporality of a sentient body caught in the alterity of perceiving, acting, and aging. Senescence is the patience of a body enduring and disintegrating over time that underlies the corporeal quality of images of duration; it is a latent material and affective condition that cannot be separated from the openness of the whole that Deleuze-Bergson connects with virtual memory.

Deleuze's recognition of the body and of senescence in particular in his reflections on the affection-image and time point suggests a reading of the "immobile element" as the fate that comes to all organisms who would die, as Freud in 1920 remarks, only in their own fashion. Senescence and mortality comprise another dimension of sociophysical unthought to the extent that they comprise a virtual body-memory that is, at once, latent potential and disavowed past. I previously alluded to the body and the drives as an unthought that haunts the limits of the frame in Deleuze's remarks on the out-of-field. From a Freudian perspective, Deleuze's "immobile element" buried in the body might be connected to tensions produced by instinctual urges that feed into the source and propulsion of the drives. Deleuze's references to the "immobile element" that the affection-image "stirs up" thus resonate with Freud's phylogenetic and metaphysical configuration of the primordial origin and radical aim of the "death drive" that seeks to neutralize unbound stimuli and thereby return the psyche to an inorganic state of matter. The immobile element might therefore be understood from a Freudian standpoint as a primal destiny to annihilate the stresses that trouble the processing functions of the perception-action circuit. In this additional sense, the virtuality of pure time can be said to share the character of inorganic matter as it does for Deleuze-Bergson.

---

32. Ibid., p. 66.

At the end of *Cinema 1* and throughout *Cinema 2*, Deleuze identifies the resurgence of this immobile element as a condition for the genesis of a direct time-image and its offshoot, the memory-image. This is the case insofar as the affection-image possesses singular "power qualities" or "potentialities" that not only anticipate the event, but also refer back to themselves as unrealized possibilities from the past. They thereby constitute the event in its "eternal aspect" as the virtual realm of memory grounding the succession and simultaneity of possibles. This delineation of the affection-image strengthens its connection to the unthought, a figure of traumatic disavowal (of the unworked-through past in the present) and potential (for unrealized possibilities from the past to be reawakened in the future).[33] Deleuze writes that "power-qualities have an anticipatory role, since they prepare for the event which will be actualised in the state of things and will modify it. . . . But in themselves, or as expresseds, they are already the event in its eternal aspect, in what Blanchot calls 'the aspect of the event that its accomplishment cannot realise.'"[34]

The transitional agency of the affection-image anticipates the return of time in still another way. In its differential expression of power-qualities, the affection-image gives rise to two signs. In the *iconic* mode specific to the close-up, the affect attaches to the faces that express it.[35] In the absence of a face, however, the affect as *qualisign* is no longer restricted to the close-up. It thus obtains a space for itself, one that, like the face, is absolutely singular, but which has lost its formal homogeneity. In Deleuze's words, "Affects are not individuated like people and things, but nevertheless they do not blend into the indifference of the world. They have

---

33. Deleuze's understanding of the concept of the unthought resonates with Maurice Blanchot's (1995) reflections in *Writing the Disaster*. Here he considers the inevitable distance from thought that is the paradoxical consequence of any attempt to think or name a traumatic event. The disastrous event always remains on reserve, like an unspoken thought.

34. Deleuze 1989a, p. 102. Citing Maurice Blanchot, *L'Espace de Littéraire* (1955, p. 161).

35. Ibid., p. 106.

singularities which enter into virtual conjunction and each time constitute a complex entity."[36] In this mode, the affection-image shows only pure powers and qualities "independently of the states of things or milieux which actualize them."[37]

This characterization of the affection-image prefigures Deleuze's discussion of the *any-space-whatever* as a type qualisign that marks the transition from the movement-image to the time-image in the evolution of cinematic thought. Deleuze adopts Robert Bresson's term to refer to a deconnected space whose parts and orientation are not determined in advance. It may also describe an amorphous, empty set that has extinguished the actions and events within it. In both senses, these deconnected or empty spaces evoke, for Deleuze, the destruction, reconstruction, and "undifferentiated urban tissue" of the postwar landscape. The "any-space-whatever" undoes the spaces wherein action might transpire, thereby leaving only the abstraction of pure optical and sound situations in its wake. According to Deleuze, the "very special extension" of the pure optical and sound situations (*opsigns* and *sonsigns*) is "to make time and thought perceptible, to make them visible and of sound." It is by virtue of this function, that a "purely optical and sound situation does not extend into action, any more than it is induced by an action. It makes us grasp, it is supposed to make us grasp, something intolerable and unbearable."[38] These situations elicit the modern affects of fear, detachment, extreme speed, and "interminable waiting" that ultimately undermine the primacy of the movement-image in prewar cinema.[39]

Deleuze interprets the proliferation of these spaces in films following the war as evidence of a crisis in the action-image, which opens a "crack" through which repressed time and memory will return. Previously, the reliance on Aristotelian plot structures guar-

---

36. Ibid., p. 103. He adds that "The close-up does indeed suspend individuation [. . .] it makes all faces look alike."

37. Ibid., p. 120.

38. Deleuze 1989b, p. 18.

39. Deleuze 1989a, p. 121.

anteed the effectivity of the relation between actions and situations; however, the second World War derailed the possibility of continuing faith in this guarantee.[40] At the close of *Cinema 1* and at the opening of *Cinema 2*, he enumerates the five principal effects of this crisis of faith. First, the Aristotelian plot structures that formerly organized the relation between situation and action have broken down. Deleuze delimits two such structures: the large form SAS' (situation-action-situation) structure whereby the plot moves "from the situation to the action which modifies the situation," and the small form ASA' (action-situation-action) structure in which an "action discloses a situation, which triggers off a new action."[41] This has the effect of weakening the characters' agency as well as the image's power to refer to global and synthetic situations. Second, insofar as the characters are caught in a dispersive reality that undermines the link between intention and action, they reflect the disconnected and lacunary situations within which these actions might emerge. Third, the stroll, the journey, and the voyage come to displace the direct relation between action and event, thereby detaching the image from the affective and active structure that supported it. Reciprocally, this detachment proliferates in the form of any-space-whatever's that disarticulate the precisely delimited spatio-temporal loci of realist cinema. The three previous effects mirror the fragmented agency of the characters whose actions no longer belong to them, but descend on them from within a dispersive disconnected universe. Hence in a world "without totality or linkage," the only unifying principal is the physical, optical, auditory, and psychic clichés that mutually feed each other. Lastly, the reign of the cliché has the corresponding effect of further decentering the action. According to Deleuze, this leads to the rise of the conspiracy film in which the center is attributed to an occult power that is itself confused with "its effects, its supports, its media, its radios, its televisions, its microphones: it now only

---

40. Ibid., pp. 205–215.
41. Ibid., p. 161.

operates through the 'mechanical reproduction of images and of sounds.'"[42] Ultimately, then, postwar cinema attests to a paralysis of action as well as to a paranoid sense that situations not only exceed control, but also delimitation.[43]

The reign of clichés is particularly significant for Deleuze's mapping of the crisis of the movement-image that will spur the cinematic thinking of an independent time. As Deleuze explains, "In order for people to be able to bear themselves and the world, misery has to reach the inside of consciousness and the inside has to be like the outside." Clichés introduce their anonymity into the spectator's

---

42. Ibid., p. 210.

43. In defining the distinctness of modern cinema in *Cinema 2*, Deleuze writes:

> What has happened is that the sensory-motor schema is no longer in operation, but at the same time it is not overtaken or overcome. It is shattered from the inside. That is, perceptions and actions ceased to be linked together, and spaces are now neither co-ordinated nor filled. Some characters, caught in certain pure optical and sound situations, find themselves condemned to wander about or go off on a trip. These are pure seers, who no longer exist except in the interval of movement, and do not even have the consolation of the sublime, which would connect them to matter or would gain control of the spirit for them. They are rather given over to something intolerable which is simply their everydayness itself. It is here that the reversal is produced: movement is no longer simply aberrant, aberration is now valid in itself and designates time as its direct cause. "Time is out of joint": it is off the hinges assigned to it by behavior in the world, but also by movements of world. It is no longer time that depends on movement; it is aberrant movement that depends on time. The relation, *sensory-motor situation → indirect image of time* is replaced by a non-localizable relation, *pure optical and sound situation → direct time-image*. Opsigns and sonsigns are direct presentations of time. False continuity shots are the non-localizable relation itself: characters no longer jump across them, they are swallowed up in them[. . . .] We can choose between emphasizing the difference between the classical and the modern. It took the modern cinema to re-read the whole of cinema as already made up of aberrant movements and false continuity shots. The direct time-image is the phantom which has always haunted the cinema, but it took modern cinema to give a body to this phantom. [Deleuze 1989b, pp. 40–41]

internal world such that "everyone possesses only psychic clichés by which he thinks and feels, is thought and is felt, being himself a cliché among others in the world that surrounds him."[44] Insofar as cinema participates in the fabrication and propagation of these clichés, it betrays the manner in which the action-image engendered a tradition "from which it could only extricate itself negatively."[45]

In occupying and disarticulating the interval between perception and action, the affection-image already embodies the possibility of their failed relation within it. The war brought this possibility to fruition because it actualized a potential for paralysis already inherent in the affect occupying the interval between them. As Deleuze suggests, the affection-image "undoubtedly contains something mental (a pure consciousness)." It therefore anticipates the advent at the end of the war of the *mental-image* "which takes as its object, relations, symbolic acts, intellectual feelings."[46]

In the hands of Alfred Hitchcock, the mental-image becomes the completion and perfection of all other images. This is the case insofar as Hitchcock employs this image to empty action of all meaning, thereby foregrounding the relation that produces the action rather than its cause. Deleuze observes that, in Hitchcock's films, "The characters can act, perceive, experience, but they cannot testify to the relations which determine them."[47] The task of this testimony consequently falls elsewhere—to the spectator. The affection-image was the image of relation that formerly represented the entry point for the spectator; however, now this function is in large part subsumed by the mental-image. Henceforth the public's reactions must come to "form an integrating part of the film." Indeed, "this is the explicit sense of suspense, since the spectator is the first to 'know' the relations."[48] In this role, the mental-image does not merely fascinate spectators, capturing them in alternating nets

---

44. Deleuze 1989a, pp. 208–209.
45. Ibid., p. 211.
46. Deleuze 1989a, p. 198. Deleuze's emphasis.
47. Ibid., p. 201.
48. Ibid., p. 202.

of glamour, pathos, and relief; its efficacy depends on its ability to implicate them in the innocent–guilty equilibrium, in the exchange between assassin and victim, hence also in murder, judgment, and the failure to judge on time.

## III. LATENCY, CRISIS, AND THE RESTORATION OF IMMANENCE: BETWEEN TRAUMATIC HISTORY AND MESSIANIC POSSIBILITY

The traumatic *topos* of the *Cinema* books is reinforced by Deleuze's description of the advent of the mental-image, which refracts the "unthought" as a latent and disavowed crisis of judgment that had previously been deferred through Aristotelian plot structures. For if the war revealed anything, Deleuze argues, it was that action, when it occurs at all, often occurs too late (in other words, after the genocide of millions had already taken place). This historical situation of failed judgment and response, and of the unthought as such, necessarily transforms cinematic expressions of the perception-action circuit along with the apperceptions of the spectator as their vehicle. As Deleuze describes it, there was no longer a "globalising situation which was able to concentrate itself in a decisive action." Instead, "action and plot were only to be a component in a dispersive set, in an open totality."[49] Likewise, insofar as there was no previous history (no grand Enlightenment narrative, no monumental historical idea) that the war had not, in some sense, annihilated, "there was no preformed action whose consequences on a situation could be foreseen."[50]

---

49. Ibid., p. 205.
50. Correspondingly, if "the cinema could not transcribe events which had already happened," it "necessarily devoted itself to reaching the event in the course of happening, sometimes by cutting across an 'actuality,' sometimes by provoking or producing it." Ultimately, then, this is the sense in which for Deleuze, "[t]here is always a moment when the cinema meets the unforeseeable or the improvisation, the irreducibility of a present living under the present of narration, and the camera cannot even begin its work without engendering its own improvisations, both as obstacles and as indispensable means" (Ibid., p. 206).

The crisis of the action-image points to a more profound paralysis at the level of judgment understood as the choice of means that would relate a perceptual horizon to an executed action. It is a crisis that historically marks the traumatic impact of World War II and the Nazi mass murders on postwar thought. Jean-François Lyotard writes that the silences that surrounded the event of mass death in Auschwitz are signs of a *"differend,"* which he defines as "the unstable state and instant of language" wherein something "'asks' to be put into phrases, and suffers from the wrong of not being able to be put into phrases right away."[51] *Differends* result from situations in which justice is left in abeyance because the rules of judgment preempt the possibility of validating the plaintiff's claims: "The one who lodged a complaint is heard, but the one who is a victim, and who is perhaps the same one, is reduced to silence."[52] A *differend*, so defined, took place in the National Socialist abrogation of deported Jews' membership in civil society and the attendant neutralization of their status as victims who could be heard. For Lyotard, this situation was made worse by the failure to believe the survivors who returned from the camps and who themselves felt guilty about surviving. This guilt intensified their reluctance to testify about experiences of suffering and brutality that were so shocking that they would likely be doubted and whose magnitude could never be represented adequately let alone rendered intelligible for an everyday world outside the death camps.

Shoshana Felman draws on Lyotard's formulation of the *differend* in *Testimony: Crises of Witnessing in Psychoanalysis, Literature, and History*, where she describes the destruction of evidence and the paralysis of bystanders who watched the genocide of the Jews, Sinti and Roma unfold and failed to prevent it.[53] This "crisis of witnessing" was exacerbated by the public's incapacity to absorb and accept the grotesque facticity of the mass murders while they were taking place and even after the liberation of the camps.

---

51. Lyotard 1988, p. 13.
52. Ibid., p. 10.
53. Felman and Laub 1992.

Felman notes that testimony only becomes possible through a crisis that transforms the onlooker. "And," as Felman suggests, "it is only through the medium of that crisis that the event can speak, and the narrative can lend its voice to history."[54]

Lyotard argues that "What is at stake in a literature, in a philosophy, in a politics perhaps, is to bear witness to differends by finding idioms for them."[55] Deleuze seemingly responds to Lyotard by depicting cinematic thought as an idiom that assumes the task of bearing witness to the differends affected by the traumas of World War II. His historical emplotment of cinema's development also resonates with Felman's analysis of this "crisis of witnessing." In effect, Deleuze converts cinema into a medium "through which the event can speak" and "give its voice to history." His figuration of the crisis of the movement-image that produces an "unbearable" experience of duration in postwar films will also transform the spectator from passive onlooker into a witness in the context of Hitchcock's films that implicate him or her in the process of judgment. The cinematic configuration of the experience of duration opens a tension-filled space that evokes the painful silences that surround the specter of justice left in abeyance: the silences of murdered and surviving witnesses; a widespread public failure to hear, to believe, and to act upon their testimonies; and the collective horror and shock in the aftermath of the crimes. This horror takes the form of an unthought that short-circuited an effective and sympathetic recognition of the victims and of the atrocities they suffered. For Deleuze, the shock that is triggered by a resurgence of this unthought is convened in the proliferation of figures of incommensurability, undecidability, and irrationality following postwar cinema's "turn" toward the problem of time. In this respect, Deleuze's explicit attention to the cinematic conceptualization of time, memory, and judgment attests to his critical recognition of the cultural and epistemological aftereffects of historical trauma.

---

54. Felman and Laub 1992, p. 110.
55. Lyotard 1988, p. 13.

As I have mentioned, Deleuze's characterization of the unthought recapitulates Blanchot's reflections on "the disaster" that traumatically wounds, surpasses, and negates the prospect of its writing or representation. The disaster is "an experience that none can undergo" because it "obliterates (while leaving perfectly intact) our relation to the world as presence or as absence." The impossibility of adequately representing the real of death compels us to live under the shadow of "the obsession with which it burdens us: others."[56] Deleuze reinscribes the deferral of this impossible obsession with the vulnerability of others in his figuration of the unthought, as a traumatic residue of the failure to take responsibility for the disaster as it transpired. In recognizing the formal status of this failure as an unrealized moral and political potential, Deleuze's invocation of the unthought also seems to attest to the influence of Walter Benjamin's critique and materialist displacement of dialectical historicism in "Theses on the Philosophy of History."[57]

In the "Theses," Benjamin identifies a consonance between bourgeois historiography, which abolishes the past without a backward glance, and dialectical historicism, which narrates the progression of consciousness toward a revolutionary aim. Against historicism, which "eternalizes" the past and "culminates in universal history" according to Theses XVI and XVII,[58] Benjamin advocates a revised notion of historical materialism that "supplies a unique experience with the past" in respecting the contingent parameters of transpired events in relation to the present and future. For Benjamin, the wreckage of past struggles contains unsettled moments whence traces of residual hope can be redeemed as a potential for new vision and action in the present.

In "The Work of Art in the Age of Mechanical Reproduction," Benjamin locates film's revolutionary function in its ability to "demonstrate the identity of the artistic and scientific uses of

---

56. Blanchot 1995, p. 120.
57. Benjamin 1969b.
58. Ibid., pp. 262–263.

photography which heretofore usually were separated."[59] In a subsequent subsection, he invokes the example of architecture to reconsider the assumption that distraction derails contemplation and with it the prospect of a politicized collective consciousness. He notes that the sudden change of film images interrupts the "spectator's process of association." This shock effect should be cushioned by "heightened presence of mind"; however, in its absence, the mass subject might still assume the role of a critic, but one who is too passive and absentminded to achieve a historically and politically determinate collective consciousness.[60]

Yet Benjamin reminds us that the "tasks which face the human apparatus of perception at this turning point of history cannot be solved by optical means, that is, by contemplation, alone. They are mastered gradually by habit, under the guidance of tactile appropriation."[61] Because the "distracted person, too, can form habits," "[d]istraction as provided by art presents a covert control of the extent to which new tasks have become soluble by apperception."[62] The issue for Benjamin who was influenced by Bertolt Brecht is whether this control sponsors habits of apperception that foment or neutralize the basis for revolutionary agency. Benjamin's consideration of the distracted subject thus challenges the assumption that contemplation is a prerequisite for collective consciousness and sociopolitical transformation while calling on us to keep in mind the dangers of manipulated distraction through films and other cultural forms that introduce "aesthetics into political life": the *Führer* cult that forces the masses to their knees and the futurist glorification of war that fetishizes the "dreamt-of metallization of the human body."[63]

---

59. Benjamin 1969a, p. 236.
60. Ibid., p. 240.
61. Ibid.
62. Ibid.
63. Ibid., p. 241. Though Deleuze seemingly alludes here to Sigfried Kracauer's (1947) *From Caligari to Hitler: A Psychological History of the German Film*, Benjamin's warnings about the introduction of aesthetics into politics in

What is striking about Benjamin's observations here is that they suggest a political motive for Deleuze's almost exclusive focus on auteur cinema. Directors such as Sergei Eisenstein, Carl Dreyer, Robert Bresson, Josef von Sternberg, John Cassavetes, Akira Kirosawa, Michelangelo Antonioni, Rainer Werner Fassbinder, Jean-Luc Goddard, François Truffaut, Orson Welles, Alfred Hitchcock, and Chantal Akerman exert the kind of "covert control" that might guide spectator apperception toward the solution of new tasks. Deleuze apparently celebrates their respective modes of subtle "guidance" because they presumably nurture task-solving habits

---

the "Work of Art" essay also appear to inform Deleuze's considerations of mediocrity in postwar cinema:

> What becomes of Hitchcock's suspense, Eisenstein's shock and Gance's sublimity when they are taken up by mediocre authors? When the violence is no longer that of the image and its vibrations but that of the represented, we move into a blood-red arbitrariness. When the grandeur is no longer that of the composition, but a pure and simple inflation of the represented, there is no cerebral stimulation or birth of thought. It is rather a generalized shortcoming in author and viewers. Nevertheless a current mediocrity has never prevented great painting; but it is not the same in the conditions of an industrial art, where the proportion of disgraceful works calls the most basic goals and capacities directly into question. Cinema is dying, then, from its quantitative mediocrity. But there is a still more important reason: the mass-art, the treatment of masses, which should not have been separable from an accession of the masses to the status of true subject, has degenerated into state propaganda and manipulation, into a kind of fascism which brought together Hitler and Hollywood, Hollywood and Hitler. The spiritual automaton became fascist man. As Serge Daney says, what has brought the whole cinema of the movement-image into question are 'the great political *mises-en-scène*, state propaganda turned tableaux vivants, the first handlings of masses of humans,' and their backdrop, the camps. This was the death-knell for the ambitions of 'the old cinema': not, or not only, the mediocrity and vulgarity of current production but rather Leni Riefenstahl, who was not mediocre. And the situation is still worse if we accept Virilio's thesis: there has been no diversion or alienation in an art of the masses initially founded by the movement-image; on the contrary the movement-image was from the beginning linked to the organization of war, state propaganda, ordinary fascism, historically and essentially. [Deleuze 1989b, pp. 164–165]

among distracted spectators and therefore establish the conditions for the growth of revolutionary agency. Of course, by largely ignoring the Hollywood entertainment industry and bypassing the sociology of its reception, Deleuze "covertly" directs his own readers to consider evidence that will always confirm and never contradict his line of argument. In light of the several decades of film production since the "Work of Art" essay first appeared in 1936, Deleuze's readers might be prone to be more jaded about cinema's revolutionary potential than Benjamin (who had only just witnessed the birth of the "talkie"). While not dialectical themselves,[64] Deleuze's *Cinema* books nevertheless seem geared to challenge clichéd dismissals of film by paying homage to Benjamin's dialectical approach in the "Work of Art" essay, where he recognizes both the limits and the value of a mass cultural medium with the power to reorganize experience by changing habits of perception.

Deleuze's debt to Benjamin is also evinced in his definition of a "modern political cinema" to come:

> In [classical] American and in Soviet cinema, the people are already there, real before being actual, ideal without being abstract. Hence the idea that the cinema, as art of the masses, could be the supreme revolutionary or democratic art, which makes the masses a true subject. But a great many factors were to compromise this belief: the rise of Hitler, which gave cinema as its object not the masses become subject but the masses subjected; Stalinism, which replaced the unanimism of peoples with tyrannical unity of a party; the break-up of the American people, who could no longer believe themselves to be either the melting-pot peoples past or the seed of a people to come [. . .] In short, if there were a modern political cinema, it would be on

---

64. In "Nietzsche's Dice Throw: Tragedy, Nihilism, and the Body without Organs," Dorothea Olkowski (1994) explains how Deleuze's Nietzschean commitment to recognizing difference and becoming counteracts the logic of the Hegelian dialectic: "For although active and reactive forces are difference at the origin, their association with the quality of will to power, that is with affirmation and negation, ultimately prevents their synthesis" (p. 132).

this basis: the people no longer exist, or not yet . . . *the people are missing.*[65]

Deleuze's reference to a missing people, who are, at once, no longer and not yet, resonates with Benjamin's Jewish-Messianic revision of the historical materialist dialectic. The passivity and failed action of the masses that permitted Hitler's and Stalin's tyrannies and the systemic disenfranchisements that divide contemporary multicultural democracies remain imbedded in the past as a missed potential. Deleuze's articulation of this potentiality adds a political dimension to the motif of latency that structures his Bergsonian construction of cinematic evolution.

Once again, Deleuze situates the movement-image that dominates the prewar period in an evolutionary process that ultimately produces the modern conception of movement in relation to an independent time. The conditions for this later development must therefore already be present in its prior incarnation in the mode of an unthought.[66] In *Cinema 2*, this unthought takes on the *topos* of an excess, previously excluded by perception, that might nevertheless "come back" (as a post-psychoanalytic version of the return of the repressed).[67] Not surprisingly, it is World War II that

---

65. Deleuze 1989b, p. 216. Deleuze adds:

The death-knell for becoming conscious was precisely the consciousness that there were no people, but always several peoples, an infinity of peoples, who remained to be united, or should not be united, in order for the problem to change. It is in this way that third world cinema is a cinema of minorities, because the people exist only in the condition of minority, which is why they are missing. [Ibid., p. 220]

66. This notion of latency also carries over into Deleuze's consideration of the talkie, which he claims, is "already implied" in and "called for" by the silent film (1989b, p. 225).

67. I already alluded above to Deleuze's remarks on the out-of-field as an absent-presence that pressures the contents of the frame. Relevant also in this connection is a passage in Freud's *Beyond the Pleasure Principle*, where he describes the unconscious in opposition to the Kantian theorem that "time and space are 'necessary forms of thought.'"

We have learnt that unconscious mental processes are in themselves "timeless." This means in the first place that they are not ordered

affects the return of this repressed, which exerts an intolerable pressure on the centrality of the movement-image. The reign of the movement-image consequently gives way to a proliferation of images that enunciate time, memory, and duration at the expense of the perception-action circuit.

This is to suggest that the prospect of viewing time as an independent variable is latent in classical cinema, but comes to the fore in the heightened employment of time-images after World War II. The postwar rise of the time-image is Deleuze's evidence for an evolved, which is to say, increasingly modern understanding of movement in relation to time. Time will be henceforth figured as the "unbearable immanence" of mechanical succession. On a corporeal level, the time-image arouses an experience of inexorable duration and with it an "immobile element": the pains and exhaustions of an aging body increasingly weighed down by the torpid eventuality of its death.

The transition from an ancient to a modern understanding of movement and time only becomes possible by virtue of the voiding of action in postwar film. On a historical level, this annulment

---

> temporally, that time does not change them in any way and that the idea of time cannot be applied to them. These are negative characteristics which can only be clearly understood if a comparison is made with the *conscious* mental processes. On the other hand, our abstract idea of time seems to be wholly derived from the method of working of the system *Pcpt.-Cs.* and to correspond to a perception on its own part of that method of working. This mode of functioning may perhaps constitute another way of providing a shield against stimuli. [Freud 1955, p. 28]

This passage is germane to the current discussion in the following respects. First, the *topos* of an "atemporal" unconscious is consonant with the timelessness and spacelessness of the elsewhere proper to the out-of-field that haunts the movement-image from the margins of the frame. In the second place, this passage self-reflexively highlights Freud's reflections on the unconscious as a perception itself subject to a selective process that negates the prospect of a transcendent, nonempirical understanding of time. Third, the acknowledgment that a conceptualization of time might serve as a defense mechanism in its own right is the theoretical condition for the historical disavowal and latent potential of the unthought that Deleuze foregrounds throughout the *Cinema* books.

and the time-images that enunciate it belatedly attest to a moral paralysis or inability to act among witnesses that permitted the Nazi mass murders (and Stalin's purges). Cinematic evolution is thus spurred by climactic historical events and is itself a symptomatic precipitate of trauma.

Significantly, the irruption of time as a traumatic aftereffect awakens another dormant Messianic–materialist element: a revolutionary promise that abides in the unsettled past. In Deleuze's characterization of it, the time-image provokes an experience of duration that stops and thereby shocks thought. This shock awakens the unthought that conjoins a traumatic disavowal of historical injustice with an opening to the future of a hope it blocked, but that remains buried within it. The rise of the time-image in postwar film thus inscribes the historical materialist method as Benjamin defines it:

> Thinking involves not only the flow of thoughts, but their arrest as well. Where thinking suddenly stops in a configuration pregnant with tensions, it gives that configuration a shock, by which it crystallizes into a monad. A historical materialist recognizes a sign of a Messianic cessation of happening, or, put differently, a revolutionary chance in the fight for the oppressed past. He takes cognizance of it in order to blast a specific era out of the homogeneous course of history—blasting a specific life out of the era or a specific work out of the life work. As a result of this method the lifework is preserved in this work and at the same time cancelled [*aufgehoben*]; in the lifework, the era; and in the era, the entire course of history. The nourishing fruit of the historically understood contains time as a precious but tasteless seed.[68]

To translate Deleuze into Benjamin, the time-image that emerges in the postwar cinematic void of action halts thought in a configuration "pregnant with tensions." The cessation of thought shocks the spectator into an immanent view of history: a Messianic–

---

68. Benjamin 1969b, pp. 262–263.

materialist standpoint that redeems impeded action as a "precious but tasteless seed" of lost possibility. Hence the latent revolutionary power of cinema is situated, not in its ability to consolidate class consciousness among distracted spectators, but rather in the capacity of its modern form to bear witness to an era whose possibilities are preserved and cancelled at once. They are "preserved" in a Messianic memory that makes them available again as an incipient hope for transforming the present. They are "cancelled" in the failure of a people to witness and act against the disappearance and genocide of another.

Cinematic thought as realized by the auteurs after World War II mirrors the belated effects of this historical wound to the agency of judgment. This wounding paralysis of judgment, which is expressed in the decentering of the perception-intention-action circuit, thus constitutes the principal trauma "worked through" in a postwar cinema. Working-through enjoins, as Benjamin suggests, that a particular lifework be preserved in its immanence, in its undoctored materiality, as an unsettled past whose possibilities might still unfold into the present and future. Deleuze narrates the crisis of the movement-image as that which gives rise to the time-image—an unbearable experience of duration that opens a window for Benjamin's preserving recognition. This is the experience of an action-emptied present as "'the time of the now' which is shot through with chips of Messianic time" in Benjamin's words.[69] While it remains submerged or latent in classical cinema, after World War II the emergence of time as an independent variable cracks the space of action and indicates by negation the promise of a people still to come. The "Now" time of the time-image thereby mobilizes a "unique experience with the past" that crystallizes an impeded possibility as "a revolutionary chance in the fight for an oppressed past." In this respect, Deleuze's Bergsonian emplotment of cinematic evolution and crisis might be read as an historical materialist attempt to restore immanence to the thinking of events, while

---

69. Ibid., p. 263.

allowing the Leibnizian monad to echo off-screen through Benjamin's felicitous politicization of it.[70]

It is worth remarking the way in which Benjamin's Messianic–materialist dialectic solves a problem for Deleuze that is created by his turn toward Leibniz's monad in order to think the form of time as becoming. Gregg Lambert observes that, for Deleuze, the core problematic in philosophy is its confrontation with the collapse of every model of truth in the face of temporal differentiation. The Leibnizian concept of the monad initially seems to offer a resolution to the problem of time for philosophy in proposing "an absolute difference (or exteriority) between the luminosity of soul and the visibility of matter, or between thought and perception."[71] As Lambert notes, this resolution is ultimately unsatisfying for Deleuze because

> the Leibnizian construction first posits an irresolvable difference or confrontation between two forms of difference, and then, as Deleuze shows, resolves this confrontation in the most bizarre manners: the creation of God, who occupies the position of the

---

70. What I am referring to as the Messianic standpoint is, perhaps, another way of understanding Giorgio Agamben's formulation of a beatific pure potentiality, or "bare life," which informs Deleuze's (1995) "Immanence: une vie. . . ." In Agamben's (1999) words, "One could say that the difficult attempt to clarify the vertigo of immanence by means of 'a life' leads us instead into an area that is even more uncertain, in which the child and the dying man present us with the enigmatic cipher of bare biological life as such" (p. 230). The Messianic valence of "absolute immanence" becomes evident in his citation of Deleuze:

> A life is everywhere, in all moments that traverse this or that living subject and that measure lived objects—immanent life carrying events or singularities that effect nothing but their own actualization in subjects and objects. This undefined life does not itself have moments, however close to one another they might be; it has only inter-times [entre-temps], inter-moments [entre-moments]. It neither follows nor succeeds, but rather presents the immensity of empty time, where one sees the event that is to come and that has already happened in the absolute of an immediate consciousness." [Deleuze 1995, p. 5; cited by Agamben 1999, p. 233]

71. Lambert 2002, pp. 12–13.

central monad, and of the *a priori* expression of a "pre-established harmony" (*harmonia praestabilita*) which Deleuze likens to an automaton. In other words, Leibniz solved the problem of time by constructing the series of incompossible worlds where divergent series could be developed without suffering contradiction; he saved truth "but at the price of damnation" (that is, by creating aborted becomings and cast-away worlds where certain singularities were assigned to spend eternity).[72]

Lambert adds that "the Leibnizian solution could only have been temporary and 'the crisis of truth thus enjoys a pause rather than a solution.'"[73] This is the case insofar as Leibniz's solution spatializes time; it also assumes an innately ethical God who sees "the whole of time stretched out across incompossible universes" and who is ideally equipped to choose the best of all possible worlds.

Yet to the extent that Deleuze is committed to an immanent standpoint, the question, as Lambert phrases it, remains as to "What happened? What could have happened to place truth, again, in crisis?" In other words, why does Deleuze feel compelled to find a solution to the problem of time for philosophy? Lambert writes:

> Taking our cue from the preface of the second cinema study, *The Time-Image*, we might reply: "The War!" In its wake, we are all survivors; our memories are stricken by an irretrievable trauma. The earth is laid waste by a paralysis of memory and zones of impossibility: death camps, burned-out cities, atomic sink-holes, summer fields yielding each year a new harvest of corpses. Today, we find ourselves in the age of Auschwitz, on which is superimposed the age of Hiroshima, under the shadow of a horrible decision, a botched and burned-out world. Although I am employing these names in a drastically abbreviated manner—that is, as signs of a kind of universal or world memory—the events they designate remain somber and cast their shadow over the idea of reason that existed prior (or a priori). In fact, they mark a *caesura* or eclipse of reason itself,

---

72. Ibid., p. 13.
73. Ibid., p. 13 (citing Deleuze 1989b, p. 131).

as a result of which "before" and "after" are no longer equal and time undergoes a profound declension and suspense.[74]

Lambert adds that if "the Leibnizian solution were adequate to determine the best of all possible worlds, then Auschwitz and Hiroshima would have been banished to incompossible worlds, instead of death zones that have emerged within our own."[75] Because "Auschwitz" and "Hiroshima" irrevocably wound reason, contemporary philosophy becomes a philosophy of the event and, more specifically, a "writing of the disaster." It is in this form that philosophy comes to represent "the default of the concept of the possible (with which it can no longer represent time, and therefore itself, since the possible has become impossible *a priori*."[76]

What is compelling about Lambert's argument in light of the foregoing discussion is that it highlights Benjamin's Messianic–materialist dialectic as an alternative solution to the "crisis of truth" precipitated by temporal differentiation and historical traumas and as a means of recovering from the "default of the concept of the possible." This dialectic permits a view of the event in relation to its era, and of the era in relation to the whole of history without reconvening a transcendental consciousness or ground and without assuming a transcendent deity bestowed with perfect hindsight in advance. A Messianic historiography refigures time through a future-oriented mode of seeing/reading that allows incompossible worlds to exist immanently, without contradiction; Benjamin's materialist dialectic consequently enables a historical rethinking of the ambivalence of the contextually bound contingencies that brought one or another of these worlds into fruition. The possibilities that lived in "aborted becomings and cast-away worlds" are cancelled yet also preserved through Benjamin's Messianic standpoint; it blasts the past out of "the homogeneous course of history" by compelling interpretation to affirm the materiality of preempted

---

74. Ibid., pp. 13–14.
75. Ibid., p. 14.
76. Ibid., p. 16.

actions and of the promise they might have yielded and still might fulfill.

Finally, a restitution of immanence to the thinking of the event is crucial in Deleuze's view if the singularity of a crisis is to be re-imagined beyond the standpoint of historical progress that reduces it to an instance of moral or political breakdown. From an imma-nent perspective, historical trauma appears as a monadic distilla-tion of the whole of time. The "precious" prospect of transformation lying nestled in the folds of an event might then be harvested for the future. It is in this sense that Deleuze's *Cinema* books illuminate Benjamin's paradoxical assertion quoted above that "The nourish-ing fruit of the historically understood contains time as a precious but tasteless seed." Deleuze's evolutionary narrative serves to restore the "tasteless" or neutral immanence of time to the cinematic think-ing of history in order to cultivate its Messianic hope. This culti-vation is the impetus and aim of a cinematic thought that ripens at a traumatic historical juncture when the passivity of spectators must be called into question.

## ACKNOWLEDGMENTS

I would like to thank Peter Canning, Tom Conley, Gregg Lambert, and Dorothea Olkowski for their comments on prior drafts of this essay.

## REFERENCES

Agamben, G. (1999). Absolute immanence. In *Potentialities: Collected Essays in Philosophy*, ed. and trans. D. Heller-Roazen, pp. 220–239. Stanford, CA: Stanford University Press.

Benjamin, W. (1969a). The work of art in the age of mechanical repro-duction. In *Illuminations: Essays and Reflections*, ed. H. Arendt, trans. H. Zohn, pp. 217–252. New York: Schocken.

——— (1969b). Theses on the philosophy of history. In *Illuminations:*

*Essays and Reflections*, ed. H. Arendt, trans. H. Zohn, pp. 253–264. New York: Schocken.

Bergson, H. (1896). *Matter and Memory*, trans. N. M. Paul and W. S. Palmer. New York: Zone Books, 1991.

———— (1907). *Creative Evolution*, trans. A. Mitchell. Boston: University Press of America, 1954.

Blanchot, M. (1995). *Writing the Disaster*, trans. A. Smock. Lincoln, NE: New Bison Book Edition.

Boundas, C. V., and Olkowski, D., eds. (1994). *Gilles Deleuze and the Theater of Philosophy*. New York: Routledge.

Canning, P. (1994). The crack of time and the ideal game. In *Gilles Deleuze and the Theater of Philosophy*, ed. C. V. Boundas and D. Olkowski, pp. 73–93. New York: Routledge.

Cohen, T. (2005). *Hitchcock's Cryptonomies, Vol. I: Secret Agents* and *Vol. II: War Machines*. Minneapolis: University of Minnesota Press.

Deleuze, G. (1989a). *Cinema 1: The Movement-Image*, trans. H. Tomlinson and B. Habberjam. Minneapolis: University of Minnesota Press.

———— (1989b). *Cinema 2: The Time-Image*, trans. H. Tomlinson and R. Galeta. Minneapolis: University of Minnesota Press.

———— (1991). *Bergsonism*, trans. H. Tomlinson and B. Haberjam. New York: Zone Books.

———— (1995). Immanence: une vie . . . *Philosophie 47.*

Deleuze, G., and Guattari, F. (1987). *A Thousand Plateaus: Capitalism and Schizophrenia*, trans. B. Massumi. Minneapolis: University of Minnesota Press.

Felman, S., and Laub, D., M.D. (1992). *Testimony: Crises of Witnessing in Literature, Psychoanalysis, and History*. New York: Routledge.

Freud, S. (1955). *Beyond the Pleasure Principle, The Standard Edition of the Complete Psychological Works of Sigmund Freud, Vol. XVIII*, trans. and ed. J. Strachey in collaboration with A. Freud, pp. 1–64. London: Hogarth.

Kracauer, S. (1947). *From Caligari to Hitler: A Psychological History of the German Film*. Princeton, NJ: Princeton University Press.

Lambert, G. (2002). *The Non-Philosophy of Gilles Deleuze*. New York: Continuum.

Lyotard, J.-F. (1988). *The Differend: Phrases in Dispute*, trans. G. Van Den Abbeele. Minneapolis: University of Minnesota Press.

Olkowski, D. (1994). Nietzsche's dice throw: tragedy, nihilism, and the body without organs. In *Gilles Deleuze and the Theater of Philosophy*, ed. C. V. Boundas and D. Olkowski, pp. 119–140. New York: Routledge.

Rosenfield, I. (1988). *The Invention of Memory: A New View of the Brain.* New York: Basic Books.

# 6

# The Phantom Effect: The Return of the Dead in Gerhard Richter's *October 18, 1977 Cycle*

Eric Kligerman

In the summer of 2004, one of the top media events in Berlin was the American blockbuster Museum of Modern Art (MOMA) exhibition that was on display at the *Neuen Nationalgalerie*. The MOMA show, with its "feel good" exhibition, emphasized the transformation of aesthetic form over the last 150 years and included the works of Cezanne, Matisse, Van Gogh, Duchamp, Picasso, and Pollock. In an interview with the *Berliner Zeitung*, the German curator of the exhibition, Angela Schneider, was asked why she began the section of the twentieth-century artworks with Rousseau's *The Dream*. She remarked that Rousseau's painting was emblematic of the twentieth century, which was defined by: "The searching for other worlds, the exotic, the search for the imagination, the simplification of form."[1] Her response suggests a particular narrative thread behind the ordering of the paintings in the exhibition.

Moving through four rooms containing such paintings as *Starry Night*, *Water Lilies*, *The Dream*, and *The Bathers*, the museum visit

1. Schneider 2004.

ended in a room culminating with the works of one of the most celebrated contemporary German artists, the painter Gerhard Richter. The spectator's untroubled and non-confrontational movement through these rooms is brought to a halt as he/she enters the last section of the exhibition: a separated cryptlike space set aside for the fifteen paintings in Richter's *October 18, 1977* series. The spectator is assaulted with the colorless images of violence and death that commemorate German terrorism of the 1970s, embodied in the figure of the Baader-Meinhof Gang.

Although Schneider admitted that "ruptures and monstrosities" were indeed part of the show, as seen in Richter's *October*, these works become emblematic of the turn in twentieth-century art's preoccupation with what she calls the "deconstruction of the body." Bypassing any influence that historical events might have had on the shaping of Richter's series, Schneider discusses *October* in relation to its aesthetic development within the traditions of western art. The show's objective, which avoided a "violent confrontation" with the spectator, was to provide the visitor with a "high aesthetic level of enjoyment."[2] According to the curator, Richter attempts to deliver back to the realm of painting the task of representing experience and history from the shadow of mass media such as film and photography. But in her various interviews, Schneider herself avoided any discussion of the impact contemporary German history might have had on Richter's artworks. Unable to get beyond the aesthetic categories of his works, Schneider interprets the *October* series as a struggle with the "most important themes of western art." Excluding from her remarks any discussion of the connection between historical catastrophe and Richter's paintings, Schneider sidesteps the import of closing the twentieth-century exhibition space with a series that had always been, according to Richter himself, a "theme of provocation" (*Reizthema*) in Germany.[3]

Despite being described by the *Frankfurter Allgemeine Zeitung* as the "central works of political art," *October*'s return to Berlin

---

2. Ibid.
3. Dettweiler 2004.

failed to elicit a political discussion, either among the curators of the exhibition or critics of the MOMA show.[4] While Richter's engagement with the RAF in 1988 visualized the symptoms of the previous generation's unassimilated trauma, such a discussion was not provoked by the paintings' homecoming in February 2004. By placing the paintings in a separate room, the curator hoped to draw attention to the uniqueness of the artworks' aesthetics, the form of photo-painting, rather than the content of the works themselves. Quite explicitly, she contends that although spectators might wish to see *October* in the frame of contemporary history (*Zeitgeschichte*), "they are absolutely not about that." Rejecting the term history paintings (*Historienbilder*) to describe Richter's works, Schneider replaces this depiction with humanity paintings (*Menschheitsbilder*).

Although in the past the paintings had been a source of provocation in Germany, the political implications of their return to Berlin in the setting of the MOMA show failed to register in its reception. *October* and its reflections on the Red Army Faction were neither used to probe nor shed light on contemporary questions regarding the politics of memory in the summer of 2004 in Germany. Rejecting the position that *October* is about contemporary history, Schneider contends that Richter is exclusively focused on questions concerning the "perception of our reality . . . the truth of our experience." She adds: "Our view of things is subject to the blurring (*Verwischung*) of our perceptual possibilities." But Richter, aware of this haunting configuration of history, blurs his *Octo-*

---

4. In the same period in Berlin, the Kunst-Werke Museum tried to put on an exhibition titled "Mythos RAF," a show that wished to explore the history of the RAF through its artistic reception in film, photography, fashion, and literature. While the city had agreed to donate 100,000 Euros for the exhibition, the funding was withdrawn as relatives of the victims of the RAF and members of the government complained that the show was glorifying the terrorists and playing down their crimes. Although Richter's paintings were not included in the show, these were the central complaints directed against his *October* series when they were first exhibited in 1989 in Krefeld. Within the context of the MOMA show, Richter's paintings failed to provoke a similar response. Their reception was viewed solely in terms of the aesthetic. One could speculate about a shift in this response if *October* was included in the proposed show at the Kunst-Werke.

*ber* paintings in order to accentuate the ghostlike status of the very history behind their images.

In the following analysis, I will move away from the aestheticization of Richter's *October* series in the context of its return to Germany in the 2004 MOMA exhibition; instead, I will draw on Abraham and Torok's concept of transgenerational haunting in order to explore the historical implications of Richter's engagement with German terrorism in 1988. My focus is on how Richter's aesthetic techniques of photo-painting and blurring encrypt the Holocaust as an afterimage upon the canvases of his RAF paintings. *October* behaves as a screen both to the traditions of western art and to the traumata of twentieth-century German history. The paintings from 1988 point back to Richter's blurred photographs and paintings from 1964–1965 that tried to represent the traumatic images of the Holocaust. While Schneider may see images of the "dead Christ" buried in the figure of the strangled Meinhof, the spectator need not go back to Holbein to grasp the import behind the three images of her corpse. In his *October* series, Richter confronts the spectator with a palimpsest of two moments of censored memory: the memory of the Holocaust that Richter tried but failed to paint in 1964 and its screen memory via the *October* paintings in 1988.

The date *October 18, 1977* is the culmination of what is referred to as the "German Autumn." On this day, the bodies of Andreas Baader, Gudrun Ensellin, and Jan-Carl Raspe were found dead in their cells in the maximum-security prison Stammheim in Stuttgart. The previous year, one of the other original members of what was called the Baader-Meinhof Gang, Ulrike Meinhof, was found dead in her cell. These four were the core members of the "first generation" of German terrorism. Their deaths were followed by the murder of the head of the West German Federation of Industries and the chairman of Daimler-Benz, Hans-Martin Schleyer, who had also been a former member of the SS during the Second World War. He was kidnapped by the second generation of the RAF on September 5, 1977, in order to obtain the release of the imprisoned RAF members. On October 13, a Lufthansa flight was hijacked to

Mogadishu and, in addition to money, the hijackers also demanded the release of the RAF members in prison. German Special Forces ultimately stormed the plane on October 18, killing the hijackers and freeing all of the prisoners. Some time shortly afterward on that same night, Baader, Ensellin, and Raspe were discovered dead in their cells. A fourth member, Irmgard Möller, was found wounded in her cell with a knife. The next day, Schleyer's kidnappers reported that he had been executed and indicated where his body could be found. The official state investigation of the deaths in Stammheim declared them suicides, but many people, particularly on the Left, believed they had been murdered by the state.[5]

Richter's paintings are based on the RAF photographs taken by the police and exhibited in the *Stern* magazine. His distortion of these photographs becomes a metaphor signifying two historical spaces. I will argue that in Richter's *October* series, we uncover the phantom of the Holocaust lurking in the paintings' background as an afterimage. The theoretical apparatus to my argument is comprised of two parts: I will employ Marianne Hirsch's concept of "postmemory" and Abraham and Torok's notion of "transgenerational haunting." Hirsch uses the term *postmemory* to describe the second generation's memory of their parents' collective trauma. For Hirsch, the Holocaust becomes the exemplary site of postmemory that is constituted by the emblematic images of the Final Solution. Auschwitz's gate, train tracks, the skeletal forms of the living dead, and the mound of corpses have become imprinted in our mnemic reservoir over the last six decades; they help form our postmemory narratives of the Holocaust.

Abraham and Torok's concept of transgenerational haunting from *The Shell and the Kernel* refers to the effect that the parents' unsuccessful mourning has on the child: the phantom passes from the parents' unconscious into the child. Abraham states: "What haunts are not the dead but the gaps left within us by the secrets of others . . . what comes back to haunt are the tombs of others . . . the phantom which returns to haunt bears witness to the existence

---

5. For a history of the Baader-Meinhof Gang, see Aust 1989.

of the dead buried within the other."[6] The phantom carries out its return through words that point to a gap or secret from within the unconscious. While Abraham and Torok describe how phantom words can rule an entire family's history, Richter's revenants are comprised of visual images.

Because of the visual component to Richter's phantom, I will use Freud's term *Deckerinnerung* (*screen memory*) to help me move away from lexical connections that invoke the phantom effect and toward the visual impressions of a screen memory that are constitutive of "an act of memory that strikes us as strange."[7] While both types of haunting involve forms of mnemic reproduction, by moving to screen memories I shift from the import behind verbal traces to visual imprints. Richter's turn to the RAF serves as a screen memory that filters the trauma of the Shoah, which he tried to on several occasions but could not paint directly. By blurring the two media and the works themselves, Richter will use his paintings of the RAF to represent the bodies of the Shoah: what he said in his journals was "unpaintable." Although Richter calls himself a "grave-digger," he is not burying the past, but digging it up.[8]

Screen memories are constructed from two distinct memories. Freud describes one memory as being indifferent and unimportant. These "indifferent" memories, from either the past or present, form out of a process of displacement and condensation, and behave as substitutes for significant childhood impressions that are repressed. Similar to the overlay structure of a screen memory that foregrounds the material traces of a latent content, transgenerational haunting relates one moment of time to another. But instead of pointing to

---

6. Abraham and Torok 1994, p. 171. Abraham's example of transgenerational haunting is quite revealing: a child acts out the fate of his mother's beloved who was sent to a labor camp and later died in the gas chamber. The mother's melancholia over the loss of her lover manifests itself in her son's actions. Abraham writes of the child, "What does our man do on weekends? A lover of geology, he 'breaks rocks,' catches butterflies, and proceeds to kill them in a can of cyanide" (Ibid., p. 175).

7. Freud 1965, p. 44.

8. Richter 1995, p. 185.

a forgotten event from one's own childhood, transgenerational haunting points to a repressed event from a preceding generation that is passed on as a secret to the child: it is the child's inherited trace of a parent's trauma. In screen memories and transgenerational haunting, something stands in place of a content that is cut off from the subject's memory.

Richter's *October* functions as a screen memory in regard to two key components. First, the screen is comprised of visual imprints that gesture toward an earlier experience. Furthermore, a resistance from this experience prevents it from being accessed directly. Yet there is nothing "unimportant" nor "indifferent" about the event operating as a screen upon the surface of *October*. Both experiences carry historical significance. Second, the affect of surprise is an essential component of a screen memory. Although Freud claims that affect is displaced in screen memories, in Richter's screening of memory there is no "wrong place" of affect. The intended affect or shock produced in the *October* series forms a bridge between two moments of historical trauma. This surprise, analogous to Abraham and Torok's phantom effect produced through haunting words, is engendered by means of visual traces that the spectator recognizes upon the canvas of the artworks. *October* becomes a screen memory in connection with the images of the camps that he re-photographed as blurs but could never paint in the early 1960s. What transpires during a screen memory is that an "intellectual feeling gives us information of interference by some disturbing factor . . . with screen memories we are *surprised* that we possess them at all."[9] Richter's goal is to provoke this surprise or disturbance in the spectator who stands before his *October* paintings.[10]

---

9. Freud 1965, p. 45.

10. In a 1988 interview, Richter was asked, "Do you see this series (*October*) as isolated, a unique parenthesis, or are you actually revising your relation to content?" He responded, "Yes, this does seem a bit outside of my work. But now when I see the gray monochrome paintings I realize that, perhaps, and surely not entirely consciously, that was the only way for me to paint concentration camps" (Interview with Gregorio Magnani in *Art Flash* 142 [October]: 97).

But while there are structural similarities between transgenerational haunting and screen memories, there is also a fundamental difference between these terms. In screen memories, an individual's experience undergoes repression; however, in transgenerational haunting the subject is haunted by *someone else's* repressed past. The phantom passes between generations, from parent to child, and Abraham and Torok affirm: "Should a child have parents 'with secrets,' parents whose speech is not exactly complementary to their unstated repressions, the child will receive from them a gap in the unconscious, an unknown, unrecognized knowledge . . . subjected to a form of 'repression' before the fact."[11] It is at this critical juncture that transgenerational haunting becomes more applicable in regard to Richter's history paintings. Richter turns the structure of screen memories into a technique to reverse and counteract the effects of an inherited repression transmitted to subsequent generations. His blurs are meant to provoke a shock effect that reanimates affectively diminished memory by requiring the spectator to connect the imprints concealed behind the blurring.

The concept of repression often arises in the discussion of Richter's works, in particular in his *Atlas* project. Such critics as Buchloh and Chevrier discuss the structures of traumatic repression that seem to be at the core of Richter's *Atlas*: an ever-expanding lexicon of images starting from the early 1960s comprised of photographs found in family albums, newspapers, magazines, and books that the artist had collected and re-photographed and, in some cases, used as material for his paintings. In his essay "Gerhard Richter's *Atlas*: The Anomic Archive," Buchloh contends that *Atlas*'s posttraumatic gaze looks back at the aftermath brought about by German fascism. He locates the original traumatic event that defines the *Atlas* project as the concentration camp photographs that have shaped postwar German memory. His central question examines how historical memory is constructed in the aftermath of trauma. Buchloh attributes *Atlas*'s absorption with banality, "the collective lack of affect," as symptomatic of a psychic armor that

---

11. Abraham and Torok 1994, p. 140.

Germany set up in the postwar period to shield itself against historical insight.[12] But moments in *Atlas* "dismantle the armor of psychic repression." Images of the concentration camps, Hitler, or the RAF are transmitted in *Atlas* in regulated doses of historical shock that bring the spectator's gaze into an historical space of traumatic events. These *Atlas* images try to provoke the spectator to see what is not visibly shown. In a similar manner, I contend that as the figures in *October* lose focus, the residue of the past increases in magnitude and depth. The psychic inscriptions of trauma in *Atlas* are strewn across the canvases of *October* as historical remnants that the spectator needs to find again.

Jean-Francois Chevrier also discusses the link between repression and *Atlas*, and remarks that the positioning of concentration camp images alongside those of pornography "were not enough to lift the repression . . . these photos could only confirm the impossibility of mourning the fascist disaster in a German culture aligned on amnesia-prone American capitalism."[13] Chevrier employs the term *screen memory* in relation to *repression* in *Atlas* and *October*. What is reproduced in the "play of a pictorial covering-over of the photographic image (in *Atlas*), is the structure of the screen, of the screen memory: painting as the screen of and against a repressed epoch of the past . . . *18. Oktober 1977* can be considered the first return to the figurative contents repressed by the institution of pictorial history."[14] Chevrier draws a parallel between *Atlas* and *October* and regards both works as depicting Richter's struggle with historical repression. Contrary to Chevrier, the screening of memory in *October* diverges from repression and lost memory, and approaches instead a transgenerational haunting. Although there seems to be a tendency to equate blurring with repression, what one might describe as repression in Germany in 1965 had significantly changed by 1988, the year Richter began his paintings.

---

12. Buchloh 2000, p. 28.
13. Chevrier 2000, p. 44.
14. Ibid.

Richter's *October* paintings operate like apparitions that elicit from the spectator a visual recognition of the grainy black and white camp photos burned inside him/her. In his essay "Photography," Siegfried Kracauer states, "The image wanders ghostlike through the present. Ghostly apparitions occur only in places where a terrible deed has been committed . . . a shudder goes through the viewer of old photographs for they do not illustrate the recognition of the original but rather the spatial configuration of the moment."[15] Richter's paintings behave like photographs developing backward, taking us from the death scenes of Stammheim into the space of the Holocaust. The abstracted bodies of the RAF function metonymically to trigger in the spectators' memories not only configurations of the other traumatized bodies he could not paint, but also the shudder of anxiety that had possibly been diminished through repeated exposure to these images. Richter brings these past images into a dynamic visual relation to those in the present, yet he maintains their historical uniqueness. Richter's artworks try to probe the ethico-historical relation between these two traumatic spaces. The spectator in turn is asked to complete the analysis. He suspends the spectator's gaze between hazy images that frustrate his/her act of looking and the very unambiguous photographs stored in the spectator's mnemic reserve that Richter tries to conjure up through his distorted paintings.

But how does *October* attempt to invoke the Holocaust? Richter is relying on a cultural archive of images stored within the spectator, black and white photos and films that documented the extermination, to stir up memory of the Holocaust. His grainy and diffuse paintings force the spectator to reconstruct the history of what occurred not only ten years after the ambiguity surrounding the deaths in Stammheim, but more than forty years after the disclosure of the camps. As Lawrence Douglas asserts in his article "Film as Witness," these films and photos have helped to shape "persistent cultural images of the Holocaust as an event that un-

---

15. Kracauer 1995, p. 56.

folded in black and white."[16] But as Marianne Hirsch argues, through the repetition of and overexposure to seeing these same images, the spectator is not becoming desensitized from their horror nor is she/he being shielded from shock; rather, "Compulsive and traumatic repetition connects the second generation to the first, producing rather than screening the effect of trauma that was lived so much more directly as compulsive repetition by survivors and contemporary witnesses."[17] The repetition of these images compels the viewer to reach a saturation point, and Hirsch questions if empathy has become exhausted at this moment.

As Hirsch tells us, one possible effect of an overexposure to these photographs is that they risk becoming clichés, divested of their symbolic power. Through their repetitive showing, they could lose their ability to induce affect (empathy). These images become re-invested with meaning and affect and become potential "vehicles of working through a traumatic past" only through their displacement and recontextualization in new media.[18] Postmemory is based not on the invisible but on the barely visible that provokes an uncanny shudder in response to what is vaguely familiar. Richter's *October* paintings try to break free from the repetitive gaze in which we behold images from the camps. He estranges these iconic scenes of Holocaust photography in order to provoke both remembrance of the past and to recuperate lost affect required for the preservation of memory.

Closely related to Hirsch's idea of postmemory and its emphasis on affect is Abraham and Torok's psychoanalytic term *transgenerational haunting*. In "The Phantom of Hamlet," Abraham asserts that during transgenerational haunting, what we could ascribe to postwar Germany's relation to the Shoah, "The shameful and therefore concealed secret always does return to haunt. To

---

16. Douglas 1995, p. 469.
17. Hirsch 2001, p. 218.
18. Ibid. Hirsch turns to Spiegelman's *Maus* to investigate the transgenerational space of remembrance in which the father's memories are "adopted" by the son. Iconic photographs from the Holocaust are reconfigured in Artie's telling of his father's story of the Holocaust.

exorcise it one must express it in words."[19] Once these haunting words are perceived as metaphors or figurative speech, the secret in the gap is transformed into memory: the phantom effect is broken. Stefan Aust reports how RAF members described themselves as being "Jews." In addition, they accused the government, which they referred to as the "Auschwitz generation," of wanting to "gas" them.[20] Yet the manner in which Meinhof or Ensellin employ these words tends to conflate their figurative with their literal usage. The children are the carriers of the phantoms, which need to be recognized as being buried within the other—the parent. It is the responsibility of the reader/analyst to put these pieces together and detect the linguistic elements of the phantom emanating from within the child's speech. The reader reconstructs the unspoken trauma inscribed within the child, transforming the literal use of words into figurative import. In the case of Richter's paintings, the spectator needs to uncover the visual imprints concealed within the blurs of the artwork.

Abraham and Torok highlight the point that the phantom is not about the return of the repressed but, "It works like a ventriloquist, like a stranger within the subject's own mental topography."[21] The phantom is their term to indicate the genealogy of a psychic history (familial or cultural), composed of secrets, gaps, or silences, inherited by the child's unconscious: it is passed from the parent and speaks through the child. Transgenerational haunting in Richter is not about words, but is comprised of visual resonances that resemble pantomime more than ventriloquism. Abraham and Torok make a connection between their concepts of the phan-

---

19. Abraham and Torok 1994, p. 188. At the end of "Notes on the Phantom," Abraham tells us that the effects of the phantom need to be placed into the social realm so that others can see them. In relation to Richter's artworks, this would be the public space of museum.

20. See Aust 1989. Such remarks become even more complex when read next to Meinhof's own anti-Zionist rhetoric, her support of Palestinian terrorism against Israel including Black September's 1972 attack on the Israeli Olympic team in Munich, and the training of RAF members in Palestinian military camps in Lebanon in the early 1970s.

21. Abraham and Torok 1994, p. 173.

tom to "cryptonymy." Cryptonymy refers to a theory of readability based on the structures of repetition, obfuscation, and erasure, where meaning is concealed behind fragments and traces. While cryptonyms are words that hide or conceal a secret, in my reading of Richter, it is the visual contours and the blurring technique of his paintings that open up a buried space of reading. Richter borrows from postmemory's iconographic images to evoke the Shoah upon his canvas.

Richter was asked in an interview where the spectator's standpoint should be when viewing these paintings. The question attests to the difficulties of seeing what transpires on the canvas. He replied that the *Standpunkt* is one of "*Trauer, Mitleid und Angst.*"[22] Richter's goal is to recover lost affect that is needed to transform the phantom effect into memory in the cells/tombs of Stammheim. In his *October* paintings, the gap becomes the mark of the phantom effect. The spectator confronts multiple gaps where the possibility of the phantom effect can rise to the surface: the media gap between painting and photography, the gap between paintings (the very spaces on the wall that juxtapose images of life and death), and the gaps in the paintings themselves (the technique of blurring). Together these gaps form the space of a censored history of which the spectator must become mindful. This site of omission or erasure is the intended space where the phantom effect is produced upon the canvas. Richter is not forming a narrative that attempts to explain what happened in Stammheim. Rather, the *October* paintings narrativize transgenerational haunting and seem to incite the spectator to recall a censored history embedded in the artworks.

Throughout his journals and interviews, Richter repeatedly discusses questions that revolve around the representation of the Holocaust. In an interview with Benjamin Buchloh, Richter dismissed the claim that the Shoah was unrepresentable, claiming that there was no *Bilderverbot* (prohibition against making images). On

---

22. Richter 1995, p. 200. In various interviews and journal entries, Richter returns to these terms of "mourning, compassion and anxiety" to describe the spectator's perspective before his paintings.

several occasions, Richter had remarked that, "There is lyric after Auschwitz."[23] The *Bilder*, he tells Prikker, already exist as photographs.[24] Richter himself re-photographed and distorted the iconographic images of the Holocaust in his *Atlas* project. In one section of *Atlas*, Richter places images of the death camps, of the dead and dying, next to pornographic photographs. Storr remarks that this juxtaposition forces the viewer "to look at 'familiar' atrocities of the Holocaust with fresh eyes."[25] I would argue that Richter seems to be making the same gesture in his *October* series. He questions the iconic function of these earlier images of the Holocaust and explores how they are potentially losing their ability to provoke "empathy, mourning and anxiety" in 1988. What becomes central to these paintings is their ability to disrupt the spectator's gaze and provoke affect during the act of looking at sites of trauma.

In 1964–1965 while the Auschwitz trial, which began in 1963, was still unfolding in Frankfurt (preceded by the Eichmann trial in Jerusalem in 1961), Richter began his attempts at representing the Holocaust. The development of German terrorism grew out of the student movement of the 1960s, which was itself a reaction by young intellectuals who felt compelled to uncover their parents' connections to National Socialism and Germany's traumatic past. Ultimately, the political and social structures of the Federal Republic of Germany were viewed by parts of the student movement as a continuation of this fascist past. Thus the Baader-Meinhof Gang becomes a historical consequence of their parents' failure to confront a traumatic past that consequently remained unprocessed.

Around the time of the Eichmann and Auschwitz trials and the early stages of the *Atlas* project, one of the first photodocumentary narratives that detailed the persecution and extermination of Europe's Jews was published: Gerhard Schoenberner's *The Yellow Star* (1960). This visual account of the Holocaust was released after a decade of silence and at a moment when anti-Semitic activ-

---

23. Ibid., p. 148.
24. Ibid., p. 185.
25. Storr 2000, p. 100.

ity was on the rise in West Germany.[26] Richter's re-photographed images in *Atlas* come from this collection. His photo-paintings and re-photographing of the Holocaust photographs occurs between the release of *The Yellow Star* and three years before the publication of Alexander and Margarete Mitscherlich's study of Germany's failure to engage with its Nazi past in *The Inability to Mourn* (1967). Richter, who is clearly aware of the function of mourning's relation to art in *October*, transforms the space of art into a place of provocation, where the traumatic past does not vanish but rises to the surface. The blur of these iconic images is left to the spectator to reconstruct.

Why would Richter indirectly paint the photographic imprint of the Shoah in 1988, twenty years after calling these very photographs unpaintable? As Habermas wrote in "On the Public Use of History" in 1986: "Contemporary history remains fixated on the period between 1933 and 1945 . . . tied up to the same point of departure: the images of that unloading ramp at Auschwitz. This traumatic refusal to pass away . . . [has] burned into our national history and entered consciousness of the general population only in the 1980s."[27] Habermas's words appeared as Germany was enmeshed in the 1986 *Historikerstreit* and Auschwitz's afterimage was being deformed in German memory. One must consider the historical-political context out of which these paintings developed. The subject of the *October* series arises during a debate concerning the centrality of Holocaust, the ultimate expression of Nazi crimes,

---

26. Schoenberner 1960. For an excellent analysis of *Der Gelbe Stern* in the context of Holocaust photography, see Chapter 3 of Cornelia Brink's (1998) *Ikonen der Vernichtung: öffenlicher Gebrauch von Fotografien aus Nationalsozialistischen Konzentrationslagern nach 1945*.

27. Habermas 1989, pp. 229–230. In addition to the ten year anniversary of the German Autumn in 1987, German newspapers, magazines, and news shows were replete with articles on the 50th Anniversary of the Degenerate Art exhibition from 1937 and the preparations for the commemorative events surrounding the 50th anniversary of Kristallnacht. The questions concerning historical repression in relation to the history of the Third Reich were reaching their pinnacle during this period with the Waldheim affair, not just in Germany but throughout Europe.

in modern German memory. During the *Historikerstreit* the link between memory and how to write the history of the National Socialist past was the crux of the debate: How was the Nazi era to be remembered and written by German historians, in particular its policies of extermination? Many saw the attempt to historicize the Shoah as a way to distance oneself from the past and thus draw a *Schlußstrich*, or narrative closure, to this "episode" of German history. It is such a *Schlußstrich* that Richter confronts obliquely through the lens of German terrorism ten years after the events of Stammheim. His interrogation in 1988 of the RAF is implicitly also an interrogation of the Third Reich, and shows his awareness that a continuity exists between the past and present.

Despite his insistence that the *October* paintings are not about ideology, I contend that Richter is inserting himself into the debates concerning postwar German memory prevalent throughout the 1980s. Richter starts his series in March 1988, directly positioned between the end of the *Historikerstreit* and Philipp Jenninger's conciliatory speech concerning National Socialism given in the Bundestag on the 50th anniversary of Kristallnacht. Richter, I believe, wants to cast doubt on one official story of the government (what happened in Stammheim) and recall the blurring of another history that was currently undergoing its own distortion by both historians and politicians.

Richter's *October*, where each painting both obfuscates and warps the original photographs, relies on the spectator's exegesis to release the family secret encrypted in Stammheim's cell. These two chapters of history—the Shoah and German terrorism of the RAF—are not separate and disconnected, but blend with one another. The images from Stammheim behave like screen memories that reconfigure components of the German past that are both displaced and disfigured by consciousness. It is the spectator who stands before the screen memories of these paintings and has the task of recuperating their original content along with their diminished affects: empathy, mourning, and anxiety. The cell of Stammheim is not a place of repressed or forgotten history, but the site where the concerns over the closure of history are put on display, are combated, and confronted by the artist. These paintings articulate the impossibility of ridding oneself of the past.

In his concept of screen memories, Freud represents consciousness as ordered by the mechanism of *Nachträglichkeit* [belatedness]: "A screen memory may be described as 'retrogressive' or as having 'pushed forward' as the one chronological relation or the other holds between the screen and the thing screened off . . . according to whether the displacement has been in a backward or forward direction."[28] In relation to his artistic development, the paintings of Stammheim take us back to Richter's effaced photographs from *Atlas* and thus to his own artistic past, but the artist is also making an historical link between the censored memory of the RAF and the position of the Holocaust in contemporary German memory. Hence the displacement in Richter's artwork moves in both directions. He confronts the legacy of National Socialism in Stammheim and forms a continuity between two historical moments: the traces of an unprocessed past are inscribed in the present. The cells of Stammheim, like Abraham and Torok's depiction of the shell, are not hermetically sealed; rather, they function as potential vehicles for moving affect into the realm of consciousness through the spectator's exegesis of the artwork.

I want to examine briefly how documentary images of the Shoah have been used as quotations in other visual media, in particular film, that are engaged with the history of the RAF. Through the insertion of photos or documentary footage, Alexander Kluge's *Germany in Autumn* (1978) and Margarethe von Trotta's *Marianne and Juliane* (1981) clearly attempt to construct or represent proximity between the two historical spaces. The continuation of these historical lines transpires through juxtaposition and cuts. Kluge makes a subtle connection between the murdered Schleyer and his Nazi past through the language of film. In *Germany in Autumn*, the opening scene of Schleyer's funeral is placed next to shots of the ESSO flags; the viewer cannot help but read the cryptonymic function of the letters "SS" inscribed in the backdrop of the funeral

---

28. Freud 1953–1974(3):320.

procession. It is the viewer's responsibility to read in this juxtaposition Schleyer's National Socialist past as a member of the SS during the Second World War. Despite Schleyer's murder at the hands of the RAF, Kluge reminds the audience of Schleyer's own tainted past.[29]

Perhaps even more striking than *Germany in Autumn* is Von Trotta's turn to Holocaust imagery in *Marianne and Juliane*. The citation of Alain Resnais's *Night and Fog* (1955), one of the first Holocaust documentaries, plays a pivotal moment in her film: it is used as a marker to establish the origins of the RAF. The temporal-spatial use of the film within the film begins in 1959 with a flashback scene in which Resnais's documentary is shown in the classroom. In the scene, the gaze of the camera alternates between three different subject positions. Our perspective constantly shifts as our point of view begins with that of the audience: the spectator sits behind the students and sees what they see. Our gaze then shifts to the screen itself: the students look at us and we watch their faces react to the film images before them. While we hear the voice-over, we are shielded from the figures on the screen: the images are withheld from the spectator.[30]

Ultimately Resnais's film takes over the entire screen. *Night and Fog* breaks out of its frame each time *Marianne and Juliane* is seen. The bodies of the dead fill the screen as the Holocaust re-

29. Nora Alter (2002) provides an excellent reading in her chapter "Framing Terrorism: Beyond the Borders," where she examines how a repressed past comes back to haunt Germany in Kluge's film *Deutschland im Herbst*. She reads the rise of the RAF as connected to the failure of a collective mourning in Germany over the crimes of the Third Reich. The children revolt against the generation of the perpetrators: their parents.

30. It is important to mention that the German translation of Jean Cayrol's commentary is from Paul Celan. In the classroom scene that preceded the viewing of *Nacht und Nebel*, the teacher asks Juliane to recite Rilke's *Herbsttag*. She responds that instead of Rilke, they should recite "Black milk of daybreak," that is, Celan's *Todesfuge*. In the scene that follows the screening of Resnais's film and takes us back to Marianne's cell, she remarks to her sister that she has forgotten the poem they used to say together, "the Celan poem," suggesting the slipping from memory of National Socialism's victims.

turns into the present. Overwhelmed by the horrific images of a mound of corpses, the sisters run into the bathroom that is meant to simulate a shower room. Juliane vomits and, through the sound of dripping water, we hear the voice-over of the film, "Who from us here will protect and warn us when the new executioners come?" The scene cuts to the present and the images of the desiccated bodies from the Holocaust turn into Marianne's gaunt face as she explains to her sister why she is partaking in a hunger strike. The two historical spaces are bridged by the cut: she is both the new guardian and victim of the state. Through this juxtaposition of scenes, the line is erased and Von Trotta clearly shows her position. What happened in the cell was murder: the RAF become Jews killed by the fascist state.

I do not wish to suggest here that Richter is comparing the dead in Stammheim to Jewish victims. In contrast to Kluge and Von Trotta, Richter rejects the position that the policy of the state is equivalent to that of the National Socialists; instead, he uses these images as a catalyst to recall the obscuring of the history of the Third Reich in contemporary German memory. The paintings, unlike the films, create an ambiguity surrounding what transpired in the cells. Richter's series shows the before and after: the members alive and then their deaths. What transpired in between is left blank on the wall. It is the spectator's responsibility to reconstruct what happened in these spaces and decipher the meaning behind *October*'s historical blur.

Over twenty years after his attempt to represent the Shoah, Richter returns in *October* for one of the first times to the aesthetic techniques of this former period: the monochrome and blurred texture of black and white photography and juxtaposition of images. Around the same time he was blurring images from the Holocaust and placing them alongside pictures of pornography in his *Atlas* project, Richter had used this method of photo-painting in three paintings from 1965: in the paintings *Aunt Marianne* (1965), her grinning brother *Uncle Rudi* (1965) in his German Wehrmacht uniform, and of *Mr. Heyde* (1965), taken from a newspaper clipping from 1959. Richter confronts Germany's Nazi past in these paintings and pulls his own personal relation to it into this space of memory. What is the significance of Aunt Marianne when she is placed alongside Uncle Rudi and Mr. Heyde? Aunt Marianne was mentally ill and was euthanized during the Third Reich. Mr. Heyde, a doctor, was the individual credited with inventing the gassing technique that killed her. He had lived in hiding in Germany until his exposure in 1959. His "discovery" revealed that the traumatic past of National Socialism was still entrenched in present-day Germany. Whether or not he was aware of this connection between Marianne and Mr. Heyde, Richter makes a correspondence, albeit private, that tries to reflect, represent, and engage with the horrors of the Third Reich. Despite their encrypted nature, these paintings show Richter's ongoing preoccupation with the history of the Third Reich and the effect that its concealment had on German society.

When asked in 1989 why he blurred his *October* paintings, Richter responded by saying, "I first paint the pictures very precisely from the photograph, sometimes more realistically than the originals . . . and the result is, of course, an unendurable picture from every point of view."[31] In one sense, blurring becomes a mode of protection needed to shield the spectator from his works and thus from the horrors of history. But a response by Jan Thorn Prikker during an interview with Richter suggests another conception of protection as it relates to the interplay between artwork and spectator: "It reminds me of the working of psychoanalysis. As if you wanted first to cancel the repression, in order to reinstate it later."[32] Blurring becomes an act of provocation. It is used not sim-

---

31. Richter 1995, p. 189. Included in Richter's notebooks from 1964, there is a mock interview that his friend Sigmar Polke had written in Richter's voice. When asked why he blurred his paintings, the response was, "I can't show them. Everyone would collapse." He goes on to describe how the death camps in Eastern Europe had used his paintings to kill their inmates. His paintings were so good that he had to hang cloth over them so as not to kill the spectator. Finally, to protect the spectator, he overpainted them all in white (Ibid., pp. 26–28).

32. Ibid., p. 189. In his notes from 1964–1965, Richter (1995) reflected on the link between looking at photographs and trauma. He worked in a photo lab in his youth and remarked, "The masses of photographs that passed through

ply to shield the spectator from what cannot be endured, but to impel him/her to remember what has been erased or edited from memory. As Kracauer states, "In order for history to present itself, the mere surface coherence offered by photography must be destroyed."[33] Richter's desire to blur, erase, or scratch away the surface of the canvas becomes a means whereby traumatic history is made perceptible through the disfigurement of the artwork.

But one wonders if trauma could potentially be universalized through this correspondence between the RAF and National Socialism. In November 1988, just as his *October* series was about to go on exhibition in Krefeld, Richter warned against such comparisons. He wrote in his journal: "To compare the Nazi crimes with other crimes is only in a superficial sense to play them down. The real way to play them down would be to ascribe them to the Nazis alone, and thus take the easy way of acquitting oneself from guilt."[34] He called such a comparison a *Verharmlosung* [playing something down], the very word used in the media the prior week to describe Jenninger's apologist speech in the Bundestag where he emphasized the "positive" changes that transpired in Germany under Hitler's rule. Richter prepares for the reception of his *October* works as if to say that he is not equating the government's response to the RAF as fascist. Rather, he reflects on the censored historical memory of both events, recalling by way of visual echoes National Socialist crimes through the deaths in Stammheim. Memory of the Holocaust should not be encrypted in the space of 1933–1945, but still recalled in October 1977, November 1988, or post-September 11,

---

the bath of the developer every day may have created a lasting trauma. There must be other reasons. I can't tell exactly" (p. 33). In the same interview, Richter stresses a belated quality to his paintings, in which their meaning is revealed to him afterward, "A picture has a logic we can't verbalize until afterwards . . . We talk about thinking a thing over, meaning over again, afterwards (*Nachdenken*). I am more and more aware of the importance of the unconscious process that has to take place while one is painting—as if something were working away in secret" (p. 195).

33. Kracauer 1995, p. 45.
34. Richter 1995, p. 173.

2001. The date "October 18, 1977," like the faces of the dead in
*October*, loses its specificity. One history is in the process of vanishing as the other history that was being distorted through recent
debates rises to the surface. Although the date might at first serve
to orient the spectator in time, Richter's goal is to disorient the
spectator temporally and spatially. What breaks censored memory's
phantom effect depends on the spectator's ability to see behind
Richter's screen.

Despite the very order of the paintings, the spectator might
anticipate that the paintings' trajectory leads toward narrative closure or *Schlußstrich*. Richter's objective is to undermine any narrative coherence. *October* offers neither a narrative about the RAF
nor of the Shoah; to be more precise, it is a critique of the sidestep-
ping of memory. If Richter is telling a story, it is that of a transgenerational haunting along with its accompanying phantom.
Richter begins *October* with a portrait painting of Meinhof as a
young woman prior to her radical political turn, and one recalls
how Barthes described portraits as a rehearsal for death. The last
painting in the series is that of the funeral. But the paintings of
Stammheim open up a space of affect—not of closure—by ruptur-
ing the spectator's gaze in order to provoke him/her to recall the
elision of historical wounds. As he repeatedly states in interviews,
these paintings are about the affects of "mourning, empathy and
anxiety."

I contend that the key elements in the series are Ensellin's gaze
and Meinhof's wound. Ultimately, Richter replaces Meinhof's and
Ensellin's gaze with their wounds in order to rupture the spectator's
own act of looking. This interplay of gaze, wound, and broken narrative takes us to Barthes's concept of the *punktum*, which is "a sting,
cut, little hole" that interrupts the spectator's absorption with the
image and forces her/him to reflect not so much on what she/he is
seeing, but on what is not shown.[35] Contemplating the recent death
of his mother, Barthes confronts the problem of mourning and
melancholia in his *Camera Lucida* as he analyzes her photograph.

---

35. Barthes 1981, pp. 26–27.

While he turns to her photograph as a space of potential consolation, Barthes concedes, "I cannot transform my grief, I cannot let my gaze drift; no culture will help me utter this suffering which I experience entirely on the level of the image's finitude . . . when it [the photograph] is painful, nothing in it can transform grief into mourning."[36] Although he reflects on and includes other photographs throughout *Camera Lucida*, the one he cannot show, the one that is withheld from the reader, is that of his mother. Barthes holds onto her body; its punctum, its wound, is for him alone. Unable to let go of her body, grief becomes something private and interior, without solace.

Contrary to Barthes's claim that nothing in the photograph can turn grief into mourning, what turns transgenerational haunting into memory or melancholic history into historical mourning for Richter is the very disfiguration of the photograph. Richter's *October* series transforms the unambiguous marks of a particular date into memory traces of other dates that need to be recalled by the spectator. Although Richter re-photographed over a hundred images of the RAF in his *Atlas*, the majority of those he decided to paint are the photographs of the dead. Despite what seems like a repetition of a traumatic scene, an obsessive reproduction of the photographs from the inside of Stammheim, Richter's paintings circumvent traumatic repetition through the process of distorting and blurring the original images. By rendering the figures of these paintings opaque, covering them in a veil of gray, the spectator's passive gaze is disrupted and beckoned to look more closely. Meinhof, Baader, and Ensellin are defaced so that the other faces that Richter could not paint can be remembered. Once the face is removed, the returning body becomes a figuration of loss, not an act of mere repetition but of memory.

In the images of Meinhof's disembodied head, Richter's painterly punctum suspends the spectator's familiar relation both to the visible world and to the temporal referent of October 18, 1977. A photograph tries to appeal to the veracity of a moment in history,

---

36. Ibid., p. 90.

time, and space. Depriving us of the individual's face, Richter configures loss that starts at one moment in history and arrives at another. His configuration of a *punktum* brings about a displacement in which October 1977 leads us to another date outside the frame: to the Holocaust and the bodies he could not paint but only photograph as blurs.

Richter focuses on the mark of the rope in his three images of Meinhof's corpse (entitled *Tote 1, 2,* and *3* respectively). Although the body and the size of the canvas slowly vanish, the wound becomes more visible. As her hair fades into the background, Meinhof's jaw becomes sharper thereby accentuating the rope line beneath it. Her eye is hollowed out. The series has the effect of a time-lapse camera depicting her decomposition. The last painting of the three appears as if she is levitating. Richter's technique matches the content of these paintings. Describing the manner in which he paints as a *"Verletzung"* [injury], Richter paints the photos and then scratches them away, leaving blurred traces of the scene behind for us to reconstruct.[37] The spectator sees nameless victims whose wounds are held together by a date. How does one read these wounds? Similar to Barthes's *punktum* that acts like a wound that interrupts the familiar relation to the visible world, there is no identification with the other in the photograph. The punktum of the paintings is itself the wound that interrupts the spectator's absorption in the image. Similar to Barthes's statement that he wants "to explore photography . . . as a wound," Richter, too, seems obsessed with the seeing, reading, and remembering of historical injuries in these photo-paintings.[38]

Richter has constructed a series of screens that are not about protection, but are, instead, part of an entrapment, a seduction that requires the spectator to sharpen his/her gaze, move toward the paintings and look for the right perspective to see what is unfolding in the series. Don DeLillo offers a keen insight into the optics of Richter's *October* paintings in a short story titled "Baader-Meinhof." The story

---

37. Richter 1995, p. 237.
38. Barthes 1981, p. 21.

takes place in the room containing Richter's fifteen paintings in the Museum of Modern Art in New York. A woman returns to the exhibition to look at the paintings, feeling as if she is sitting "in a mortuary chapel" keeping watch over a friend.[39] A man whom she meets in the room asks her what she sees when she looks at them: "Tell me what you see. Honestly. I want to know." Her words convey what the spectator's struggle is before these paintings. "I realize now that the first day I was only barely looking. I thought I was looking, but I was only getting a bare inkling of what's in these paintings. I'm only just starting to look."[40] These paintings draw in the visitor, not simply beckoning him or her to approach the canvas and find the right place to stand; they also coerce the spectator to return again to the paintings themselves. When asked what she feels standing before these works, her first response is, "I don't know," but then she answers, "Helpless." Her answer captures what Richter wishes to elicit from the spectator. A feeling of visual helplessness compels the spectator to return to the site of mourning in order to uncover what is encrypted in the blurs. Any attempt by the spectator to control the images upon the canvases would therefore fail. Neither the gaze of the state-controlled camera nor the spectator's voyeuristic look can mortify the figures in the paintings. The bodies belong to a traumatic past that resists both petrification and closure.

It is the first painting in the "Confrontation" series that interests me here in its relation to questions concerning postmemory and the Holocaust. The viewer occupies the position of the camera as Ensellin appeared in court after her arrest (see Fig. 6–1). Richter frames her in three different ways as she moves from left to right. Her face slowly dissipating, Ensellin simultaneously develops and vanishes before our eyes. She appears to be forming out of her shadow projected on the wall. Like stills from a film, Richter freeze-frames her walking. But Ensellin resists stasis. Arresting the spectator's voyeuristic gaze, her look paradoxically freezes him/

---

39. Delillo 2002, p. 78.
40. Ibid., pp. 79–80.

Fig. 6–1. *Confrontation* (1), 1988. Gerhard Richter. Digital Image © The Museum of Modern Art/Licensed by SCALA/Art Resource, NY.

her while breaking the series' flow. Trying to reach across the surface of paint, she defiantly catches us looking and, in the last frame, she turns her face away.

In looking at Ensellin, one particular Holocaust photograph comes to mind, not one invoked by her hanged body, but by her gaze. I am thinking of the Jewish woman arriving at the loading ramps of Auschwitz during selection, apparently taken right before her death (see Fig. 6–2). How can this image help us understand

Fig. 6–2. *Selektion, The Yellow Star*, Gerhard Schoenberner. Permission: Imperial War Museum BU 3760.

what is happening in Richter's *October* in relation to postmemory and the Holocaust? Where do these two figures intersect to trigger the phantom effect? First, a visual correspondence opens up between the two images taken by the state as a means of documentation: each glances up at the camera and looks at us, mouths parted, faces blurred. One is identified by her yellow star, and the other by her institutional prison garb. Both walk toward their respective places of death.[41] Richter shows where Ensellin marches off to as she exits the frame of "Confrontation." Like an image of someone being led toward an execution, the spectator anticipates what is coming. In his interview with Prikker, Richter asserts, "People can't

---

41. On the opposite page of Schoenberber's *Gelbe Stern*, where the image of the woman appears with the title *Selektion*, her trajectory follows that of a photo of a mother and her five children walking along the selection ramp. Its caption reads, "On the way to the gas" (pp. 206–207).

wait to see corpses,"[42] and he will not disappoint us: Ensellin steps into her hanging, Baader lies in a pool of blood, and Meinhof's body is laid out before us. The between of the living and the dead, a space to which the spectators have no access except through the gaps between the paintings themselves, is left concealed. Such echoes between the optics of Holocaust victim photography and Richter's paintings of Ensellin also provoke reflections about the function of the gaze in state photography: the subject of the picture becomes a mere record of state surveillance. In Harum Farocki's film *Images of the World and the Inscription of War*, the figure of the Jewish woman on the loading ramps plays a significant role when he examines her return gaze to her Nazi photographer. Farocki titles this section of the film, "How to Face a Camera." This title along with Farocki's observations about the woman's relation to the camera can be applied to Richter's paintings of Ensellin: "The camp run by the SS shall bring her to destruction and the photographer who captures her beauty for posterity is from the same SS. . . . How the two elements interplay, preservation and destruction."[43] I am not trying to equate the two governments or their respective policies with one another; instead, I am investigating the similarities of the state's use of photography and how both photographed subjects try, in their acts of standing before the camera, to resist its gaze. What seems to be an inhumane act of the "lineup" is subverted by Ensellin's pause before the camera: it is her act of resistance.

Richter, like Farocki's analysis of camp photographs, is critiquing the state's use of photography in watching and identifying its citizens, a critique similar to what Benjamin referred to as an "administrative process of control." As Benjamin states: "In the history of methods of identification, the invention of photography represents a breakthrough . . . photography makes possible for the first time the preservation through time of a person's unequivocal traces [*eindeutige Spuren*]."[44] Benjamin's rejection of photography

---

42. Richter 1995, p. 185.
43. Silverman 1995, p. 151.
44. Benjamin 1980, p. 550.

stems from his concern that it will be abused by the state. While photography is used by the state to record, document crime scenes and criminal records, it is also used to watch civilians. The photographic record stands for the "single truth" of the individual. Through the technique of distortion, Richter questions the gaze of the state. Richter vehemently rejects and undermines such unequivocal traces with regard to how the RAF was portrayed. The state used the unequivocal traces of the RAF images displayed in the *Stern* magazine as clinical proof of their deaths and thus as an end to the narrative of the German Autumn. But instead of closing this history, Richter inserts into his paintings a series of punktums that suspend the state's narrative. Rejecting a totalizing narrative of the RAF and the Shoah, Richter wishes to expose the very deceptiveness behind such narratives.

How does the state want the spectator to see the woman on the platform or Ensellin before the courtroom? The intended objective of the National Socialist photography was to depict the Jew as less than human [*Untermenschen*] and to cancel out any empathy with the victims. But when the woman on the selection ramp looks back at the camera, her gaze defeats this goal. How does Ensellin face the camera, or more specifically, how does Richter represent her facing the camera? Richter frames her in three different ways as she moves from left to right. By cropping the bottom half of the photograph, Richter focuses on her gaze. Richter does not interrogate Ensellin's gaze, but rather, he allows her gaze to interrogate the spectator. Her pose becomes an act of resistance as she catches the spectator looking and draws attention to his/her voyeuristic gaze. Similar to the intended effect of Richter's positioning of pornography alongside concentration camp photographs, the spectator's passive consumption of images is broken as he/she becomes conscious of the act of looking.

There is a possibility that one might try to access Richter's *October* through a theological lens that incorporates the Stammheim dead into a redemptive narrative of martyrdom comprised of fifteen stages of the cross: the empty cell qua tomb, the Christ-like triptych of the dead Meinhof, the two crucified images of Baader, the cross that might or might not be there in the trees of the funeral painting. But despite this analogy between cell and cenotaph, which suggests a missing body, the series overflows with the dead: seven out of the fifteen paintings revolve around the theme of the corpse. Any mythopoetic narrative that might suggest redemption, heroism, or closure is exactly the type of reading that Richter attempts to subvert through his distortion of the original photographs. Narrative constantly gives way to the punktum.

The body that most suggests such a redemptive reading would be Baader in "Man Shot Down" (1 and 2) (see Fig. 6–3). In what might appear at first to be a figuration of martyrdom, crucifixion, and redemption, we behold Baader's outstretched body. How does Richter undermine such an analysis? Through the technique of photographic cropping applied to painting, Richter obscures the background of Baader's cell and directs our gaze to the body in the foreground. In the first painting, Baader's body appears to be suspended in an ethereal swirl of black paint. His arched body seems to be floating or elevating out of the frame. Despite the correspondence between the painting and police photographs in terms of scale and position of the body, Richter adds a dimension of transcendence to the first painting. Yet such a transcendence is undermined in the second painting where the figure begins to recede. There is both a spatial and temporal change occurring between the two paintings.

While the first painting depicts more closely the original police photograph, in the second painting the face, traces of blood, and Baader's wide-open eyes are erased. In spite of the repetition in canvas size, it is now the figure in the frame that is vanishing. His truncated legs fade into floor. The features of his face become desiccated as his body withers away and the folds of his shirt make the corpse appear skeletal. Instead of lifting upward, the body now appears to sink both downward and toward the spectator. Baader's figure becomes more centered and the space around him more defined as he himself undergoes a vanishing. The scene is more temporal, the body more terrestrial as it becomes subject to the effects of time. The intensification of perspective contributes to the spatial-temporal quality of this space. Thus the image loses its transcendent features and becomes more historically grounded. The hand, the traces of self-inflicted wound, and the watch are exactly where the painting ends. Richter crops the photograph at the mark of time. As Richter observed, these paintings are about "leave-taking."[45] He takes leave of one moment in history and arrives at another.

Richter uses paint like a semi-transparent screen not in order to conceal something but to entice the spectator to penetrate it. By constantly subverting our gaze, Richter's method of painting keeps the spectator at a distance. The image is difficult to grasp and the spectator assimilates its meaning by way of content and visual organization: one might turn to art history, to Richter's past works, or to corresponding historical images to gain access to the artworks. Relying on visual echoes that recall a distinct historical moment, Richter resurrects the memory of other wounds and bodies. I read Richter's paintings of Baader next to a similar image of crucifixion and the pieta from another photo-narrative. With Richter's removal of the face and obsessive look at corpses, I return to *Atlas* and *The Yellow Star*. The order in which the following image from *The Yellow Star* (see Fig. 6–4) appears sheds light on the narrative structure the text wishes to convey. In Schoenberner's closing chapter titled "Liberation," the reader is confronted with decomposing corpses: what the allies saw when they entered the camps. Several of the photographs used by Schoenberner depict piles of corpses that center around one body with arms spread.[46] In one particular image, a decaying corpse with spread arms, suggesting the crucifixion, is shown. On the facing page, a female inmate sits like Mary in the *Pieta* and gazes at him. But like Richter, Schoenberner's *The Yellow Star* subverts this redemptive use of the image by means of

---

45. Richter 1995, p. 178.

46. Richter's last re-photographed image in his *Atlas* series on the camps is based on one of these photographs. Also, *Nacht und Nebel* toward its end will focus on a body in a Christ-like pose and *Die Bleierne Zeit* will replay these closing images in its use of Resnais's film.

his cynical inscription: *Ecce homo 1945*. Any notion of a redemptive narrative is undone by the caption.

I would like to conclude my analysis by returning briefly to the MOMA exhibition, which culminated with Richter's *October* paintings. In the article "Torpedo auf Zeitreise," published in the *Süddeutsche Zeitung*, February 20, 2004, Holger Liebs described *October*'s presence in Berlin as an "adequately worrying conclusion to the show," which ends "suddenly in the unmastered German present." The present is unmastered, because the past still has not been properly incorporated into memory. In a press conference, the curator of the show remarked that in *October*'s return to Germany, "This most recent work of the exhibition shows both the way towards the future and towards, *um* [*äh*] . . . I would like to thank our American friends."[47] The opportunity to situate these

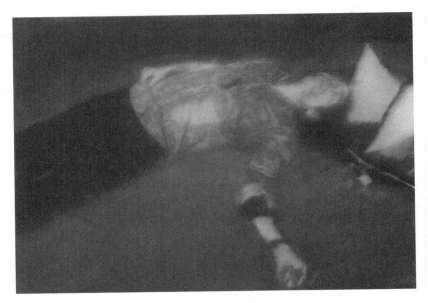

Fig. 6–3. *Man Shot Down* (1), 1988. Gerhard Richter. Digital Image © The Museum of Modern Art/Licensed by SCALA/Art Resource, NY.

47. Reich 2004.

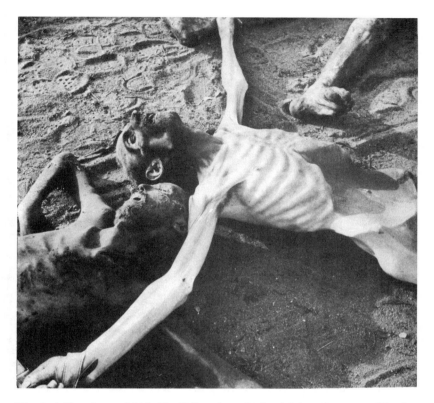

Fig. 6–4. Ecce homo 1945. *The Yellow Star*, Gerhard Schoenberner. Public domain, from the "Auschwitz Album" in the Yad Vashen Archive.

works within the context of Germany's past is not simply left unspoken, but is censored by Schneider. One could infer that the concealed, not forgotten, word is "*hintern*" [backward or the past], and Schneider catches the import behind what she has just said. While her words were meant to be hopeful with respect to the innovative aesthetic quality of Richter's paintings, Schneider recognizes the ominous implications of her statement: the paintings point toward more terror. The disruption of her sentence does not get her out of the trap of history that she had attempted to avoid. Instead, the linguistic gap calls attention to the very point she tried to evade. There is a doubling of the trap: the path to which these paintings lead (both to the future and past) is, in each direction, a heading toward more historical violence. Schneider's previous circumvention of the past, as seen in the obscuring of historical trauma through her emphasis on aesthetics, now manifests itself in the disarticulated word "äh." Her stutter functions as an involuntary translation of Richter's blur back into the phantom effect of language.

Nicholas Rand describes the language of those who find themselves under the sway of the phantom as afflicted with a concealed signification of words—what he names in his introduction to *The Shell and the Kernel* a "psychic aphasia."[48] Through the obfuscation of speech, or the "cryptonymy of language," meaning is concealed. In Abraham and Torok's theory of readability, the analyst/reader is required to convert silence into speech, thereby reintegrating the crypt's secret into consciousness. Likewise, the spectator who stands before *October* needs to reconfigure or refocus Richter's cryptonymic blurs, the visual equivalent of psychic aphasia, into historical consciousness. The phantom, whether it be the secret occluded in language or in Richter's distorted images, is an "unspeakable fact" that points to the gap in memory of an unintegrated traumatic past.[49] It is the task of the reader/spectator to both recognize and convert these linguistic and visual imprints into historical memory. In Richter's use of postmemory, the bodies of the Holocaust left unburied, unmourned, and unpainted in *Atlas* rise to the surface almost twenty-five years later on October 18, 1977. The shudder, shock, or punktum is the moment when the spectator becomes conscious of this temporal-spatial displacement and is made aware of its phantom effect.

## ACKNOWLEDGMENTS

I would especially like to thank Julia Hell who presented a paper on Gerhard Richter, Peter Weiss, and W. G. Sebald at a DAAD seminar at Cornell University on visualizing the Holocaust, sum-

---

48. Abraham and Torok 1994, p. 17.
49. Ibid., p. 171.

mer 2003. Her work on Richter has been a great influence on my own reflections regarding Richter and postmemory of the Holocaust.

## REFERENCES

Abraham, N., and Torok, M. (1994). *The Shell and the Kernel*, ed. N. Rand. Chicago: University of Chicago Press.

Alter, N. (2002). Framing terrorism: beyond the borders. In *Projecting History: German Nonfiction Cinema, 1967–2000*, pp. 43–75. Ann Arbor: University of Michigan Press.

Aust, S. (1989). *Der Baader-Meinhof-Komplex*. Munich: Goldman.

Barthes, R. (1981). *Camera Lucida: Reflections on Photography*. New York: Hill and Wang.

Benjamin, W. (1980). *Gesammelte Schriften*, ed. R. Tiedmann and H. Schwepenhuser. Frankfurt/Main: Suhrkamp.

Brink, C. (1998). *Ikonen der Vernichtung: öffenlicher Gebrauch von Fotographien aus Nationalsozialistischen Konzentrationslagern nach 1945*. Berlin: Akad. Verlag.

Buchloch, B. (2000). "Gerhard Richter's *Atlas*: the anomic archive." In *Photography and Painting in the Work of Gerhard Richter: Four Essays on Atlas*, pp. 11–30. Barcelona: Consorci del Museu d'Art Contemporani de Barcelona.

Chevrier, J.-F. (2000). Between the fine arts and the media. In *Photography and Painting in the Work of Gerhard Richter: Four Essays on Atlas*, pp. 31–60. Barcelona: Consorci del Museu d'Art Contemporani de Barcelona.

DeLillo, D. (2002). Baader-Meinhof. In *The New Yorker*, April 1, 2002, pp. 78–82.

Dettweiler, M. (2004). RAF-Gemälde in Berlin: Wenn Terroristen-Bilder Verwischen. *Spiegel-Online*, February 20.

Douglas, L. (1995). Film as witness: screening Nazi concentration camps before the Nuremberg Tribunal," *Yale Law Journal* 105(2):449–481.

Freud, S. (1953–1974). Screen memories. In *The Standard Edition of the Complete Psychological Works of Sigmund Freud*, Vol. III, trans. and ed. J. Strachey, pp. 299–322. London: Hogarth.

——— (1965). *The Psychopathology of Everyday Life*, ed. J. Strachey. New York: W. W. Norton.

Habermas, J. (1989). *The New Conservatism: Cultural Criticism and the Historians' Debate*, trans. and ed. S. Nicholsen. Cambridge, MA: MIT Press.

Hirsch, M. (2001). Surviving images: Holocaust photography and the work of postmemory. In *Visual Culture and the Holocaust*, ed. B. Zelizer, pp. 215–246. New Brunswick, NJ: Rutgers University Press.

Kracauer, S. (1995). Photography. In *The Mass Ornament: Weimar Essays*, trans. and ed. T. Y. Levin. Cambridge, MA: Harvard University Press.

Reich, A. (2004). Kaufhaus-Kunst-Kanon. *Junge Welt*: http://www.jungewelt.de/2004/02-23/021.php. (February 23).

Richter, G. (1995). *The Daily Practice of Painting. Writings and Interviews, 1962–1993.* London: Thames and Hudson and Anthony d'Offay Gallery.

Schneider, A. (2004). Interview conducted by Anita Wünschmann: Die Demut vor der Kunst. *Berliner Zeitung* 10 (April).

Schoenberner, G. (1960). *Der Gelbe Stern* [*The Yellow Star*]. Hamburg: Verlag Rütten und Loening.

Silverman, K. (1995). *The Threshold of the Visible World.* New York: Routledge.

Storr, R. (2000). *Gerhard Richter October 18, 1977.* New York: Museum of Modern Art.

# 7

# The Unbridgeable Distance to the Self: Sarah Kofman's Revision of Philosophy

Astrid Deuber-Mankowsky
Translated by Dominick Bonfiglio and Ole Gram

## LIFE AND PHILOSOPHY

Philosophy cannot be severed from life just as the philosopher cannot be severed from his or her body and desires. The truth of this easy assertion, however, is not as evident as it first appears. Following Sarah Kofman, the history of western metaphysics can be partly understood as a grandiose project to censure or even erase this assertion in order to posit in its place the opposition between life and philosophy. Philosophy cannot be severed from life; Sarah Kofman was deeply convinced of it and her work grew out of this belief. She practiced it in her writing: she subverted the metaphysical opposition between life and philosophy, she blurred its borders and crossed it out, she infected philosophy with life and life with philosophy.

In place of the opposition of life and philosophy, Kofman opposes metaphysics and philosophy, assigning the latter the task of deconstructing all the false and delusional ideas of metaphysics.

Doing philosophy consists of "uncovering the desires at work in all discourse and of asking oneself what morality, what politics a given 'theoretical' piece of writing means to arrive at."[1]

Thus, when Kofman writes on theoretical texts, she inevitably speaks of the author's life and personal fantasies. Whether it is the psychoanalysis of Sigmund Freud, the educational program of Jean-Jacques Rousseau, the scientific theory of August Comte, the philosophical system of Immanuel Kant, or the philosophy of Friedrich Nietzsche, we always learn something about the life of the author, about his "masculinity" and his relation to women, about his ambivalent desire for "feminization," and his confrontation with death. In short, we learn about *das Unheimliche*—about that which the text conceals.[2]

To speak of the uncanny is particularly apt. The metaphysical attempt to separate philosophy from death occults the opposition between philosophy and life. Kofman shows that, by keeping death at a distance from life, metaphysics not only censures the feminine, but projects the uncanny aspects of self onto the foreign and thereby exiles them to an external front.

Misunderstandings, however, should be carefully avoided. On no account can metaphysics be simply copied from life, nor can philosophy be reduced solely to biography. If philosophy cannot be severed from life, then life in turn cannot be purged from philosophy. One of the consequences of this understanding is an ability to embrace the idea of a philosophy "contaminated" by traces of subjectivity and sexuality. As Kofman writes, "Whether the author of a 'pedagogical novel,' a philosophical system, or a psychoanalytic work with scientific pretensions, one is never a transcendental and objective, sexually neutral subject."[3]

Kofman's philosophical method is the reading. Her approach consists in disorienting texts in order to discover the effects of life

---

1. Kofman 1984b, p. 184. (All English translations of quotations in French from *Lectures de Derrida* [1984a,b] are my own—DB.)

2. Cf. Sigmund Freud, "The Uncanny" (Freud 1953–1973, p. 244).

3. Kofman 1986a, p. 358 (translation by D.B.).

from a new "slanted" perspective—effects that are utterly "uncanny." In its indifference and nondifferentiability, life not only threatens the subject's integrity but pulls it out of joint. This subversion affects every individual in his or her "unbridgeable distance"[4] from others. Life puts the subject into an "unbridgeable distance" from itself.

The word *other* is rarely capitalized in Kofman's books. Such capitalization calls to mind the "One" rather than its opposite. She prefers such expressions as "radical alterity," "relation without relation," and "the infinitely Distant." These are paradoxical expressions—expressions that actually cannot be thought. But Kofman uses them for that very reason. These paradoxes allude to that which precedes all thinking in oppositions and establishes the possibility of such thought: a nondifferentiability, an undecidable, original ambivalence, in which nothing is secured and life is always already connected with death. The thinking of radical alterity therefore entails confronting philosophy with life.

Here lies the philosophical motive behind Kofman's crucial attention to the "personal" fantasy of the author. Her aim is not to pathologize the author but to reveal how philosophy is generated from a traumatic experience that she describes as the "unbridgeable distance" separating us from ourselves and above all from others. A communication that addresses the other is only possible under the condition that this original, infinite distance is taken into account. This isolating experience must be shared if what Kofman calls an "authentic relation" is to become possible.

In her many books, Kofman speaks accordingly not only of others' trauma, but also of her own. This sets her philosophical writing apart from those of the philosophers she examines. She takes great pains to configure the unmasterable elements of her own life with those in her writing.

Connecting Kofman's own life with philosophy are two works that might be called "autobiographical." In *Rue Ordener, Rue Labat* (1994) she writes of her childhood and of her mother. *Smothered*

---

4. Kofman 1998, p. 30.

*Words* (1998) is devoted to her father, who died in Auschwitz. In a 1991 interview with Sarah Kofman about *Smothered Words* that I conducted with Ursula Konnertz, Kofman insisted that her work was neither a biographical gesture nor a personal drama, but an attempt to understand an historical fact:

> It is true that I speak of my father in my book, and it was very important for me to be able to write his name in a book. During a program for *France Culture*, Laure Adler (*Nuits magnétiques*) asked me to read aloud this biographical passage. I was not able to read more than two lines—she ended the reading with a totally expressionless voice, something that cut off all those feelings that had prevented me from reading to the end. I haven't written a biographical account insofar as I believe that my personal history is only of public interest to the extent that it touches collective history, to the extent that "my absolute" overlaps with the "absolute" of history. Besides, my father was not deported because he was "my" father, but quite simply because he was a Jew.[5]

The overlapping of the absolute of the private with the absolute of history connects Kofman's personal trauma with the traumatic history of the twentieth century. This history ties the unmasterable aspects of Kofman's life with the traumatic historical fact of Auschwitz. By tying the unmasterable elements of private life with writing, Kofman introduces trauma into a philosophy turned historical, thereby unsettling all previous philosophy. Philosophy itself thereby becomes transitory, that is to say, historical. Although Sarah Kofman put a premium on philosophical rationality, her attempt to understand the historical fact of Auschwitz, conditioned by her personal history and the demands of survival, made it impossible for her to exclude the experience of historical trauma from philosophical reflection. This is precisely what lends her philosophical writing that historical indexicality that grounds the enduring relevance of her work.

---

5. Deuber-Mankowsky and Konnertz 1991, p. 104f.

This philosophical conviction establishes the relentless "authenticity" of Kofman's writing. In what follows, I want to touch on three vehicles of its expression. The first is Kofman's reading of Rousseau. Using an exemplary instance, I want to show how Kofman reconstructs the repressed desire for life in metaphysical texts. As Kofman carefully demonstrates, Rousseau's educational novel becomes haunted by a trauma that manifests itself as an anxiety in the face of "too much" life. Concretely, it is the anxiety generated at that terminal point where life and death converge and become indistinguishable. In Rousseau's case, this anxiety leads back to the circumstances surrounding his own birth, which he only narrowly survived and during which his mother died. Mothers not only give life, they also bring death. To be sure, this obvious conclusion is not one that Rousseau draws. On the contrary, he does whatever he can to avoid this conclusion and develops a complex system of thought in which he argues exactly the opposite. As Kofman shows, the figure of the "good mother" directs the son's repression of this perceived dangerous conjunction between giving life and bringing death. Rousseau's metaphysical system is thus revealed as a defensive model that not only forms the basis for thinking gender difference as this began to develop in the eighteenth century, but also for thinking the distinction between nature and culture.

The second vehicle I consider is Kofman's relationship to psychoanalysis. In central passages of her reading of Rousseau, Kofman draws upon psychoanalytical concepts and figures of thought. Psychoanalysis is central to Kofman's deciphering of trauma in the philosophical text, yet she distances herself from the notion that her readings are psychoanalytical. How, then, does she situate her philosophy in relation to psychoanalysis? Kofman repeatedly engaged herself with Freud's writings in order to free psychoanalysis from metaphysics. Life is, as Kofman understands it, radically different from Freud's sense of the unconscious. Life cannot be mastered, neither by the therapist's analysis nor scientific description. Life subverts the author and his language.

In the last part of this essay, I pursue the question of how Kofman's own personal trauma—the nightmare that is tangent to the absolute of history—has left a mark on her work: how, in other words, the memory of the Shoah is written into her own books. In this context, her two autobiographical books, *Rue Ordener, Rue Labat* and *Smothered Words*, are key. An examination of these books will illuminate her interpretation of "the highest ethical exigency"[6] and lead, ultimately, to the concept of the sublime in Kofman's configuration of Kant and Nietzsche.

## ROUSSEAU AND WOMEN

Kofman's deconstructive readings aim to discover the point where the personal fantasy of the author converges with the illusions of metaphysics in order to expose the desires bound to the author's own body. Unrecognized and repressed, these desires secretly—like specters—haunt the texts of speculative knowledge and transform them into delusional constructs. The perception of these desires requires a finely tuned sense of hearing and a double-sided vision. Kofman's close reading skills are nowhere more apparent than in her analysis of Jean-Jacques Rousseau's discourse on women. Listening carefully, she passes through Rousseau's texts, extracting from his words that meaning they are meant to conceal at all costs. How and where does Kofman think fantasy replaces philosophical insight?

> Such passages from *Lettre à d'Alembert*, *Emile*, or *la Nouvelle Héloïse*, which depict the sadistic spectacle of the male para-lyzed, suffocated, and imprisoned, call to mind certain passages of the *Confessions*. How can one not think, for example, of the passage where Jean-Jacques states that for him to remain seated in a room, arms crossed, inactive, chatting with others, "mov-ing only his tongue," is an "unbearable torture"?[7]

In *Emile*, Rousseau likens domestic life to imprisonment, unbear-able for a man, since "he needs the open air, movement, and fa-

---

6. Kofman 1998, p. 41.
7. Kofman 1986a, p. 355; trans. version 1992, pp. 55–56.

tigue . . . ; he is disturbed and agitated; he seems to be struggling; he stays because he is in chains."[8] "These are the words of Emile's private tutor," Kofman continues, "but they betray all the fantasies of Jean-Jacques as endlessly repeated in the *Dialogues*: his fear, his horror of the dark, the belief that his persecutors have surrounded him with a 'triple enclosure of darkness,' entombed him behind impenetrable walls of darkness; his fantasy of being weighed down with chains, of being unable to say a word, take a step, move a finger without the knowledge and permission of his enemies; of being enclosed in an immense labyrinth where tortuous and subterranean false paths lead him further and further astray; and finally, the fantasy of being buried alive."[9]

These images of persecution express both a puerile and masochistic wish to be punished by returning to the womb and the terror of being buried alive as its uncanny inversion. Kofman observes how,

> caught in the grip of his persecutors, he barely tries to escape. Surrounded by falsity and darkness, he waits, without a murmur of protest, for truth and light. Finally, buried alive in a coffin, he lies still, not even thinking of death. Is this the tranquility of innocence? Or the tranquility of masochistic pleasure at being punished, immobilized, possessed like a woman and by women, the pleasure of being suffocated and humiliated by women, of being made into their thing, their property when they refuse to be mothers wholly at the service of the man, mothers who show him pity and tenderness and who would otherwise be responsible for his death, his degradation, his perversion, his expropriation, his emasculation.[10]

Were women not tender, they would be held responsible for Rousseau's degeneration, his perversion, his emasculation, his feminization. To prevent this degeneration, women have to be educated

---

8. Rousseau 1966, pp. 567–568. *Emile* passage quoted in Kofman, "Rousseau's Phallocratic Ends," p. 56.

9. Kofman 1986a, pp. 355–356; trans. version 1992, p. 56.

10. Ibid., p. 56. (DB's translation).

and disciplined. Rousseau, of course, does not argue in his own name, but appeals constantly and urgently to Nature itself. Yet by calling on Nature, does he not actually mean again the mother, the good Mother Nature? Doesn't he find in her the most intimate associate who, only as a tender mother can, acts completely in the interests and on the side of the son—the one who, in looking after her son, insists accordingly that women are completely different from men? Doesn't he find in Nature the good mother herself? Mistrustful of the imploring tone in Rousseau's texts, Kofman suggests the following interpretation: "insofar as these dissymmetries [between the sexes] favor the masculine sex, as they always do, we might wonder if good Mother Nature doesn't serve as a mere pretext here, if the ends of Nature don't in fact dissimulate the ends of man (*vir*), rationalizing his injustices and violences."[11]

Even while idealizing the mother in nature and in the natural woman, Rousseau condemns the "threat" to and of the feminine in his battle against urbanite women. The part of the feminine that is threatening is excised and projected onto the "dolls," those intellectual, made-up Paris women, who are infertile, denatured, and emasculating. In Rousseau's texts, they become the emblem for the uncanny, the denatured, the foreign, the degenerate, the unliving, for evil, death, and castration.

## THE UNCANNY SEX

An *apotropaic* is a magic ritual or formula designed to avert evil. Kofman uses the expression "apotropaic defense" as the *terminus technicus* to describe the cover-up tactics and defense mechanisms of metaphysics. The metaphysical text hence functions like a dream "unbeknownst to those who wrote it, like a place for the fulfillment, more or less censured, of repressed desires."[12] There lies in the metaphysical text a further, hidden text that becomes legible

---

11. Ibid., pp. 342 and 347.
12. Kofman 1984a, p. 99.

when attention is drawn to the disparity between declaration and description, between what the author claims to do and what he actually does: "The rift between the declaration and the description, which makes appear another text, in contraband, reveals that a desire has lodged itself within the declared text."[13] In Rousseau's speculative philosophy about the sexes, Kofman discovers an apotropaic, spellbinding gesture meant to offer protection from the "*unheimlich*": from the uncanniness of life, from the uncanniness of one's own ambivalent desire to become a woman. It is a desire that merges together in its ambivalence with the traumatic circumstances of Rousseau's own birth—that the infant Jean-Jacques almost suffocated in his mother's womb, that his mother brought him into being as "weakly and infirm," while she herself died.[14] For Kofman, reflecting on this traumatic birth entails an admission that the life-giving mother also brings death. It also means that all humans, men and women, are always already—if one wants to use this word—castrated in entering the world as mortals. From a psychoanalytic standpoint, the "respect" for women, demanded not only by Rousseau but also by Kant and the entire eighteenth century, protects the son from discovering that his mother lacks a phallus. Women are kept at a "respectful distance"[15] in order to protect the men from the threat of castration, leaving them with nothing more to fear, not least of all death.

In order to avert the uncanny and castration, the mother is split into the figure of the virgin and of the whore. This splitting enables tidy distinctions between good and bad, natural and artificial, right and wrong, *heimlich* and *unheimlich*. Such valuations persist in the metaphysical oppositions between being and non-being, inside and outside, the familiar and the foreign, life and death, man and woman. For Kofman, these metaphysical binaries are grounded, as I will discuss below, in the same act of violence

---

13. Ibid., p. 104.

14. In the first book of the *Confessions*, Rousseau writes, "My birth cost my mother her life, and was the first of my misfortunes."

15. Cf. Nagl-Docekal 1990.

as the separation of the "good" from the "bad" mother. In all cases, both terms of the opposition repress an original undecidability, the ambivalence preceding the separation. Since the undecidability of life and death, masculine and feminine, *heimlich* and *unheimlich* threatens the subject with death, the subject protects itself through the splitting and externalization of the threatening force. That which is threatening is projected onto the "others," the women, the foreigners, the Jews, the poor, all who, as emblems of the uncanny, must be ultimately disciplined, fought, or killed.

Out of this defense mechanism emerges a knowledge saturated with power. Those trapped in this power are unable to recognize the other independent of its image, to recognize the other in its radical difference and distance beyond all power relationships. Although Rousseau speaks ceaselessly about the mother, he is never concerned with the mother, rather only about his own masculine intactness.

Just as philosophy cannot be severed from life, neither can it be severed from a sexuality that is essential to life; Kofman's deconstruction of metaphysics thus necessarily leads her to the subject of sexual difference and psychoanalysis. The chain of metaphysical oppositions can be seen as an infinite reproduction of a single, always identical binary model: masculine/feminine. Following Nietzsche, Kofman understands concepts such as "the Woman" or "the Eternally Feminine" as male fictions, invented at a certain point in history when men divided humanity into stronger and weaker sexes in order to ascribe to themselves the strength they had already lost. What one calls "woman" is nothing other than the world of images that falls under the heading "the Eternally Feminine." For Kofman, the notion of "Woman" is an illusion, a product of repressed desires crystallized into a unified image. These desires themselves, however, are inextricably bound up with life and the fear of death.

And women? As Kofman emphasizes, they are in no way protected against neurosis formation. Why should they have less to fear of life than men? Women, nevertheless, have more reasons to turn metaphysics and metaphysical oppositions on their heads. It is not, after all, their illusion that constrains them as "women." And since "Woman" is nothing other than a male fiction, it seems only logical for Kofman to disband and blur the opposition between masculine and feminine. This does not mean that sexual difference stops being thematized. On the contrary, in order to wear away sexual difference, it must be thematized until a void opens that allows the other in her irreducibly human singularity to be heard. For the sake of the otherness of every single human, one must refuse the splitting into masculine and feminine categories.

Turning back now to the relationship between life and philosophy, Kofman's attention to the fantasies of individual philosophers sets up her exposure of the fantasies that constitute metaphysics, which, like neurosis, are products of a repression. This fantasy serves as an apotropaic gesture protecting the subject from a confrontation with the damage inflicted by life—death. In this context, Sarah Kofman speaks of a "complicity . . . between philosophic Reason and 'paranoiac' madness."[16]

It is significant that she avoids employing the concept of the unconscious. Freud's understanding of this concept remains, as Kofman emphasizes, itself metaphysical, caught in oppositions and divisions: "The unconscious, a negative term, refers to consciousness, of which it is merely the negation."[17] Kofman wants to neither project psychoanalysis onto the reading nor reduce the text to the neurosis of its author. Her aim rather is to dislodge the text from metaphysics and expose its heterogeneity in order to lay bare the effects of the "original ambivalence."[18] One could also formulate it thus: in her readings, Kofman tries to free philosophy from its calamitous alliance with power. It is an ethically motivated reading committed to the demand "to keep one's word by letting the other speak instead of killing him."[19]

---

16. Kofman 1986a, p. 353; trans. version 1992, p. 54.

17. Kofman 1984a, p. 55 (DB's translation).

18. Freud's speculation becomes particularly clear in his theories on women. Cf. Kofman 1980. On Kofman's readings of Freud see Kofman 1970, 1986b, 1987, 1991.

19. Deuber-Mankowsky and Konnertz 1991, p. 104.

Insofar as Freud's psychoanalysis remains caught in the system of classical metaphysical oppositions such as unconscious/conscious, primary/secondary, dark/light, masculine/feminine, Kofman puts it in quotation marks and cites it in order to rattle it. She shifts the meaning of psychoanalysis to extract it from metaphysics and bring its critical force in this new modality to bear on philosophy. She alters it until the "unconscious" finally appears as "an old name for expressing/saying absolute and radical alterity in Levinas's sense."[20] Kofman wants to extricate "unconscious" from the presumption that it can be mastered, that is to say, from the comprehension of the psychoanalyst. Only when the unconscious becomes untranslatable, unthinkable, does it have a share in life and death. Only then can it be freed from the metaphysical context: "It is truly *unheimlich*, death, the death drive that works in silence, whose work is not the opposite of the clamor that undermines all clamor: the death drive, the mark of radical alterity, of the absolute outside."[21] "Radically other" means existing outside of every relation. Even Levinas's notion of unthematizable alterity is not sufficiently radical in its reliance on a conscious relationship with God; Kofman's thinking of a still more radical alterity forces Levinas's own thought from its theological context. Following Nietzsche, she relocates radical alterity in a this-world humanism. Yet, like Levinas, Kofman also believes that if a new ethics can be founded at all, then it is possible only on the condition of a recognition of "radical alterity."[22] As I propose in the following, she arrives at this conclusion in *Smothered Words*, the book dedicated to her father's memory and in which Kofman poses the question about how to speak about Auschwitz. I intend to connect *Smothered Words* with the later autobiographical text *Rue Ordener, Rue Labat* as both texts display an attempt to write about that which eludes writing and speaking and thus defies integration: the coincidence between the absolute of history and the absolute of Kofman's life history marked by the Shoah.

---

20. Kofman 1984, p. 56.
21. Ibid., p. 89.
22. Cf. Deuber-Mankowsky and Konnertz 1991, p. 107.

## BIOGRAPHY AND PHILOSOPHY

In his introduction to *Enigmas. Essays on Sarah Kofman*, Jean-Luc Nancy remarks that "Sarah wrote for her living, as we say of those who make it their profession, but in her case, over and above the profession, it was not just a question of ensuring a subsistence but of attesting to an existence."[23] Kofman devoted two of her many books to her own life. *Smothered Words* concerns the death of her father in Auschwitz. *Rue Ordener, Rue Labat* (1994), published a year before her death, tells the story of her childhood in occupied France. Neither book is merely biographical. *Rue Ordener, Rue Labat* is above all a book about mothers. Kofman insists repeatedly and quite unequivocally that her personal story "is only of public interest to the extent that it touches collective history."[24] That she discloses these points of contact to her own life protects Kofman from the fall into speculation and should not be understood as a departure from philosophy. Rather, it lends her writing that decidedly historical valence, allowing her personal history to concern all her readers. She exposes her life just as she secures her own existence through writing. She took on the responsibility not only for herself but also for her readers, for our historical existence. Unfortunately, this is remarked on all too seldom. Jean-Luc Nancy also appears not to have noticed.

In a plain and straightforward language, the 23 short segments of *Rue Ordener, Rue Labat* shed light on the stations [*Stationen*] of a traumatic childhood. It all began on the 16th of July, 1942, the day Kofman's father, a rabbi of a small Paris synagogue in the 18th arrondissement, was arrested at his apartment and deported to Auschwitz—taken right from the midst of his family, from his wife and six children. At the time, Kofman was seven years old. She remembers how she and her siblings stood on the street pressed close together, crying. And she remembers how she caught her mother lying that day for the first time. Perhaps in order to protect

---

23. Nancy 1999, p. viii.
24. Deuber-Mankowsky and Konnertz 1991, p. 107.

her husband from deportation, the mother told the police officer that her youngest child had not even turned two yet. But in reality the child's birthday had been two days before. The mother lied (although the lie didn't help) and "the idea that my mother could lie" filled the daughter with shame.[25] Was this humiliated, imperfect mother supposed to be the same mother who had strictly adhered to the laws of the father and who had scared the children into submission with her puppets and stories?

The 16th of July, 1942 is the date on which the "absolute of history" overlaps with the "absolute" of Kofman's personal history[26]: the date when her father was deported to Auschwitz. After this day, everything changed in the child's life. Until that point, the family life had been governed by the holidays, prescribed rites, and kosher prohibitions. The Polish emigrant parents were not assimilated; among themselves they spoke no French, only Yiddish. Kofman acknowledges, "At home a religious atmosphere prevailed."[27] The old life, filled with the presence of the father, whose presence had filled the life of Sarah in turn, ceased on this date.

After the 16th of July, 1942, the children were called "dirty Yids" at school. Jewish communist organizations helped the mother give the children new identities and hide them in the countryside. Sarah was taken up by a farmer, who gave her pork to eat. She cried all the time and refused to eat entirely. Yet Sarah was no hero, she was a child: "This refusal, whose pretext was obedience to my father's law, must have served, without my being completely aware of it, as a means of returning to my mother."[28] Sarah the child was not sensible. She wanted to be with her mother; history did not interest her. "The real danger," she writes, was "separation from my mother."[29]

In recalling her childhood, Kofman neither idealizes nor reproaches herself. Rather she lets the child appear in all of her pa-

---

25. Kofman 1994, p. 7.
26. Kofman 1998, p. 10.
27. Kofman 1994, p. 13.
28. Ibid., p. 24.
29. Ibid., p. 27.

thetic desperation, in all of the obstinacy that brought herself and her mother into mortal danger. It was her demand to be happy that, despite the absence of the father, despite the war and devastation, continued to persist. The wishes of a child are beyond good and evil.

Little Sarah was sent back to her mother in Paris. For a short time, she lived in the old apartment on the Rue Ordener until it was destroyed by the German Gestapo. The mother asked a child-doting former neighbor for help. This is how the mother and daughter moved in with the "the lady on the Rue Labat," where the actual drama of *Rue Ordener, Rue Labat* begins. Rue Ordener was the world of the mother, of the ritual laws of the father, of kosher prohibitions, of the old life, of Judaism, of strictness, of poverty. Rue Labat stood for the lady with the fair and friendly eyes, the rescuer who gave books to Sarah, never screamed, and knew no laws; the one who was certain, sovereign, and sure of victory. Soon the lady had Sarah call her "Mémé," let her pass for her own child, dressed her differently, changed her haircut, and gave her "healthy" food—raw horsemeat in broth—until Sarah didn't vomit anymore. The lady brought about a real transformation in Sarah. And Sarah liked it. While the mother suffered alone in her room, Sarah learned from Mémé that she had a Jewish nose, that Jewish food was unhealthy, and that the Jews had crucified "our" Lord Jesus. The "lady on the Rue Labat" was, as Kofman tells us, not without anti-Semitism. Although she took in the Jewish woman and her daughter, she did it just as she would have taken in and fed a cat; her help was not political. Her "tour de force" was to detach Sarah from her mother and from Judaism right under her mother's nose. The child wanted to be happy, and with "Mémé" she could be.

So, in the middle of a war, her father doomed to die in Auschwitz, Sarah lived with two mothers, a good one and a bad one, in an idyll from which she was to be shaken suddenly on the day of liberation. The "bad" mother wanted her daughter back. The child didn't want to go back. There was a trial. The "good" mother won, but the "bad" one refused to recognize the court decision and took her child back by force. Kofman writes that, deep down, she felt relieved.

Sarah spent the rest of her childhood arguing with and fleeing from her mother. She was often sick and had long stays in
hospitals and boarding schools. Only much later did the experiences with her two mothers become interpretable and describable.
In coming to terms with these experiences, Kofman is no less critical
of herself than others. She makes no exception for herself when
she asserts that an author is "never a transcendental and objective,
sexually neutral subject." It stands to reason that the drama of "Rue
Ordener, Rue Labat" represents a paradigmatic experience that
Kofman lived through and wrote down again and again, a supposition that is supported by Kofman's own allusion to this experience.
In recalling the memory of one of her favorite films, Hitchcock's *A
Lady Vanishes*, she focuses on a particular scene that seizes her. One
of the main female leading roles, the good old Miss Froy, turns out
to be a secret agent for the Intelligence Service. "The part that is
always unbearable for me is to perceive, all of a sudden, instead of
the good maternal face of the old lady . . . the face of her replacement. . . . It is a horribly hard, shifty face, and just as one is expecting to see the good lady's sweet, smiling one, there it is instead
—menacing and false." Using a pictorial metaphor, Kofman alludes
to why the scene is so unbearable while conveying that knowledge
about it does nothing to diminish its unbearability: "The bad breast
in place of the good, the one utterly separate from the other, the
one changing into the other."[30]

Unlike Rousseau, Kofman is an extremely exacting listener and
critical reader. She knows how quickly desire leads the text into
phantasmagoria and narcissism. Her own writing becomes, accordingly, a writing turned against itself, a writing against repression,
a writing that reveals that the experience with the good and the
bad mother amounted to a trauma. And only this insight makes it
possible for Kofman to redeem both mothers from their being split
apart, thereby keeping to her formulation of an "ethical exigency"
for a "writing without power."[31]

---

30. Ibid., p. 66.
31. Cf. Kofman 1998, pp. 10, 35, 41.

If Kofman's childhood memory is a labor of love for the mother, then it is not through reparation, but through her refusal to distinguish between her good and bad mothers. Only on the condition of this refusal is love conceivable and possible as a relation that excludes all relation, as a gift without expecting something in return.[32] "It is that which separates, leaves at an unbridgeable distance (in a relation which maintains a caesura such that the other forms neither a duality nor a unity with the self), which forms an authentic relation."[33]

"Authentic relation" means recognizing the other in her radical alterity, in her infinite distance, in her irreducible humanity: it means, in short, "keeping one's word to the other."[34] This love is the alternative to killing, to forgetting the other. This love does not come by itself but presupposes, as all ethical behavior does, a decision. It is the decision to make no image of the other for yourself.

In contrast to an idealistic ethics, however, one can neither expect thanks nor reward from such a love. Nor can one expect punishment, when it comes to an end. The ethics meant by Kofman has to do neither with God nor with Reason. On the contrary, Kofman breaks radically with the idea of an ethical subject of reason identical with itself. One should not imagine oneself as an angel, but as a wounded, living being, affirming life in order to let the other live.

## WRITING WITHOUT POWER

After the war, all that Kofman's mother heard of her father was the news of his death. Introducing the account of her childhood memories in *Rue Ordener, Rue Labat*, Kofman observes the following about her father and her writing:

---

32. Cf. Kofman 1993, p. 66; the chapter "Le psychologue de l'Éternel feminin" (pp. 49–72) in which the passage appears has been translated by Madeleine Dobie as "The Psychologist of the Eternal Feminine (Why I Write Such Good Books, 5)" (Kofman 1995, p. 185f).

33. Kofman 1998, p. 30.

34. Deuber-Mankowsky and Konnertz 1991, p. 107.

Of him all I have left is the fountain pen. I took it one day from my mother's purse, where she kept it along with some other souvenirs of my father. It is a kind of pen no longer made, the kind you have to fill with ink. I used it all through school. It "failed" me before I could bring myself to give it up. I still have it, patched up with Scotch tape; it is right in front of me on my desk and makes me write, write. Maybe all my books have been detours required to bring me to write about "that."[35]

Under difficult circumstances, in spite of poverty and her mother's resistance, Sarah Kofman went to the Lycée and then studied philosophy at the university. Why philosophy?

Everything that happened demanded an explanation. But for years I repressed all problems, all thoughts of the terror. I was unable to pronounce the name of my father. The theoretical work helped me with the repression: I had no image of the horror. Philosophy is the most abstract of all disciplines, one can speak about something without having to see it. I speak about death, but I can't see it. I made no images for myself—that saved me.[36]

Between 1970 and 1994, Sarah Kofman published 25 books. She spoke of death again and again, just as she spoke of life. She never stopped insisting, along with Freud, Derrida, and, time and again, Nietzsche, that life can only be affirmed when death is accepted as part of the deal. Yet it was not until 1987 that she wrote about her father's death, about her "absolute, which communicates with the absolute of history."[37] In Smothered Words, Kofman ties the biographical—the death of her father—with her reading of two literary texts, Maurice Blanchot's "The Idyll" and Robert Antelme's report about the horrors of the concentration camps, The Human Race.

Smothered Words begins with Theodor Adorno's reformulation of Kant's categorical imperative. Adorno demands that we "arrange

35. Kofman 1994, p. 3.
36. Cited in Altweg 1988, p. 16.
37. Kofman 1998, pp. 9–10.

. . . [our] thoughts and actions so that Auschwitz will not repeat itself, so that nothing similar will happen." As always, when Kofman cites, she places the quotation in a new context; she "shakes" it and gives it a new meaning. She introduces the Adorno quotation with an "if": "If, since Auschwitz, the categorical imperative has become the one which Adorno has formulated in the style of Kant, though ridding it of its abstract and ideal generality . . . ," then

> it behooves me, as a Jewish woman intellectual who has sur-
> vived the Holocaust, to pay homage to Blanchot for the frag-
> ments on Auschwitz scattered throughout his texts: writing
> of the ashes, writing of the disaster which avoids the trap of
> complicity with speculative knowledge, with that in it which
> is tied to power, and thereby complicit with the tortures of
> Auschwitz.[38]

Kofman reads Adorno with Blanchot and Blanchot with Adorno in order to pose once again Adorno's reformulation of the categorical imperative as a question. Her book about Auschwitz is dedicated to this question, which she shifts from action to writing and language. How, she asks, can one remember, how can one speak about what happened in Auschwitz, a name "which designates that which has no name"?[39] Kofman specifies the question yet again: "To speak: it is necessary—*without (the) power*: without allowing language, too powerful, sovereign, to master the most aporetic situation, absolute powerlessness and very distress [sic], to enclose it in the clarity and happiness of daylight."[40] As the title of *Smothered Words* implies, language has to be turned against itself.

Because he recognized this necessity, Blanchot deserves homage. Before Kofman comes to speak of the 1935 story "The Idyll," she recalls that after *The Folly of the Day*, Blanchot eliminated the word *story* from all of his texts. *The Folly of the Day* was written in

---

38. Ibid., pp. 7–8.
39. On Kofman's implicit reference to traditional patterns of remembering, see Erdle 1995.
40. Kofman 1998, pp. 9–10.

1941 and deals with the impossibility of telling a story after Auschwitz or about Auschwitz. After Auschwitz every story—any coherent history of events—will be a story from before Auschwitz. By
implication, even the story of "The Idyll" cannot be understood to
anticipate the "unimaginable" of Auschwitz.

In the 1991 interview cited above, Kofman remarks:

> Originally, I had written *Smothered Words* for a special num-
> ber of *Cahiers de l'Herne* to be devoted to Blanchot (but which
> then didn't happen). For this reason my reflection on the con-
> centration camps began with Blanchot's view of the Jews and
> the interpretation he suggests of Antelme's book. This point of
> departure explains the fact—surprising for some—that, in a text
> where I speak about the death of my father and Antelme's con-
> centration camp experience, I could also conduct a reading of
> a literary text, Blanchot's "The Idyll." The reading was almost
> never mentioned by the press. For myself, however, the con-
> nection between the biographical (my father) with my reflec-
> tion on Antelme's unique and excellent book and the reading
> of a literary text was essential: indeed, I wanted to show that,
> according to Blanchot, literature cannot foresee the horror of
> the camps; for, whatever situation literature describes, it is by
> its nature idyllic; the comparison between a lived experience
> of the camps and a literary work, however full of expression it
> may be, can only be an insult to the misery.[41]

"The Idyll" tells the story of a stranger arriving in a community. The community forces him to renounce his foreignness because it threatens to destroy the idyll. Upon his arrival, he has to
clean himself in a large showering facility until, exhausted, he loses
consciousness. Instead of offering him something to eat, as hospi-
tality would demand, the community gives him a forced baptism.
Before he is allowed into the community, he has to rid himself of
all mud, of everything which comes from the "outside"; he must
purge himself of his foreignness. In subjugating him to discipline

---

41. Deuber-Mankowsky and Konnertz 1991, p. 104.

and the order of the house (order and hygiene being the hallmarks of idylls), they make him perform the absurd task of hauling stones into a pit from which they will be taken away anyway by trucks.

In her reading, Kofman focuses on the moments of the story that could be understood as anticipating the concentration camps in order to deny this possibility all the more categorically. No story can anticipate Auschwitz or be about Auschwitz. In its apparent similarity with Auschwitz, "The Idyll" is particularly suited to show this impossibility. For the story makes apparent how language itself is idyllic. Language is always directed toward uncovering the existing, the universal, and meaning—everything that remains and not that which disappears, that which becomes foreign. In Blanchot's story, it is the nightly cries that give voice to what Kofman calls the "affliction intrinsic to language," "to the loss of death, of difference, of the outside and the alien."[42] Already the opposition of day and night, happiness and death, inside and outside, of the foreign and the familiar—all binary opposites that structure the story—are signs for the denial of the undecidability preceding those oppositions. By means of "beautiful names,"[43] language covers up its forgetting and masters it. Kofman speaks accordingly of the "lie which [language] dissimulates."[44] The "affliction inherent in language"—its striving for sense and meaning—makes it into an accomplice of metaphysics and speculative knowledge. In order to speak of Auschwitz, language must be turned against language itself. In order to speak without power, one needs to make a detour via the written word.

Auschwitz is the absolute of power, the absolute of history.[45] Citing Blanchot, Kofman writes that this event inflicted on the whole of humanity "the decisive blow which left nothing intact,"[46] least of all language. Faced with the absolute of power, one can only swallow his words and close them in his breast. And yet they

---

42. Kofman 1998, pp. 26–27.
43. Ibid.
44. Ibid.
45. Ibid., p. 10.
46. Ibid.

must be spoken for the sake of the victims so as not to concede to the perpetrators that they were right.

Why does language have this weight? Because only in language —even if turned against itself—can a relation be remembered that escapes all power, a relation therefore that escapes even Auschwitz. It is the relation to the "infinitely Distant," to the "absolutely foreign," to "radical alterity"; it is the relation that connects each individual with death, with his or her own mortality. This paradoxical relation to the truly *unheimlich*, to the individual, to indivisible death, connects each subject with the "absolute outside," thereby releasing the subject from the clutches of power, and, indeed, constituting the subject as an individual in the first place. Power becomes absolute at the point at which it crosses the limit of the individual. Accordingly, in order to become literal masters of death, the SS henchmen tried to de-individualize the concentration camp prisoners, to dehumanize them, to transform them into animals and beasts.

This is where Kofman's biography coincides with the absolute of history. This coincidence of the biographical with the absolute makes definitely clear why, after Auschwitz, Kofman thinks an autobiographical text that tells the story of a life as history, a life history, is just as impossible and linked with power as every idyll. Just as the self cannot be removed from life through writing, so, conversely, life cannot be described without death. Otherwise life itself is immediately sacrificed. Speaking without power, one has to speak so as not to forget the dead, so that one "does not forget the other." In order to do this, one has to speak of (one's own) life without forming that life into a story.[47]

---

47. Unlike Marguerite Duras who, in her novel *La Douleur*, wrote an autobiographical text about her separation from Robert Antelme after his return from the concentration camp, Kofman is interested in the connection between reading and life in order to avoid the immediacy of autobiographical gestures. Kofman distances herself explicitly from Duras's text: "My aim was not, as was Marguerite Duras's, to put myself at the center of a drama, it was rather to understand an historical fact." However dramatic it may be, a directly autobiographical text is an idyllic text; it is always a form of speculation, making it unsuitable for remembering the dead. In this context, Kofman points out that after Antelme died, one could only hear talk of Duras: "R. Antelme has just died (25 October, 1990), almost all newspapers have taken the opportunity of this death to speak of Duras." See also Erdle 1995, p. 46.

The biographical for Kofman is "my father."[48] Her father was buried alive, because, while in the death camp, he wanted to observe Shabbat. He was killed because he wanted to reestablish "in this situation of extreme powerlessness and violence, a relation beyond all power."[49] Degraded to a bundle of bodily needs by the SS officers, he respected Jewish monotheism at this unmentionable "place." In doing so, Kofman writes, he "maintain[ed] a relation to that which excludes all relation: the infinitely Distant, the absolutely Foreign."[50] For Kofman, maintaining this relation shows the limits of power. Because no form of power can overcome this relation to the infinite ". . . other than by denying it, burying it in a pit with a shovel, without ever having encountered it."[51] It shows the limit of what humans can do to others humans. Yet, at the same time, it reveals that there is no limit to the destruction of humans.

Thus when she speaks of her father and the other prisoners, she does it only in a language that gives space for the recognition of the relation connecting every human with the "absolutely foreign" or "infinite." Kofman specifies what writing without power entails in the following: "When writing, one must try to leave room for the silence of those who cannot speak: such is a writing 'without power.' It must allow the immeasurable, the irreducible of man to appear, beyond all the force and violence that have attempted to reduce him, or even to wipe him out."[52]

## ALTERITY AND THE SUBLIME

Twice Kofman calls Robert Antelme's *The Human Race* "sublime."[53] His book about the experiences of concentration camp prisoners is not "beautiful" but "sublime" because

---

48. Cf. Deuber-Mankowsky and Konnertz 1991, p. 104.
49. Kofman 1998, p. 34.
50. Ibid.
51. Ibid., p. 35.
52. Deuber-Mankowsky and Konnertz 1991, p. 104.
53. Kofman 1998, p. 40.

it can make us understand the silence of those who could not speak, the "true speech" that is one with the silent presence of the other (*autrui*), prevented from expressing itself in the camps; forbidden, yet also withheld, preserved, protected against all straying, all corruption, against all violent abuse that might have exposed it to the suspicion of playing along with the boundless violence, and therefore have discredited it forever and "definitely compromised the future of communication."[54]

It is no accident that Kofman invokes the notion of the sublime and quotes Blanchot's concern about the "future of communication" in connection with her call for a writing without power. All three formulations in different ways bring up questions about ethics, humanism, and the possibility of a "we," "we people," after Auschwitz. Kant had already associated the sublime with the formation of the idea of humanity that leads beyond the singular human. Nature's immeasurability, according to Kant, not only exposes human powerlessness, but also "reveals a faculty of estimating ourselves as independent of nature, and discovers a superiority above nature that is the foundation of a self-preservation of quite another kind from that which may be impugned and brought into danger by external nature. This saves humanity in our own person from humiliation, even though as mortals we have to submit to external violence."[55] Has this idea of humanity not been entirely corrupted by the fact of the Shoah?

Kofman seconds Antelme when he writes against this ultimate corruption of the idea of humanity. His book is sublime because he fulfills the ethical demand latent in the "humankind" of the title. The book makes clear that in man there is "a multiplicity of powers, none of which is ever sure to triumph."[56] Belonging to these forces, Kofman writes, is the power to kill and forget the other. Yet at the same time, there is also the power to acknowledge the other, to keep one's word, recognizing the other in his humanity and radi-

---

54. Ibid.
55. Kant 1952, Book II, B. "The Dynamically Sublime in Nature," p. SS 28.
56. Ibid., p. 72.

cal alterity while not making him into an emblem, not making him into a nonhuman, letting him live.

Another reason that Antelme's book is sublime according to Kofman is that his memory has given space to the silence of the voiceless prisoners. Unlike Kant, Kofman does not connect the idea of the sublime with establishing boundaries between humankind and nature, but rather with the possibility of a form of communication in which a space is returned to those who were excluded and reduced to their physical nature. Antelme's book is a writing without power, because he shows how the prisoners resisted the power with which the SS tried to make them subhuman. Antelme tells how "the deportees constantly felt that their belonging to the species was challenged, because the will of those who were supposed to belong to a 'higher' species, that of the gods, was to make them confuse themselves with animals by forcing them to 'live' in conditions worse than those of animals."[57]

Ultimately, then, Antelme's book is sublime because it illuminates, without compromising the vulnerability and suffering of the prisoners or diminishing the brutality of the SS officers, the question of why the prisoners, even under such conditions, still wanted to live. The book reveals where the SS members did not succeed in turning themselves into gods and the deportees into nonhumans. By holding on to life, the prisoners demonstrated that the irreducibly human consists in the will to live. By wanting to survive, the prisoners attested: "We men: we the detainees, we are not animals; and you the SS are not gods. We are all nothing more or less than men, and there is nothing inhuman or superhuman in man."[58]

Kofman's reading of *The Human Race* celebrates the prisoners' will to survive. Insofar as they wanted to live and to continue to live, they affirmed the unity of the human race. Kofman asks at the end whether Antelme's book perhaps vouches for the old humanism. Do we not run the risk of denying the difference between

---

57. Ibid., p. 58.
58. Ibid., pp. 60–61.

perpetrator and victim when we insist on the unity of the species? She answers this question in the negative. To insist on the unity of the human species is to stipulate that precisely no confraternity is possible with the SS men who did everything in their power to destroy this unity. The strongest community, argues Kofman, is the community of those without a community. This community is not founded upon a difference or a boundary against something else, but alone "on a shared power to choose, to make incompatible through correlative choices, the power to kill and the power to respect and safeguard the incommensurable distance, the relation without relation."[59]

As Kofman insistently makes clear, to hold onto the concept of the unity of the species is to enjoin a writing without power and, conversely, to affirm the power to safeguard the unfathomable distance. For this reason, the possibility of a new ethics cannot be founded upon an overcoming of the trauma, according to Kofman, but rather on the possibility of a "we" that is always already dissolved and destabilized.

Kofman's tremendous achievement in *Smothered Words* is to remove the aesthetic of the sublime from the context of Kant's philosophy and, in a Nietzschean move, relate it to life as the radical alterity that establishes the "unity" of the human race.[60] Following Blanchot, Kofman understands Jewish Monotheism, the religion of her father, as "the revelation of the word as the place in which men maintain a relation to that which excludes all relation"[61]: the infinitely Distant. According to Kant, it is the infinite that escapes all representation; and according to Nietzsche, it is life which, as the *"wahrhaft Unheimliche,"* [the true uncanny] cannot be distinguished from death. Following Kofman's articulation of

---

59. Ibid., p. 70.
60. For the discussion on the sublime triggered by Jean Francois Lyotard in the 1980s, see Christine Pries (1989) and Renate Homann (1994). In contrast to Lyotard's understanding of the sublime, which cannot be further elaborated here, Kofman relates the sublime to Nietzsche's concept of life as "Baubô," thereby removing the sublime of its Idealism and divesting it of its idyllic moments.
61. Kofman 1998, p. 52.

Kant and Nietzsche, that which cannot be represented is exactly this undecidability between life and death that precedes all oppositions. Hence the new unity of the human race means nothing other than that there is nothing inhuman. Kofman's recourse to Kant circumvents every new attempt to yoke the concept of humanity to a process of elimination, in which others, foreigners, are made into nonhumans. The new unity of humanity reduces the concept of the human to the basic facticity of life and death.[62] The "human" thus becomes a concept no longer suitable for grounding oppositions.

Radical alterity is that which stands outside of every relation. It is *that of which no one can make an image.* In this way, Kofman's thinking of radical alterity goes back surprisingly and unsuspectingly to the Second Commandment as interpreted by Kant, who, in the Third Critique, binds the feeling of the sublime with an infinity that demands an imageless presentation and who accordingly adds to his reflections on sublime presentation the following thought: "Perhaps there is no more sublime passage in the Jewish Law than the commandment: Thou shalt not make unto thee any graven image, or any likeness of any thing that is in heaven or on earth, or under the earth, &c."[63]

If Kofman reduces the concept of human to the irreducible, to the facticity of life, then the demand to recognize the other, the highest ethical exigency for writing without power, can be attributed to the oldest biblical commandment: You will not make any image for yourself of God.

## REFERENCES

Agamben, G. (1999). *Remnants of Auschwitz: The Witness and the Archive*, trans. D. Heller-Roazen. New York: Zone Books.

---

62. For a more recent exploration of this concept of the human, see Agamben 1999.

63. Kant 1952, Book II, B. "The Dynamically Sublime in Nature," "General Remark upon the Exposition of Aesthetic Reflective Judgments," p. SS 29.

Altweg, J. (1988). Introduction. In *Smothered Words* [German trans.: *Erstickte Worte*], by S. Kofman. Vienna: Edition Passagen.

Deuber-Mankowsky, A., and Konnertz, U. (1991). Schreiben ohne macht. Ein gespräch mit Sarah Kofman. *Die Philosophin. Forum für feministische Theorie und Philosophie* 3.

Erdle, B. R. (1995). Bezeugen, verstehen, vergleichen: Spuren der Tradition der Erinnerung in Sarah Kofman's 'Paroles suffoquées.' *Die Philosophin* 12:38–53.

Freud, S. (1953–1973). The uncanny. *Standard Edition of the Complete Psychological Works of Sigmund Freud*, Vol. XVII, trans. and ed. J. Strachey, pp. 217–252. London: Hogarth.

Homann, R. (1994). Zu neueren Versuchen einer Reaktualisierung des Erhabenen. Lyotard's Utilisierung einer ästhetischen Kategorie für eine neue Ethik. *Zeitschrift für philosophische Forschung* 48:43–68.

Kant, I. (1952). *The Critique of Judgment*, trans. J. C. Meredith. Oxford, UK: Clarendon.

Kofman, S. (1970). *L'enfance de l'art: Une interpretation de l'esthétique freudienne*. Paris: Payot. [Trans.: *The Childhood of Art: An Interpretation of Freud's Aesthetics*, trans. W. Woodhull. New York: Columbia University Press, 1988.]

——— (1980). *L' enigme de la femme, la femme dans les textes de Freud*. Paris: Galilée. [Trans.: *The Enigma of Woman: Woman in Freud's Writings*, trans. C. Porter. Ithaca, NY and London: Cornell University Press, 1985.]

——— (1984a). Graphématique et psychanalyse. In *Lectures de Derrida*. Paris: Galilée.

——— (1984b). Philosophie terminée, philosophie interminable. In *Lectures de Derrida*. Paris: Galilée.

——— (1986a). Les fins phallocratiques de Rousseau. *Cahiers de l'ACFAS* 44 (special number: "Égalité et différence des Sexes"):358. [Trans.: Rousseau's phallocratic ends. In *Revaluing French Feminism: Critical Essays on Difference, Agency, and Culture*, trans. M. Dukats, ed. N. Fraser and S. L. Bartky. Bloomington and Indianapolis: Indiana University Press, 1992.]

——— (1986b). *Pourquoi rit-on? Freud et le mot d'espirit*. Paris: Galilée.

——— (1987). *Conversions*: Le Marchand de Venise *sous le signe de Saturne*. Paris: Galilée. [Trans.: Conversions: *The Merchant of Venice* under the sign of Saturn. In *Literary Theory Today*, trans. S. Whiteside, ed.

P. Collier and H. Geyer-Ryan, pp. 142–166. Cambridge, UK: Polity, 1990.]

———— (1991). Il n'y a que le premier pas qui coûte. In *Freud et la speculation*. Paris: Galilée. [Trans.: It's only the first step that costs. In *Speculations After Freud: Psychoanalysis, Philosophy and Culture*, trans. S. Wykes, ed. S. Shamdasani and M. Münchow, pp. 97–131. London and New York: Routledge, 1994.]

———— (1993). *Explosion II: Les enfants de Nietzsche*. Paris: Galilée.

———— (1994). *Rue Ordener, Rue Labat*, trans. A. Smock. Lincoln and London: University of Nebraska Press.

———— (1995). The psychologist of the eternal feminine (Why I write such good books, 5), trans. M. Dobie. *Yale French Studies* 87 (special number: "Another Look, Another Woman: Retranslations of French Feminism"):185f.

———— (1998). *Smothered Words*, trans. M. Dobie. Evanston, IL: Northwestern University Press.

Nagl-Docekal, H., ed. (1990). Die ökonomie der achtung. In *Feministische Philosophie*, pp. 41–63. Vienna: Oldenbourg.

Nancy, J.-L. (1999). Foreword. Run, Sarah! In *Enigmas. Essays on Sarah Kofman*, ed. P. Deutscher and K. Oliver. Ithaca, NY, and London: Cornell University Press.

Pries, C., ed. (1989). *Das Erhabene. Zwischen Grenzerfahrung und Grössenwahn*. Weinheim: VCH, Act Humaniora.

Rousseau, J.-J. (1966). *Emile*. Paris: Garnier-Flammarion.

# 8

# Transnational Adoption: The Ethics and Politics of New Family Stories

DRUCILLA CORNELL

If you are an adopting parent, a birth parent, or an adopted person, you are part of the story of adoption, but you are also one of the people who shape the story. From the moment one decides to become an adopting parent, all the details of one's life are exposed to the legal systems of the states involved in the adoption process. The process of adoption, for an adopting parent, is about becoming passable and acceptable as a parent. For the mother who relinquishes her baby, it is very different: it's about divesting herself of her parental role. Adoption agencies and prospective parents frame children through the law and other political means. And while the frame establishes the scope of possible relationships and the stories that can accompany them, adoption stories and relationships can create new pathways of love that defy the exclusionary and hierarchical systems that seem to inform them in the first instance. To the degree that they ever become "ours," the stories and relationships of adoption are ones of disruption. They proceed from embattled engagements with the international and transnational institutions that pigeonhole citizens of the world into triangulated positions—birth parents, adopting parents, adopted children. These institutions create such a triangle through strict adherence to heterosexual and culturally specific norms of kinship—norms that, for many involved in the adoption process, are anything but normatively desirable.

My adopted daughter, Sarita Graciela Kellow Cornell, was born in Paraguay in 1992. I adopted her from Paraguay in April 1993. In 1997, my daughter became a naturalized U.S. citizen. At the naturalization proceedings, I was one among a group of several hundred adopting parents from the United States. After our naturalization papers had been verified, both the adopting parents and the adopted children were given flags of the United States and allowed to join a ceremony. The mood was celebratory. An official from the Immigration and Naturalization Services[1] congratulated us for our generosity of spirit, our good will, and our courage. After all, we had traveled to a "third world country" in order to adopt our babies. As the official droned on, I kept imagining the struggle of Gladys Gomez to have her baby returned to her. In 1996, Diane Jean Schemo had written a *New York Times* article about how babies were being stolen in Paraguay and described Gomez and her plight:

> Gladys Gómez's shoes are torn, her fingernails ragged and her blouse threadbare. But the picture she keeps in her pocket, of the daughter who disappeared almost three years ago, is still crisp, wrapped in plastic like a personal shrine. Miss Gómez, 23, said she left her daughter, Cintia Carolina, then 14 months old, in the care of a cousin while she went to visit her godmother nearby on the night of Aug. 28, 1993. When Miss Gómez returned a few hours later, her only child had disappeared. Relatives told her that the cousin, who is being detained on charges of stealing the child, had sold Cintia for international adoption.[2]

---

1. The former INS has been integrated into the Department of Homeland Security.
2. Schemo 1996.

I imagine Gomez trying to get her daughter back. I imagine the horrible, earth-shattering panic and anxiety that she must feel over her daughter's disappearance and her attendant hope that maybe she can be recovered. But then the tragic realization hits that she is gone. What follows are the lost years—the years marked by radical absence and despair that she will never get back. But despite all odds and obstacles, Gomez remained determined. She did not give up and, at the time Schemo wrote her article, Gomez believed that she had discovered that a couple from the United States had adopted her daughter in 1994. But did she ever get her daughter back? I wonder. I try to reassure myself that I followed the letter and spirit of Paraguayan law. Sarita was not kidnapped. Or rather, Mabel Delgado Barrio was not kidnapped—that was the name Gabriella Delgado Barrio gave to the little girl I renamed Sarita.

I listen to the INS official talk about the adopted Paraguayan children having won in "the great lottery" of life because we had given them the ultimate prize, U.S. citizenship—a prize coveted throughout the world. The official presumes they would have had little chance for a meaningful life because of the poverty, cultural deprivation, and corrupt government in their country of origin. But the presumption goes one step further: "our" children were worse off than even normal downtrodden, third world children because they had been born to women who could not take care of them and abandoned them. The official is absolutely confident that this is a salvation story, and that these children have won. Clearly, Gomez did not think that the kidnapping of her daughter was an act of deliverance—either for herself or for her daughter.

After the speech, the parents read the citizenship oath because the vast majority of the children cannot read. I leave out the phrases that do not apply to my daughter. I had petitioned to have my daughter retain her Paraguayan citizenship. The petition was granted, and when Sarita turns 21, she will have to choose whether she wants to keep her Paraguayan citizenship. I want to get outside as quickly as possible to escape what I see as an orgy of disrespect for the diverse peoples to which these children had initially been born. I go from feeling embarrassed, to guilty, to completely horrified by the thoughtlessness of the INS official, who seems to have no idea about the political and ethical complexity of a transnational adoption. A transnational adoption implicates all the layers of global injustice that I try to fight against, but as an adopting mother, I am also a participant in this system. That is the inescapable paradox that Gayatri Spivak captures in her extraordinary phrase "enabling violation." Due to the extreme economic inequalities that separate countries in the global North and the global South, many children are left in serious poverty. These inequalities are created and sustained by the very countries that allow some of us the resources to adopt in the first place. Thus, what can be enabling for certain children—parents who adopt them and, in many cases, enable them to stay alive—is inseparable from the violation perpetuated through systematic inequalities. Throughout her work, Spivak speaks of the postcolonial condition as itself an enabling violation. Being part of the scene of adoption forces us to acknowledge the great extent to which the postcolonial predicament is about the continuing legitimation of inequalities between the global North and global South.

By 1997, I had realized that there was no avoiding the enabling violation inherent in a transnational adoption. Both my relationship to Sarita and the frame of that relationship had to be confronted. My critique of the official story does not prevent me from being part of the official story of Sarita's citizenship and U.S. global political hegemony. At the time of Sarita's adoption, I was so scared of the adoption process, what with all its state trappings. I saw this and yet didn't see it. I had myopic vision: I could see only the next step in what seemed an endless process. Much of what I knew about the egregious inequalities that define so many of the relations between nations of the world blurred in the frightening whirl of the adoption process.

When I first arrived in Paraguay in April 1993 to adopt my daughter, I was shattered by the fact that I was on the wrong side of the adoption issue. I was staying at the Gran Hotel del Paraguay. It was a hot night. The street outside the hotel was full of throngs of demonstrators, who held up placards that exclaimed: "Yankees go Home!"; "Child Kidnappers!"; "Paraguayan children for Paraguay!" U.S. citizens were told that if they left the hotel, they would be in danger. There was to be an election on May 9. All the parties had one thing in common: they promised to outlaw all adoptions to the United States. I tried my best to hear the message of the demonstrators. It took two years for the new government to suspend adoptions to the United States. By 1995, Paraguay, a nation of only 4 million people, had become the largest supplier of adopted children to the United States. The suspension honored all adoptions that were in process. Paraguay was not alone in implementing anti-adoption legislation. The Hague Convention on the Protection of Children and Cooperation in Respect of Intercountry Adoption (THC) had been passed in 1995. THC was recommended by the Hague Convention on international law, which facilitates and oversees treaties. The goals of the THC are to "set minimum standards for intercountry adoption that will allow recognition among the party countries, protect the interests of children, both birth parents and adoptive parents, and prevent illegal trafficking."[3] The United States has yet to ratify the THC. Examination of the official U.S. government statistics confirms that, between 1996 and 1997, Chile, Costa Rica, the Dominican Republic, Ecuador, Honduras, El Salvador, and Peru significantly diminished or altogether banned adoptions, regardless of whether countries have ratified the THC. By the time of my daughter's naturalized citizenship ceremony in 1997, the existence of the THC already had a worldwide impact on the politics of transnational adoption.

Although it may be true to some degree that "a wrong life cannot be lived rightly"—as Theodor W. Adorno wrote—most of us try to live life rightly, making judgments of right and wrong because we have no choice but to make them. I was thrown into the political and ethical fray of transnational adoption when I participated in Sarita's citizenship ceremony. I had to make a decision about how to proceed politically and ethically. I did not have the option of suspending judgment. I was an adopting mother but also a lifelong leftist. These warring identities were the product of the

---

3. Simon and Altstein 2000, p. 33.

enabling violation of the adoption process. I continue to tell Sarita the following: You can live a good life in Paraguay if you want. You might well choose to do so. You have that option. The official story, of course, tells her precisely the opposite: only an adopting mother from the U.S. can give her a future; only assimilation into the receiving country will give her a rebirth and allow her to live happily ever after as a U.S. citizen.

The simple, linear narrative of assimilation may indeed be a soothing story to some adopting parents. Nevertheless, I suspect that many of the adopting parents I met at the citizenship ceremony felt as uneasy as I did at being cast as supporters of U.S. hegemony. They probably felt no less uneasy about the moralistic fervor fueling the notion that "children are being saved." After all, as soon as a child is brought from one country to another, the child's own life story inevitably changes. Indeed, in our thoroughly racialized society, a transnational adoption necessarily becomes a transracial and transethnic adoption. The new country deploys different markers of race and ethnicity that make the child conspicuously different from his or her adopting family. Until about fifteen years ago, parents and children were matched so that the adopting family and its new child looked "as if" it were a natural family. No one was supposed to see the difference. And the adopting families could only be a "normal" heterosexual couple with women accepting their "proper" domestic role. In other words, women who wanted to adopt could not work. Single mothers were out of the question as prospective adopting parents. Gay, lesbian, and transgendered parents were also completely excluded because, by definition, they did not remotely resemble the "normal" heterosexual couple. The transnational adoption of children of color creates families that cannot pass "as if" they were natural families. In this way, both the U.S. naturalized citizenship ceremony and the "American" assimilation narrative belie the full impact and complexity of the prefix "trans." As Aihwa Ong notes, "[T]rans denotes both moving through space and across lines, as well as changing the nature of something. Besides suggesting new relations between nation states and capital, transnationality also alludes to transversal, the transactional, the translational, and the transgressive aspects of contemporary behavior and imagination that are incited, enabled, and regulated by the changing logics of states and capitalism."[4]

Transnational adoption thus shows how idealized the traditional adoption narrative is. This is important since that narrative is hardly innocuous. In fact, it has caused great suffering and what Betty Lifton calls "cumulative trauma" in adopted children, even in those adoptions that do not cross racial, ethnic, and national boundaries. Herself an adoptee, Lifton was one of the first writers to define adoption as a trauma for the adopted child and as a scene of haunting for all the people involved in the adoption. Lifton searched for her own birth mother and ultimately found her, even though her adoption records were sealed. Lifton has devoted much of her life to testifying to the inhumanity of "sealed records," particularly the way they erect a seemingly insurmountable barrier to the child's past. Initially, the public justification for sealed records was to guarantee that children could avoid being labeled illegitimate. As Lifton explains,

> [t]he original purpose . . . was to protect the newborns from the stigma of being born out of wedlock. . . . Social workers urged the courts to seal away the baby's birth certificate, which was stamped illegitimate, and to issue an "amended" one that substituted the names of the adoptive parents for those of the birth parents. As the policy of sealing records spread rapidly from state to state after World War II, however, it lost sight of its original purpose and became a means of protecting the adoptive family from interference by the birth family. Secrecy effectively pitted adoptive mothers against birth mothers and kept adopted children separated from their birth families.[5]

In the justification that the birth mother's privacy is being protected, we still hear the echoes of the purported shamefulness of the act that brought the illegitimate baby into the world. In

---

4. Ong 1999, p. 2.
5. Lifton 1995, p. 24.

Lifton's own case, her birth mother did not want to meet with her publicly because she did not want her son or even her neighbors to know of her shameful past. The secrecy is a symptom of the culture of legal normalization in which certain children and parents are deemed illegitimate while others are not. Even though the problem remains with us today, many birth mothers, adopted children, and adopting parents organizations have fought against sealed records, and, increasingly, states accept open adoptions or at least give information to adopted children about their birth parents. But these changes have only occurred within the last twenty-five years. Lifton's own analysis of the dilemma of adoption sometimes wistfully yearns for a story other than the one she describes as a ghostland. Lifton thus ends her memoir: "[w]hat if all these things came to pass: unsealed and updated records, agencies treating adoptees as clients instead of enemies, adopted children knowing that when they are grown they will have the chance to search out their origins freely? I tried to imagine what those future adoptees growing up in such utopian circumstances would be like. Already I envied them. Or would they have problems too?"[6]

But her engagement with the story of adoption, both as she lived it and as it was passed down to her, contains a highly imaginary world of idealized heterosexuality and lineage. As Lifton muses,

> [a] friend of mine recalls that when his seven-year-old (biological) daughter was a little younger, she would approach him four or five times a year with "tell me the story." And then he would tell her once again about how he met her mother through a friend, and how they started dating, and how they got married, and how they loved each other, and how she began growing in her Mommy's tummy. It made his daughter very happy and secure to hear the story that began not with her but with her parents who created her. Sometimes her grandparents and other relatives showed up in the details of the story of before she was born. The child knew without having to be told that her narra-

---

6. Lifton 1975, p. 255.

tive was connected to the narrative of her parents, grandparents, and great-grandparents down through the generations, and so she was connected. Her narrative revealed her identity. It told her who she was. If there had been essential people missing from her narrative—her Mommy, Daddy, grandparents, and other members of her clan—it would have been difficult for her to feel as connected as she did. For most children, like my friend's daughter, their narrative is as much a part of them as their shadow; it develops with them over the years and cannot be torn away. Unless, of course, they are adopted.[7]

For Lifton, her adoption breaks the chain of narration because "the Mommy and Daddy and baby makes three" is the narration of "normal," non-adopted children. It is the biological bloodline that holds the story together. What is broken for her though is precisely this family lineage. And yet this brokenness, this shattering, would occur regardless of whether adoptions were open. Lifton recognizes that other traumatic situations can break up the family line: divorce, war, famine, and so on. But her point is that the break—no matter what its cause—is in itself traumatic.

Indeed, for Lifton, adoption itself is a trauma because it breaks up the bloodline, which she idealizes as the origin of a coherent narrative of family and roots. This idealization leads her to view adoption as second best—a compensation for infertility—and adopted children as perpetually suffering. Only in view of Lifton's claim that infertility is the main reason that parents adopt can we understand her sketch of the shadowy and ghostly scene of adoption. Specters and shadows hover around the loss of the normal heterosexual family.

Who are the ghosts? The adopted child is always accompanied by the ghost of the child he might have been had he stayed with his birth mother and by the ghost of the fantasy child his adoptive parents might have had. He is also accompanied by the ghost of the birth mother, from whom he never completely

---

7. Lifton 1995, pp. 36–37.

disconnected, and the ghost of the birth father, hidden behind her. *The adoptive mother and father are accompanied by the ghost of the perfect biological child they might have had, who walks beside the adopted child who is taking its place.* The birth mother (and father to a lesser extent) is accompanied by a retinue of ghosts. The ghost of the baby she gave up. The ghost of her lost lover, whom she connects with the baby. The ghost of the mother she might have been. And the ghosts of the baby's adoptive parents.[8]

In the case of the adopted child, the "perfect" child her parents might have had accompanies her as a mirror of her own failure—her failure to be the perfect child for her parents. The adopted child comes to mimic the child who never actually existed, except perhaps as part of the unconscious fantasy in the psychic life of the adopting parents. On Lifton's account, this becomes futile mimicry because it involves buttressing the fantasy projected onto the adoptive parents at the expense of the adopted child's own separate existence. This is Lifton's "good adoptee," whom she identifies as herself prior to her search for her birth parents. Yet from within her own perspective of despair and despondency, Lifton imagines the adopted baby knowing that it can never be the real object of its parents' affection—knowing that it is a fraud:

> [I]deally the wicked changeling would be gone when the mother awoke, and in her place would be the good sweet, obedient child, all curly haired and dimpled like Shirley Temple. Of course, the real child was never returned, for adopted children are permanent changelings who are doomed to impersonate the manners and fidelity of the natural child who might have been. As if she understood this the changeling fled into herself and, since fairies are shape shifters, this one assumed the guise of a docile daughter eager to please.[9]

---

8. Ibid., p. 11.
9. Lifton 1975, p. 15.

This is an imagined picture of the adopted child's artificial self, divided not only from the fantasy child of her adopting parents' psychic life, but also from her own fantasy about who she might have been had she stayed with her birth mother. If adopting parents deny their adopted child the right to discuss the actual history of her birth mother, the child identifies with the gap at the very heart of herself that prevents her from becoming a whole person. In this way, Lifton identifies the quest for the identity of the birth mother and the quest for a unified identity as one and the same. Once this quest is foreclosed to the child, the child becomes melancholic, holding onto her entire identity in the form of a lost object that never was allowed to exist. Although Lifton does not refer to Freud, traumatized adopted children are best understood as melancholic in Freud's sense. Let me be very clear that I do not agree with Lifton that adoption is in and of itself a trauma. Of course, it can become a trauma under the condition of sealed records. The ego fragility that Lifton often describes as characteristic of adopted children keeps the lost object intact precisely at the expense of the ego's own organization and growth. In his classic study of mourning and melancholia, Freud defines the distinguishing features of melancholia as "a profoundly painful dejection [and] abrogation of interest in the outside world, loss of the capacity to love, inhibition of all activity, and a lowering of the self-regarding feelings to a degree that finds utterance in self-reproaches and self-revilings, and culminates in a delusional expectation of punishment."[10]

Bringing this Freudian psychoanalytic insight to bear on Lifton, I would suggest that, for Lifton, the adopted child's loss of its birth mother becomes the loss of its own ego due to the ambivalence that underlies the child's relationship to its adoptive parents. Since Lifton does not speak of melancholia directly, she cannot confront her own view of her adopting parents as desiring a labyrinth of secrets from which she cannot escape. This is why, over and over again, Lifton claims that she is "indentured" to her adoptive mother.

---

10. Freud 1959, p. 153.

[I]t is one thing to have a story (she writes) and another thing
to tell it. I could not put it on paper. The adopted child in me
felt a traitor. The child reminded me that her adoptive parents
had taken her when she was helpless and raised her with the
innocent hope that she would never look back. The unspoken
debt was to be paid with acquiescence and silence: it is a form
of emotional indenture even though it is made in the name of
love. Adoptive parents demand that their stories end happily
ever after, although they must know that families with blood
ties cannot be promised such a simple-minded plot, that even
blood children must one day go off on their own lonely jour-
neys of self-discovery.[11]

Through melancholia, the adopted child at once colludes with and
resists the secret. Indeed, it is this unique combination of collusion and resistance that distinguishes melancholia from mourning.
Though Lifton, despite her caveats to the contrary, seems ultimately
to believe that melancholia is the fate of the adopted child, I believe there is no such inevitability.

Freud notes that while many of the attributes of melancholia
are shared by mourning, the loss of self-esteem is purely melancholic in origin. "Now the melancholic displays something else,"
he argues, "which is lacking in grief—an extraordinary fall in his
self esteem, an impoverishment of his ego on a grand scale. In grief
the world becomes poor and empty; in melancholia it is the ego
itself."[12] The lack of self-esteem that Lifton describes as part of the
good adoptee's emotional experience of indenture is inseparable
from a young child's inability to express the ambivalence of early
childhood. For Lifton, the adopting mother cannot handle the
"truth." So the adopted child must conceal it from her. But of course
the truth of the child's origins is bound up with her unique history—her utter singularity. Paradoxically, under Lifton's tale, a
melancholic adopted child's lack of self-esteem is an act of love
directed at the vulnerable adoptive mother. Yet within the child's

---

11. Lifton 1975, p. 5.
12. Freud 1959, p. 155.

psychic life, this generates not only self-imposed erasure of the ego, but at the same time resistance to it. "If one listens patiently to the many and various self-accusations of the melancholic," Freud observes,

> one cannot in the end avoid the impression that often the most violent of them are hardly at all applicable to the patient himself, but that with some insignificant modifications they do fit someone else, some person who the patient has loved or ought to love. . . . There is no need to be greatly surprised that among those transferred from him some genuine self-reproaches are mingled: they are allowed to obtrude themselves since they help to mask the others and make recognition of the state of affairs impossible; indeed they derive from the "for" and "against" contained in the conflict that has led to the loss of the loved object. The behavior of the patients too becomes much more comprehensible. Their complaints are really "plaints" in the legal sense of the word; it is because everything derogatory they say of themselves at bottom relates to someone else that they are not ashamed and do not hide their heads. Moreover, they are far from evincing towards those around them the attitude of humility and submission that would alone befit such worthless persons; on the contrary, they give a great deal of trouble, perpetually taking offence and behaving as if they had been treated with injustice. All this is possible only because the reactions expressed in their behavior still proceed from an attitude of revolt, a mental constellation which by a certain process has become transformed into melancholic contrition.[13]

Melancholic contrition rather than docility or the artificial self most accurately describes Lifton's account of the complex relationship of adopted children to their adoptive parents—a relationship that harbors within it both blame and revolt that cannot be expressed other than as collusion. The adopted child feels literally torn between collusion and betrayal. But since this contrition follows from a deep ambivalence of love and hate, it need not culminate in suicide.

---

13. Ibid., p. 159.

It can lead to forms of mania, some of which produce extremely active and successful, if overdriven, people. Not surprisingly then, many of the adopted children who sought Lifton's counseling were people who led productive lives. But the forms of behavior that elicit considerable attention are those that Lifton associates with the forbidden self—problems in school, substance abuse, and criminal activity. Implicit in these forms of behavior, along with Lifton's evil changeling, is the self-berating confession, "I am a bad person." The revolt turns against the ego from which it emerged, thereby confirming its worthlessness.

When Lifton was seven years old, her mother told her that she had been adopted and that her parents were dead. Lifton was ill with scarlet fever and her mother stayed by her bedside. From what Lifton remembers of the story she was told, her father was shell-shocked and her birth mother died grieving for him. None of the story was true, Lifton later discovered. Even so, when she was first told this fable, it did not give her comfort. As she simply admits, "From that day I felt apart from other people."[14] Adding insult to injury, her adoptive mother demands that Lifton become part of the secret and that it be kept from her adoptive father. Describing her colluding self in the third person, Lifton writes,

> [s]he and her mother are conspirators now. They are collaborating on a labyrinth, a fearsome maze worthy of the great Daedalus himself. The mother shows the child how to place the secret, her bull demon, in the center. Over the years the child will faithfully guard this monster of whom she is both ashamed and afraid; and only in the stillness of the night will she imagine wandering down those tortuous passageways to throw some part of herself to it. Sometimes the monster lies waiting there in the center of the labyrinth, but at other times seems to be one with it. The child understands that she is the sacrifice on which the monster feeds.[15]

---

14. Lifton 1975, p. 7.
15. Ibid., pp. 10–11.

The secret is not just about concealment. It is also about a child being "unclean." In the system of modern adoption, Lifton's mother "had no such way of cleansing her adopted child of that evil deed that hangs over most adoptions."[16] In her psychic struggle against her own ambivalence and rage, the "sacrifice" of Lifton's mother becomes indistinguishable from her birth mother's evil "deed." The adopting mother effectively kills off the birth parents. According to Lifton's adoptive mother, the birth mother dies of grief. Therefore the implicit message to the child was that her baby was not enough to keep her alive. Her birth mother abandoned her, but Lifton's adoptive mother cannot save her. Hence, for Lifton, both mothers are equally "bad."

Supplementing Freud's understanding of mourning and melancholia, Melanie Klein argues that a depressive position emerges in which a child cannot realign its "good" and "bad" mothers through the reparative work of the imagination. "Ultimately, in making sacrifices for somebody we love," Klein argues,

> and in identifying ourselves with the loved person, we play the part of a good parent, and behave towards this person as we felt at times the parents did to us—or as we wanted them to do. At the same time, we also play the part of the good child towards his parents, which we wished to do in the past and are now acting out in the present. Thus, by reversing a situation, namely in acting towards another person as a good parent, in fantasy we re-create and enjoy the wished-for love and goodness of our parents.[17]

The mother being split into good and bad is at once normal and desirable since it enables the child to find a way out of depending on its fantasized, omnipotent mother. Following Klein, I would suggest that, in our struggle to claim our own person, we all need an internalized good mother or some other good object in her place in order to heal the wounds of a split and divided ego. The state of

---

16. Ibid., p. 11.
17. Klein 1984, p. 312.

mourning depends on an already internalized field of objects in which the lost object can find its place. Thus, mourning is a repetitive struggle of both the loss of the fantasized omnipotent mother —the figure Jacques Lacan will later name the phallic mother— and the recovery of the mother as the child comes to link the image of the good mother with the actual mother that cares for her. Mourning repeats the struggle of the alignment of the lost object with the internalized field of good objects.

"While it is true that the characteristic feature of normal mourning is the individual's setting up the lost loved object inside himself," Klein argues, "he is not doing so for the first time but, through the work of mourning, is re-instating that object as well as all his loved internal *objects* which he feels he has lost. He is therefore *recovering* what he had already attained in childhood."[18] When this struggle is thwarted or blocked, melancholia ensues or what Klein describes as depressive states, in which there is an inability to internalize good objects and a psychic forfeiture of the "good" mother. However, in normal mourning,

> the early depressive position, which had become revived through the loss of the loved object, becomes modified again, and is overcome by methods similar to those used by the ego in childhood. The individual is re-instating his actually lost loved object; but he is also at the same time reestablishing inside himself his first loved objects—ultimately the "good" parents—whom, when the actual loss occurred, he felt in danger of losing as well. It is by reinstating inside himself the "good" parents as well as the recently lost person, and by rebuilding his inner world, which was disintegrated and in danger, that he overcomes his grief, regains his security, and achieves true harmony and peace.[19]

The difference between mourning and the depressive position for Klein turns on the ongoing work of imaginative reparation that

---

18. Klein, "Mourning and Its Relation to Manic-Depressive States," in Klein 1984, p. 362.
19. Ibid., p. 369.

sustains the affirmative dimension of identification. The reparative work of the imagination in mourning when there is an actual death, though, should not be confused with an easy repose in which we simply dream away the death of the person we loved. It demands rather that, through identification, we come to see that person both differently and more complexly. In this way, we can hopefully both forgive her and take responsibility for our own aggressive fantasies of the other person that may have wounded and injured her. At once ethical and imaginative, this labor is bound up with the psychic method of mourning that Klein describes. It allows the individual to transform her shattered reality into a better reality and a more promising future, in which what is good about the lost object can be preserved in a different and higher configuration. There is no simple "reality-testing," as Freud called it, where the mourner comes to accept the object as lost. On the contrary, there is a re-imagined relationship with the object, which is recollected as part of a reality that must continue without the actual presence of that object.

In Lifton's case, her collusion with her "bad" adoptive mother against her "bad" birth mother prevented her from being able to repair or re-imagine her relationship with either one. When Lifton finally reconnected with her birth mother, she wanted a relationship with Lifton, though not one that could make Lifton proud of her. The woman did not want her other family to know anything about Lifton. Excited that her daughter had found her, Lifton's birth mother sent her a sentimental mother's day card. But Lifton's disappointment that her mother was not the strong, proud woman she had dreamt her to be turns into anger and then abjection when her mother—Rae is her name in the story—sends her a generic greeting card that celebrates mother's day. Lifton offers a characteristically ambivalent response: "She should have known there were no Hallmark Cards for a relationship such as ours. Imagine seeing on the rack in the drugstore tucked in among Get Well, Valentine, Birthday, and anniversary greetings, a section entitled: To the child I gave Away or to the Mother I never knew. My card to her would read:

The day that's known as
Mother's day
Is Adoption Day to me
A Day for wondering and regret
In which again I see
That laughing little babe
Of yours
Who grew into the orphan girl
Who would search you out, Dear, one day.[20]

Lifton does not send this card to her birth mother. Tragically for Lifton, she could not embrace either one of her mothers. And in death, neither can be mourned. Hence the dedication of *Journey of the Adopted Self*: "To the memory of my adoptive mother Hilda and my birth mother Rae who might have known and liked each other in another life in another adoption system."

Lifton frequently identifies with Oedipus, who sought after his birth mother as a means of discovering whence his unique being came. Recently, Adriana Cavarero has argued that the story of Oedipus continues to resonate for us because of the connection made between narration and the need to know the beginning of a story, the narration of a unique and embodied life always beginning with the mother. "The story of one man's life," Cavarero writes,

always begins where that person's life begins. We are not speaking of Man in his disembodied and universal substance, but rather of a particular man, a unique being who bears the name of Oedipus. . . . [H]e was born of a mother. The uniqueness of his identity, his daimon, has its origin in the event of this birth. . . . [T]he link between personal identity and birth, according to Oedipus, is materially founded as it is indubitable. His daimon is rooted in his being born of a mother, this and not another; a mother who, by giving birth to him, has generated the "seasons" of his entire existence, this existence and not another. By being ignorant of the factual truth of his birth, he has been able

---

20. Lifton 1975, p. 140.

to believe himself to become another; but he was never able to become another.[21]

Here, we are returned to Lifton's central anguish, that the system of sealed records keeps the adopted child from knowing who she really is. It is important to note here that in her dedication, Lifton perhaps unconsciously recognizes a different outcome for adopted children if they are allowed the chance to struggle through their own history with both their birth and adopting parents. Let me stress again that it is the system of sealed records and normalized heterosexuality that sets up a scene of melancholia rather than one of mourning. What is crucial is that the child be given the material from which she can tell her own story that allows her to confront and engage her own idealizations of and identification with both birth and adopting parents.

Unlike Lifton, Cavarero understands that it is a loss of narration, not the loss of an actual object, that creates the plight of someone who is cut off from his or her own history. Cavarero complicates Lifton's own narrative because Cavarero's understanding of the narratable self can actually help us understand that robbing a child of her story wrongs that child. Cavarero is careful to remind us that, with our birth, with the fact that we are born from the womb of one particular woman, our mother inaugurates our full exposure to the world as the unique beings we are. Cavarero distinguishes the question "Who am I?" from the more abstract question "What is a human being?" For Cavarero, as for many other feminists, this abstract question conflates the universality of humanity with the sexual and gender particularity of human beings, thereby identifying the masculine with the human and disavowing the feminine within sexual difference. Without being able to answer the initial question "Who am I?"—that is, the question, "From whom was I born?"—Lifton felt that she could not know, let alone tell, her story. The story of the "good parents" that the adopting mother told her, which was an attempt to give her a "legitimate history," ironically

---

21. Cavarero 2000, p. 11.

concealed her daimon from her. In the ancient Greek religions and mythology, the daimon is the identity that actually hovers behind us: others see it but we ourselves do not. It is the sign of our uniqueness. Cavarero beautifully defines uniqueness as follows:

> Difference is absolute because each human being is different from all those who have lived, who live and who will live. Not because she is free from any other; on the contrary, the relation with the other is necessary for her very self-designation as unique. We come to suspect therefore that the bad reputation from which the term uniqueness suffers, both in the moderns and the postmoderns, depends upon the erroneous way in which it is mistaken for an idea of romantic origin. On the contrary, in the uniqueness of the who there is no homage to the self-centered and titanic subject of romanticism. The who does not project or pity herself, and neither does she envelop herself within her interiority. The who is simply exposed; or, better, finds herself always already exposed to another, and consists in this reciprocal exposition.[22]

At birth, the uniqueness emerges as the new baby is already a who that can be no one else even though the story of her life has barely begun. One need not sentimentalize the role of mothers or the difficult labor of giving birth to accept the fact that we are all initially tied to a woman and born through her labor and that our existence as a self with a story includes this co-existence with her and thus her story. Nevertheless, this means that from the very beginning of our lives, our stories and subjectivities are already positioned by another. We can now understand the hopelessly sentimental story told to the seven-year-old about how Mommy and Daddy fell in love and "did it" under just the right circumstances. At a deeper level, we can understand why Lifton romanticized the story told to the child of her friends, for it is purportedly this story that allows that other seven-year-old to participate as a spectator in her own birth and retrieve at least some semblance of

---

22. Ibid., p. 89.

the unity that was promised by her birth. Since Lifton was denied, on Cavarero's account, the desire for one's story, she grasped on to any story to pick up a supposedly continuous narrative thread. We are dependent on others to help us enact our own projects of remembrance, which is why adopted children need to have access to their history and adopting parents must accept responsibility for providing such access. "Autobiographical memory," Cavarero claims, "always recounts a story that is incomplete from the beginning. It is necessary to go back to the narration told by others, in order for the story to begin from where it really began: and it is this first chapter of the story that the narratable self stubbornly seeks with all of her desire."[23]

The temporality of a narratable self bears within it a circular turn to the past, to the others who can return this promise of unity to us. Recognizing as our own the stories that others tell about us requires that we acknowledge the "you" who recounts what we cannot remember. Cavarero traces the desire of the narratable self to the inevitable incompleteness of the autobiographical memory. According to Cavarero, we know that we all have stories, that who we are is at best presentable as a unique story by our living through the very incompleteness of our own story, our shadow, our daimon:

> [i]ndeed, the first and fundamental chapter of the life-story that our memory tells us is already incomplete. The unity of the self—which lies in the miracle of birth, like a promise of its naked uniqueness—is already irremediably lost in the very moment in which that same self begins to commemorate herself. This loss of unity gets turned into the lack that feeds desire. If everyone who is born, from the start—and with a promise of unity that the story inherits from that start—then no recounting of a life-story can in fact leave out this beginning with which the story itself began. The tale of her beginning, the story of her birth, nevertheless can only come to the existent in the form of a narration told by others. The beginning of the narratable self and the beginning of her story are always a tale told by others. Poor

---

23. Ibid., p. 39.

Oedipus knows it well, he who would not give up that story for anything in the world. Oedipus is therefore special only for his misfortune, because there is perhaps no one alive who does not understand what an inalienable right this narration is.[24]

The desire for unity coalesces into an ideal that provokes and sustains the desire to hear one's story so that one can know that there is indeed an answer, if always a tentative one, because any narration must be sensitive to the question "Who am I?" The story sought sustains the promise of unity and a sense of a meaningful life. But the desire arises from the inevitable exposure of ourselves to others throughout our lives. Because we are exposed, we are at once narratable and vulnerable to others' narration of us. As Cavarero suggests,

> [i]t nonetheless seems to us that, more than immutability, it is the unity of the self made tangible by the tale, which moves the desire of the narratable self to seek the narration of the life-story. In other words, the narrative familiarity of memory, which constitutes the self as a narratable identity, has, in the unity of this identity, the ideal of her desire. The unity is therefore the figure of an in-born and inexhaustible tension; it is the design promised, from birth, to a unique existent, in so far as she exposes herself to the world, leaving behind herself a story. The one who is unique is also one in the very act of self-exhibition. She is this way first of all in her birth, when she is already a who without yet being a what; when, in her very new beginning, she is unique unity, about whom multiplicity, or fragmentation or discontinuity, cannot yet be predicted.[25]

The who appears in the world both through the mother and through her withdrawal. In this sense, the orphan's ontological condition is simply a more fragile exposure: "This exposure is, in the case of the orphan, simply more fragile. The mother, who embodies the *ex-* of existent, despite having been there at the origin

---

24. Ibid.
25. Ibid., p. 72.

of the child's existence, is now no longer there. Existence as exposure becomes, in this case, the perceptible truth of every existent, made more acute by the immediate loss of one's own origin."[26]

We want our desire for a narratable self recognized by all others but particularly by those on whom we depend for narration and memory. In this way, a closed adoption system does more than just wound a child, as in Lifton's case, by foreclosing the narratable conditions of its life. It denies the adopted child her desire for a narratable self. If the adopting parents are to be faithful to the desire for narration and selfhood—for a self with a story—there is an escape from Lifton's labyrinth, otherwise the adopted child will inevitably try to follow the clues that lead her back to her own history without ever knowing what she is looking for. "What does one do?" she asks. "Does one spend the rest of one's life playing Sherlock Holmes, following clues, looking in old phonebooks, rummaging through old records and graveyard listings, knocking on all the doors of old addresses—hoping that some action will magically spring the lock which holds the door to the labyrinth? One does—there is no choice."[27]

It is the loss of the narratable self that is the trauma that Lifton endorses. Lifton finds her birth mother; ultimately, she finds someone who knew the story of her father and can narrate a version of her father's relationship to her mother. She can finally patch together her story, but only incompletely. It is not enough. At the end of *Twice Born*, Lifton is still waiting "for the Great Unsealing Day,"[28] because she cannot find a story that she can claim as her own. This vulnerability is more than just an ontologically more fragile experience of how we all are exposed and narratable because of that exposure. "I think about Jean's words for the adopted a lot in the next few months," she writes.

> Orphan. I never thought of myself as an orphan before. I go to the dictionary: an orphan is a child who has lost both parents

---

26. Ibid., p. 19.
27. Lifton 1975, p. 101.
28. Ibid., p. 258.

through death . . . or less commonly one parent/an orphan is a young animal who has been deserted or lost its mother/an orphan is a person or thing that is without protection, sponsorship/an orphan is bereft of parents. Nowhere in the dictionary does it say that an orphan is someone who has been adopted. We [who are] adopted are not bereft of parents. Do we not have those "psychological parents" who raised us? But now that I think about it honestly, the orphan wind has been blowing relentlessly through me all my years, although I've tried to masquerade about like other more insulated mortals.[29]

The only insulation comes from the "you" that tells your story. Obviously, many biological parents fail to be that "you" that Cavarero believes is the one who ultimately sustains our story by telling it to us, making up for the lacunae in our own autobiographical memory. But adopted children in a closed adoption system are supposed to disavow their very desire for a narratable self. Indeed, it is this narratable self that becomes taboo. Lifton's adopting mother reinforces this taboo, causing a rift between them that never heals. By demanding that her daughter not ask her about her father and their relationship, Lifton's birth mother imposes her own version of the same taboo. Neither one could give her what she desired so desperately—her own story narrated to her by her mothers. Taking to heart the theoretical insights of Klein and Cavarero, we can see that, within Lifton's own imagination, reparation through realignment of the actual mother with the good mother could not take place. The notion that Lifton's birth mother was in "hiding" kept her from offering and exposing herself. Lifton describes a phone call to her birth mother where she actually hangs up because she knows that her birth mother does not want her half brother to know about her. Howie, her half brother, answers the phone:

For a moment I was tempted to say "Hello, Howie, this is your sister" to blow everything. Instead I put the receiver down, just like the heavy breather. It was all so tawdry. Again I was

---

29. Ibid., p. 170.

the dirty secret, the bastard, the polluter who would put a plague on my mother's house if I were discovered. The resentment I thought I didn't feel toward her now overwhelmed me. Did she think, like Jocasta, that once she had put her baby out on the mountain she was truly rid of it? That it wouldn't return to fulfill the prophecy of her sin: reveal her as a fallen woman? Did all natural parents really think that signing the release form is the equivalent of making the baby magically disappear: Now it's here, now it's gone? How dare she! How dare she what? How dare she not be my strong, beautiful, fantasy mother![30]

For Lifton, the fantasy mother of her imagination was the Rae that actually struggled to hold onto her after she was born. Lifton imagines this mother as strong and determined, willing to defy society. Indeed, even after Rae put Lifton in an orphanage, she continued to see her. It was only after considerable pressure from the orphanage and social services that Rae gave her up. As a result, Lifton was not adopted until she was two and a half years old. The circumstances of Lifton's early childhood clearly disrupted the psychic trajectory in which the mother as lost object is slowly replaced by the mother as a whole—the mother as her own individuated person. Although I agree with Cavarero that we are all exposed at birth to the loss of our mothers in that her body is no longer part of us, I also agree with Klein that giving meaning to that loss has everything to do with how we avoid becoming melancholic. For Klein, we must lose the mother's body and later her breast. But we can live through this loss by introjecting good objects that allow us to risk love and to take responsibility. As Esther Sanchez-Pardo succinctly defines the Kleinian position,

[a]ll subsequent losses that threaten the precarious stability of this psychic system can be mimetically negotiated so to speak if the individual were re-instating his or her inner objects anew but with the backdrop of the memory that he or she once succeeded

---

30. Ibid., pp. 225–226.

in doing it. The opposite holds true for manic depressive states. The violence of sadistic impulses and paranoid anxieties does not leave room for establishing good (whole) internal objects. The individual is overwhelmed by the sense that there is nothing good to hold onto, nothing good inside, and therefore nothing to recuperate. The feeling of emptiness and nothingness that the melancholic exhibits is due to a failure in introjection and to the infinite doubts and uncertainties that assail a subject who was unable to firmly establish his or her good internal objects.[31]

That Lifton experienced a break in the process of introjection and projection is clear from her story. In her work on adoption, Nancy Verrier, argues that the very act of early separation leaves traumatic traces because the child develops a relationship to the mother in the late stages of pregnancy. Scientific studies are pursuing this connection and what it means for adopted children.[32] One does not need to idealize pregnancy or essentialize its meaning to accept that the separation of adopted children from the mother's body is different and more trau-matic than the separation experienced by children who continue to have that first love object in their lives. "Adoption," Verrier claims,

> . . . is in fact a traumatic experience for the adoptee. It begins with the separation from his biological mother and ends with living with strangers. Most of his life he may have denied or repressed his feelings about this experience, having had no sense that they would be acknowledged or validated. . . . Somewhere within him, however, he does have feelings about this traumatic experience . . . he is wounded as a result of having suffered a devastating loss and . . . his feelings about this are legitimate and need to be acknowledged, rather than ignored or challenged.[33]

---

31. Sanchez-Pardo 2003, p. 131.
32. See Verrier 1993, Ch. 1.
33. Ibid., p. 16.

But the question arises: Can traumatic wounds be healed or at least acknowledged within the psychoanalytic terms of mourning and reparation? Clearly, the trauma cannot be worked through if it is simply denied. Verrier encourages adopting parents to allow their children the space to symbolize the specificity of their loss, even if this involves primordial fantasies of the remembered other mother. That the fantasies focus on the other mother is not surprising since it is her body that is lost and recuperated in fantasies. The adopting mother is entrusted with these fantasies and with the attempts at symbolizing the loss of the other mother in exactly Cavarero's sense. The child tells the mother these fantasies in order for the adopting mother to protect them and ultimately return them to the child as part of its story.

The adopting mother is both the storytaker and the storyteller. Part of the task imposed by adoption (understood as entrustment of the child's story to the adopting parent) is that the child's story be recovered as part of her relationship to her past, to her birth mother, so that the child can imagine herself as witnessing her own birth as the beginning of her unique existence. What is crucial, then, is the adopting parents' commitment to and recognition of the child's desire for a narratable self as irreducibly part of the unique self he or she is. Lifton becomes bitter toward her adopting mother because she feels that she did not care about her desire for narration and selfhood and instead distorted the facts of her story. The distortion was that Lifton was legitimate, and that her parents were dead. Everybody is given a stereotypically "good" role: her father is the good soldier, the mother the mourning wife. As a sanitized fictitious tale, the story made Lifton feel imprisoned in the role of a docile little girl who was not given the psychic space to take responsibility for her own aggression and reattach herself to her first love objects—her two mothers as whole people, separate from her.

Adoption agencies have long advocated some version of this sanitized story. The "official story" of the U.S. embassy is a classic example of the sanitization of the story of transnational adoption. These "official" stories always violate the uniqueness of the narratable self. Lifton's unwillingness to abandon "the orphan" should be understood as part of her psychic rebellion against the social system that prevented her from exploring her desire for a narratable self and against her mothers who had internalized its values. Bitterly, Lifton pays heed to the adoption taboos embraced by her mothers:

> [l]et us now pay homage to taboos: They guard the rituals of the community—birth, initiation rites, marriage, childrearing, burial against interference. They guard adoptive parents from natural parents, natural parents from adoptive parents, adoptees from natural parents, natural parents from adoptees. They guard everybody from everybody. They enable us to live in armed citadels safe from each other. They protect us from our deepest impulses, from that to which we are most naturally drawn. The violated taboo is programmed to avenge itself, but should it fail benevolent society takes over the punishment of the hapless offender. In my case I didn't need society: I was doing a fine job myself.[34]

To lift the taboo clearly demands the end of the closed system of adoption. Within that system, an orphan holding onto the abjected part of herself can be understood as resistant and the melancholic position of adopted children as rebellion against an unjust system that denies them their desire for a narratable self. Sanchez-Pardo defines the Kleinian understanding of the relationship between melancholy and systems of social exclusion and taboos:

> [t]he character of receptivity or exclusion of the external environment is decisive for the future adaptation or maladjustment of the individual and determines standards of health and illness. Melancholia arises as an acute response to the dangers and lethal traps with which external reality threatens our objects of love, admiration, and idealization. In a desperate attempt to safe-guard the object at risk, its incorporation and preservation inside the psyche seems to be the most effective maneuver, but it has a very high cost. Along with the loss, the effacement of

---

34. Sanchez-Pardo 2003, p. 137.

the object, a retreat of the subject from reality is also present in acute melancholic states—manic depression and involutional melancholia. Melancholia is a measure of the intolerance and rejection that external reality imposes upon the individual.[35]

In their recent essay on racial melancholia, David Eng and Shinhee Han argue that stereotypes of model minorities breed melancholia because they are determined by the necessarily failed mimicry of whiteness. The ideal Asian American is as close as a minority can get to being white, but in the very act of mimicry, whiteness remains unattainable. The stereotype itself is an ideal envisioned as a means of containing particular minority populations. As Eng and Han explain,

[w]hile Asian Americans are now largely thought of as model minorities living out the American dream, this stereotyped dream of material success is partial . . . The success of the model minority myth comes to mask our lack of political and cultural representation. It covers over our inability to gain full subjectivities—to be politicians, athletes, and activists for example—to be recognized as "All American". . . . This near successful assimilation attempts to cover over the gap—the failure of well roundedness—as well as that unavoidable ambivalence resulting from the tacit comparison in which the Asian American student is seen as lacking. This material failure leads to psychic ambivalence that works to characterize the colonized subject's identification with dominant ideals of whiteness as a pathological identification. It is an ambivalence that opens upon the landscape of melancholia and depression for many of the Asian American students with whom we come into contact on a regular basis. Those Asian Americans who do not fit into the model minority stereotype (and this is probably a majority of Asian American students) are altogether erased from—not seen in—mainstream society.[36]

---

35. Ibid., p. 69.
36. Eng and Han 2002, p. 351.

Eng and Han's insight into racial melancholia is directly relevant to Asian American adoptees. But there is the added dilemma, that these children are being "sold" to white parents on the basis of their model minority status and hence their purported ability to assimilate more easily into mainstream white society. The story of immigration can never be the same for a child as it is for an adult because children seldom choose to emigrate to other countries. If white parents simply assume and demand assimilation from adopted children, then psychic conflict over loss and abandonment is not given adequate space for articulation and reparation. Coupled with the imposition of stereotypes of race and ethnicity, this conflict can clearly result in racial melancholia as the only possible position of resistance to assimilation. But what can be the beginning of institutional change that affords transnationally adopted children the psychic and narrative space in which to grapple with their own unique and frequently tragic histories? Obviously, the adopted child's country of origin, along with the social processes of encoding racial and ethnic difference in the U.S., has everything to do with the answer to this question. Yet as "sending" countries slowly come to terms with their historical roles as such, interesting experiments involving their grown adoptees in the diaspora have begun to occur. These experiments and the reactions of adoptive and birth parents to them will become part of the story of transnational adoption.

In 1997, the South Korean government welcomed South Korean adoptees back to South Korea, guaranteeing them a special class of quasi-citizenship. The ceremonies were called marriages and received much political attention. Some of the adoptees were Amerasians produced by the United States' occupation in the Korean War. The "mixed" appearance of these children within South Korean society had been a reminder of the shameful U.S. occupation. But "Amerasian" children comprise only a small percentage of adoptions. South Korea continued to have an extremely high rate of adoption until very recently. But South Korea's struggle to become a "modern" nation led to the decrease in adoption. Currently, its foreign adoptions are down to 2000 per year. Yet between 1955 and 1997, over 197,000 Korean children were adopted overseas.[37] The wedding ceremonies were one way for the government to show that South Korea was no longer the kind of country that would send its own children away. Many South Korean adoptees felt stifled by these awkward ceremonies. But the stifling is inseparable from the forgetting of the trauma—that these children were sent away and that this is part of their story. In terms of the narratable self, the forgetting of the uniqueness of their history frustrates the desire of the adult adoptee to retell her story, which undoubtedly includes coming to terms with "Koreanness." Eleana Kim has conducted a study of Korean adoptees and tracked their response to the government's effort to change its image and the meaning of being a "sending" nation. She argues that

> [f]or some adoptees who go to South Korea, the past weighs heavily, whether as something to actively explore through birth family searches or as something to defer. Many confront their individual histories and understandings of cultural identity and belonging in ways they may never have done before. This sense of belonging is of course connected to "Korea" as a nation state and ethnic cultural paradigm, but it is also produced out of disjuncture with "Korea." The social memory of transnational adoptees is necessarily fractured and diverse, deterritorialized. And as Korean adopteeness is increasingly articulated by a collective, global, and deterritorialized community, collective histories, constructed through shared storytelling, constitute a disidentificatory practice out of which Korean adoptees' cultural citizenship emerges.[38]

Kim emphasizes the complex process of identification and disidentification—belonging to, being rejected from, and then being welcomed back to Korea. As she observes, "[c]ommon feelings of disorientation and alienation from Korean culture are expressed by adoptees who go back to Korea and desires for

---

37. Kim 2003, p. 63.
38. Ibid., p. 61.

authentic personhood frequently surface in adoptee activities of self-narration. These narratives suggest that the ideal of building bridges, of being flexible 'citizens' or postcolonial hybrid subjects may be more compelling in theory than it is in lived practice."[39] In 1996, Korean adoptees, many caught between conflicting idealizations, held their first conference called The Gathering. The South Korean government idealized them as part of its own attempt to become a modern state. Some adoptees, however, were ostracized because they were viewed as radically different from other South Koreans. Yet despite the mixed feelings that were expressed, there was also an acknowledged sense of belonging to a society in which everyone looked like them. On the other hand, they spoke of their experiences of racism in the United States and the complex relationship to whiteness and the stereotype of the model minority Eng and Han so eloquently describe. "A survey of the participants at the Gathering," Kim writes,

> found that 40% of respondents said they identified as Caucasian in their adolescence and perceived Asians as "the Other." For adoptees who grew up isolated from others like them and who identified primarily as Americans, therefore, racial discrimination posed a particularly difficult form of double consciousness. Even the most emphatic parents were perceived as unable to fully relate to the experience of racism, thereby intensifying feelings of alienation and racial difference. Some described it as a pendulum swinging back and forth between "Korean" and "American" sides. Many agreed with one attendee's sense that Koreans reject the American side, Americans reject the Korean side, adding that Koreans reject the adoption side.[40]

Well-meaning white parents who actively tried to get their children to pursue their Korean heritage were also seen as aggravating the alienation by remaining caught up in the orientalization of the adoptees' cultural and ethnic difference. Those white par-

---

39. Ibid., p. 66.
40. Ibid., p. 71.

ents who tried to amplify the Koreanness of their children during adolescence were seen as only further exacerbating the problem of assimilation at an age when it was already proving difficult for the adoptees to identify and pass as white. The adoptees saw their parents' enthusiasm for their difference as just another indication of how they did not truly belong and how their parents did not understand the difficulty of identifying with that difference in a thoroughly racialized society. Since whiteness is the color that erases itself, the parents saw themselves as without a color, as without an ethnicity other than American. Thus, in the very attempt to recognize their children's uniqueness, the parents thwarted their need to identify as Americans "like them."

But The Gathering can be viewed as political if we follow Cavarero's understanding of the political as the space of exposure in which we make sense of our life stories. In the case of South Korean adoptees, that story could only be told among themselves, since they were differently Korean precisely because of their history in the United States with primarily white identified parents. The South Korean adoptee movement, according to Kim,

> has been both a community-building project and a political one, exhibiting concerns with both cultural struggle and social policy. Sites of collective articulation and the searches for self and identity through different aspects of adoptees' experience contribute to what Teshome Gabriel refers to as a multigenerational and transindividual biography . . . a symbolic autobiography where the collective subject is the focus. A critical scrutiny of the extended sense of autobiography (perhaps hetero-biography) is more than an expression of shared experience; it is a mark of solidarity with peoples' lives and struggles. The Gathering . . . help[s] to illuminate some of the translocal conjunctures that form the broader context for the emergence of Korean adoptee heterobiography, constituted by discursive and symbolic practices.[41]

---

41. Ibid., p. 67.

The South Korean adoptees who gathered together presented stories different from the official story of adoption, whether promoted by the U.S. embassy (as in my daughter's citizenship ceremony) or the South Korean government. Their unofficial story challenges conventional notions of national and ethnic belonging as well as traditional patterns of heterosexual kinship. Although she observes the complexity of the response of Korean adoptees to the highly ritualized marriages between South Korea and adoptees in the diaspora, Kim also notes the importance of the South Korean government's attempts to open up space for these adoptees to further explore their relationship to Korea. Indeed, Kim recognizes that post-national hybridity may be a privilege for those who already take for granted a "home" in a nation-state:

> In discussing issues of national identity with adoptees from Germany and from France, I asked rather naïvely if they couldn't imagine themselves as being both Korean and German, or French and Korean. The French adoptee asserted: "You need to be situated in a nation. It's too idealistic to think that you can live in between." . . . [H]ybridity or dual belonging . . . is often felt to be an uncomfortable in-between state that is an undesirable or even untenable location. Unable to be fully "French" in France or even American in the United States, they are likewise unable to be fully Korean in South Korea or in the Korean diaspora. For another young French adoptee who declared "I don't like France and I don't like Korea," the question still remains, Where can I go?[42]

Yet it is in the imagined community of The Gathering that Kim finds the potentially radical political solution to feelings of "homelessness" described by Lifton as well as by the Korean adoptees. Homelessness is a current that runs through much adoption literature, irrespective of whether adoption involves actual dislocation from a specific country. Lifton describes herself as homeless, and indeed, her comfort in "Asian cultures" she attributes to her

---

42. Ibid., p. 75.

status as an adoptee. Lifton's experience shows how deeply heterosexual kinship is bound up with national belonging, hence the Korean adoptees' sense that they do not belong in South Korea because they do not have a family history in the traditional Korean sense. But is holding onto this homelessness an expression of melancholia? Here again we return to Eng and Han's insightful essay. Their whole point is that melancholia may be the only available psychic response to the erasure of the uniqueness of the narratable self. But events like The Gathering open the political space for mourning and for repairing the conditions of belonging that Korean adoptees can claim as their own.

As parents, we all have to mourn our children as they travel into worlds where we cannot follow them. For adopting parents, this is often painfully obvious. White parents were not invited to The Gathering. They were not offered the chance by the South Korean government to "marry" South Korea, nor are they called by their position in society to negotiate the multiple meanings of what it means to be Korean. The effort of some parents to hold onto their children results from these parents' feeling that their children are not actually their own. Parenting involves learning to accept that a child never belongs to the parent. With this acceptance, adopting parents will be able to let their children return to the worlds from which they hailed and enter new worlds they create with others out of "gatherings." Although Lifton is particularly sensitive to the plight of transnational and transracially adopted children, she fails to fully address the other scene of mourning that haunts transnational adoptions. At the time I adopted my daughter, I believed myself to hold no illusions about the role of the United States in South America. But the full ethical and political ambiguity did not hit me until I stood on that balcony in Paraguay. There it was: in 1993, there was no way for an adoption from Paraguay to the United States to be just. I mourned for a more just world where the adoption of my daughter did not have to be an enabling violation. After I went home, I supported the Paraguayan government in their effort to suspend adoption. To mourn for a more just world does not mean to immerse oneself in guilt or the self-beratement of melancholia. But it does mean that adopting parents are called to recognize the injustice of the closed system of adoption, to make their own reparations, starting with making that injustice part of the story of adoption. Gabriella Delgado Barrio did not give up her daughter because I was destined to raise her. She gave her up because she could not be a single mother in the Paraguay of her time. In the story and image of Gabriella I give my daughter, I imagine a woman who courageously faced the worst odds and obstacles. If we deny the conditions in which the other mother gave up her child, we fail to recognize the injustice of those conditions, along with the uniqueness of our adopted child's narratable self and her relationship to us. As a matter of reparations and indebtedness, mourning for justice is the very least we owe our adopted children. Of course, the mourning of adopting parents involved in confronting the enabling violation that allowed them to become parents can by no means resolve the adopted child's own struggle against the melancholic loss of a narratable self that Lifton so movingly describes. It simply makes the loss symbolizable as one that can enter the shared history of the adopting parents and their children. For only through that mourning may we be able to join them in dreaming up new family stories.

## REFERENCES

Cavarero, A. (2000). *Relating Narratives: Storytelling and Selfhood*, trans. P. A. Kottman. New York: Routledge.

Eng, D. L. and Han, S. (2002). A dialogue on racial melancholia. In *Loss: The Politics of Mourning*, ed. D. L. Eng and D. Kazanjian. Berkeley and Los Angeles, CA: University of California Press.

Freud, S. (1959). Mourning and melancholia. In *Collected Papers Vol. IV: Papers on Metapsychology*. New York: Basic Books.

Kim, E. (2003). Wedding citizenship and culture: Korean adoptees and the global family of Korea. *Social Text* 21(74):57–81.

Klein, M. (1984). *The Writings of Melanie Klein, Vol. 1: Love, Guilt, and Reparation and Other Works 1921–1945*. New York: Free Press.

Lifton, B. J. (1995). *Journey of the Adopted Self: A Quest for Wholeness*. New York: Basic Books.

———— (2006). *Twice Born: Memoirs of an Adopted Daughter*. New York: Other Press.

Ong, A. (1999). *Flexible Citizenship: The Cultural Logics of Transnationality*. Durham, NC: Duke University Press.

Sanchez-Pardo, E. (2003). *Cultures of the Death Drive: Melanie Klein and Modernist Melancholia*. Durham, NC: Duke University Press.

Schemo, D. J. (1996). Adoption in Paraguay: mothers cry theft. *The New York Times*, March 18, 1996. http://www.nytimes.com.

Simon, R. J., and Altstein, H. (2000). *Adoption Across Borders*. Lanham, MD: Rowman & Littlefield.

Verrier, N. (1993). *The Primal Wound: Understanding the Adopted Child*. Baltimore, MD: Gateway.

# 9

# Politics in the Age of Sex: Clinton, Leadership, and Love

Juliet Flower MacCannell

## OBJECT OF LOVE OR OBJECT A?
## LEADERSHIP AFTER FREUD AND LACAN

> *Let us venture . . . to correct Trotter's pronouncement that man is a herd animal and assert that he is rather a horde animal, an individual creature in a horde led by a chief.*
>
> —Freud, *Group Psychology*

Perhaps because Lacan had the misfortune of a longer experience than Freud's of Nazism and other totalitarian formations, he was much blunter about the drawbacks of being "socialized" to "asocial" behavior by such regressive societal groups—by gangs, packs, mobs, fascists, and so on. Neither analyst harbored that faint fondness for the gangster ego some Americans have recently exhibited. Freud simply delineated objectively the mob ego's structure while Lacan (with more sophisticated tools of social analysis at his disposal than Freud's Le Bon, McDougall, and Tarde) adopted a consistently severe position toward any ego[1] that

---

1. The distinction between ego and subject is absolute in Lacan; they are never the same thing. "Ego," for Lacan, is a creature of the imaginary, of mimicry

excuses its ethical lapses by referring to "social forces" that over-whelm it.[2]

Yet for Freud, compulsion is a primeval feature of human society. In his *Group Psychology and the Analysis of the Ego*,[3] Freud describes the original welding of people into social groups as both "uncanny" and "coercive." (Anyone who has ever attended an American high school, joined a fraternity or sorority, participated in activist movements, or simply watched a sports team can see why.) This welding is "uncanny" because whatever galvanizes humans into collective formations makes it so that they no longer have anything in common with simple animal flocks ("herds") and everything in common with "hordes" (a less charming figure), that is, with packs, gangs, mobs with their alpha males, bosses, and leaders (see Freud's epigraph above). Group formations are "coercive," Freud says, because their original impetus proceeded from a primal father who not only "had prevented his sons from satisfying their directly sexual impulses," he had also "forced them into abstinence and consequently into the emotional ties with him and with one an-other which could arise out of those impulses that were inhib-

---

and synthetic lure; the ego is defined by its antagonistic relation to an "*other*" (*a-a'* in the L Schema) wherein the symbolic (social pact) dimension is back-grounded. The *subject's* relation, on the other hand, is primarily to the Other. Lacan's subject, however, is not the legal, juridical, or social subject, but its hollowing out: the subject is always the subject of the unconscious for Lacan. The unconscious is the precipitate of the symbolic (whose foundation is the signifier). In the symbolic, the imaginary is backgrounded (see Lacan's L Schema, R Schema, and I Schema).

2. To French social theorists, "Society" clearly had an extra-individual life and force all its own. Over the two centuries following Rousseau, Hegel and Marx, Emile Durkheim, and others (Marcel Mauss, Maurice Halbwachs, et al.) had made as strong a case as possible for the "social" as an independent factor and force—a new dimension—in human existence. Claude Lévi-Strauss, Lacan's close friend, counted Freud, Marx, Durkheim, and Mauss as his forebears while Jean-Paul Sartre (Levi-Strauss's philosophical opponent otherwise) likewise focused on the existentiality of group life—albeit mostly its inauthenticity. Louis Althusser more or less synthesized psychoanalytic, Marxist, and Rousseauian theses concerning the reality of the symbolic social dimension.

3. Freud 1920.

ited in their sexual aim. He forced them, so to speak, into group psychology."[4]

As primal human hordes evolved into complex civilizations, the original violence enforcing the societal pact was muted, but never fully lost. In the heart of symbolically organized civil society, Freud suggests the uncanny horde still lurks. But what constitutes its present menace? It is apparently no longer the threat of an ur-father, since the "modern" group is bound together, Freud tells us, by egalitarian "brotherly love" and by its collective passionate attachments to a benevolent Leader, not by fraternal fear. If a reversal of the horde-character "seems to occur under the influence of a common affectionate tie with a person outside the group"— "the Leader"[5]—this pale, "symbolic" outsider cannot completely veil its fearsome familial root. For, of course, Freud dryly remarks, such warm attachments are "simply an idealistic remodelling of the state of affairs in the primal horde, where all of the sons knew that they were equally *persecuted* by the primal father, and *feared* him equally."[6] Still, Freud describes modern Leader-focused groups as, to all appearances, harmonious and characterized by the unruffled fit among their members.

In his relatively underinterpreted *Group Psychology*, Freud (1920) showed that a "group" is structured around love for its Leader—not just any kind of love, but *excessive* "love"—hypnotic, weird, extravagant. Magnetic love is critical to group formation; members must all hold the very same "love-object" in common; they are "fellows" only because each has put this unique object (the Leader) in the place of their own ego-ideals (see Fig. 9–1). The "group" loves its Leader if and because he is this "object." Members also expect to have their love returned—a back-and-forth mirroring that is the source, Freud tells us, of the Leader's supposed "hypnotic" quality. Group love is thus displaced ego-love run through

---

4. Ibid., p. 124.
5. Ibid., p. 121.
6. Ibid., p. 125.

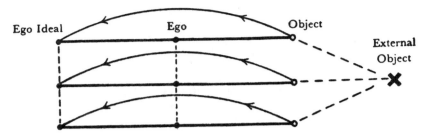

Fig. 9–1.

the magnifying relay of the Leader. It is also the opposite of "sexual love"[7] or what Freud otherwise calls "object love" (love for some object external to the ego). Even though the Leader appears as an external object, he is only a disguised modality of the ego.

Freud's analysis of the "group" (sometimes translated as "crowd," "mob," or "mass"—more fleeting than the English word) has found relatively few followers, although Wilhelm Reich and the Frankfurt School saw in it adumbrations of the mass psychology of fascism. Freud, however, did not limit his remarks to pathological groups. While the elementary structures of groups are crystallized in their modern "artificial" form, Freud found the role and structure of leadership comparable from ancient to modern times. Groups neither deviant nor aberrant may follow the same patterns as pathological ones. Modern "artificial" groups do, however, bring out clearly what is at stake in group life and leadership: *love*.

In this paper, I try to envision the grounds of the kind of group we call "democratic," dwelling on where it may deviate significantly from Freud's models and examining the psychic source of democracy's power to diverge from the ideal or norm of "group psychology."

Because this smooth-running group is, however, ultimately anchored *by the ego*, Freud finds it never represents true social concord, no matter what pains its stranger/Leader takes to harmonize it. Freud thus quickly rejoins Lacan's critical and theoretical

7. Freud, *Group Psychology*, p. 143.

rejection of any society modeled on the ego. Like Lacan, Freud's social ego is paranoid and aggressive, truly unfit for and unsuited to social life. It is deeply rivalrous with its fellows, albeit in a way hidden by its *esprit de corps* and group feeling. Freud confirms, for example, that superficially unified groups tend to regress and will often lend themselves to especially base actions, particularly against rival groups. They energize members with the élan of collective (mob) action, thereby allowing normal constraints to lift off. Their members will sometimes suddenly band together in overcharged crowds and mobilized packs to engage in acts otherwise unthinkable for them as individuals. Immoral, violent, and illegal actions are often undertaken in such groups with a sense of authorized impunity. So much for peace and love through conformity.

Freud realized also that the Leader (a precursor of Lacan's *Other*) was not really "other." The Leader must be, Freud says, only a disguised version of the ego, for the only thing the ego ever loves without ambivalence (and with such strong and lasting attachment) is itself. The Leader, to whom the individual member of a group addresses its love, is thus only a mirror that inverts the love remitted to it and returns it to the sender. The individual thus receives his own address upside down: i.e., it is he, not the Leader, who is the ultimate addressee of the love he emits. Freud's Leader thus becomes a collective *love-object*, a virtual focal point for all social ties to him and through him. But he is also a mask or a blind for the voracious primal father.

Taking his cue from this insight of Freud's, Lacan made a further analytic improvement. He noted that the (love)-messages to and "from" the Other return to the subject in the form of the *voice*: as intimate commands, demands, imperatives—in short, as the (object a) voice of the *superego*. The superego appears when oedipal myths wane; it fills in the void they leave. According to Freud, this event inaugurates the castration complex. In the reign of the superego, the Leader's "paternalistic" protection is questioned while a new version of the old "father" tightens its obscene grip.

Lacan extrapolated further the politically traumatic nature of the superego, stretching to the breaking point Freud's analytic notion that mass hypnotic love for an anodyne Leader bent people pliantly toward social unity and caused them to wed themselves freely to group psychology. Lacan recognized the *extimate* super-ego hidden in the ego at the center of Freud's group. It vitiates as much as it forges the social link. For Lacan, the superego reopens the subject internally to the terrifying jouissance of the Real, that is, to the fantasy return of a persecutory primal father who repeats its original "coercion."[8] The extimate superego functions to recall the real "force of law": the primal father's fearsome power to en-force his obscene commands. As "voice of conscience" then, the superego supposedly holds society together; but as a domineering, insistent, obscene, invasive, sadistic voice, it eats into the subject's heart, inverting all the imperatives required for life in common.

Indeed, Lacan (in *Seminar XI*) singularly speaks of the prov-enance of such extimate commands as "zones of shades"[9] issuing forth from a netherworld whose ghosts must be "fed with blood."[10] The superego thus *traumatically* recalls the all-consuming primal father still lodged in the unconscious of the group. Lacan says there is always a temptation to nourish this abusive Other, a temptation to sacrifice to this "dark god."[11] Sacrifice what? Your desire.

Freud's and Lacan's equally keen sense of the "totemic root" of group life (the persecutory ur-father who has it all, the *père jouissant*), together with their common experience of accelerating, excess so-cial energy, showed them that obscenity drives the unconscious of group life just as the obscene superego haunts the individual uncon-scious. When the group models itself on a Leader who is a pure re-flex of the ego, the process intensifies: we are in Drive.

---

8. Lacan 1956–1957, p. 212. Lacan calls the superego ("tyrannique, foncière-ment paradoxal et contingent") the signifier *of* the signifier's castrating work in the human.

9. Lacan 1977, p. 23.

10. Ibid., p. 32.

11. "The offering to obscure gods of an object of sacrifice is something to which few subjects can resist succumbing . . . the sacrifice signifies that . . . we try to find evidence of the presence of the desire of this Other that I call *the dark god*" (Ibid., p. 275).

The new face Lacan put on the Leader of group (mass, mob) psychology (the face of Drive over Desire) and on the Love he commands is particularly disturbing from the viewpoint of democracy, which has so often been thought of as mass or even mob rule. As such, it demands closer review. This should clarify some crucial distinctions, whose key elements surround the nature and status of Leaderly Love, so central to Freud's thesis on group formation. The democratic focus demands equal attention to the matter of sex. For Freud, in *Group Psychology*, showed us that in ego-based groups, sexuality does not exist:

> There is scarcely any sense in asking whether the libido which keeps groups together is of a homosexual or of a heterosexual nature, for it is not differentiated according to the sexes, and particularly shows a complete disregard for the aims of the genital organization of the libido.[12]

We must now ask if the modern democratic group is or is not formed around the ego; and, if not, how does its Leadership relate to love and sexuality?

## LEADERLY LOVE

For Freud, Leaderly love was only a variant of ego-love (disguised auto-affection). Its asexuality was thus assured: Other-love is always secondary to One-love as the ego's first love is (and remains) *itself*. While Freud accented love and harmony, Lacan refused to see the social as anything other than (at bottom) a field of rivalry and antagonism, and therefore he accented the lush underside of envy, primal competition to Freud's social feeling. While he accepted Freud's contention that Social love and Leaderly love were "asexual," Lacan did not view sexuality in the social context in quite the same way as his predecessor. For Lacan, the sexual root of the

---

12. Freud 1920, p. 140.

subject lies not in the logic of the signifier but, more crucially, in its precipitate, the object a, or the signifier's remainder of inassimilable jouissance.

Global, idealized figures of Leaders or Fathers are not what bind group psychology for Lacan; instead, an almost indiscernible, half-real, half-phantasmic object is the true social root, the actual focal point, the real Leaderly pivot. Lacan, like Freud, saw the communal/singular/Leaderly love-object as indeed the ego in disguise; but he also found in group-life the vivifying presence of a new kind of object: the object a. Lacan cites "*le petit moustache du Führer*" as just such a bit of the "real," the thing on which Hitler's followers were hooked. By what? By the lure of imagined jouissance seemingly bodied forth in this minor "unary trait" of the Leader.

How so? This trait hints at a promise of jouissance—and suggests a measure of fear. The Leader mesmerizes and appeals through the object a (e.g., the unary trait, the mustache) because it signals the presence of jouissance: but a jouissance *in* the Leader, not an enjoyment pledged *to* his followers. It underscores that only their Leader stands between the group and the threatening primal father, the One who alone enjoys.

Object a is thus the site of the unconscious remainder/reminder of obscene enjoyment that lingers beneath a unitary social feeling that creates this jouissance by repressing it. Far from an assurance of peace, love, and harmony "uncannily" binding and bonding the members of a modern group to it and to each other, then, it is rather a hypnotic investment in the object a that welds them into one.

Those invested in Freud's type of group thus find no relief in the unconscious from the primal father who incites to action those egos it cannot do without. In Freud's type of "group," the imperative, superego voice traumatically recalls the abusive, obscene father through the *invocatory drive*, that inner voice that is never really one's own: an internal alien object, a voice on the radio, the Führer's voice, and so on. This drive demands a strong public disavowal of any relation to the obscene enjoyment that the object a bears (i.e., the traces of paternal enjoyment); indeed, for Freud's group, sexuality is completely banished.[13] That does not, of course, defend against its obscene return.

Does this structure, however, really govern the *democratic* bond, a bond that seems to me a brilliant counterinvention to Freud's modern group psychology? While the two appear to resemble each other, there remain many crucial differences. Freud's typology seems, for example, more relevant to the political/religious factions that recently lined up to oppose William Clinton; the millions of people who supported Clinton's request to keep his private sex life separate from politics seem more apposite to the "democratic" position. If indeed democratic group formation turns out to be largely incompatible with the imperatives of Freud's group type and if democratic psychology can be distinguished from Freud's mass psychology, it is on the basis of several key components: sexuality, the position of the subject, and its object a.

Perhaps the case of William Jefferson Clinton's presidency, which was deeply marked by conflicting imperatives on sex, may enlighten us here on differences between the two social groups. One group implicitly demands that the Leader mark himself as largely asexual; the second tolerates and even encourages sexual pleasure in its Leader. One can only speculate why.

Clinton's presidency was indeed characterized from the outset by that very thing Freud's group psychology does not tolerate: sexuality. Clinton's quasi-openness about his own sexual nature evoked intense reactions. Perhaps, in the minds of some, Clinton's sexuality represented a primal father returning to take over the horde. The mere hint Clinton possessed more than a single sexual object (Hillary? Gennifer Flowers?) was enough to set off irrational, unchecked speculation, conjectures whose unconscious referent had to be the *père jouissant*, the *Ur-Vater* possessor of all sexual objects. Time and again, even before the Lewinsky scandal, Clinton was reported to have hundreds and hundreds of mistresses, or to have ordered murders and sexual favors at will—accusations that

---

13. See footnote 12 above as well as footnotes 32 and 33 below.

could only stem from a fearful fantasy, whose referent had to be the primal father's unwelcome return. Clinton veritably fleshed out the fantasy of a menacing Father/Leader-figure.

This fear nearly sank his presidency, but it was largely restricted to those who hail from the American variants of Freud's type of group, a group that requires abrogating the public/private split the democratic group cherishes. As a true democrat, Clinton had been handed, unwittingly or even unwillingly, an extraordinary task. He was called upon to exemplify something with no prior model: a Leader whose tenure did not depend on repressing a threatening sexuality.

Why does Freud (and much of traditional society) insist that sex be refused an acknowledgment in collective life? Wherever groups can survive through recruitment, adoption, or even conquest, rather than through sexual reproduction, sex becomes not only unnecessary *to* group life, it becomes a useless evocation of the "obscene" root of social being. Whence this psychic terror of sex? The answer lies in democracy's relation to the subject.

The subject and not the ego is the hinge point for democracy. And this subject is intimately tied to sex; a relation to its own jouissance forms the subject, an ethical relation whose logical expression is sexual. In Lacanian terms, sex evokes the existence of a subject where only the ego had imagined itself to be. The subject's sexuality need not only or predominantly be connected to the abusive primal father's obscene enjoyment, nor is its ethical position exclusively guided by superego pressure. Its object a may certainly bear the obscene traces of the *père jouissant* (for Lacan, *le père jouissant* is more central to masculine than to feminine sexuation). But the subject's position toward this Jouissance of the Other is resistive rather than compliant. Another way to put this is that the subject is formed around its own singular object a, which need not be the superego's voice and need not contain the menace of the urfather to sustain life in common.

I now pose the question of politics in the "age of sex" and engage the problematic Clinton was forced to exemplify—sexual Leadership.

## AMERICA'S TWO SOCIAL BODIES

The perplexities of William Jefferson Clinton's tenure as the president of the United States and leader of the free world dramatized a consummate clash between two root forms of social group. The first, Freud's, is psychically structured by a focus around the ego. The second type (something new, really) is based entirely on a subtraction of the ego from the public sphere of engagement. Both forms of group coexist in historic forms of democracy (roughly speaking, Hobbesian and Rousseauian in polarity). In the first, any withdrawal of ego is completely unthinkable: the group would fall apart. In the second type, the ego is not the cornerstone of society; the subject is. The first is a passional social group of Freud's type; the second is a democratic type whose structure is not yet well understood.

Stendhal once opined that the best and most unique feature of "American" democracy was entirely negative: America, he says, granted its citizens the right to be left alone by their government.[14] (He nonetheless noted with amusement that minding one's neighbor's business seemed to be our national passion.) Stendhal's precious "negative right" has long been valued by liberal and conservative Americans alike. So fundamental did such a right to privacy seem that even in his role as Leader, William Jefferson Clinton took it quite evidently to heart, and made both his personal and political policy "don't ask, don't tell."

Despite the distinctively *ego-negative* democratic society that Stendhal thought dominated the United States, however, the American landscape has always yielded the other, ego-syntonic kind: the *ego-positive* group. In these, the group becomes the site of special, passional attachments—to a particular cause, crowd, or person. Early radical social experiments (e.g., the Oneidas, the Shakers, et al.), dreams of founding a pantisocracy, and varied attempts to found theocracies take their place in this pantheon alongside their seeming

---

14. "A free government is the one who does its citizens no harm . . . in America . . . the government fulfills its functions as it should and harms no one" (Stendhal 1822, pp. 163–164).

opposite: highly conformist clubs, fraternities, sororities, fraternal orders, political parties, and sports teams. On more than one occasion, passional groups have propelled their leaders into political prominence: think of Malcolm X, but think also of today's religious right, which owes its public force to this kind of group ardor. (So did Richard Nixon, who had an enduringly magnetic effect on his followers, notwithstanding his cold war passions and hint of crookedness.)[15]

Avowed sexualness is, of course, the biggest "no-no" for leader and follower alike under this type of group, for even if the rallying cry of passional groups is "the personal *is* the political" (to invoke for a moment early feminism), what this often means is that the personal is open to public inspection: all traces or stains of obscene jouissance are to be purged. In other words, the public/private split is suspended or abrogated for special causes.

Bill Clinton's Leadership, in contrast, bore the mark of the negative ego of Rousseau's type of democracy: he mounted a strong defense of his right to a private life full of sexuality. Even in his role as chief of state, it was also a right for which millions supported him. Moreover, where Freud says that when a Leader singles out one person for special sexual attention, the act brings back to the surface the primitive envy that group life suppresses and renews alarm at the return of the One who possesses All. Clinton violated this imperative, yet the democratic group failed to collapse around him. Why not? A comparison of Watergate and Monicagate proves instructive.

## FROM WATERGATE TO MONICAGATE: LEADERSHIP AND TRAUMATIC SEXUALITY

In the biggest scandal the U.S. presidency ever endured, the Watergate scandal, sexuality was not an issue at all. The so-called national

---

15. Even Ronald Reagan's buoyant rise to the presidency on an antigovernment platform was tied to his long-term support for investigating the private opinions of private citizens suspected of political deviance. (See his tenure as head of the Screen Actor's Guild, where he freely cooperated with the FBI to ferret out actors who were "communist sympathizers.")

trauma of the Clinton–Lewinsky scandal and of the president's impeachment by the House of Representatives, though overtly about sex, was actually a restaging of President Richard M. Nixon's guilt and exposure in the Watergate affair—and of Nixon's missed encounter with impeachment. Bill Clinton was being made to pay for Nixon's traumatic unmasking of the "truth" of group life when it is rooted in the ego.

The conservative-looking Nixon had embraced a "Silent Majority" as a fictional embodiment of stable society. His White House entourage resembled "straight" fraternity boys (e.g., the crew-cut Haldemann) far more than the antiwar "radicals" and the long-haired "hippie freaks" that were then shaking up America (with whom few Americans could identify, the ones Vice President Agnew loudly disdained). Yet this "stable" president (who did decisively take the reins and who did lead the nation out of the war) prepared a near-fatal blow to the aspirations and claims of the American ego as the pivot point and greatest beneficiary of our social bond. With Nixon, the American people were shocked to find that the conservative paternalist they hoped would return their fractured country to the "wholeness" and "harmony" of the Eisenhower years was, instead, as the scandal revealed, the paranoid ego on which such false harmony inevitably rests.

With Nixon, the people had wanted a true conservative to return them to a peaceful, orderly, rational status quo ante; instead they got a ruthless warrior whose aggressive covert actions created a greater national upheaval than anyone would have predicted. Nixon's tragic adventure in internal political warfare—the break-in he authorized at the Democratic National Committee's Watergate offices—struck the American soul at its weakest point: its desire for social harmony, for things to go smoothly. The strongly individualistic leader the public had wanted emerged instead as a cartoonish mobster, the putative boss of a gang Raymond Williams once called the "Orange County Mafia."

As the shape and scope of the Watergate break-in by White House operatives unfolded, our Leader no longer reflected the self-image we the people wished to see: a calm, collective self. Instead, bit by bit, a paranoid, narrow-minded, bigotry-laden man emerged at our social center, who was focused on a political enemies list and launched preemptive strikes against imagined political foes; we the people could no longer identify either with him or, more important, with each other through him, à la Freud's model.

The realization was jarring, but in some ways salutary. Americans were not traumatized *as a people* by the revelations of the rot at the center. The *institutions of democracy*, while obviously at risk, remained intact: proper mechanisms of succession, of orderly transition, and of legal process were followed; there were pardons and convictions and elections to right a system that had gone off course. Some Americans began to realize that democracy may not be best anchored in the ego if it is long to remain democracy, that indeed our institutions are more than a little in debt to the Rousseauian doctrine that ego-will must be excluded from general-will. After all, it is our institutions that get us through our crises, not personalities (like Al Haig's).

Unlike the nation, however, the political party the miscreant president represented—the Republicans—may have suffered a traumatic blow to its group psychology. Republicans were obviously taken off guard by the president they had supported enthusiastically and who abused his powers under cover of the office for which they had clearly chosen him. While the cheerleading gloss of the Reagan years allowed the country to "stand tall" again after the moral ambiguities of Vietnam, the Reagan–Bush presidencies did nothing really to remedy the underlying wound that Nixon's transgressions inflicted on the party of Lincoln. It quickly transformed itself into a party in the mold of Freud's group: impassioned, aggressive, ardent in its attachments to its new Leaders, like Reagan.

Now, the very definition of "psychic trauma" is that its understanding is precluded *while the traumatizing event takes place*. Nor can it consciously be recalled. In trauma, a death drive in the subject has manifested itself that can only be "remembered" through repetition—allusive restagings of the trauma in altered and obscured form. Although the repetition may take place unbidden in dreams and sexual fantasies, it also frequently appears in acts that reiterate, stutteringly, the originating event. These repetitions are attempts to make up for the jouissance lost in the trauma, for what has been exacted from its victim. In repetition, the victim changes roles, plays the part of the abuser or occupies that of a bystander deriving a measure of enjoyment from rewitnessing (in disguise) the original, unbearable pain.

In the articles of impeachment for Clinton, *Nixon's* short-circuited impeachment was being replayed as fantasy—and as farce. Beneath the Clinton prosecution lay a strange, unconscious institutional fantasy, a Republican fantasy in which its Nixon-induced trauma was reduced. Here the Watergate drama was repeated, but this time the American people were frankly assigned the role of helpless victim of the subversion of authority perpetrated by their popularly chosen president—the "victim" role the people had refused to play in Watergate. The Democratic Party was made the unwitting accomplice-instrument of presidential abuse, while Republicans, this time, were chosen to save the people from their humiliatingly foolish choice of Leader.

Fantasies, unconscious, are always one-sided in their perspective. They demand that things be seen from a controlled viewpoint because their aim is to redistribute the power, the pain, and the enjoyment in a historical event. Even without pop psychologizing the principle actors in this event (Clinton as "sex addict," Starr as "pervert," Monica as "hysteric" with fantasies of seduction), we can see that indeed something more than simple political revenge for Watergate was going on. Something excessive was being repeated for the purpose of a gain entirely unconscious in character: a trauma was being restaged to retrieve a jouissance lost under the most painful conditions. The agent who had brought the news of Nixon's transgressions—the Democratic Party—was being made to share Republican shaming in a scenario that seemed to everyone "odd" and excessive simply because it was a *fantasy*.

In the compulsion to repeat and master their original trauma, however, the Republicans risked creating a new one entirely of their own making. Until the tabloidization of daily life in America, one of the fundamental materials of fantasy—sex—was implicitly out of bounds as far as the figure of the president was concerned. Our head of state was tacitly allowed his flirtations in recompense for the enormous responsibilities he bore in representing the free world. FDR, Eisenhower, JFK, LBJ (and even George Bush, apparently) enjoyed "openly" secret affairs—some with staffers. Vicki Morgan's sensational accusations that she had taped sadomasochistic sex acts with the "highest officials in the land" in Reagan's White House and rumors that Nancy Reagan was sleeping with Frank Sinatra in her private White House bedroom caused little more than fleeting public stir.

Officially, the president (and his wife) had no sex; no sitting president was open to detailed public speculation about his sex life, which in turn (until Clinton) was virtually never the subject of federal investigation (although among John F. Kennedy's mistresses, Judith Exner's mob connections might have made it fair game). This was a crucial evasion for the sake of allowing the two types of groups to coexist: presidential dalliances had to be treated as private travails for presidential husbands and wives, without public knowledge or political consequence.

But the presidential wife in this case was a public figure in her own right, with a professional career and a political history of her own: Hillary. For this she was dragged insistently into the center of the controversy on every level, personal and political. No one ever thought to probe the feelings of Jackie, Lady Bird, Mamie, or Barbara over their husbands' presumed affairs. Yet in Clinton's case, the compulsion to cloud his leadership with extreme guilt spread *to* his wife, who was singularly enveloped in a dense cloud of suspicion—we heard murder and more implied.[16]

Once sex became the sole center of the traumatic restaging of Watergate, it revealed something of the unconscious logic at play

---

16. True, Harding's wife is still suspected of having poisoned him over his Senate cloakroom mistress. But rumors of the Clintons' hiring assassins in their Arkansas days, as well as Linda Tripp's suspicions that Hillary had Vince Foster killed over his knowledge of Whitewater-gate, swelled into a tide of imputation intended to drown the Clintons in an ocean of absolute guilt. (Tripp was sole witness to the supposed mysterious White House comings and goings on the night of Vince Foster's suicide.)

in Watergate, but it also indexed how drastic and even traumatic the sex-change in our society was felt to be. The Monicagate fantasy tried to return sex to something knowable, predictable, and quite one-sided (i.e., masculine): to return sex entirely to men by making Monica into a helpless female victim (she wasn't quite) and Hillary into a long-suffering, betrayed, but supportive "wifey." It tried to turn sex, that is, into something that was not-sex.

What Starr sought—a strict, narrow, legal definition of "sexual relations" that could be used to punish and convict in the public arena—is precisely what sex never admits. In the hundreds of pages of testimony on sexual-ish activities released over the Internet worldwide by Starr and the House, never once did we catch a glimpse of the only truth possible in sexuality: the obscure "truth" of a desiring subject.

## NIXON VS. CLINTON: SHAME AND SEX IN THE WHITE HOUSE

The Nixon disclosures were shocking but not ultimately traumatic to the nation because Nixon himself was so wrapped up in the definition of "truth" as something that could be hidden and distorted up to a final moment of disclosure—a disclosure for which he was fully prepared. (Why else tape his own illegal moves to consolidate power and political advantage?) But the kind of truth Kenneth Starr demanded of Clinton—sexual truth—is absolutely unrevealable, the most truth-less of any truth.

To have elicited and enunciated such a truth would have required the skill not only of a Freud, but also of a Tiresias, a Stendhal, a Roland Barthes, an Annie Ernaux. And to paraphrase Senator Lloyd Bentsen, Kenneth Starr is no Annie Ernaux. Who but a Stendhal could have conveyed the significance of the romantic signs to which, like any subjects in love, the unhappy figures of Monica and Bill were reduced—the wearing of particular ties, the reading of ambiguous glances, the "meaningful" timing of certain phone calls? A thousand pages of Special Prosecutor's reports, countless media probings of all angles of the affair, even Monica's own one-sided tell-all book, have done nothing but miss the essential: that sexual love is radically a dependence on uncertain signs communicated between two divided subjects, that sexual love is a way of making up for the trauma of being human by locating itself outside the limits of the law.[17]

In one way, however, the fantasy repetition of Watergate succeeded. As Starr and the House Managers pursued the overly oral Monica to gain access to her "Deep Throat," few Americans indeed failed to feel that *they* were being victimized—vicariously through her. An exceptional threat to the people—as a democratic body— seemed to hang over us from day one of the investigation. Thus, we the people eventually began to speak of our own elected representatives as a "Jihad caucus," the term "sexual McCarthyism" came into wide currency,[18] and images of totalitarianism and worse became commonplace in the media, private gossip, and comments by the principals. Lewinsky later wrote that Starr made her feel like "Hitler's whore" for coercing her to betray her lover.[19] Her parents thought only Hitler-era Germany, the Inquisition, and Stalinist tactics could reference how deeply disturbing to individual liberties and democratic practices the Special Prosecution of their family seemed.[20]

Individual civil liberties and personal discomfort at the thought of the public airing of one's intimate fumbles and romantic successes were not the only issues, however. Through Starr, the American people discovered what they "knew" all along—that Democracy's "Symbolic" had a flaw. But they were less horrified at the thought of its sacred space (the Oval Office) being used as a "sexual playpen"

---

17. See my chapter "Love Outside the Limits of the Law," in MacCannell 2000. See also Lacan 1977, p. 276.

18. See Dershowitz 1998.

19. Morton 1999, p. 210.

20. Ibid., p. 219. Lewinsky's mother called Starr a new Stalin; her father saw Starr as "un-American" and likened his tactics to those of the "Inquisition" and the "Hitler era."

(Pat Robertson's phrase) than at the thought of zealots trying to "fix" that flaw for good. Without knowing their Lacan, the people seemed spontaneously to feel that their Symbolic Order *required* the existence of a crucially empty private space for jouissance. To think otherwise would mean dismantling a whole way of life simply because its *necessarily* obscene underside had now been discovered.

Our "civilization," with its sometimes torturous constraints, has always granted us the remedy of a private jouissance not held fully accountable to the law. By turning a searchlight on the space of obscene jouissance necessarily hidden at the core of Symbolic Law, Kenneth Starr and the House Managers risked damaging something the people seemed to find surprisingly crucial to their existence as a people. The people resisted Starr as if a kernel of their own being were catastrophically laid bare, as if something crucial to our collective existence as political subjects was about to be radically undermined. He had set in motion a radically risky area of inquiry.

We may well wonder how and why a president's sexuality had come to be the defining issue of his term in office. But I find it equally difficult to fathom how men and women of conservative bent (whose education, legal training, and/or simple political horse sense ordinarily would have prevented them from it) stepped into such quicksand. Only two completely different unconscious attitudes toward what constitutes a group and its Leader account for it. What else explains Starr's self-contradiction (e.g., his earlier pronouncement that "Public media should not contain explicit or implied descriptions of sex acts.")[21] unless it came from some inner conviction that overt sexuality is dangerous in a Leader? Why else did Starr suddenly deem presidential sex suitable for widespread public consumption? Starr, after all, forced tremendous

---

21. See Kenneth Starr's (1987) comments to Diane Sawyer on *Sixty Minutes*: "Public media should not contain explicit or implied descriptions of sex acts. Our society should be purged of the perverts who provide the media with pornographic material while pretending it has some redeeming social value under the public's 'right to know.'"

ethical choices on unwilling parents who struggled over how to explain oral sex or semen stains to their five-year-olds.[22]

Many people simply thought of Starr as "sick"—as a prurient voyeur. But in forcing morality against both legal reason and ethics, Starr was not necessarily obtaining obscene enjoyment for himself. He was also trying to secure the ground for retrieving Republican pride from the blackening Nixon had given it, acting for all the world as if he were rallying everyone against a despot.

It is also possible to attribute unconscious institutional motives to the virulence of the anti-Clinton attack as well. In relentlessly exposing a sitting president, the prosecutorial team and the House Managers were politically clever at masterminding the discrediting of the Democrats and their presidential choice. But they themselves seemed mastered by something beyond their individual control. Henry Hyde defended his dogged, highly unpopular pursuit of the president this way: "I wake up every morning with that little voice in my ear that says, 'Duty, duty, duty!'" Any Kantian duty here was being put, however, in service of what Kant found the most violent human act: the stripping away of another's dignity. Yet even Hyde's own dignity (the disclosure of his affair with a hairdresser) and those of his fellow House members suffered in the process. Something irrational pressured the otherwise sober, even boring, Republican men and women to sacrifice their own dignity (along with the president's, Monica's, Hillary's, Chelsea's, and Linda Tripp's).

In focusing on Clinton's sexual misstep, Starr and company were neither legally out of line nor out of synch with a larger trend toward skepticism regarding the government, law, and political institutions—with what I call the "perverse ethic" of our time.[23] But they so inflated the national import of the intimate personal issue and so exaggerated the dangers to society posed by Clinton's

---

22. From private correspondence between a doctoral student-mother and the author.

23. I discuss the perverse ethic in Chap. 2 of *The Hysteric's Guide* (MacCannell 2000). See also footnotes 24 and 27 below.

sexual trespass that their accusations often seemed to lack the weight of serious moral conviction. While Clinton's accusers may have been conscientious, many felt they were just out to do maximum political damage: their moral outrage looked like a flimsy excuse to publicize embarrassing details, what sociologist Erving Goffman once called "fake righteous indignation" (outdone only by a countering "fake fake righteous indignation," which at times was certainly exhibited by the Democratic side).

The rationale the actors imagined they had—political paybacks for Clinton's "stealing their issues," for Watergate, Iran-Contra, and Clarence Thomas—turned out to be perhaps not entirely rational. What propelled them beyond politics, money, and morality has, I believe, to do with the structure of an unexplored region of trauma: institutional trauma. Something more was at issue than the hope of ousting a man they considered an inadequate president and a political danger to their party, something more than satisfying constituents, donors, and the silent majority Nixon had invented.

The Special Prosecutors and House Managers gave the impression of being impelled by an obscure demand they were ultimately prepared to sacrifice themselves to. The demand stemmed partly from their party's Nixon trauma, which introduced a superego structure into their political and legal practice and put their group psychology in harm's way. The element of Drive in Starr and company— betrayed in their frustrated pleadings and their oft-stated rigorous devotion to (an unobtainable, impossible sexual) Truth—"the whole truth"—pushed them beyond political and legal concerns into the realm of phantasm.

On one level, of course, the attack was just politics. Although it was not easy to expand dirty details extracted from grudging, hearsay witnesses into constitutional crises, Starr made Clinton squirm. And he forced Clinton to repeat the unappetizing tactical defenses the country had scoffed at when they were employed by Nixon, Oliver North, and even Clarence Thomas. To resist legally the Special Prosecutor's dismantling of the traditional firewalls guarding presidential privacy, Clinton found that he had to resort to executive privilege, a Nixon device. When he carefully avoided

incriminating himself in the Jones deposition, he was seen as setting himself "above the law"—a phrase used by Fawn Hall in her
shockingly fascistic-sounding defense of Oliver North's illegal acts
in Iran-Contra. (She later apologized for expressing this sentiment.)
The ridiculousness of the sexual details Starr released was intended
to humiliate Clinton as Clarence Thomas had been humiliated by
Democratic-controlled Senate confirmation hearings.

The simple tactical components of the conservative's political game went even further, though: they forced these particular
legal responses from Clinton to demonstrate concretely that *no one*
was ever any less guilty than anyone else; that Democratic leaders
were as fallible as Republican ones. In playing this out, though, the
Starr team unleashed the notion of a guilt beyond measure, exor-
bitant, ineradicable, one no longer simply confined to explicit acts
of trammeling the law and violating fundamental ethics the way
Richard Nixon had. They unleashed superego guilt.

No one should ever be forced to face his or her traumatic core:
no person, without having freely chosen to undergo psychoanalysis or having elected to write an autobiographical confession, should
ever be made to endure the agonizing scrutiny of their private
jouissance, their guilty kernel, their death drive. In the effort to
sully everyone and to ensure that no one was "above the law," Starr
undercut an elementary principle crucial to democracy: individual
responsibility. This translates, in psychoanalytic terms, as the necessary assumption of your own subjectivity: the acceptance of your
own traumatic core, of the existence of an unconscious that escapes
the confines of your own unruffled ego (who misrecognizes this
kernel of enjoyment and thus remains vulnerable to its traumatic
return as superego pressure). To say individual responsibility is to
say that a subject's relation to jouissance is an ethical, not a moral
matter. Jouissance is an existential fact that must be ethically faced,
not a delict to be exposed and condemned as a moral failing.

Yet a moral judgment on a psychic structure is precisely what
Starr essentially demanded. The implicit claim in his rhetoric was
that because *all* are *guilty, none are* (to exculpate Nixon, e.g.). Yet
was public misconduct like Nixon's (even if rooted in psychic dif-

ficulties) on a par with Clinton's personal inability to handle his private relation to jouissance gracefully? It is time to submit this psychoanalytic question to political philosophy.


## DEMOCRACY IN THEORY

In the theory descended from Rousseau, modern democracy depends on excluding private jouissance from the "general will."[24] In founding our democracy on the "will of the people," our framers sought anxiously to foreclose special interests from claiming that their private good conveniently dovetailed with the "good of the whole." The American founders thus, with perhaps unwitting prescience, structured our society on what we might call *desire—collective desire*—precisely by excluding private passions (what we would now call their *lethal jouissance*) from public, political acts. That is why Starr's insistent demand for exposure did not come from *the people*, who found the picture of Bill and Monica engaged in heavy petting disgusting, decidedly unromantic, and not even very "juicy."

In a way, Starr was virtually forced into the confrontation—not just by his private anxieties but also by the provocation Clinton represented (however unwillingly). How far should the exclusion of private passion from public will extend? Few had ever ventured to test the limits; after all, no modern president ever permitted himself much of a sexual tonality. Until Clinton. (Even JFK's love life did not loom very large in the public imagination until well after his assassination.)[25] For reasons not entirely clear, Bill Clinton always played politically with his sexiness, even before being caught in Starr's headlights. He had allowed one sexual rumor after another to swirl unanswered as part and parcel of a political appeal to younger veterans of the sexual revolution, to Americans not

---

24. See my chapter "Race/War," in *The Hysteric's Guide* (MacCannell 2000).

25. Surprisingly, Jimmy Carter had spoken of "lusting in his heart" (in a *Playboy* interview), though it was taken as a ploy to show voters he was not just an "uptight" micro-managerial type.

descended from puritans, and to romantic people everywhere. "At last you have a president who is a real man," one French waiter declared.[26]

Yet it is possible that Clinton could not really do otherwise. To refer once again to Lacan's terms, the Leader can and even must embody the group's object a, the kernel of its fundamental fantasy. Clinton, however, was neither the magnetic leader of Freud's type of group nor the totalitarian whose object a represents the menacing Other. Whatever Bill Clinton's object a was, it was clearly his and his alone (remember all the jokes about "big hair" or Monica Lewinsky's lawyer speculating he must like dark pubic hair?). As such he (it) represented the way *the people* in democracy experience the object a: as a relationship between them, as subjects, to their own jouissance, not only that of their Leader.

Thus it was Clinton's fate to challenge, however unwillingly, the way that the object a had imperceptibly come to be embedded in a group ego during the conservative era. As that era drew to a close, Clinton emerged as the polar opposite of Nixon's (and Reagan's) type of love-object. He thus reflected the traumatic object a that uniquely relates us to the democratic group. If the object a is the condition of possibility of the subject, then the political body the subject produces is not really the conformist "melting pot" group, the one that, from the 1950s on, Americans were told they were supposed to be. The shift is dramatic.

In the Lewinsky matter, Clinton therefore seemed strangely sympathetic, less caught than caught off guard by the surprising loss of aura ordinarily attending the person as well as the office of president. The public rightly admonished Clinton for being "dumb" enough to pursue an extramarital involvement while he was a defendant in Paula Jones's civil suit for sexual harassment. But by and large they didn't fall in with Starr's attack on his sexuality.

Why did Starr pursue this unpopular attack so very doggedly? In refusing Clinton the traditional discretion afforded the commander in chief—the privilege of having his sexuality politely

---

26. Thanks to Manya Steinkoler for this anecdote.

ignored—Starr seemed to be striking at privilege itself—the ulti-mate privilege of the One who has it all. In the Clinton–Starr wrangle, democratic politics risked entering openly the region of jouissance, of the superego and its administrators.[27] The public sphere sud-denly became an arena for the politics of jouissance—and envy and theft of jouissance are the basic stuff of trauma. (This is the long-standing claim made by Jacques Lacan in *Seminar III* on psychosis, 1955–1956, and in *Seminar VII* on ethics, 1960–1961, on which the theses of Jacques-Alain Miller and Slavoj Žižek concerning paranoid envy and *Lebensneid* at the root of social life are based.)

Did the Clinton–Starr battle succeed in foreclosing the demo-cratic politics of desire, or did it strengthen them by opposition? Clinton proved remarkably resilient in the face of Starr's demand for absolute disclosure. But the social body Clinton represented may not have remained untouched. Although the silly banality of the exposures Clinton suffered personally embarrassed him, his fam-ily, and his lover, they were relatively minor compared to a larger evil that banality risked inflicting on our maturing democracy.

## WHY WAS CLINTON OUR OBJECT A?

While Watergate and Monicagate enjoyed the figural resemblance Starr forced on them, their legal and political parallelism was never more than superficial. The legal precedents (e.g., executive privi-lege), the substantive charges, the national security issues, were all radically dissimilar. What Clinton and Nixon had in common exclusively was their reputation for dishonesty. For Clinton, how-ever, this charge was always aimed at his sexual persona, not at his political one. For Nixon, the opposite was true. Yet ultimately the hidden linkages among love, sexuality, and leadership do forge a

---

27. Copjec 1994, pp.181–190. Copjec writes that we live in a society that "commands *jouissance* as a cure"; it is a "duty" that has disrupted our attempts to "safe-guard the empty 'private' space" necessarily produced as the residue of culture.

traumatic link between Presidents Nixon and Clinton. While their style and manner of leadership differed radically, each embodied the group as Leader in some way. This ties Nixon and Clinton together while distinguishing them absolutely.

Few have ever really given much thought to Nixon's sexuality, and fewer still ever contemplated Clinton's sexy, "mesmerizing" gaze in a political rather than exclusively sexual frame. Yet when Clinton assumed national leadership, the two frames collided in an unprecedented (and, for many, calamitous) way. For, according to Freud, the Leader of a group *must* be loved by it irrationally, and *he* must also love *it* unconditionally in return in order for the group to be. Its Leader becomes a group's irrational, absolute, asexual yet strangely obscene point that hooks his followers together and commands their loyalty, conformity, and harmony. In contrast, the person of Bill Clinton had come to represent, in a highly overdetermined way, not social harmony, but nearly all the difficult social conflicts and social changes the country had coped with in the five decades prior to his election.

This is not surprising. American democracy was convulsed in the latter half of the twentieth century by events everyone deemed national traumas: McCarthyism, the King and Kennedy assassinations, the horrifyingly televisual Vietnam War, the My Lai massacre, the Watergate scandal, and the Iran-Contra hearings. Such political shocks were not easily absorbed by public consciousness; they seemed deeply foreign to our optimistic, progressive, democratic state.

These events accompanied large-scale social changes equally difficult to assimilate: disrupted generational ties, altered social mores, shifting gender status and power, and crucial transformations in race relations. These last changes were amazingly orderly given their enormous structural scope: reformist legal challenges instituted civil rights for all—that is, for more than white (Protestant, mostly male) citizens that many had considered the "real" American citizens. If they also showed a violent edge—urban conflagrations, the murder of whites alongside blacks (Schwerner, Goodman, *and* Chaney *and* the four Little Rock girls in the 1960s)—ultimately it was still the Law, not the Violence that was determinative of the outcome. The Benjaminian style of violence that "institutes" the Law (the Law of the social as instituted by the violence to nature of language and culture) was not at work in this case, where another level of legal work was being accomplished.

The violence of the 1960s, that is, was an *occasional* cause of progressive social legislation. But its unintended effect was also to mobilize various behind-the-scenes efforts to "South Africanize" our educational and social institutions. "Apartheid" style thinking, in the 1980s and 1990s, was always excused by reference to violence. Thus, in the end, progressive social outcomes were installed despite (and I believe not because of) the various militancies urging them on or attempting to halt them.

The sexual revolution likewise deeply disturbed our society, but, unlike the racial one, it proved much less amenable to legislative resolutions and to the discourse of rights. Perhaps violence might have caused legal changes to be implemented on sexual issues, but because sexuality is so implicated in the problematics of group life (detailed here), complications remain.

I suggest that large-scale, dramatic (though most often slow-moving) changes in American society were traumas only in a quasi-medical sense—the sense of serious injuries suffered by an otherwise intact body. Whatever violence these events may have done to the fabric of American society, they never approached the level of bitter virulence, say, of the Civil War (which affirmed our wholeness as a political and social necessity). Deep down, we did accept these changes as obligatory growing pains and abrasions incurred as our land of freedom, justice, and equality, and (above all) good will grew to maturity.

Undeniable socio- and psychopathologies did, it is true, erupt alongside these glacial legal changes. Serial killers, one after the other, emerged steadily from the shadows of the house next door—Charles Manson, Ted Bundy, John Wayne Gacy, Wayne Williams, Henry Lucas, Jeffrey Dahmer—bearing titles like the Hillside Strangler, the Night Stalker, and more.[28] Mass murderers sought out

---

28. As well as more recent femmes fatales serial killers.

cheap chain restaurants and schoolyards to attack. Derelict military-industrial-bureaucratic complexes poisoned large populations without displaying a hint of conscience, either rapidly (Bhopal) or over time (tobacco companies, atomic testing, Love Canal, medical experiments on prisoners). It was as if the reserve power of a democratic society—its popular self-correcting power—was being tested by impersonal associations (corporate bureaucracies) and lone individuals (Ted Kaczynski) who amassed their own kind of excessive firepower to produce huge damage.

As insistent, unaccountable irrationality burst forth in public life alongside the larger but generally orderly social changes I have mentioned, Bill Clinton stepped up to government. His mere existence stirred memories of the very real and wrenching changes that the Reagan–Bush years had smoothed over. Clinton was a Southern white who, on his own, had made obvious his personally happy accommodation with blacks—some of his "closest friends" really were black (and also, quite evidently, Jewish). He was the first president who had been born after World War II and was thus part of an untested and mistrusted younger generation. He married a woman who was his intellectual peer (or even superior), to whose judgment he often publicly deferred. His academic accomplishments had permitted him to avoid serving in a war he opposed—the Vietnam War that disproportionately took men of his own class and background who had not achieved similar success. He also bore the brunt of a larger revolutionary interchange of public for private in which no one, however much they were swathed in symbolic mantles (like Prince Charles or Richard Gere), seemed able to evade disclosing their intimate being, their jouissance.[29]

---

29. I suggest the reader consult Copjec 1994, pp. 181–182. I also recommend her brilliant essay "The Strut of Vision," in *Qui Parle* (1996), which details the scopic drive as perverse in the sense that it demands the displaying of jouissance at the expense of shadowy, "backlit" desire. The matter of privacy is not a question of elite privilege; it is a structural requirement of democratic social and civic life to acknowledge that a "bit" remains forever outside that civil, social life. See my essay "Perversion in Public Places," *New Formations* (March 1999), which also appears as a chapter in *The Hysteric's Guide* (2000).

Clinton also occupied his symbolic post in a peculiar way that uniquely wedded him to two of the greatest social revolutions of the previous decades—race and sex—and he thus seemed to incorporate their irrational remainders into his public persona, his symbolic character as Leader. According to Freud's theory of the group, neither sexuality nor visible, physical differences (like race and biological sex) can be sustained within group life (see footnotes 32 and 33 for Freud's thoughts)—and no Leader can become the group's object a if he permits explicit differences to become foregrounded. Clinton, however, for all his whiteness, achieved a measure of both racializing and sexualizing the Leader, thereby undoing the Leader's dependence on the unary trait.[30] He was perhaps the first to bear openly the mark of an irrational, indefinable "x" factor that was no longer embedded in the gaze, voice, or other ego-reflex of Freud's mesmeric Leader. Clinton thus placed his bets not on a group that was balanced on a fragile ego (and tormented by a superego) but on a group composed of subjects. The greatest stake of Clinton's leadership was precisely to be the first person to recast Leadership in the "age of sex"—the age of sexual difference. He was the first thereby to reflect the *democratic* social group.

The right wing reacted against this fundamental change in the stakes of political leadership in a more than political way: for to them, the very stakes of group life itself were at risk. To the majority of the democratic people he led, Clinton's adoption of a sexual character

---

30. Clinton was simply not a traditional "white" man in the older sense, and perhaps not even a "man" at all. Toni Morrison noted in the *New Yorker* that Clinton's practical sympathy with a "black" viewpoint had made him into "our first 'black president'"—and thus left him open to the humiliation any accomplished black man may endure—having his worth reduced to the size of his bare(d) genitals. (Think of the FBI "sex files" kept on Martin Luther King or the dramatic reduction of the Clarence Thomas hearing to his pornography-viewing habits rather than his legal views.)

Moreover, Monica Lewinsky's account pictures a Clinton who was far from a classic male predator/aggressor. She shows him playing rather the "feminine" part in the affair, refusing sexual advances, at last giving in to enormous seductive pressures, and never "going all the way." In Monica's picture, Clinton is the 1950s prom queen the jocks eagerly kiss—and tell on.

was unthreatening, but for others, it was the cause of great alarm. Clinton's presidency meant a radical transformation of the face—literally—of our society and of the presidential image. It was now a face made up of difference and desire, rather than unity and love. The Nixon presidency, by contrast, had invented a "moral majority" to recast the democratic group around an average center. It relegated all oddballs—the "nattering nabobs of negativity," the "pointy-headed intellectuals" (and thus the women, the people of color, and the poor)—to the no-man's-land of the group's periphery.

New dimensions of Leadership opened by people like Clinton make necessary a second reading of Freud: we can now accept that it is in the nature of Leadership to be "traumatic" in character, but the trauma does not necessarily mean that Leadership must constantly refer to the fearsome primal father it staves off or allows to be foregrounded at will. Can we not say more broadly instead that in Clinton we found a shift from group psychology to Democratic psychology?[31] And does not the allegory of Clinton—or the Clintons—demonstrate that a group's object a can (or may) alter its unconscious referent? Let us look at Leaderly love once again to draw some conclusions.

---

31. One reader of this essay resisted my thesis that the democratic group now being born may be characterized as specifically sexual in nature (not just liberal-tolerant à la Judith Butler's sanitized gender-play, but rawly, frankly, dirtily sexual). No matter how we liberalize it, the Christian-Augustinian-Thomist version of the city of God remains our mainstream model for society—even democratic society. Democracy is supposed to be a universal wherein all may be uniformly included—but there's always a catch. Some are always excluded where an enclosed universal is aimed at (the ones Marguerite Duras enumerates in *Hiroshima, mon amour* as vagabonds, madmen, and dogs who roam outside the city walls). These exceptions are broadly designated in Lacan's *Encore* as sexual others (i.e., feminine, nonphallocentric) made unwelcome in the Thomist city except as servants or slaves.

Despite the fact that the Jewish Freud chose to characterize the excluded mainly by their sexual behavior rather than by their racial, religious, or sexual difference, none are fully acceptable to groups invested in uniformity, harmony, and conformity. Democracy ought to deviate from this model and remain open to sexual as well as other differences.

## LEADERLY LOVE ENCORE

Richard Nixon commanded, until his death and even since, the kind of hypnotic loyal love from the people he mirrors that Freud's group Leader does—for after all he stands between them and the primal fear of a persecutory father. But Bill Clinton gave and received his Leaderly love on an entirely different model. Clinton broke the rule of the late modern group: he had favorites. He broke this rule not only with his mistresses; more crucially, he broke it by having a strong relationship, intellectual, partnering, whatever, with another sexual subject: his wife.

Freud says that "two people coming together for the purposes of sexual satisfaction, in so far as they seek for solitude, are making a demonstration against . . . group feeling."[32] Freud tells us that sexual love is absolutely excluded in modern artificial groups: sexual couples must form outside the group, which (along with its other demands for uniformity) requires the deletion of all sexual difference.[33]

How can we update Freud's view of the group *for* democracy? Slavoj Žižek has theorized that all group formations have a necessarily traumatic core that constitutes the group's greatest (lost) jouissance as well as its greatest (potential) pain. But in democracy, what do we really fear? The return of the despotic ur-father? Or the return of political despots who have such a figure only as their ideal-ego? What constitutes the indelible trauma of the democratic group's origination, and what forms the unknowable, non-dialectizable cause of this Group's being? What is the kernel of the democratic group's fundamental fantasy, the obscene kernel of its

---

32. Freud 1920, p. 140. Freud's sense of strict egalitarianism is that it is founded on primal envy; his example is a group of girls swooning collectively over a crooner to prevent him from singling out one for special notice.

33. Ibid.: "in the great artificial groups, the Church and the Army, there is no room for woman as a sexual object. The love relation between men and women remains outside these organizations. Even where groups are formed which are composed of both men and women, distinction between the sexes plays no part."

jouissance, the absence/presence at the center of democracy's fundamental fantasy? What binds this new kind of group together? Is it that its object a is both its substance and its defense against it?

We cannot say *what* the democratic object a is; only *that* it is. How we relate to the obscene point of enjoyment that forms our fundamental fantasy, and the Leader that may embody it, matters politically, however. It impacts our life in common. Do we envy the imputed possession of our object a by others? Do we see it as an unconscious fulcrum of power—like the Führer's mustache? Let us note minimally that Clinton was a sexualized Leader who was nonetheless not a despot. Clinton's manner of inhabiting Leadership jarred these "group psychology" assumptions and implicitly challenged these (Hobbesian/authoritarian) conventional ways of coping with the traumatic object a:

*Power.* Leader-love brooks no internal antagonisms and permits no open conflicts over the object of desire. Its social bond is governed by an implicit claim to innocence: that its social contract is free of conflicts. Freud tells us that the group's unity is illusory, however. Its air of glossy falsity (see Adorno) stems from an ego-driven need to deny the original trauma from which it arose: the primal conflict with the ur-father over the object of desire. While Leader-love submerges it, this conflict is repressed. Clintonian democracy unearthed buried social conflicts.

*Envy.* Clinton's special (and long-overdue) recognition of blacks provoked a primal envy in the all-white group image, the melting pot that Adorno and Lacan alike objected to, in which all others were conformed to an image of the One. Once any white, of whatever political party, could assume a basic similarity with all the objects of a Leader's love. Starr tried to separate sexual love from the Leader's sustaining love for the group; but in bringing it so far into the light, Starr himself risked dissolving the bonds of love crucial to this version of group life. Clinton permitted visibly distinctive others—blacks, women—into the American image. This was potentially devastating to the group-self constituted by uniformity and conformity. But in the relatively young and untried structure of a modern democracy, showcasing difference is necessary even at the risk of inciting unconscious envy. The American people actually cut Clinton some slack: he could care for them as a people *and* he could care for any number of individuals. They permitted him to single out Monica Lewinsky the way Freud's Leader cannot.

*Sexuality*. Kenneth Starr's hounding of Clinton and Lewinsky for disclosure was rooted in a desire to remove from office someone who deviated from his notion of a Leader—the kind Freud's book analyzed. Starr overstated the threat of sexuality in the Leader. He found to his surprise that the "democratic group" was not only forgiving of sexuality in its Leader, it seemed to welcome its presence.[34] Finally, it was Hillary who was (and remains) the real target of the attack on Clinton's "sexuality."[35]

## CONCLUSION

The commentators who were so quick to brand the president's banal, truncated flirtation a national *trauma* even while the facts were still unfolding were not entirely off base. For although the Clinton–Starr–Lewinsky tangle was a minor, risible footnote to the later history of the twentieth-century American republic, and quite unworthy of the extraordinary attention it drew at its height, it was also of exceptional importance to the future life of our democracy.

In the idiosyncratic and original way Clinton embodied the democratic object a—democracy's traumatic excess—we learned something of the structure of the democratic "group." We also discovered the ultimate shortcomings of the stubbornly perverse efforts—by Starr among others—to bring this object a out of the

---

34. Ibid., p. 120.

35. It remains undecided whether even a democratic people can ultimately tolerate and forgive their president—their commander in chief—his partnership with a woman whose judgment he may, on occasion, defer to. We should also note (to follow the traumatic repetition of Watergate to its sad conclusion) that Hillary was the only principal in this Democrat/Republican war to have served on the Senate Watergate committee (as junior counsel).

demidark and into the light. The real trauma connected to this affair had to do with the constitutive trauma in which the democratic collective subject arose (the direct overthrow of tyranny). Democracy has demonstrated a fundamental desire to keep this traumatic object and the drive it evokes activated by sheltering it from a perverse scopic drive.

The Clinton affair ultimately did do more than sell newspapers and television ads, which of course it also did: a public puzzled by modern sexuality was anxious for crumbs of information to form the very judgments official pundits failed at. Yet the politicians who listened closely (they thought) to that public and made excessive responses on that basis, the partisan politicians who fanned the flames ("a vast right-wing conspiracy") and showed moralistic outrage (the "sexual playpen" quotation), were wrong. The out-of-kilter responses to Clinton (and to the Clintons) indexed more than media overreach, more than political advantage seeking. The hysterical response to Clinton even seemed inevitable to those of us of a certain age who half-expected an antisexual, antidemocratic backlash to the civic gains made by women and blacks.

Many—not only on the extreme right—appeared to half-hope or half-fear that Clinton would at last be found out for a rapist, murderer, or just plain sex addict/serial philanderer (of gigantic proportions)—to be found out as a totemic father who needs to be slain again. Whoever assumed Clinton to be a totemic father, however, was secretly reacting to the terrific change in the modality of Leadership that Clinton represented. This change, though, only reflected the changes in our society that no Leader had yet found the means or the courage to face—let alone tried to symbolize.

To have seen Clinton as embodying horrendous excess is a bit of a stretch, given Clinton's truly bland personality, his boyishness, and his Horatio Alger biography. Yet in his accusers (and a lot of his supporters), he excited a demand for light to be shed on a mysterious "x" factor, a traumatic "ex-cess" otherwise unaccounted for, that was obviously plaguing our lives and bedeviling his.

That "x" factor turned out to be only the object a at the core of anyone's life. It also turned out to be something nearly everyone wished to keep offstage, out of the light. It thus emerged as a new way for the democratic group to anchor its unique form of identification. The highly charged lynchpin of social feeling (Leaderly ego love) may never recover its former supremacy of the Nixon years and since.

The mob and democracy are often confused for each other— democracy has always contended with being called "mob rule" or "mass society." This paper has been a modest effort to distinguish the two by using the psychoanalytic toolkit. We democratic peoples can ignore neither democracy's continual fascistic temptations nor the magnetic attraction Freud's mob exerts on us (why *do* we love Mafia movies so much?). Not if we wish to discover, patiently, the root principles of *our* kind of group (even if they dwell in the unconscious).

## REFERENCES

Copjec, J. (1994). *Read My Desire: Lacan against the Historicists*. Cambridge, MA: MIT Press.

Dershowitz, A. M. (1998). *Sexual McCarthyism: Clinton, Starr and the Emerging Constitutional Crisis*. New York: Basic Books.

Freud, S. (1920). Group psychology and the analysis of the ego. In *The Standard Edition of the Complete Psychological Works of Sigmund Freud*, Vol. 18, trans. J. Strachey. London: Hogarth, 1955.

Lacan, J. (1956–1957). *Le Séminaire, Livre IV, La Relation d'objet*. Paris: Seuil, 1994.

———— (1977). *The Four Fundamental Concepts of Psychoanalysis, Seminar XI*, trans. A. Sheridan. New York and London: W. W. Norton.

MacCannell, J. F. (2000). *The Hysteric's Guide to the Future Female Subject*. Minneapolis: University of Minnesota Press.

Morton, A. W. (1999). *Monica's Story*. New York: St. Martin's Press.

Starr, K. (1987). Interview by Diane Sawyer. *Sixty Minutes*. CBS.

Stendhal. (1822). Love in the United States. In *Love*, trans. G. Sale and S. Sale. Harmondsworth, England: Penguin, 1975.

# 10

# The Subject of True Feeling: Pain, Privacy, and Politics

Lauren Berlant

*Liberty finds no refuge in a jurisprudence of doubt.*[1]

## PAIN

Ravaged wages and ravaged bodies saturate the global marketplace in which the United States seeks desperately to compete "competitively," as the euphemism goes, signifying a race that will be won by the nations whose labor conditions are most optimal for profit.[2] In the United States, the media of the political public sphere regularly register new scandals of the proliferating sweatshop networks "at home" and "abroad," which has to be a good thing, because it produces *feeling* and with it something at least akin to *consciousness* that can lead to *action*.[3] Yet even as the image of the trauma-

---

1. *Planned Parenthood of Southeastern Pennsylvania v. Casey* 1992, at 2803.
2. See, for example, DeMartino and Cullenberg 1994.
3. Take the case of the talk show host Kathie Lee Gifford, whose clothing line at the U.S. low-price megastore, Wal-Mart, generated for her ten million

tized worker proliferates, even as evidence of exploitation is found under every rock or commodity, it competes with a normative/utopian image of the U.S. citizen who remains unmarked, framed, and protected by the private trajectory of his life project, which is sanctified at the juncture where the unconscious meets history: the American Dream.[4] In that story, one's identity is not borne of suffering, mental, physical, or economic. If the U.S. worker is lucky enough to live at an economic moment that sustains the Dream, he gets to appear at his *least* national when he is working and at his most national at leisure, with his family or in semipublic worlds of other men producing surplus manliness (e.g., via sports). In the

dollars of profit in its first year. During May and June of 1996, Gifford was exposed by Charles Kernaghan, of the National Labor Education Fund in Support of Worker and Human Rights in Central America, for allowing her clothes to be made by tragically underpaid and mistreated young Honduran children, mostly girls. A Lexis/Nexus search under the keywords *Kathie Lee Gifford/Child Labor* nets close to two hundred stories, from all over the world, reporting on this event. A few main plots emerge from these stories: it is cast as a revenge story against privilege from the ranks of the less well-off, which strips from Gifford the protection of her perky, populist, and intimate persona to reveal the entrepreneurial profiteer beneath; it implicates an entire culture of celebrity-centered consumerism (Jaclyn Smith/K-Mart, The Gap, Spike Lee/Michael Jordan/Nike) that is organized around a "virtuous" role modelesque public figure or label that seems to certify healthy conscientious social membership for consumers; it becomes an exemplum of the banality of sweatshop labor in the United States and around the world; and a call to belated conscience. Through Gifford's apparent intimacy with her devoted audience, a "public" outraged by child exploitation seemed instantly to emerge, which led in turn to a kind of state action, involving an intensified federal push for voluntary covenants against child labor and subminimum wages (measured by "local," not U.S., standards of remuneration). It also eventuated in the development of a new label, "No Sweat," to be put on any clothes produced by adequately paid workers—a sad substitute for the union labels of years past. This issue has quickly joined child abuse as an ongoing zone of fascination and (mainly) impotent concern in the political public sphere. See, for a relatively unjaded extended example, Schamberg 1996. For a more general view of the political/media exploitation of the exploited child figure, see Wark 1995.

4. For more exposition on the ways political cultures that value abstract or universal personhood produce privileged bodies and identities that travel unmarked, unremarkable, and free of structural humiliation, see Berlant 1993, 1997, Dyer 1993, and Phelan 1993.

American dreamscape, his identity is private property, a zone in which structural obstacles and cultural differences fade into an ether of prolonged, deferred, and individuating enjoyment that he has earned and that the nation has helped him to earn. Meanwhile, exploitation only appears as a scandalous nugget in the sieve of memory when it can be condensed into an exotic thing of momentary fascination, a squalor of the bottom too horrible to be read in its own actual banality.

The exposed traumas of workers in ongoing extreme conditions do not generally induce more than mourning on the part of the state and the public culture to whose feeling-based opinions the state is said to respond. Mourning is what happens when a grounding object is lost, is dead, no longer living (to you). Mourning is an experience of irreducible boundedness: I am here, I am living; he is dead, I am mourning. It is a beautiful, not sublime, experience of emancipation: mourning supplies the subject with the definitional perfection of a being no longer in flux. It takes place over a distance: even if the object who induces the feeling of loss and helplessness is neither dead nor at any great distance from where you are.[5] In other words, mourning can also be an act of aggression, of social deathmaking: it can perform the evacuation of significance from actually existing subjects. Even when liberals do it, one might say, "others" are ghosted for a good cause.[6] The

---

5. The essay of Sigmund Freud's summarized here is "Mourning and Melancholia" (1963).

6. The best work on the civilized barbarism of mourning has been done on AIDS discourse in U.S. culture: see Crimp 1990 and virtually every essay in Crimp 1988. Crimp is especially astute on the necessary articulation of sentimentality and politics: because processes of legitimation cannot do without the production of consent, and empathetic misrecognition is one tactic for creating it. The question is how, and at what cost, different kinds of subjects and contexts of empathy are imagined in the struggle for radical social transformation. See also Nunokowa 1991. Judith Butler's (1990, 1993) work has also been a crucial intertext here, notably its representation of heterosexual melancholia (the disavowed experience of loss heterosexuals endure as a consequence of having to divert ongoing same-sex love/identification/attachments), a condition that expresses itself through gender normativity, heterosexual hegemony, misogyny, homophobia, and other forms of disciplinary order. This opened a space for thinking about

sorrow songs of scandal that sing of the exploitation that is always "elsewhere" (even a few blocks away) are in this sense aggressive songs of mourning. Play them backward, and the military march of capitalist triumphalism (*The Trans-Nationale*) can be heard. Its lyric, currently crooned by every organ of record in the United States, is about necessity. It exhorts citizens to understand that the "bottom line"[7] of national life is neither utopia nor freedom but survival, which can only be achieved by a citizenry that eats its anger, makes no unreasonable claims on resources or control over value, and uses its most creative energy to cultivate intimate spheres while scrapping a life together flexibly in response to the market world's caprice.[8]

In this particular moment of expanding class unconsciousness that looks like consciousness, emerges a peculiar, though not unprecedented, hero: the exploited child. If a worker can be infantilized, pictured as young, as small, as feminine or feminized, as starving, as bleeding and diseased, and as a (virtual) slave, the righteous indignation around procuring his survival resounds everywhere. The child must not be sacrificed to states or to profiteering. His wounded image speaks a truth that subordinates narrative: he has not "freely" chosen his exploitation; the optimism and play that are putatively the rights of childhood have been stolen from him. Yet only "voluntary" steps are ever taken to try to control this visible sign of what is ordinary and systemic amid the chaos of capitalism, in order to make its localized nightmares seem uninevitable. Privatize the atrocity, delete the visible sign, make it seem *foreign*. Return the child to the family, replace the children with adults who can look dignified while being paid virtually the same revolting wage. The problem that organizes so much feeling then regains livable proportions, and the uncomfortable pressure of feeling dissipates, like so much gas.

---

the social function of mourning in similar contexts of normative hierarchy in which intimacies appear to have to be constructed, not suppressed.

7. On the "bottom line" as a site of political articulation and struggle, see Alexander 1995.

8. On the structures and rhetorics of coercive flexibility in transnational times, see Harvey 1989, Martin 1994, and Rouse 1995.

Meanwhile, the pressure of feeling the shock of being uncomfortably political produces a cry for a double therapy—to the victim and the viewer. But before "we" appear too complacently different from the privileged citizens who desire to caption the mute image of exotic suffering with an aversively fascinated mourning (a desire for the image to be *dead*, a ghost), we must note that this feeling culture crosses over into other domains, the domains of what we call identity politics, where the wronged take up voice and agency to produce transformative testimony, which depends on an analogous conviction about the *self-evidence* and therefore the *objectivity* of painful feeling.

The central concern of this essay is to address the place of painful feeling in the making of political worlds. In particular, I mean to challenge a powerful popular belief in the positive workings of something I call national sentimentality, a rhetoric of promise that a nation can be built across fields of social difference through channels of affective identification and empathy. Sentimental politics generally promotes and maintains the hegemony of the national identity form, no mean feat in the face of continued widespread intercultural antagonism and economic cleavage. But national sentimentality is more than a current of feeling that circulates in a political field: the phrase describes a longstanding contest between two models of U.S. citizenship. In one, the classic model, each citizen's value is secured by an equation between abstractness and emancipation: a cell of national identity provides juridically protected personhood for citizens regardless of anything specific about them. In the second model, which was initially organized around labor, feminist, and antiracist struggles of the nineteenth-century United States, another version of the nation is imagined as the index of collective life. This nation is peopled by suffering citizens and noncitizens whose structural exclusion from the utopian-American dreamscape exposes the state's claim of legitimacy and virtue to an acid wash of truth telling that makes hegemonic disavowal virtually impossible, at certain moments of political intensity.

Sentimentality has long been the means by which mass subaltern pain is advanced, in the dominant public sphere, as the true core of national collectivity. It operates when the pain of intimate others burns into the conscience of classically privileged national subjects, such that they feel the pain of flawed or denied citizenship as their pain. Theoretically, to eradicate the pain, those with power will do whatever is necessary to return the nation once more to its legitimately utopian odor. Identification with pain, a universal true feeling, then leads to structural social change. In return, subalterns scarred by the pain of failed democracy will reauthorize universalist notions of citizenship in the national utopia, which involves believing in a redemptive notion of law as the guardian of public good. The object of the nation and the law in this light is to eradicate systemic social pain, the absence of which becomes the definition of freedom.

Yet since these very sources of protection—the state, the law, patriotic ideology—have traditionally buttressed traditional matrices of cultural hierarchy, and since their historic job has been to protect universal subject/citizens from feeling their cultural and corporeal specificity as a political vulnerability, the imagined capacity of these institutions to assimilate to the affective tactics of subaltern counterpolitics suggests some weaknesses, or misrecognitions, in these tactics. For one thing, it may be that the sharp specificity of the traumatic model of pain implicitly mischaracterizes what a person is as what a person becomes in the experience of social negation; this model also falsely promises a sharp picture of structural violence's source and scope, in turn promoting a dubious optimism that law and other visible sources of inequality, for example, can provide the best remedies for their own taxonomizing harms. It is also possible that counterhegemonic deployments of pain as the measure of structural injustice actually sustain the utopian image of a homogeneous national metaculture, which can look like a healed or healthy body in contrast to the scarred and the exhausted ones. Finally, it might be that the tactical use of trauma to describe the effects of social inequality so overidentifies the eradication of pain with the achievement of justice that it enables various confusions: for instance, the equation of pleasure with freedom or the sense that changes in feeling, even on a mass scale, amount to substantial social change. Sentimental politics makes these confusions credible and these violences bearable, as its cultural power confirms the centrality of interpersonal identification and empathy to the vitality and viability of collective life. This gives citizens something to do in response to overwhelming structural violence. Meanwhile, by equating mass society with that thing called "national culture," these important transpersonal linkages and intimacies all too frequently serve as proleptic shields, as ethically uncontestable legitimating devices for sustaining the hegemonic field.[9]

Our first example, the child laborer, a ghost of the nineteenth century, taps into a current vogue to reflect in the premature exposure of children to capitalist publicity and adult depravity the nation's moral and economic decline, citing it as a scandal of citizenship, something shocking and un-American. Elsewhere I have described the ways the infantile citizen has been exploited, in the United States, to become both the inspiring sign of the painless good life and the evacuating optimistic cipher of contemporary national identity.[10] During the 1980s, a desperate search to protect the United States from what seemed to be an imminently powerful alliance of parties on the bottom of so many traditional hierarchies —the poor, people of color, women, gays and lesbians—provoked a counterinsurgent fantasy on behalf of "traditional American values." The nation imagined in this reactive rhetoric is dedicated neither to the survival nor emancipation of traumatized marginal

---

9. One critic who has not underestimated the hegemonic capacities of state deployments of pain is Elaine Scarry in *The Body in Pain: The Making and Unmaking of the World* (1985). This book remains a stunning description of the ways control over actual physical and rhetorical pain provides the state and the law with control over what constitutes collective reality, the conjuncture of beliefs and the material world. See especially Part 2, on pain and imagining. Like the legal theorists and jurists whose writing this essay engages, Scarry works with a fully state- (or institutionally) saturated concept of the subject, a relation more specific and nonuniversal than it frequently seems to be in her representation of it.

10. See Berlant, *Queen of America* (1997). The following paragraphs revise and repeat some arguments from this book. For an essay specifically on scandalized childhood in the contemporary United States, see Ivy 1993.

subjects but, rather, to freedom for the American innocent: the adult without sin, the abducted and neglected child, and above all, and most effectively, the fetus. Although it had first appeared as a technological miracle of photographic bio-power in the mid-1960s, in the post-Roe era, the fetus became consolidated as a political commodity, a supernatural sign of national iconicity. What constituted this national iconicity was an image of an American, perhaps the last living American, not yet bruised by history: not yet caught up in the excitement of mass consumption or ethnic, racial, or sexual mixing, not yet tainted by knowledge, by money, or by war. This fetus was an American to identify with, to aspire to make a world for: it organized a kind of beautiful citizenship politics of good intention and virtuous fantasy that could not be said to be dirty, or whose dirt was attributed to the sexually or politically immoral.

By *citizenship* I refer here both to the legal sense, in which persons are juridically subject to the law's privileges and protections by virtue of national identity status, but also the experiential, vernacular context in which people customarily understand their relation to state power and social membership. It is to bridge these two axes of political identity and identification that Bernard Nathanson, founder of the National Abortion Rights Action League (NARAL) and now a pro-life activist, makes political films starring the traumatically post-iconic fetal body. His aim is to solicit *aversive identifications* with the fetus, ones that strike deeply the empathetic imaginary of people's best selves while creating pressure for the erasure of empathy's scene. First, he shows graphic images of abortion, captioned by pornographic descriptions of the procedures by which the total body is visibly turned into hideous fragmented flesh. He then calls on the national conscience to delete what he has created, an "unmistakable trademark of the irrational violence that has pervaded the twentieth century."[11] The trademark to which he refers is abortion. He exhorts the public to abort the fetal trademark so as to save the fetus itself and, by extension, the national identity form and its future history. In this sense, the fetus's sanc-

---

11. Nathanson speaks this line in the film *The Silent Scream* (1984).

tified national identity is the opposite of any multicultural, sexual, or classed identity: the fetus is a blinding light that, triumphant as the modal citizen form, would white out the marks of hierarchy, taxonomy, and violence that seem now so central to the public struggle over who should possess the material and cultural resources of contemporary national life.

It will be clear by now how the struggle over child labor takes on the same form as fetal rights discourse: revelations of trauma, incitements to rescue, the reprivatization of victims as the ground of hope, and, above all, the notion that the feeling self is the true self, the self that must be protected from pain or from history, that scene of unwelcome changing. The infantile citizen then enfigures the adult's true self, his inner child in all its undistorted or untraumatized possibility. But to say this is to show how the fetal/infantile icon is a fetish of citizenship with a double social function. As an object of fascination and disavowal, it stands in for (while remanding to social obscurity) the traumatized virtuous private citizen around whom history ought to be organized, for whom there is not a good-enough world. (This currently includes the formerly tacit, or "normal," citizen and the sexually and racially subordinated ones.) In addition to its life as a figure for the injured adult, the fetus has another life as a utopian sign of a just and pleasant socius, both in pro-life, pro-family values rhetoric, and in advertisements and Hollywood films about the state of white reproductive heterosexuality in the United States during an era of great cultural, economic, and technological upheaval. Its two scenes of citizenship can be spatialized: one takes place in a traumatized public and the other in a pain-free intimate zone. These zones mirror each other perfectly, and so betray the fetish form of sentimental citizenship, the wish it expresses to signify a political world beyond contradiction.[12]

---

12. This intensification of national-popular patriotic familialism has taken place at a time when another kind of privatization—the disinvestment of the state economically and culturally in promoting public life—characterizes almost all the activity of the political public sphere. The economic defederalization of citizenship downsizes the public so drastically that it begins to look like "the private,"

I have elaborated these basic Freudian dicta about mourning, the theory of infantile citizenship, and this account of U.S. political culture to make a context for four claims: that this is an age of sentimental politics in which policy and law and public experiences of personhood in everyday life are conveyed through rhetorics of utopian/traumatized feeling; that national-popular struggle is now expressed in fetishes of utopian/traumatic affect that over-organize and over-organicize social antagonism; that utopian/traumatized subjectivity has replaced rational subjectivity as the essential index of value for personhood and thus for society; and that, while on all sides of the political spectrum, political rhetoric generates a high degree of cynicism and boredom,[13] those same sides manifest, simultaneously, a sanctifying respect for sentiment. Thus, in the sentimental national contract, antagonistic class positions mirror each other in their mutual conviction about the *self-evidence* and *objectivity* of painful feeling, and about the nation's duty to eradicate it. In the conjuncture "utopian/traumatized," I mean to convey a logic of fantasy reparation involved in the therapeutic conversion of the scene of pain and its eradication to the scene of the political itself. Questions of social inequity and social value are now adjudicated in the register not of power but of sincere surplus feeling: worry about whether public figures seem "caring" subordinates analyses of their visions of injustice; subalternized groups attempt to forge alliances on behalf of radical social transformation through testimonial rhetorics of true pain;[14] people believe that they know what they feel when they feel it, can locate its origin, measure its effects.

---

its nineteenth-century antithesis (only this time mass-mediated and thus publicly sutured in a more classic Habermasean sense). Yet all too frequently the analysis of the institutions of intimacy is kept separate from the considerations of the material conditions of citizenship.

13. On cynicism and citizenship, see Slavoj Žižek, *The Sublime Object of Ideology* (London: Verso, 1989), pp. 11–53.

14. On pain's place in forming the political imagination of subjects during the epoch of U.S. identity politics, see Wendy Brown's (1995) powerful essay "Wounded Attachments: Late Modern Oppositional Political Formations."

The traffic in affect of these political struggles finds validity in those seemingly superpolitical moments when a "clear" wrong— say, the spectacle of children violently exploited—produces a "universal" response. Feeling politics takes all kinds: it is a politics of protection, reparation, rescue. It claims a hard-wired truth, a core of common sense. It is beyond ideology, beyond mediation, beyond contestation. It seems to dissolve contradiction and dissent into pools of basic and also higher truth. It seems strong and clear, as opposed to confused or ambivalent (thus: the unconscious has left the ballpark). It seems the inevitable or desperately only core material of community.

What does it mean for the struggle to shape collective life when a politics of true feeling organizes analysis, discussion, fantasy, and policy? When feeling, the most subjective thing, the thing that makes persons public and marks their location; takes the temperature of power; mediates personhood, experience, and history; takes over the space of ethics and truth? When the shock of pain is said only to produce *clarity* when shock can as powerfully be said to produce panic, misrecognition, the shakiness of perception's ground? Finally, what happens to questions of managing alterity or difference or resources in collective life when feeling *bad* becomes evidence for a structural condition of injustice? What does it mean for the theory and practice of social transformation when feeling *good* becomes evidence of justice's triumph? As many historians and theorists of "rights talk" have shown, the beautiful and simple categories of legitimation in liberal society can bestow on the phenomenal form of proper personhood the status of normative value, which is expressed in feeling terms as "comfort;"[15] and, meanwhile, political arguments that challenge the claim of painful feeling's

---

15. On rights talk and normativity, see the volume *Identities, Politics, and Rights*, ed. A. Sarat and T. R. Kearns (Ann Arbor: University of Michigan Press, 1995). See especially Wendy Brown's contribution, an indispensable discussion of the ways "rights talk" enables the production of traumatized political identities: "Rights and Identity in Late Modernity: Revisiting the 'Jewish Question,'" pp. 85–130.

analytical clarity are frequently characterized as causing further violence to already damaged persons and the world of their desires.

This essay will raise uncomfortable questions about what the evidence of trauma is: its desire is to exhort serious critical, but not cynical, attention to the fetish of true feeling in which social antagonism is, frequently, being worked without being worked through. My larger aim is to bring into being as an object of critique the all-too-explicit "commonsense" feeling culture of national life, evident in the law, identity politics, and mass society generally: it is about the problem of trying juridically and culturally to administer society as a space ideally void of struggle and ambivalence, a place made on the model of fetal simplicity. I am not trying to posit feeling as the bad opposite of something good called thinking: as we will see, in the cases to follow, politicized feeling is a kind of thinking that too often assumes the obviousness of the thought it has, which stymies the production of the thought it might become.

In particular, our cases will derive from the field of sexuality, a zone of practice, fantasy, and ideology, whose standing in the law constantly partakes of claims about the universality or transparency of feeling, a universality juridically known as "privacy." We begin by addressing the work of feeling in Supreme Court decisions around sexuality and privacy. But the tendency to assume the nonideological, nonmediated, or nonsocial status of feeling is shared by opponents of privacy as well, with consequences that must equally, though differently, give pause: the following section interrogates the antiprivacy revolution legal radicals have wrought via the redefinition of harm and traumatized personhood. The paradoxes revealed therein will not be easily solved by ignoring or condescending to the evidence of injustice provided by the publicized pain of subordinated populations: the essay's coda focuses on a twelve-step book about reproduction, *Peaceful Pregnancy Meditations*, by Lisa Steele George, (1993) whose commitment to therapy for pregnant women and whose paranoia about the world of identity politics in the present moment does *not* produce an image of the just world. Its properly paranoid politics of intimacy rejects the mirroring logics of posttraumatic national subjectivity. It promotes, instead, a deeply felt but stubbornly uncongealed form of person-hood whose way of inhabiting politics, publicness, personhood, and power suggests how much work it would take, and what kinds of changes it would bring, to induce a break with trauma's seduction of politics in the everyday of U.S. citizenship.[16]

## PRIVACY

It would not be too strong to say that where regulating sexuality is concerned, the law has a special sentimental relation to banality. But to say this is not to accuse the law of irrelevance or shallow-ness. In contrast to the primary sense of banality as a condition of reiterated ordinary conventionality, banality can also mark the experience of deeply felt emotion, as in the case of "I love you," "Did you come?," or "O' Say, Can You See?"[17] But for an occasion of banality to be both utopian and sublime, its ordinariness must be thrust into a zone of overwhelming disavowal. This act of optimis-tic forgetting is neither simple nor easy: it takes the legitimating force of institutions—for example, the nation form or heterosexuality—to establish the virtue of forgetting banality's banality. Take a clas-sic instance of this process, an entirely forgettable moment in *The Wizard of Oz* that precedes an unforgettable one. Auntie Em says to Dorothy, who has been interfering with the work on the farm (no child labor there: Dorothy carries *books*): "Find yourself a place

---

16. *Intimate discipline* is Richard Brodhead's term for the coercions of sen-timental culture in nineteenth-century United States. See "Sparing the Rod: Dis-cipline and Fiction in Antebellum America," in *Cultures of Letters: Scenes of Reading and Writing in Nineteenth-Century America* (Chicago: University of Chi-cago Press, 1993), pp. 13–47.

17. Jean Baudrillard posits banality as the affective dominant of postmodern life: see *In the Shadow of the Silent Majorities . . . Or the End of the Social and Other Essays* (1983); and "From the System to the Destiny of Objects," in *The Ecstasy of Communication* (1987). See also Morris 1990, Mbembe 1992, and Mbembe and Roitman 1995.

where you won't get into any trouble." Dorothy, in a trance, seems to repeat the phrase but misrepeats it, sighing, "a place where there isn't any trouble," which leads her then to fantasize "somewhere over the Rainbow." Between the phrase's first and second incarnations, the agency of the subject disappears and is transferred to the place: the magic of will and intention has been made a property of property.

The unenumerated relation between *the* place where *you* won't get into trouble and *a* place where, definitionally, *there is no trouble*, expresses the foggy fantasy of happiness pronounced in the constitutional concept of privacy, whose emergence in sexuality law during the 1960s brought heterosexual intimacy explicitly into the antagonistic field of U.S. citizenship. Privacy is the Oz of America. Based on a notion of safe space, a hybrid space of home and law in which people will act legally and lovingly toward one another, free from the determinations of history or the coercions of pain, the constitutional theorization of sexual privacy is drawn from a lexicon of romantic sentiment, a longing for a space where there is no trouble, a place whose constitution in law would be so powerful that desire would meet moral discipline there, making real the dreamy rule. In this dream, the zone of privacy is a paradigmatic national space too, where freedom and desire meet up in their full suprapolitical expression, a site of embodiment that also leaves unchallenged fundamental dicta about the universality or abstractness of the modal citizen.

Much has been written on the general status of privacy doctrine in constitutional history, a "broad and ambiguous concept which can easily be shrunken in meaning but which can also, on the other hand, easily be interpreted as a constitutional ban against many things other than searches and seizures."[18] Privacy was first conceived as a constitutionally mandated but unenumerated right of sexual citizenship in *Griswold v. Connecticut* (381 U.S. 479 [1965]). The case is about the use of birth control in marriage: a nineteenth-century Connecticut law made it illegal for married couples to use

---

18. Black 1965, at 509.

contraceptives for birth control (oral arguments suggest that the "rhythm method" was not unconstitutional in that state);[19] they were only allowed prophylaxis to prevent disease. To challenge this law, Esther Griswold, director of Planned Parenthood in Connecticut, and Lee Buxton, the chief physician there, were arrested, by arrangement with the district attorney, for giving "information, instruction, and medical advice to *married persons* as to the means of preventing conception."[20]

These arguments made in *Griswold* stress the Due Process clause of the Fourteenth Amendment, because denying the sale of contraceptives "constitutes a deprivation of right against invasion of privacy."[21] This kind of privacy is allotted only to married couples: Justice Goldberg quotes approvingly a previous opinion of Justice Harlan (*Poe v. Ullman*, 367 U.S. 497, at 533), which states that "adultery, homosexuality, and the like are sexual intimacy which the State forbids . . . but the intimacy of husband and wife is necessarily an essential and accepted feature of the institution of marriage, an institution which the State not only must allow, but which always and in every age it has fostered and protected."[22]

We can see in Harlan's phrasing and Goldberg's citation of it the sentimental complexities of making constitutional law about sexual practice in the modern United States. The logic of equivalence between adultery and homosexuality in the previous passage locates these antithetical sexual acts/practices in an unprotected public space that allows and even compels *zoning* in the form of continual state discipline (e.g., laws).[23] In contrast, marital privacy is drawn up here in a zone elsewhere to the law and takes its authority from tradition, which means that the law simultaneously protects it and turns away its active disciplinary gaze. At this juncture of space, time, legitimacy, and the law, Gayatri Spivak's distinction

---

19. Guitton and Irons 1995, p. 4.
20. Douglas 1965, at 480.
21. Ibid., 5.
22. Goldberg 1965, at 499.
23. I borrow this rhetoric of zoning, and specifically its relation to the production of normative sexuality, from Berlant and Warner 1998.

between *Time* and *timing* will also clarify the stakes of privacy law's optimistic apartheid where sexuality is concerned. Spivak argues that the difference between hegemonic and "colonized" conceptions of imperial legal authority can be tracked by graphing Time as that property of transcendental continuity that locates state power to sustain worlds in the capacity to enunciate master concepts such as liberty and legitimacy in a zone of monumental time, a seemingly postpolitical space of abstraction from the everyday. In contrast, timing marks the always processual, drowning-in-the-present quality of subaltern survival in the face of the law's scrutiny and subject-making pedagogy.[24] Mapped onto sexuality law here, in privacy's early and most happy conceptualization, we see that nonmarital and therefore nonprivate sex exists in the antagonistic performance of the law's present tense, while the marital is virtually antinomian, Time above fallen timing. It is not only superior to the juro-political but also, apparently, its boss and taskmaster.

The banality of intimacy's sentimental standing in and above the law is most beautifully and enduringly articulated in the majority opinion in *Griswold*, written by Justice William O. Douglas. Douglas argues that a combination of precedents derived from the First, Fourth, Fifth, Ninth, and Fourteenth Amendments[25] supports

---

24. Spivak 1991.

25. Douglas writes: "Various guarantees create zones of privacy. The right of association contained in the penumbra of the First Amendment is one, as we have seen. The Third Amendment in its prohibition against the quartering of soldiers 'in any house' in time of peace without the consent of the owner is another facet of that privacy. The Fourth Amendment explicitly affirms the 'right of the people to be secure in their persons, houses, papers, and effects against unreasonable searches and seizures.' The Fifth Amendment in its Self-Incrimination Clause enables the citizen to create a zone of privacy which government may not force him to surrender to his detriment. The Ninth Amendment provides: 'The enumeration in the Constitution, of certain rights, shall not be construed to deny or disparage others retained by the people'" (*Griswold v. Connecticut*, at 484). Justice Goldberg's concurring opinion, while mainly running a legal clinic on the Founders' relation to unenumerated rights, adds the Due Process clause of the Fourteenth Amendment to this constitutional congeries (Ibid., at 488).

his designation of a heretofore unenumerated constitutional right for married persons to inhabit a zone of privacy, a zone free from police access or the "pure [state] power" for which Connecticut was arguing as the doctrinal foundation of its right to discipline immorality in its citizens.[26] The language Douglas uses both to make this space visible and to enunciate the law's relation to it shuttles between the application of *stare decisis* (the rule of common law that binds judicial authority to judicial precedent) and the traditional conventionalities of heteronormative Hallmark-style sentimentality:

> The present case, then, concerns a relationship lying within the zone of privacy created by several fundamental constitutional guarantees. And it concerns a law which, in forbidding the *use* of contraceptives rather than regulating their manufacture or sale, seeks to achieve its goals by means having a maximum destructive impact upon that relationship. Such a law cannot stand in light of the familiar principle, so often applied by this Court, that a "governmental purpose to control or prevent activities constitutionally subject to state regulation may not be achieved by means which sweep unnecessarily broadly and thereby invade the area of protected freedoms" [*NAACP v. Alabama*, 377 U.S. 288, at 307]. Would we allow the police to search the sacred precincts of marital bedrooms for telltale signs of the use of contraceptives? The very idea is repulsive to the notions of privacy surrounding the marriage relationship. We deal with a right of privacy older than the Bill of Rights—older than our political parties, older than our school system. Marriage is a coming together for better or for worse, hopefully enduring, and intimate to the degree of being sacred. It is an association that promotes a way of life, not causes; a harmony in living, not political faiths; a bilateral loyalty, not commercial or social projects. Yet it is an association for as noble a purpose as any involved in our prior decisions.[27]

---

26. Guitton and Irons 1995, p. 7.
27. Douglas 1965, at 485, 486.

Douglas bases his view that sexuality in marriage must be constitutionally protected—being above the law, prior to it, and beyond its proper gaze—on a sense that "specific guarantees in the Bill of Rights have penumbras, formed by emanations from those guarantees that help give them life and substance."[28] A *penumbra* is generally a "partial shadow between regions of complete shadow and complete illumination," but I believe the sense in which Douglas uses this dreamy concept is more proper to its application in the science of astronomy: "The partly darkened ridge around a sunspot." In other words, privacy protections around even marital sexuality are the dark emanations from the sunspot of explicit constitutional enumeration, and the zone of privacy in which marital sexuality thrives is the shadowland of the "noble" institution of marriage, with its sacred obligational emanations of social stability and continuity, intimate noninstrumentality, and superiority to the dividedness that otherwise characterizes the social. To back him up, Justices Harlan's and Goldberg's opinions invoke the state and the Court's propriety in pedagogically bolstering the institutions of traditional American morality and values: after all, the theater of marital intimacy is "older than our political parties, older than our schools."

Justice Hugo Black's dissent in *Griswold* blasts Justices Douglas, Goldberg, Harlan, and White for the unethical emotionality of what he calls the "natural law due process formula [used] to strike down all state laws which [the justices] think are unwise, dangerous, or irrational." He feels that it introduces into constitutional jurisprudence justifications for measuring "constitutionality by our belief that legislation is arbitrary, capricious or unreasonable, or accomplishes no justifiable purpose, or is offensive to our own notions of civilized standards of conduct. Such an appraisal of the wisdom of legislation is an attribute of the power to make laws, not of the power to interpret them." He finds precedent in this critique in a Learned Hand essay on the Bill of Rights that reviles judges' tendency to "wrap up their veto in a protective veil of ad-

---

28. Ibid., at 484.

jectives such as 'arbitrary,' 'artificial,' 'normal,' 'reasonable,' 'inherent,' 'fundamental,' or 'essential' whose office usually, though quite innocently, is to disguise what they are doing and impute to it a derivation far more impressive than their personal preferences, which are all that in fact lie behind the decision."[29] In this view, whenever judges enter the zone of constitutional penumbra, they manufacture euphemisms that disguise the relation between proper law and personal inclination. Patricia Williams has suggested that this charge (and the countercharge that at the heights of feeling it is no different than reason) is at the heart of the fiction of *stare decisis* that produces post-facto justifications from judicial or social tradition for judges who inevitably impose their will on problems of law but who must, for legitimacy's sake, disavow admission of the uninevitability of their claim. The virtually genetic image legal judgment has of itself in history veils not only the personal instabilities of judges but also the madness of the law itself, its instability and fictive stability, its articulation at the place where interpretive will and desire mix up to produce someone's image of a right/just/proper world.[30]

After sexual privacy is donated to the U.S. heterosexual couple in *Griswold* by way of the sentimental reason the Court adopts— through the spatialization of intimacy in a bell jar of frozen history— a judicial and political nightmare over the property of sexual privacy ensued, whose mad struggle between state privilege and private liberty is too long to enumerate here. We can conclude that the romantic banality that sanctions certain forms of intimacy as nationally privileged remains hardwired into the practice of sex privacy law in the United States. Almost twenty years later, however, *Planned Parenthood of Southeastern Pennsylvania v. Casey* (112 S. Ct. 2791 [1992]) recasts the force of its machinery remarkably, replacing the monumentality of sexual privacy that *Roe* had established as a fundamental condition of women's liberty with the monumentality of *Roe* itself as evidence of the Court's very authority.

---

29. Ibid., at 517, n. 10.
30. Williams 1991, pp. 7–8, 134–135.

In their majority opinion, Justices O'Connor, Souter, and Kennedy recognize the sovereignty of the zone of privacy as a model for freedom or liberty, returning explicitly to the method of penumbral enumeration and *stare decisis* introduced in *Griswold*. But the real originality of *Planned Parenthood v. Casey* is in the extent to which it supplants *entirely* the utopia of heterosexual intimacy on which sexual privacy law was based in the first place, putting *women's pain* in heterosexual culture at the center of the story of privacy and legal protections. In this sense, the legitimating force of deep juridical feelings about the sacred pleasures of marital intimacy are here inverted and displaced onto the woman, whose sexual and political trauma is now the index of the meaning and value of her privacy and her citizenship.

Briefly, *Eisenstadt v. Baird*, 405 U.S. 438 (1972) extended *Griswold* to unmarried women through the equal protections clause, transforming sexual privacy from its initial scene—the two-as-one utopia of coupled intimacy—into a property of individual liberty. This muted the concretely spatial aspects of the "zone of privacy," dismantling the original homology between the marital/sexual bedroom and the citizen's sense of self-sovereignty. It placed the focus on the space of the woman's body, which includes her capacities, passions, and intentions. But the shift from reframing contraception to adjudicating abortion required the discovery of more emanations from constitutional penumbra: in *Roe v. Wade* (410 U.S. 113 [1973]), the right of privacy remains the *woman's* right but here one that has internal limits at the juncture where state interest over potential "life" and social self-continuity overtake the woman's interest in controlling her sexual and reproductive existence. Gone from that decision is *Griswold*'s rhetoric of the Court's moral pedagogy or its chivalry toward sexually sacred precincts: indeed, Justice Blackmun writes that, because of the "sensitive and emotional nature of the abortion controversy," he wants to adhere to "constitutional measurement, free of emotion and predilection."[31] (There is not a sexuality/privacy case in which such

---

31. Blackmun 1973, at 708.

a caveat against emotion is not passionately uttered.) *Roe* attempts to achieve its postemotionality by deploying knowledge, plumbing the juridical and historical archive on abortion: its emphasis is not on expanding liberty by thinking through the contexts of its practice but, rather, by massaging precedent and tradition.

*Planned Parenthood v. Casey* was widely seen as an opportunity for a new set of justices to overturn *Roe*. The Pennsylvania Abortion Control Act of 1982 (amended in 1988–1989) did not abolish abortion in the state but intensified the discursive contexts in which it happened, seeking to create around abortion a state-sanctioned, morally pedagogical *zone of publicity*. Provisions included a twenty-four-hour waiting period, minor notification of parents and wife notification of husbands, and intensified standards of "informed consent" (including a state-authored brochure condemning abortion). The majority opinion has two explicit aims: to affirm the fundamental holdings of *Roe* on behalf of the sovereignty of women's citizenship, the unity of national culture, and the status of the Court's authority; and to enumerate what it felt was underenumerated in *Roe*, the conditions of the state's sovereignty over the contexts of reproduction. In other words, as Justice Scalia's dissent argues, the Court's majority opinion seeks to affirm *Roe* while also significantly dismantling it. Its technical mechanism for achieving this impossible feat is the substitution of an "undue burden" rule for a whole set of other protections that *Roe* provides: especially by dismantling the trimester framework that determined the woman's sovereignty over reproduction in a pregnancy's first six months and substituting for it a rule that favors the state's right to place restrictions on the woman's reproductive practice (restrictions that can then be weighed by courts that will determine whether a given law mounts egregiously burdensome obstacles to the woman's exercise of her constitutional right to abortion).

Scalia claims that the majority pulls off this impossible feat (in its claim to refuse a "jurisprudence of doubt" while making equivocal legal judgments) by disguising its own muddy impulses in a sentimental and "empty" rhetoric of intimacy:

The best that the Court can do to explain how it is that the word
"liberty" *must* be thought to include the right to destroy human
fetuses is to rattle off a collection of adjectives that simply deco-
rate a value judgment and conceal a political choice. The right
to abort, we are told, inheres in "liberty" because it is among "a
person's most basic decisions" (*ante*, at 2806); it involves a "most
intimate and personal choic[e]" (*ante*, at 2807); it is "central to
personal dignity and autonomy" (*ibid.*); it "originate[s]" within
the zone of conscience and belief" (*ibid.*); it is "too intimate and
personal" for state interference (*ante*, at 2807); it reflects "intimate views" of a "deep, personal character" (*ante*, at 2808); it
involves "intimate relationships" and "notions of personal autonomy and bodily integrity" (*ante*, at 2810).[32]

Correctly, Scalia goes on to point out that these very same qualities meant nothing to the Justices when they heard *Bowers v. Hard-
wick* (487 U.S. 186 [1986]), "because, like abortion, they are forms
of conduct that have long been criminalized in American society.
Those adjectives might be applied, for example, to homosexual
sodomy, polygamy, adult incest, and suicide, all of which are equally
'intimate.'"[33]

But Scalia's critique is trivial, in the sense that the majority
opinion does not seek to rethink sexual privacy or intimacy in any
serious way. The rhetoric of intimacy in the case is part of its argument from *stare decisis*,[34] but the majority justices' originality is
located in their representation of the specificity, what they call the
"uniqueness," of the material conditions of citizenship for women
in the United States. Because the right to sexual privacy has been
individuated by *Roe*, privacy no longer takes place in a concrete zone
but, rather, a "zone of conscience"—the place where, as Nietzsche

---

32. Scalia 1992, at 2876–2877.

33. Ibid. Scalia also blasts Justice Blackmun (n. 2, at 2876) for using the
same intimate rhetoric that means nothing, constitutionally, at least to Scalia.

34. A passionate and creative argument about what cases constitute precedent for *Roe* takes place between Justices O'Connor, Kennedy, Souter (ibid., at
2808–2816), and Scalia (at 2860–2867).

tells us, the law is painfully and portably inscribed in subjects.[35] The justices refer to women's "anxieties," "physical constraints," and "sacrifices [that] have since the beginning of the human race been endured by the woman with a pride that ennobles her": they contend that a woman's "suffering is too intimate and personal for the State to insist . . . upon its own vision of the woman's role."[36] Therefore, abortion definitively grounds and sustains women's political legitimacy: their "ability to participate equally in the economic and social life of the Nation has been facilitated by their ability to control their reproductive lives."[37]

The Justices here concede that femininity in the United States is virtually and generically an undue burden, however ennobling it might be. The de-utopianization of sexual privacy established in *Griswold* and the installation of female citizenship at the juncture of law and suffering is further reinforced by the one part of the Pennsylvania law that the majority finds unconstitutional: the clause that commands women to notify their husbands of their intention to abort. The segment in which this happens exposes women's suffering in the zone of privacy, where, it turns out, men beat their wives. They cite evidence, supported by the American Medical Association, that men are raping their wives, terrorizing them (especially when pregnant), *forcing* them to inhabit a zone of privacy that keeps secreted men's abuse of women. In short, the "gruesome and torturous" conditions of marital domesticity in battering households requires the Court *not to protect privacy* for the couple but to keep the couple from becoming the unit of modal citizenship where privacy law is concerned.[38]

Catharine MacKinnon deems privacy law a tool of patriarchal supremacy:

---

35. Nietzsche 1967. On the ways Nietzsche reproduces the individuating limits of pain-centered politics, see Brown 1995.

36. O'Connor, Kennedy, and Souter, Opinion of the Court, *Planned Parenthood v. Casey*, at 2807.

37. Ibid., at 2809.

38. Ibid., at 2827.

> Women in everyday life have no privacy in private. In private,
> women are objects of male subjectivity and male power. The
> private is that place where men can do whatever they want
> because women reside there. The consent that supposedly de-
> marcates this private surrounds women and follows us every-
> where we go. Men [in contrast], reside in public, where laws
> against harm exist. . . . As a legal doctrine, privacy has become
> the affirmative triumph of the state's abdication of women.[39]

MacKinnon's arguments in these essays—which purport to be
about "women" and "men" but which to my ear are more profoundly about heterosexuality as a virtual institution and a way of
life—derive from Court practice through the late 1980s and do not
consider the work that jurists such as O'Connor have done to
deprivatize privacy. But it should be no surprise that the citizen
imagined by even moderates these days is no longer a complex
subject with rights, needs, reciprocal obligations to the state and
society, conflicting self-interests, or prospects for happiness in
realms beyond the juridical: the citizen now is a trauma effect who
requires protection and political reparation, whether or not that
citizen can be fully described by the terms in which historically
subordinated classes circulate in the United States. The Opinion of
the Court in *Casey* answers the dissenters' argument—which asserts
that so few women are battered in the United States that the husband notification principle stands within constitutional norms—by
arguing that "the analysis does not end with the one percent of
women upon whom the statute operates: it begins there."[40] Here their
jurisprudence is not so far from Mari Matsuda's when she claims that
"looking to the bottom" of social hierarchy and making reparative
law from there is the only politically ethical thing to do.[41]

In the twenty years between *Roe* and *Planned Parenthood v.
Casey*, the general scene of public citizenship in the United States
has become suffused with a practice of making pain count politi-

---

39. MacKinnon 1995, pp. 117–118. See also MacKinnon 1989.
40. *Planned Parenthood v. Casey*, at 2829.
41. Matsuda 1995.

cally. The law of sexual privacy has followed this change, registering with symptomatic incoherence a more general struggle to maintain the contradictory rights and privileges of women, heterosexuality, the family, the state, and patriarchalized sexual privilege. The sheer ineloquence of this jumble of categories should say something about the cramped space of analysis and praxis to which the rhetoric and jurisprudence of sexual privacy has brought us—a place where there *is* much trouble: a utopia of law.

## POLITICS

In *Griswold*, I have argued, we see codified the assurance of some jurists that the intimate feelings of married sexual partners represent that zone of privacy and personhood beyond the scrutiny of the law, whose value is so absolute that the law must protect its sovereignty. Between *Griswold* and *Roe*, these intimate feelings and their relation to liberty were still assumed as the sovereign materials of the law of sexual privacy. Now, however, many of the political and juridical contexts have dissolved that once sustained the fantasy of a core national culture, threatening the capacity of sentimental politics to create feeling cultures of consensus that distract from the lived violences and fractures of everyday life in the polis. The class, racial, economic, and sexual fragmentation of U.S. society has emerged into the vision of the law and the public not as an exception to a utopian norm but as a new governing rule of the present. The legal struggles over affirmative action, welfare, abortion, and immigration the courts currently worry are also about whether the utopian or the traumatic story of national life will govern jurisprudence and the world it seeks to confirm. Trauma is winning.

Central to the legal emergence of the politics of trauma against the scene of liberal-patriotic disavowal has been a group of activists from within (mainly academic) legal studies who speak from feminist, gay and lesbian, antiracist, and anticapitalist movements. They take their different but generally painful experiences of social hierarchy in the United States to require a radical rhetorical and conceptual transformation of legal scholarship that embraces "subjectivity of perspective," asserts the collective nature of subject formation (around stereotypical social identities), and refuses traditional liberal notions that organize the social optimism of law around relatively unimpeded individuality, privacy, property, and conventional values.[42] At stake in this transformation of law is the importance of antinormativity to counterhegemonic critical theory and practice: since liberal law has long recognized a particular and traditionally sanctioned form of universal personhood as that around which society, theory, forms of discipline, and aspirational pedagogies should be organized, antiliberal activism has had strategically to *ground* law in experience (in all senses of the pun) and particular identities.

In this sense, critical legal praxis is the opposite of national sentimentality, which pursues collective cohesion by circulating a universalist currency of distress. At the same time, the structure of reparation central to radical legal politics suggests an unevenness in this general tactic of making legal notions of subjectivity historically and corporeally specific. Subaltern pain is not considered *universal* (the privileged do not experience it, they do not live expecting that at any moment their ordinarily loose selves might be codified into a single humiliated atom of subpersonhood). But subaltern pain is deemed, in this context, universally *intelligible*, constituting objective evidence of trauma reparable by the law and the law's more privileged subjects. In other words, the universal value is here no longer a property of political personhood but, in-

---

42. Critical Legal Studies, critical race theory, radical feminist legal theory, and an emergent body of work on gay and lesbian culture, power, and the law encompasses a huge bibliography. Rather than dump a stupidly big omnibus footnote here, let me metonymically signal the archive via a few recent helpful anthologies or extended works: Williams 1991, 1995, Matsuda and colleagues 1993, Smith 1993, West 1993, Becker, Bowman, and Torrey 1994, Danielsen and Engle 1995, Delgado 1995, Duggan and Hunter 1995.

stead, a property of a rhetoric that claims to represent not the universal but the true self. But, if historical contexts are incomparable across fields of simple and complex distinction, how can someone's pain or traumatized identity produce such perfect knowledge? And, if the pedagogies of politics were necessary to reframe a set of experiences, knowledges, and feelings as the kind of pain that exposes injustice, what is "true" about it, exactly?

In this political model of identity, trauma stands as truth. We can't use happiness as a guide to the aspirations for social change, because the feeling of it might well be false consciousness; nor boredom, which might be depression, illness, or merely a spreading malaise. Pain, in contrast, is something quick and sharp that simultaneously specifies you and makes you generic: it is something that happens to you before you "know" it, and it is intensely individuating, for surviving its shock lets you know it is your general survival at stake. Yet, if the pain is at the juncture of you and the stereotype that represents you, you know that you are hurt not because of your relation to history but because of *someone else's* relation to it, a type of someone whose privilege of comfort depends on the pain that diminishes you, locks you into identity, covers you with shame, and sentences you to a hell of constant potential exposure to the banality of derision.

Pain thus organizes your specific experience of the world, separating you from others and connecting you with others similarly shocked (but not surprised) by the strategies of violence that constantly regenerate the bottom of the hierarchies of social value you inhabit. In this sense, subaltern pain is a public form because its outcome is to make you readable, for others. This is, perhaps, why activists from identity politics generally assume pain as the only sign readable across hierarchies of social life: the subaltern is the surrogate form of cultural intelligibility generally, and negated identities are pain effects. Know me, know my pain—you caused it: in this context, paranoia would seem adaptive and would make understandable a desire for law to be both the origin *and* end of my experience of injustice. It might even make a wish that I have to see even subaltern suffering as something more mediated seem, per-haps, cold or an effect of the leisure of privilege. Who has time, after all, to query violence between shock and the moment it becomes true meaning?

These dicta ground much current countertraditional legal argument. Take, for example, an original and impassioned work such as Robin West's *Narrative, Authority, and Law*,[43] which sees as its task the production of moral criticism and transformation of the law from the point of view of its and a society's victims. West wields narratives powerfully throughout the book that reveal the law's fundamental immorality (and therefore its fundamentally immoralizing effect on the subjects who are educated to its stan-dards) where women's lives are concerned, and her powerful femi-nist arguments for the need to deprivatize women's structurally induced pain testify to the radical changes in the law and other institutions of intimacy that would have to happen if women are to attain legitimacy as social subjects. But West assumes that women's pain is already available as knowledge. To her it *is* meaning and the material for radical pedagogy. To think otherwise is to be ei-ther misogynist or guilty of shallow and overacademic postmodern-ism. Empathy is an ethical rule. Not surprisingly, as it happens, one example of pain's pure force that she uses to summarize her argument comes from a child: "We must be able to say, to quote my two-year-old, 'don't do that—you're hurting me,' and we must be able to hear that utterance as an ethical mandate to change course."[44]

Not all radical legal theorists so simplify pain as to make the emblem of true wisdom about injustice and its eradication some-thing as sentimental and fictive (to adults) as a child's conscious-

---

43. West 1993.

44. Ibid., pp. 19–20. Much the same kind of respect and critique can be given to Catharine MacKinnon's promotion of juridical reparation on behalf of women's pain under patriarchy: in her work, the inner little girl of every woman stands as the true abused self who is denied full citizenship in the United States. For an analysis of antipornography rhetoric's depiction of pain's place in women's citizenship, see the essay "Live Sex Acts," in *Queen of America* (Berlant 1997).

THE SUBJECT OF TRUE FEELING  **333**

ness,[45] yet the desire expressed in its seeming extreme clarity signals a lost opportunity for rethinking the relation of critique and
culture building at this juncture of identity politics and legal theory.
Would the child build a just world from the knowledge he gleans
from being hurt? What would the child need to know for that to
happen? How could this child learn to think beyond trauma, to
make a context for it? It seems hard for this group of legal theorists to imagine the value of such questions, for a few reasons. One
may be due to the centrality of "pain and suffering" to tort law,
which endorses a construction of the true subject as a feeling subject whose suffering disables a person's ability to live at his full
capacities, as he has been doing, and thus requires reparations from
the agents who wielded the force. A great deal has been and will be
written on this general area, for feminist antipornography and
antiracist hate speech litigation borrows much of its legitimation
from this hoary jurisprudential domain:[46] their tactic here is to
challenge local purveyors of structural violence in order to make
racism and misogyny *less profitable*, even symbolically, and meanwhile to use the law to debanalize violence by making illegal that
which has been ordinary practice, on the model, say, of sexual
harassment law or even more extremely, using the constitutional
model of "cruel and unusual punishment" to revoke legitimation
from social relations of violence traditionally authorized by the state
and the law.

---

45. Another instance in which a generic child's nonideological relation to
justice is held as the proper index of adult aspiration is to be found in Patricia
Williams's (1991) *Alchemy of Race and Rights*. This brilliant book is fully dedicated to understanding the multiple contexts in which (Williams's) legal subjectivity inherits, inhabits, and reproduces the law's most insidious violences: its
commitment to syncretic modes of storytelling about these conjunctures leaves
open some questions about the relation between what she represents as the madness of inhabiting legal allegories of the self in everyday life and certain scenes of
hyperclarity in which children know the true scale of justice and the true measure of pain (in contrast to adults, with their brains twisted by liberal ideologies
of property and contract [pp. 12, 27, e.g.]). Perhaps this is because, as she says,
"Contract law reduces life to fairy tale" (Ibid., p. 224).
46. See Finley 1989; see also Scarry 1985, Williams 1991, West 1993,
Matsuda 1995, and MacKinnon, *op. cit.*

Kendall Thomas has made this latter point, in an essay on privacy after *Bowers*.[47] He takes up Elaine Scarry's model of torture as a vehicle for the legitimating fiction of state power and claims that the Cruel and Unusual Punishment clause of the Eighth Amendment should be applied to state discrimination against gays and lesbians. The strength and clarity of his vision and the sense that his suggestion seems to make brings us to the second reason it seems hard for theorists who equate subjectivity in general with legal subjectivity to work beyond the rule of traumatic pain in imagining the conditions for progressive social change. Thomas's model only works if the agent of violence is the state or the law; it works only if the domain of law is deemed interchangeable with the entire field of injury and reparation, and if the subject of law is fully described by the taxonomies that law recognizes. This position would look awkward if it were rephrased: subjects are always citizens. But the fact is that the notion of reparation for identity-based subordination assumes that the law describes what a person is, and that social violence can be located the way physical injury can be tracked. The law's typical practice is to recognize kinds of subjects, acts, and identities: it is to taxonomize. What is the relation between the (seemingly inevitable) authoritarianism of juridical categorization, and the other, looser spaces of social life and personhood that do not congeal in categories of power, cause, and effect the way the law does? Is the "cruel and unusual punishment" tactic merely a reversal in extremis that points to the sublime banality of state cruelty, or is it a policy aspiration seeking a specific reparation for the specific violation/creation of gay and lesbian identities? Would the homeopathy of law against its own toxins in this domain of state cruelty work for women or the poor African Americans, Hispanics, and immigrants who are currently being economically disenfranchised from the resources that state capitalism manages?

Without making a ridiculous argument that the state is merely a mirage or a fetish that represents networks of inchoate forces that control, without constituting the realm of society, it should be pos-

---

47. Thomas 1995.

sible to say that radical counterpolitics needs to contend with notions of personhood and power that do not attain the clarity of state
and juridical taxonomy, even across fields of practice and stigma.
The desire to find an origin for trauma, and to rework culture at the
violating origin, effectively imagines subjects only within that zone,
reducing the social to that zone (in this case, the state and the laws
that legislate nonnormative sex) and covertly reauthorizing the hegemony of the national. The desire to use trauma as the model for
the pain of subordination that gets congealed into identities forgets
the difference between trauma and adversity: trauma takes you out
of your life shockingly and places you into another one, whereas
structural subordination is not a surprise to the subjects who experience it, and the pain of subordination *is* ordinary life.

I have not meant to argue that identity politics has become a
mode of "victim politics" too reductive to see the world clearly or
to have positive effects. In its most tawdry version, this accusation
reads that a politics organized around publicizing pain constitutes
a further degradation of subaltern selves into a species of sub-
civilized nonagency. The people who make this argument usually
recognize structural social inequality and the devastating impacts
it has on persons, but continue to believe that the United States
operates meritocratically, for worthy individuals. In contrast, Wendy
Brown's deconstruction of contemporary U.S. identity rhetorics
places skepticism about traumatic identity in the context of imagining a more radical politics. Brown sees people who claim their
pain and build collective struggles around it as potentially over-
identifying with their pain then identifying with it, becoming passive to it, becoming addicted to seeing themselves as virtuous in
the face of bad, unethical power. She follows Nietzsche's dicta
against a passive-aggressive politics of *ressentiment*:

> Politicized identity thus enunciates itself, makes claims for it-
> self, only by retrenching, restating, dramatizing, and inscrib-
> ing its pain in politics, and can hold out no future—for itself or
> others—which triumphs over this pain. The loss of historical
> direction, and with it the loss of futurity characteristic of the

> late-modern age, is thus homologically refigured in the struc-
> ture of desire of the dominant political expression of the age—
> identity politics. . . . What if we sought to supplant the language
> of "I am"—with its defensive closure on identity, its insistence
> on the fixity of position, its equation of social with moral posi-
> tioning—with the language of "I want"?[48]

The critical clarity of a subordinate population's politicized pain has
provided crucially destabilizing material that disaffirms the organization of liberal national culture around a utopian form of personhood that lives in zones of privacy and abstraction beyond pain, and,
as a counterhegemonic *tactic*, this logic of radical juridicality affirms
more powerfully than anything the fragile and violent disavowals that
bolster hegemonic worlds of reason and the law.

But to say that the traumatized self is the true self is to say that
a particular facet of subjective experience is where the truth of history lies: it is to suggest that the clarity of pain marks a political map
for achieving the good life, if only we would read it. It is also to imply
that in the good life, there will be no pain. Brown suggests that a
replacement of traumatic identity with a subjectivity articulated
utopianly, via the agency of imagined demand, will take from pain
the energy for social transformation beyond the field of its sensual
experience. For this to happen, *psychic pain experienced by subordinated populations must be treated as ideology*, not as prelapsarian
knowledge or a condensed comprehensive social theory. It is more
like a capital letter at the beginning of an old bad sentence that needs
rewriting. To think otherwise is to assert that pain is merely banal,
a story always already told. It is to think that the moment of its ges-
tation is, indeed, life itself.

## CODA: PREGNANCY, PARANOIA, JUSTICE

The world I have tried to telegraph here, in this story about privacy's
fall from the utopia of normal intimacy, finds the law articulating

---

48. Brown 1995, pp. 220–221.

its subjects as public and American through their position within a hegemonic regime of heterosexuality, which involves coordination with many other normative social positions that are racially and economically coded toward privilege. I have argued that the split between the patriotic context of national metaculture and the practical fragmentations and hierarchies of everyday life has become powerfully mediated by a discourse of trauma, which imagines "relief" through juridicalized national remedies because, in fighting against the false utopia of privacy, it imagines subjects wholly created by law.

Too often, and almost always in the work of legal radicals, the nation remains sanctified as a political "zone of privacy" in *Griswold*'s sense: it holds out a promise that it can relieve specific subjects of the pain of their specificity, even as the very project of nation formation virtually requires the public exposure of those who do not structurally assimilate to the national norm (so, if population *x* is relieved of the obstacles to its juridical and cultural citizenship, a given population *y* will almost inevitably come to bear the burden of surrogacy that expresses citizenship's status as *privilege*). Fighting for justice under the law in the face of these normative strategies is crucial, a tactic of necessity. If it means telling half-truths (that an experience of painful identity shocks a minoritized subject) in order to change juridical norms about that kind of subject, it still must be a good thing. But thinking that the good life will be achieved when there is no more pain but only (your) happiness does nothing to alter the hegemonic structure of normativity and mourning, whose saturation of the diminished expectations for liberty in national life I have sketched out in this essay. The reparation of pain does not bring into being a just life.

Usually this point is made in studies of testimony and the Holocaust, the unspeakable national violence that generates horrific evidence that will always fail to represent the brutal totality of its referent and that can never be repaired, reparated.[49] The cases addressed in this essay, in contrast, are ever so banal, cruel but not

---

49. See Lyotard 1988, Felman and Laub 1992.

unusual, an ordinary part of everyday citizenship for subordinate populations in the United States. Such a difference advises replacing the model of trauma I have been critically describing as inadequate material for world or nation building with a model of *suffering*, whose etymological articulation of pain and patience draws its subject less as an effect of an act of violence and more as an effect of a general atmosphere of it, peppered by acts, to be sure, but not contained by the presumption that trauma carries, that it is an effect of a single scene of violence or toxic taxonomy. Thus where certain ordinary identity forms are concerned, the question of suffering's *differend* might be drawn and drawn out differently, without the danger of analytically diffusing any population's subordination into some parodically postmodern miasma of overdetermination and pseudo-agency. (But even *suffering* can sound too dramatic for the subordinated personhood form I am reaching toward here: imagine a word that describes a constantly destabilized existence that monitors, with a roving third eye, every moment as a potentially bad event in which a stereotyped someone might become food for someone else's hunger for superiority and connect that to a term that considers the subjective effects of structural inequalities that are deemed inevitable in a capitalist nation. *Suffering* stands in for that compound world.)

I can provide here only a sketch of this model of pain, subjectivity, and politics. We might start in a place not defined by taxonomic identity, an image of the subject as heterotropic, distracted, or what I have called "loose." Earlier in this essay, privacy law was a place of intensified gendering and sexualization: women versus fetuses, wives versus husbands, the law versus the sanctity of the marital couple. Identity was clear; it was bounded; it was opposed to counteridentity. But (as Denise Riley argues), when women are not in any kind of court defending their gender, they experience the relation between their juridicalized femaleness and other scenes of womanhood and identity-style attachment in inconsistent ways.[50] Barbara Duden, Emily Martin, and Rayna Rapp's three ethnogra-

---

50. Riley 1988.

phies of the racial, class, and ethnic contexts of reproduction in the United States tell constantly of the minoritization of pregnant women in the face of medical and state expertise about fetuses, health, cleanliness, monitoring.[51] It is as though these women are even more incompetent to the scene of their survival than ordinary consumers, whose desires are at least constantly rerendered as self-expertise by the pedagogies of capitalist culture. Yet the reproducing women have created a sentimental culture of their own, which coexists with the zones of their subordination: it is not that radical, yet it is very critical and, above all, skeptical about the relation between knowing about women's material struggles and making them uninevitable.

I take as an example the book *Peaceful Pregnancy Meditations*. This 1993 book epitomizes much contemporary feminine self-help literature. It merges insights about women's expertise over their bodies from the feminist health movements of the 1970s and the sentimental feminine self-help movement of the 1980s, which emphasizes women's expertise over intimate suffering. It takes pregnancy as the condition of ordinary femininity writ large; it uses twelve-step language to partition and make livable the predictable but excruciating changes of pregnancy; it provides on each page space for the reader to become an author through a routine of daily affirmations that enable pregnant women to apportion their anxieties through a life lived one day at a time. It actively disaffirms the political public sphere as the source of emancipatory public making. It is paranoid about the ceaselessness of women's caretaking burdens in the family and affective burdens in society. Its paranoia is entirely banal about the conditions of women's ordinary lives.

*Peaceful Pregnancy Meditations* begins with a defensive nod to the world of fetal politics. Day 1, whose title is "Beginnings," begins: "When does pregnancy really begin? At conception? Years ago when we started yearning for a family of our own? Yesterday when our home pregnancy test turned positive? For each mother-

---

51. Martin 1987, Rapp 1990, 1991, Duden 1993.

to-be, it is different. But no matter where we define our beginning, we know it is truly that: a new beginning."[52] The beautiful tautologies and open questions of this passage provide for the pregnant gender a way of negotiating a complex set of contexts for maternal paranoia and the undue burdens of femininity in the contemporary United States. Pregnancy advice books have long made the woman responsible for fetal health. They have long made the woman feel that the development of her managerial skills is crucial to the happiness of everyone who depends on her to provide clarity for them. But the current public mistrust of women's competence to the maternal service economy has intensified the disciplinary aspects of these discourses and has made women even more defensive.

George's refusal to accede to the priority of fetal personhood or any norm of femininity remains resolute throughout the text. What she does prioritize is ameliorating the shame at the center of the experience of modern pregnancy. She releases women from shame about the ambivalence they feel toward the fetus and the theft of ordinary life that the fetus engenders; she acknowledges women's ambivalence toward the couple form and supports their need to build a social world to soften the blows and stresses of a marital intimacy that can only be enjoyed in random moments of repose. Above all, she confirms the rationality of women's ambivalent feelings about the pressure not to have a self that is a part of what structural pain demands of dominated persons.

On each page of the book, which represents one day, pregnant femininity is de-shamed by way of a dialectic between the anger/frustration/discomfort of the reader's complicated social meaning and the assurance and comfort of the poetic affirmation that George writes on each page. The affirmation, a kind of lay prayer, enables the reader to endure that life of which she surely is not master. Formally, this is signified by a top paragraph (with titles such as "Privacy," "Manly Pride," "Chronic Uncertainty," "Ultrasound") that expresses the zone of discomfort that this day's meditation depicts; a middle paragraph that graphs an affirmation of the

---

52. George 1993, p. 3.

reader's desire not to be defeated by today's degree of pain (as in "I try to remain positive toward those around me, seeing their attention as love");[53] and then a bottom third made up of four empty lines for women to write on, which begin with the three words "Today I feel. . . ."

The book does offer the suffering women a dependable space of feeling and temporal freedom from the cramped conditions of social value and everydayness that pregnant women negotiate: women's culture, a survival mechanism that involves forming a relationship with particular commodity forms and, through them, with other women who feel the way they feel, because they are regendered as pregnant women. In this way, this book, and the culture of affectivity and opinion that produces other commodities in support of its project of consolation and buttressing, keeps maternity/femininity in the United States from being merely a humiliating, isolating/collectivizing scene of personal struggle, public embarrassment, and alienated nonrepresentation in the political public sphere. This is what makes it a part of sentimental culture. Its aim, however, is not to change the law but to confirm the sheer difficulty of being made its subject while existing in so many strange relations undescribable by the terms *power/powerlessness, pain/happiness, equality/inequality*.

The suffering that George represents neither clarifies into a single struggle nor confuses the immediate sources of discomfort as the totality of actual sources. She sees a whole structure and a set of different ideologies in place, situating and destabilizing women and the contexts they inhabit: she cannot imagine freedom in these contexts but merely survival. She suffers gendering, and not just for her married self—but imagines the different contexts of struggle occupied by single mothers-to-be, lesbian mothers-to-be, working mothers-to-be, and the most conventional married mothers-to-be. Linked to one another by a collective experience of being public and scrutinized in pregnancy, they can live the unique change from the positions they were in when they were

53. Ibid., p. 167.

nonreproducing gendered, sexual, and economic subjects. In their intimacy with and alterity to the reduced versions of their gender, the women imagined in this book imagine no outside to history, no radically different future from the one they are presently suffering (and also finding sustenance in), but an ongoing present in which they are fragmented agents whose strange social value forces a constant improvisation and scraping together of a viable existence.

The binary trauma/reparation would not satisfy the conditions of genuine social oppression that (pregnant) women in the U.S. endure. Their issues are neither with the past nor with events marked by the scars of trauma. Their issues are with the material conditions of intimacy and the normative ideologies of desire; with having more symbolic than social value, derived from their expertise in realms of feeling; and with having no place for and therefore only a weak commitment to their anger, which pulsates instead as a muffled tone of resigned resentment. The heavily symbolized are always supposed to take whatever social value that status accords and hoard it for an always deferred future, meanwhile coping, if they can, in the everyday.

Sentimental culture takes its strength from this recognition, and in this case, by framing normative femininity and reproduction as processes of labor, it establishes gender praxis as a ground of solidarity. But because this labor is so mixed up with intimacy, and therefore with the grounds of optimism, a political response would threaten the only domain of experience that women "control": contemporary national/capitalism has made a bargain with "the personal," after all, which is that people can have dignity in its domains only insofar as they inhabit the world passively, through the negativity of trauma and the optimism held out by that Oz over the mountaintop, a (nation-) state of amelioration. The liberal-radical solution to such positioning has been to deploy an ethics of storytelling about trauma against the normative world of the law, to change the conditions of what counts as evidence, and to make something concrete happen in response, something that pays for the past that is the present. As Derrida has recently argued, however, the dialectic between situated expression that challenges universalist norms and the categorical universalism of law itself constitutes an incommensurateness already within the law that cannot be overcome by law.[54] This suggests why the reparative use of the law I have been tracking is finally, and wearily, sentimental.

Political optimism requires a future, any future that might not be more drowning in the present. This requires a violation of the sentimental contract by an analytically powerful and political rage, a discourse of demand and radial critique, a sacrifice of short-term coalition building to a politics of the long haul. It requires a refusal to be humiliated by its "irrelevance" to policy in an era of transnational capitalist triumphalism, class-bound racism, and sentimental misogyny. It requires a refusal of the seeming rationality of diminished expectations. Most important, at the moment, it requires a refusal of the juro-politics of affect, which uses trauma and stigma to measure injustice through a *feeling* someone has. The everyday struggle is a ground that must be fought for and expanded to include nonsensual experience and knowledge as a part of any "personal" story. This is what was meant by "the personal is the political," a sentence virtually impossible to understand at the present moment. It did not mean that there is only the personal, no such thing as the political. It meant to say that feeling is an unreliable measure of justice and fairness, not the most reliable one; and that new vocabularies of pleasure, recognition, and equity must be developed and taught. And that the everyday of struggle, where people live, is a ground on which ecstasy and theory and unpredicted change can be mapped into a world that will not look like the opposite of the painful one.

Who gave anyone expertise over the meaning of feelings of injustice? I was sympathetic to the cultural politics of pain until I felt the violence of sentimentality: presented as a horror at momentous mass trauma that unifies a fractured society, national sentimentality is too often a defensive response by people who identify with privilege yet fear they will be exposed as immoral by their tacit sanction of a particular structural violence that benefits them. I was

---

54. Derrida 1992, pp. 3–67, esp. 61–63.

a wholly sympathetic participant in practices of subaltern testimony and complaint, until I saw that the different stories of trauma wielded in the name of a population's political suffering not only tended to confirm the state and its law as the core sites of personhood but also provided opportunities to isolate further these dominated populations by inciting competitions over whose lives have been more excluded from the "happiness" that was constitutionally promised by national life. Meanwhile, the public recognition by the dominant culture of certain sites of publicized subaltern suffering is frequently (mis)taken as a big step toward the amelioration of that suffering. It is a baby step, if that. I have suggested, in contrast, that the pain and suffering of subordinated subjects in everyday life is an ordinary and ongoing thing that is underdescribed by the (traumatic) identity form and its circulation in the state and the law. If identity politics is a literacy program in the alphabet of that pain, then its subjects must also assume that the signs of subordination they feel also tell a story that they do not feel yet, or know, about how to construct the narrative to come.

## REFERENCES

Alexander, E. (1995). "Can You Be BLACK and Look at This?": reading the Rodney King video(s). In *The Black Public Sphere*, ed. by Black Public Sphere Collective, pp. 81–98. Chicago: University of Chicago Press.

Baudrillard, J. (1983). *In the Shadow of the Silent Majorities . . . Or the End of the Social and Other Essays*, trans. P. Foss, P. Patton, and J. Johnston. New York: Semiotexte.

——— (1987). From the system to the destiny of objects. In *The Ecstasy of Communication*, ed. S. Lotringer, pp. 77–96. New York: Semiotexte.

Becker, M., Bowman, C. G. and Torrey, M. (1994). *Cases and Materials on Feminist Jurisprudence: Taking Women Seriously*. St. Paul, MN: West.

Berlant, L. (1993). National brands/national bodies: *Imitation of Life*. In *The Phantom Public Sphere*, ed. B. Robins, pp. 173–208. Minneapolis: University of Minnesota Press.

———— (1997). *The Queen of America Goes to Washington City: Essays on Sex and Citizenship*. Durham, NC: Duke University Press.

Berlant, L., and Warner, M. (1998). Sex in public. *Critical Inquiry* 24 (Winter):547–566.

Black, H. (Justice). (1965). Concurring. *Griswold v. Connecticut*. 381 U.S. 479.

Blackmun, H. (Justice). (1973). Opinion of the Court. *Roe v. Wade*. 410 U.S. 113.

Brown, W. (1995). Wounded attachments: late modern oppositional political formations. In *The Identity in Question*, ed. J. Rajchman, pp. 199–227. New York: Routledge.

Butler, J. (1990). *Gender Trouble: Feminism and the Subversion of Identity*. New York: Routledge.

———— (1993). *Bodies That Matter: On the Discursive Limits of Sex*. New York: Routledge.

Crimp, D., ed. (1988). *AIDS: Cultural Analysis/Cultural Activism*. Cambridge, MA: MIT Press.

———— (1990). Mourning and militancy. In *Out There: Marginalization and Contemporary Cultures*, ed. R. Ferguson, M. Gever, T. T. Minha, and C. West, pp. 233–245. Cambridge, MA: MIT Press.

Danielsen, D., and Engle, K., eds. (1995). *After Identity: A Reader in Law and Culture*. New York: Routledge.

Delgado, R. (1995). *Critical Race Theory: The Cutting Edge*. Philadelphia, PA: Temple University Press.

DeMartino, G., and Cullenberg, S. (1994). Beyond the competitiveness debate: an internationalist agenda. *Social Text* 41:11–39.

Derrida, J. (1992). Force of law: the "mystical foundations of authority." In *Deconstruction and the Possibility of Justice*, ed. D. G. Carlson, D. Cornell, and M. Rosenfeld, pp. 3–67. New York: Routledge.

Douglas, W. O. (Justice). (1965). Opinion of the Court. *Griswold v. Connecticut*. 381 U.S. 479.

Duden, B. (1993). *Disembodying Women: Perspectives on Pregnancy and the Unborn*. Cambridge, MA: Harvard University Press.

Duggan, L., and Hunter, N. D. (1995). *Sex Wars: Sexual Dissent and Political Culture*. New York: Routledge.

Dyer, R. (1993). *The Matter of Images*. New York: Routledge.

Felman, S., and Laub, D. (1992). *Testimony: Crises of Witnessing in Literature, Psychoanalysis, and History*. New York: Routledge.

Finley, L. M. (1989). A break in the silence: including women's issues in a torts course. *Yale Journal of Law and Feminism* 1:41–73.

Freud, S. (1963). Mourning and melancholia. In *General Psychological Theory*, Intro. P. Rieff, pp. 164–179. New York: Collier.

George, L. S. (1993). *Peaceful Pregnancy Meditations: A Diary for Expectant Mothers*. Deerfield Beach, FL: Health Communications.

Goldberg, A. (Justice). (1965). Concurring. *Griswold v. Connecticut*. 381 U.S. 479.

Guitton, S., and Irons, P., eds. (1995). *May It Please the Court: Arguments on Abortion*. New York: New Press.

Harvey, D. (1989). *The Condition of Postmodernity*. London: Basil Blackwell.

Ivy, M. (1993). Recovering the inner child in late twentieth century America. *Social Text* 37:227–252.

Lyotard, J.-F. (1988). *The Differend: Phrases in Dispute*, trans. G. Van Den Abberle. Minneapolis: University of Minnesota Press.

MacKinnon, C. A. (1989). *Toward a Feminist Theory of the State*. Cambridge, MA: Harvard University Press.

——— (1995). Reflections on law in the everyday life of women. In *Law in Everyday Life*, ed. A. Sarat and T. R. Kearns, pp. 117–118. Ann Arbor: University of Michigan Press.

Martin, E. (1987). *The Woman in the Body: A Cultural Analysis of Reproduction*. Boston: Beacon.

——— (1994). *Flexible Bodies: Tracking Immunity in American Culture—from the Days of Polio to the Age of AIDS*. Boston: Beacon.

Matsuda, M. J. (1995). Looking to the bottom: critical legal studies and reparations. In *Critical Race Theory: The Key Writings That Formed the Movement*, ed. K. Crenshaw, N. Gotanda, G. Peller, and K. Thomas, pp. 63–80. New York: New Press.

Matsuda, M. J., Lawrence, C. R., III, Delagado, R., and Crenshaw, K. W. (1993). *Words That Wound: Critical Race Theory, Assaultive Speech, and the First Amendment*. Boulder, CO: Westview.

Mbembe, A. (1992). Prosaics of servitude and authoritarian civilities. *Public Culture* 5(Fall):123–148.

Mbembe, A., and Roitman, J. (1995). Figures of the subject in times of crisis." *Public Culture* 7(Winter):323–352.

Morris, M. (1990). Banality in cultural studies. In *Logics of Television: Essays in Cultural Criticism*, ed. P. Mellencamp, pp. 14–43. Bloomington: Indiana University Press.

Nietzsche, F. (1967). *On the Genealogy of Morals*, ed. W. Kaufmann. New York: Vintage.

Nunokowa, J. (1991). AIDS and the age of mourning. *Yale Journal of Criticism* 4(2)(Spring):1–12.

Phelan, P. (1993). *Unmarked: The Politics of Performance*. New York: Routledge.

*Planned Parenthood of Southeastern Pennsylvania v. Casey*. (1992). 112 S.Ct. 2791.

Rapp, R. (1990). Constructing amniocentesis: maternal and medical discourses. In *Uncertain Terms*, ed. F. D. Ginsburg and A. L. Tsing, pp. 28–42. Boston: Beacon.

———— (1991). Chromosomes and communication: the discourse of genetic counseling. *Medical Anthropology Quarterly* 2(2):143–157.

Riley, D. (1988). *"Am I That Name?": Feminism and the Category of "Women" in History*. Minneapolis: University of Minnesota Press.

Rouse, R. (1995). Thinking through transnationalism: notes on the cultural politics of class relations in the contemporary United States. *Public Culture* 7 (Winter):353–402.

Scalia, A. (Justice). (1992). Dissent. *Planned Parenthood v. Casey*. 112 S.Ct. 2791.

Scarry, E. (1985). *The Body in Pain: The Making and Unmaking of the World*. New York: Oxford University Press.

Schamberg, S. (1996). Six cents an hour. *Life* (June):38–48.

Smith, P., ed. (1993). *Feminist Jurisprudence*. New York: Oxford University Press.

Spivak, G. C. (1991). Time and timing: law and history. In *Chronotypes: The Construction of Time*, ed. J. Bender and D. E. Wellbery, pp. 99–117. Stanford, CA: Stanford University Press.

Thomas, K. (1995). Beyond the privacy principle. In *After Identity: A Reader in Law and Culture*, ed. D. Danielsen and K. Engle, pp. 277–293. New York: Routledge.

Wark, M. (1995). Fresh maimed babies: the uses of innocence. *Transition* 65 (Spring):36–47.

West, R. (1993). *Narrative, Authority, and Law*. Ann Arbor: University of Michigan Press.

Williams, P. J. (1991). *The Alchemy of Race and Rights*. Cambridge, MA: Harvard University Press.

———— (1995). *The Rooster's Egg*. Cambridge, MA: Harvard University Press.

# 11

# Trauma Envy

JOHN MOWITT

## SHAKEN, BUT ALSO STIRRED

The call to which this essay answers characterized its prospective topic via the antemetabole: "Theorizing Trauma/Traumatizing Theory." At the pivot of this rhetorical figure, literally around the virgule, spins trauma. Seizing the opportunity presented by the play conditioning all such pivots, this essay seeks, while acknowledging the attendant methodological risks, to traumatize trauma. Because theory too is caught up in this antemetabolic spin, and in that sense can no longer be all that it can be, trauma will be approached through its study. Specifically, my aim is to present Trauma Studies with a sketch of its genealogy. To the extent that trauma has, through its study, come to designate an expressive limit—the unspeakable event—confronting the tendency within Trauma Studies to speak of History and/or Memory, while exhibiting a certain reticence about its own history, subjects Trauma Studies to trauma. At first glance, of course, there is a profound difference between "the unspeakable" and the "as yet unspoken," but it will be the argument of this essay that this glance, in the very obviousness of its immediacy, misses something crucial. To spell this out, it will be necessary to reflect upon the institutional context of the emergence of Trauma Studies and the importance there of psychoanalysis as a theoretical practice, indeed a practice claiming specialist knowledge of both the limits of speech and traumatic injury. Ultimately, the gesture of traumatizing trauma, by charting the envy at work in the analytic debate over castration, will help to illuminate what I regard as the troubling contemporary tendency to displace the political with the ethical; a tendency—though hardly unique to Trauma Studies—that, to my mind, speaks volumes about the failure of its institutional success.

The issues at the core of this essay first attracted my attention as I was writing about drumming and the "new" men's movement during the fall of 1995. In that study—now the concluding chapter of *Percussion: Drumming, Beating, Striking*—I found "trauma envy" analytically productive as a way to frame the affective dimension of the relation between an emergent (or merely alternative, as Williams might have insisted) politics of masculinity and "second wave" feminism. Adorno's bold gloss on Nietzsche's aphorism *"Du gehst zu Frauen? Vergiß die Peitsche nicht!"* provides the gist of the matter.

> Whatever is in the context of bourgeois society called nature, is merely the scar of social mutilation. If the psychoanalytical theory is correct that women experience their physical constitution as a consequence of castration, their neurosis gives them an inkling of the truth. . . . Without a single exception feminine natures are conformist. The fact that Nietzsche's scrutiny stopped short of them, that he took over a secondhand and unverified image of feminine nature from the Christian civilization that he otherwise so thoroughly mistrusted, finally brought his thought under the sway, after all, of bourgeois society. He fell for the fraud of saying "the feminine" when talking of women. Hence the perfidious advice not to forget the whip: femininity itself is already the effect of the whip.[1]

---

1. Adorno 1974, p. 96.

Though unnamed, the "neurosis" invoked here would appear to be, given the reiterated thematization of castration, *Penisneid*, that is, penis envy. In his critique of Nietzsche, what Adorno seizes upon is the now familiar feminist insight that "femininity," as a designation for the essential nature of women, represents little more than the gesture of consolation offered to the victims of male supremacy by its beneficiaries. In confusing femininity with women, Nietzsche reputedly misses the social character of the violation enacted through such a gesture. I take Adorno's point, though I think the matter is complicated by a detail that he overlooks. Specifically, Adorno misses that it is a woman who is represented as articulating the aphorism in question. This detail suggests that, in fact, Nietzsche wanted everyone and no one to read that Zarathustra's demand had produced a deeply ironic, if not openly contemptuous, retort. This, however, is a diversion. It is more important that Adorno discerned the logic of *ressentiment* in the repudiation of femininity missed by Nietzsche, and did so in a way that enabled me to understand something important about the men's movement, namely, the fact that its adherents felt wounded by a feminism that had deprived them of what Lacan would no doubt call the phallus, that is, the mark of meaning or, to put the point more provocatively, the capacity to naturalize male supremacy by rendering it synonymous with the logic of signification. This led to my characterization of the men's movement as mobilized by castration envy, that is, the desire—perhaps even the drive—to take possession of the wound fantasized as that which allowed women to make men answerable for the wound of castration.

The "new" men do not, however, want what psychoanalysis took from women. Instead, they seek the specifically moral authority that is now invested in this injury. To acquire it, another prior and preferably greater injury must be made to belong to men. Odd though it may seem, a blatantly masochistic drive, indeed a certain desire for suffering, appears now to have acquired a pronounced political value. Those familiar with Wendy Brown's provocative *States of Injury* (1995) will recognize its discussion of "wounded attachments" in such formulations and, needless to say, this is not entirely by chance. Indeed, the framing of my subsequent remarks relies, in significant ways, on her account of the sociopolitical and historical moment in which wounds come to be invested with moral authority, thus justifying a brief elaboration of her project, particularly as it comes to thematize the Nietzschean problematic of *ressentiment*.[2] For the sake of expediency, let us say that Brown is attempting, among other things, to situate identity politics within the discursive antinomies of liberalism. She nowhere pretends either to account fully for or to judge such politics, but her study moves inexorably toward the conclusion that identity politics is hopelessly compromised by its "wounded attachments" to liberalism, that is, the very sociopolitical discourse through which the reprehensible violence of contemporary social relations is legitimated. In this, her argument shares much with the Judith Butler of *Excitable Speech* and with Slavoj Žižek's various attacks on "multiculturalism" (I will revisit this matter at length in my concluding section). Lest I be misunderstood, this kind of pushing of the Left's political envelope represents a terribly important political initiative, and, while Brown and I apparently disagree over the legacy and viability of contemporary Marxism, her account of the enabling conditions of identity politics bears repeating.

In Brown's contribution to Gordon and Newfield's *Mapping Multiculturalism* (1996), this account appears in summary form. It is elaborated under two headings: capitalism and disciplinarity.

---

2. It should be said, of course, that Brown's study was preceded by William Connolly's *Identity/Difference: Democratic Negotiations of Political Paradox* from 1991. Indeed, in focusing on the vicissitudes of identity politics, Brown can be read as an elaboration of and response to Connolly. In this vein, it is appropriate to acknowledge the impact on this essay of Carl Gutiérrez-Jones's "Injury by Design" (1998) that appeared in the pages of this journal two years ago. Gutiérrez-Jones and I share an interest in disciplinary objects, though his study is focused on American Studies. And since, in his words, trauma "is more singularly oriented toward addressing the victim's experience of loss" (p. 77), he leaves it to the side of his discussion of injury. I argue that he remains more confident, as a consequence, about psychoanalysis and concentrates his political analysis on the remedy of "inclusion" even as he acknowledges its ethical, and therefore politically ambiguous, cast.

Both are deployed to establish how in the era of late modernity (conspicuously not postmodernity), identity is at once disinterred and dispersed: disinterred because capitalism has unmasked the aggressively particularist character of the state while at the same time uprooting its relation to national territory; dispersed because, through concomitant proliferations of disciplinary investments— at once bureaucratic, commercial, and cultural—recognition (both personal and political) has been indexed to a logic of hyperdifferentiation where, alas, size again matters. To wit, the smallest differences have assumed enormous importance. Although, as I have argued elsewhere,[3] disciplinarity bears immediately upon the institutional organization of academic knowledge production, Brown prefers not to take advantage of this aspect of the concept, keeping the broadly political character of liberalism in the foreground instead. This allows her to argue that all political discourse that is recognized as such, and which appeals to the labor of specifying identity's minute particulars, invariably repeats the conditions of its own elaboration, thus aligning itself—in the name of satisfaction —with the very cause of discomfort. Identity politics is, for Brown, the consummate embodiment of such a discourse, and despite its persistent donning of the mantle of radicality, this politics folds neatly back into the impasses of classic liberalism that, for Brown, is a perspective that engulfs the distinction between democrats and republicans.

Perhaps with the now forgotten passing of Lucien Goldmann, who, it will be remembered, was given to situating theoretical projects (especially those of his opponents) within their often unspoken sociohistorical contexts, we feel compelled to separate political discourses from theories (whether critical or traditional) about them. To be sure, we have come a long way from Part 1 of *The German Ideology*, where Marx and Engels situated Feuerbach's secular humanism within the "ruling ideas" of nineteenth-century Germany. We recognize the bedeviling complications that arise when drawing material links between ideas and institutions. However, if it makes

---

3. Mowitt 1992.

sense to situate liberalism in relation to capitalism and the micro-politics of everyday disciplinarity, then surely it makes similar sense to situate *States of Injury*, which, after all, at no point presents its analysis as emanating from any "other scene." Aware that projects in cultural studies are often dismissed as fatuously ensconced in performative contradictions, Brown maneuvers to theorize, to be-come response-able to/for, such charges. Whether she succeeds or not is best left to her readers, but her dialogic anticipation of this sort of dismissal sets a standard worth preserving. In particular, such a standard invites us to think similarly about the concept of trauma itself, not in order to determine whether its various elaborations are free of performative contradictions, but to reflect upon the relation between trauma—especially our comparatively recent theoretical preoccupations with it—and the logic of *ressentiment*. Indeed, the remainder of this essay will strike out toward this end.

What are the stakes involved here? First, of course, there are the genealogical issues that arise as one seeks to situate a particular movement within contemporary academic (though not exclusively so) theoretical practices and the mode of production conditioning them. To borrow Foucault's diction: What inscription and destruc-tion of the body is articulated in the "moment of arising" of Trauma Studies? Which lines of force converged to condition this moment and what capacity for cultural critique finds its limits there? Sec-ond, given that for Nietzsche (as well as for Brown) *ressentiment* belongs to a genealogy of morals, what symptomatic status does Trauma Studies have with regard to what I earlier called the dis-placement of the political by the ethical? Precisely to the extent that it embodies a certain disavowed politics, does this displace-ment itself not represent a privileged moment in the contempo-rary struggle over the critical character of cultural critique?

## THE GAIN OF PAIN

When Cathy Caruth spoke in 1999 at the University of Minnesota, she addressed herself to, among other things, loss. This loss of life among troubled teens, the loss of death in *Beyond the Pleasure Principle*, the loss of her mother. To this somber list one might also have added the loss of trauma, for it was clear that Caruth was keenly aware of the academic (but not merely academic) "trauma industry" that had risen up around her work, depriving it, in a certain sense, of its ontological dignity. With the precise sense of timing that renders existence itself perverse, the loss of her own mother was made to coincide with the loss of her disciplinary object, that is, the literary work ravaged and adorned by trauma. I say this not out of any disrespect for Caruth (whose *Unclaimed Experience* I admire enormously), nor in order to exaggerate her importance, but simply to draw attention to the genealogical fact that the problematization that had made Trauma Studies possible appears, of late, to have suffered a structural transformation. But this is putting the proverbial cart before the no less proverbial horse. What, after all, made Trauma Studies possible in the first place? My colleague Tom Pepper has proposed that we include the following enabling events in a description of the field's emergence: the publications of Caruth, Felman and Laub, LaCapra et al.; the de Man scandal and its impact on the cultural politics of literary criticism; the return of historicism and the pruning back of Theory; the advent of Holocaust studies; and, perhaps most important, the perception shared by many academic intellectuals that a certain ekstasis buckled us to the moment, now lost, when, to use Heidegger's zinger, we had actually begun to think. All of this makes a great deal of sense to me, and yet if we are to avoid the vaguely theological narrative wherein trauma, at a certain moment, falls into its industry, then it is necessary to grasp the possibility, indeed the likelihood, of this development in the very emergence of Trauma Studies. Of course, in the loneliness of the last instance, this possibility derives from the increasingly corporate character of the university within contemporary capitalism. But ultimately, in thereby saying everything, one ends up saying very little. Here, Brown's analysis of liberal political discourse strikes me as invaluable, for I see no point in treating academic thought as somehow above or beyond the ideological fray, since, as Kant reminds us, its very autonomy was bestowed upon it by an imperial state. This does not imply that thought is somehow *merely* ideological, only that its concerns—even when utterly inaccessible to taxpayers—are forged in conflict. Trauma Studies, precisely to the extent that it articulates the unspeakable, crafts itself on a discursive field it does not and cannot control. While this suggests, rather obviously, that trauma theory can be read as a wounded attachment, its "fall" into industry, or more particularly the pathos associated with that fall, might actually constitute something else. About this there is, of course, more to say, but the dependence of trauma upon its study, that is, the source of both its ontology and its "voice," produces a structure that necessitates, nay invites, capitalization. To be continued.

Thankfully, the matter I now wish to broach has been beaten to death. This, no doubt, peculiar expression of gratitude reflects the fact that I can be spared a certain rehashing of the all too familiar, while at the same time exploiting it, knowing full well that a certain danger has passed. I am thinking, of course, of the so-called Culture Wars and in particular of those skirmishes that, in the works of Alan Bloom, William Bennett, Dinesh D'Souza, and Roger Kimball, centered around the reputed decline of the university, a decline indexed directly to the supposed incursion there of "tenured radicals." For me, and for many others, this is all part of a protracted national struggle over the political and cultural legacy of the 1960s, a legacy that, in being emblematized in the resignation of Nixon in 1974, has been resuscitated in the failed coup d'état or revenge farce called "Monicagate." Why is it important to frame these issues in this way? There are essentially two reasons. First, when attempting to situate an event like the emergence of Trauma Studies, it is vital that one engages the discourses contending for legitimacy in the very site of this field's emergence. They help us conceive what is at stake in the struggle over new intellectual initiatives within the university, even when such initiatives do not immediately pose the question of the university. This is because nine times out of ten, legitimacy is purchased through the cultivation of studied silences. Second, beneath the forensic cliché—that in charging tenured radicals with having politicized knowledge, neoconservatives were themselves engaging in political work—lies an important "affective" element in the emergence of Trauma Studies, one worth lingering over as an element of the liberalism challenged by Brown. If embarrassment were actually capable of halting the forward march of Christian soldiers, then perhaps it would be enough to establish the hypocritical character of the neoconservative stance on postsecondary education. Unfortunately, it is not. Moreover, what such an emphasis potentially misses is the *ressentiment* at work in the neoconservative attack on the academic Left. Just as there is some truth in the claim that what the Left was blocked from gaining at the national political level during the 1960s, it later sought to gain academically, it is likewise true that neoconservatives in the 1980s (the decade of Trauma Studies' emergence) resented the cultural influence enjoyed by Left academics whose teachings sought to engage the cultural political map redrawn during the '60s. For neoconservatives, the political crises of the '60s retained their menace as long as their cultural supports maintained their legitimacy. Confronted with this sort of challenge, it is indeed worth denouncing the hypocritical character of a position that decries the political character of culture while elaborating a cultural politics that draws its energy from this very power source. But, as I said, hypocrisy is not the issue.[4]

Instead, if one concentrates on the dynamics of *ressentiment*, what comes into focus is the way that the particular resentments agitating the neoconservative meditation on the university belong to a national discourse persistently involved in the moralization of "wounded attachments." To elaborate this, it will be necessary to engage the theme of trauma envy directly, drawing upon it to

---

4. Here, it is again appropriate to acknowledge that Gutiérrez-Jones, in his reading of D'Souza's *The End of Racism*, has, in examining the significance of D'Souza's conflation of race and racism, pinpointed a key later articulation of what I'm calling "hypocrisy." In linking this articulation to the resentful liberal account of race relations, he underscores the urgency of displacing the critique of hypocrisy by exposing its often unacknowledged investment in normativity. This is a start, but the relation between this investment and the general accumulation of something we might call "moral capital" needs to be elaborated.

recontextualize the preceding discussion of the legacy of the '60s. As anyone who was involved in the Left during the '60s knows (and I am speaking here, obviously, of the so-called New Left, thereby acknowledging that there is a much more complicated story to tell here), it did not make its gains as a result of effective organization. Indeed, one might even say that it made its political gains almost in spite of itself. If gains were indeed made (and they were), it was because the movements the Left sought to engage and organize (especially the Civil Rights movement and the Women's Liberation movement) were out ahead of it, even if today these movements are struggling, as it were, to stay in the streets. These movements won ground because their members were able to demonstrate that the paradox of democracy (its formal abstraction from all the particulars it is understood to protect) could be made to register their differences and the demands that gave voice to them. If neoconservatives regard these gains as having definitively "leveled the playing field," it is not because race relations have indeed been fully democratized but because they are promulgating a discourse driven by a self-sustaining logic of, yes, *ressentiment*. Which means what? With regard to racism, it means that neoconservatives want to equate it with a painful past that has now been lived through. For them, only racists or perverts would want to relive this pain by, as we say, playing the race card. More generally, neoconservatives wish desperately to foster a link between traumatic injury and moral authority, a link that can be forged out of the conflicted legacy of the '60s.

What one recognizes in the neoconservative stance on the Culture Wars is something like an envy for what neoconservatives construe as the moral authority ceded to the Left during the '60s. Note that especially today, as Michael Eric Dyson would no doubt insist, the national memory of Dr. King pivots around his "promised land" speech in Memphis instead of those speeches in which he elaborated the political analysis that made him an ally of striking sanitation workers. As we shall see, envy shares a volatile border with guilt, and it is this sharing that invites us to consider whether the Right in general, and contemporary neoconservatives in particular, remain wounded by the guilt their partisans were made to feel as a result of the gains won during the '60s by the "new social movements." A certain white, middle-class, and predominantly heterosexual male perception and experience of the United States was effectively exposed and shaken during the '60s. As a result, the struggle over this legacy on the part of neoconservatives has driven itself on the energy generated by envying the efficacy of guilt by, in effect, seeking the opportunity to visit upon the Left the guilt, perhaps even the shame, "inflicted" upon the Right during the '60s. Two points: First, it is vital here that one recognizes the distinctly moral character of the feeling of guilt that arises when it is articulated within a discourse inflected by what Nietzsche would call the Judeo-Christian tradition. In other words, guilt is the mask worn by neoconservative partisans seeking to snatch victory from the jaws of defeat while at the same time denying the existence of hostilities. Second, it is equally vital to recognize the stakes of any move to reduce trauma to a moral problem. In short, inscribed in such a reduction is the recipe for generating a desire to experience that which authorizes the specifically moral condemnation of others, or what I am calling the envy of trauma.

Lest I be misunderstood, I am not suggesting that the new social movements of the '60s moralized the traumas of racism, sexism, class, and sexual privilege. On the contrary, my proposal is that Benjamin was right. History, now as before, remains in the hands of the victors, and, regardless of how shaken it was by the crises of the '60s, the Right has retained its right to write history. The work of Noam Chomsky, among many others—all devoted to exposing the illusion of a liberal media bias—has made this point well, and though this work might be usefully supplemented by that being done on the ideological narrowcasting of contemporary television (take, for example, Avital Ronell's [1994] essay "Trauma TV"), nothing I might say here could render it any more compelling. To put the basic point very reductively: the issue is not whether, for example, sexual promiscuity is condoned on television, but whether heteronormativity is. The very fact that the debate over alleged bias is cast in such narrow terms (Is adultery punished? Are fathers "bashed?") is the evidence of a certain cultural hegemony of the Right. Under such circumstances, our collectively mediated memory of the '60s becomes subject to an agenda that profits from the moralization of trauma, from, that is, a reconstruction of the '60s as a nationally traumatic decade lacking the "moral compass" neoconservatives now carry. Thus it is precisely in the representation of trauma that the work of moralization begins. To grasp what is at stake here, it is important that one recognizes the neoconservative desire to deny that its partisans bear any properly political responsibility for the traumas inflicted upon blacks and women (in strictly juridical terms, this introduces the specter of "compensation"). Surely I am not alone in my continual astonishment over the aplomb with which fervent believers in "original sin" insist that they are innocent of the crimes of their fathers, that only those "directly responsible" for hate crimes and the like are answerable to the charge of racism. Privilege, as it were, has its privileges. At work here is an interest, perhaps even a desire, to deprive the guilt produced by, say, the charge of racism, of any sociopolitical cause, any basis either in the political behavior of neoconservatives or the survival of capitalism now confused both here and abroad with democracy itself. As is well known, these relations are often reconciled with a certain evangelical Christianity through the exertions of management gurus like Mack Hammond, whose televised "Winner's Minute" daily exhorted CEOs to teach their employees how, in effect, to wriggle through the eye of a needle.[5]

---

5. A recurrent segment of the morning news and weather program broadcast by the local ABC affiliate in Minneapolis, the "Winner's Minute" is now off the air. For nearly two years, however, it buttonholed sleepy middle-class commuters, beseeching them to bring biblical principles to bear on their careers. Addressing specifically managers, the host/sponsor, Mack Hammond, used his sixty seconds to propose, in a tone utterly devoid of irony, that a strict analogy obtained between Christ's relation with his disciples and a manager's relation with "his" employees, thereby distancing himself from those who simply insist that the Bible does not oppose the accumulation of wealth. Some of his juxtapositions were quite chilling, so chilling in fact that his "ministry" has now morphed into the more typical format of the business seminar, having lost his television audience. Real TV indeed.

Once deprived of any social provenance or dimension, all traumas become grist for moral discourse, not just in the sense that they are treated as resulting from the moral failings of their perpetrators (when human), but more decisively in that they authorize a mode of criticism that necessarily calls for moral redress. Trauma serves in such a context to name the stunning wound that produces moral authority. As such, it facilitates the constitution of a plane upon which "reverse discrimination" becomes not only commensurable with racial discrimination, but the very conceptual means by which one might reduce protest about the latter to the morally suspect logic of "tit for tat." In relation to such a plane, one can argue that a far more serious trauma is inflicted when privilege and competence are subordinated to the morally "primitive" desire for compensation than when privilege was first secured. The second state of affairs is deemed innocent, perhaps even naïve, whereas the first is regarded as deliberately vindictive. The refusal to offer the other cheek, in its repudiation of sublime alterity, is made to verge on immorality. By teasing out the logic of *ressentiment* at the heart of contemporary liberalism, Brown's *States of Injury* argues precisely that the current avatar of the new social movements of the '60s, namely, identity politics, is caught up in this political nightmare, a nightmare in which the struggle for radical democracy authorizes itself through "wounded attachments," or, in my terms, trauma envy. In this sense, the circle has now been closed: envy for an authority defensively construed as moral on the part of neoconservatives now expresses itself in an envy for the end of "mere" politics, that is, for an ethics of difference that, in recasting the political as mere might, steers us away from the task of rethinking it. The circle must be broken.

A more thorough genealogy of the phenomenon I am tracing would have to take up Isaac Ray's *The Medical Jurisprudence of Insanity* (1838) and the still controversial McNaughton Rules. These last are the procedural guidelines developed in Britain for pursuing the now much-used and much-maligned "insanity defense" first deployed by Daniel McNaughton when he was arraigned, in 1843, on the charge of attempted assassination. And this is not because

insanity is the standard to which all so-called extenuating circumstances aspire, but because by admitting the prior history of the
perpetrator, the British courts made it possible for defense attor-
neys throughout the Anglophone world to deploy the forensic strategy of comparative trauma calculation. Thus, when more than a
century later Leslie Abramson sought to confront the jury of the
Menendez brothers with the abusive history of their childhood, she
was explicitly asking its members to weigh the two traumas of
parricide and child abuse. What is of interest here is not the legal
reasoning at stake (Abramson's was proven wrong), but rather the
symptom that it represents. When the law itself is traumatized, that
is, when it is confronted with an unspeakably infinite regress of
violations, each one madder than the next, trauma acquires transcendental status. Everything is potentially traumatic. Under these
circumstances, trauma has come to be invested with such authority and legitimacy that it elicits a concomitant desire to have suffered it, or if not the unspeakable event itself, then the testimonial
agency it is understood to produce. The fact that Nicole Simpson
did not survive the trauma of domestic abuse did not stop Clark
and Darden from attempting—in advocating in her (and, let us not
forget, Ron Goldman's) absence—to weigh the traumatic character of her experience off against the trauma of institutional racism
proffered continually by her husband's defense team. In the end, one
might even argue that the reassuring reiteration of mixed couples
(Nicole and O.J./Marcia and Chris) ultimately worked to intensify
the specific gravity of institutional racism as a traumatic element.
Certainly few would be shocked to learn that parties sympathetic
to O.J. were keen on having the rumors of a relationship between
Clark and Darden circulate as widely as possible.

But what specifically does this have to do with Trauma Studies? Some might argue that, to the extent that coming to terms with
the Holocaust was a crucial aspect of its emergence, Trauma Studies is very much aligned with a distinctly academic incarnation of
identity politics. My point is somewhat different, however. In accordance with a strictly dialectical dynamic, the very banalization
of trauma that renders it unspeakable in daily life and the euphe-

misms of medical jargon ("repetitive trauma syndrome") finds its antinomy in academic obsession. To no historical materialist's surprise, this dialectic, indeed its very sublation, is to be found in the concept of trauma. In this sense, trauma was always inclined toward capitalization. In a social context where its centrality to political debate has rendered it subject to the verbal equivalent of a *Bildverbot*, it was necessary, perhaps even inevitable, that this strategic reticence be counteracted by a certain explicitness. That this explicitness has been tinged with a certain desperation might well reflect the fact that the preoccupation with it emanated from an institution that seemed destined for ruin throughout the decades of the 1980s and 1990s, indeed an institution where the relation between speech and freedom has become variously politicized. That scholars in danger of losing their careers would turn to the task of thinking through and inventorying the traumatic character of their lives is hardly surprising. Nor is it particularly problematic. What is unsettling is the way that the academic study of trauma, perhaps in an act of sublime defiance, has rarely if ever sought to reflect upon the turf it shared with what Brown calls liberalism. In saying this I am, of course, aware of how politically charged the legacy of liberalism itself has become. However, if we are ever to find "the real killers," it will be because a movement has emerged that refuses to argue with the Right on its own terms. There is no danger in letting liberalism go, once we recognize that democracy and capitalism are not synonyms.

## TRAUMATIC COLONEL

There is, obviously, a great deal more to say here about the unsettling character of the academic study of trauma. I will not be able here, if indeed anywhere, to say it all. However, to say some of what needs to be said and, in the process, to further illuminate my association of trauma with envy, it is essential that the centrality of psychoanalysis to Trauma Studies be addressed squarely. Rather than assume the burden of engaging the entirety of the often brilliant work being done on this front, I will instead concentrate on the justly influential rereading of psychoanalysis (especially Lacanian psychoanalysis) still underway by Slavoj Žižek. Although his work is not typically included within the Trauma Studies canon, what makes it especially pertinent here is Žižek's persistent recourse to the concept of trauma. Indeed, whereas Freud was more inclined to invoke trauma (for example, "war trauma") as a repercussive event (however complex), Žižek has moved to render trauma as something of an ontological category. In the brilliantly provocative rearticulation of Marx and Freud that organizes *The Sublime Object of Ideology*, this move occurs as the motor of ideological identification comes to be lodged not in the realm of the imaginary, but in the subject's structural relation to the limits of symbolization. Additionally, Žižek's work has the virtue of being involved in a historical reading of Lacan that, on the one hand, facilitates the "plotting" of the concept of trauma, while on the other, it prompts us to think about the moment, the situation, of Žižek's reading.

Conditioned by the serendipitous fusion between a word processor and "schtick," Žižek's writing invites a reading attentive to the rhythms of serial variation. Even a casual glance over "The Object as a Limit of Discourse: Approaches to the Lacanian Real" (1998) and "Which Subject of the Real?" from *The Sublime Object of Ideology* (1989) reveals that whole sections have been lifted from the earlier essay to the later one, a fact duly noted in the acknowledgments. No doubt because a later preoccupation with the subject replaces that with the object, the sequencing of subsections is changed, but—as if to supplement the statement of his point with its enunciation—the Real returns repeatedly, and the question that his analysis prompts us to pose is: Which instance of the Lacanian Real is this? Is it the McGuffin/MacGuffin or, perhaps, the mute embodiment of an impossible jouissance? Though interesting in their own way, such questions are not mine. Instead, let us try to make sense of two things: (a) the link between trauma and the Real, and (b) the political value of such a link in the context of what I have called the trauma industry.

As concerns the link between trauma and the Real, consider the following formulations:

> The real is then at the same time the hard, impenetrable kernel resisting symbolization *and* a purely chimerical entity which has in itself no ontological consistency. . . . As we have already seen, this is precisely what defines the notion of a traumatic event: a point of failure of symbolization, but at the same time never given in its positivity. It can only be constructed backwards, from its structural effects. All its efficacy lies in these effects, in the distortions it produces in the symbolic universe of the subject. The traumatic event is ultimately just a fantasy-construct filling out a certain void in a symbolic structure and as such the retroactive effect of this structure.[6]

The déjà vu to which this citation refers is triggered in a prior section where the aim was, through a discussion of "traumatism,"[7] to persuade us that during the '60s and '70s, Lacan's approach to the Real resembled more his approach to the Imaginary as elaborated in the '50s. This invites two comments. First, not only is the Real "actually" linked to traumatic events, but, as these remarks make clear, it is conceptually linked to them as well. In other words, the Real is like trauma in that the latter's cause—like the Real itself—is subject to the work of metalepsis, or retroactive construction. Moreover, this "likeness" is rendered intelligible through an apparently necessary appeal to Lacan's account of traumatism, as though without such an appeal the Real would lack definition. To be sure, other appeals could have been made, but one of the risks consistently taken by Žižek requires that the gesture of exemplification be transferable. Here, this implies that traumatism can serve as a metonym for a series of which it may also be nothing more than a member. Žižek's appeal to traumatism warrants scrutiny

---

6. Žižek 1989, p. 107.
7. Ibid., p. 103.

under the broad heading of what might be called the "politicization of theory," about which more will have to be said.

The second of my two comments bears on the historical register of Žižek's reading. Throughout Žižek's work, one finds him engaged in a low-intensity but nevertheless steady conflict with poststructuralism. When this conflict rises above the quick and dirty thrills of caricature, it seems clear that it is driven by Žižek's desire to cast poststructuralism as the thief of his (or perhaps psychoanalysis's) enjoyment. In accord with a logic specified by Žižek himself, what the former enjoys is an obscene relation to the Real that it refuses to psychoanalysis. To wit, instead of the specific impossibility of the Real constituting its reality, poststructuralism posits the impossibility of any Real intelligible to us. To expose this theft of defect, Žižek outmaneuvers the most extant Lacanian criticism—criticism that has long centered around the conceptual bric-a-brac of the imaginary and the symbolic—by setting out to unearth the Lacanian Real. Almost immediately he discovers that this Real has a history, indeed the very decade-graduated timeline charted in the discussion of traumatism. Here, too, an enabling disjunction between the statement and its enunciation is exploited if not exactly pronounced: just as the Real is theorized as that which arises, as it were, after the fact, it is shown to be returning to where it always was in every decade prior to the '80s, that is, prior to the publication of the text in which its inevitable return is cast as an expression of its ontology. Its dialectical status as both kernel and chimera, predicting as it does the very procedures of Žižek's reading, is difficult to regard as anything other than an effect of that very reading, and no accumulation of "illustrations" (whether from film, opera, or contemporary geopolitics) can erase this bond with poststructuralism, which must then be cast as what deprives Lacanian psychoanalysis of its full enjoyment of the Real Thing. What interests me here is not, however, the question of Žižek's critique of poststructuralism. Instead, what is crucial is the appeal to trauma as the concept (and, presumably, the experience, since lately we have been treated to more and more of Žižek's "army stories") through which one gains access to the Real or, to cleave closer to the terms of the citation, through which the dialectical character of the Real is made manifest through a failure of symbolization that is, properly speaking, traumatic, if not trauma itself.

When all is said and done, Žižek's appeal to trauma is not really driven by a theoretical need to clarify the concept of the Real, but instead by a political need to forge a link between the Real and trauma that allows psychoanalysis to have, as it were, the last word about trauma. That word is "void." To the extent that "void" also designates the inessential essence of the subject, thereby grounding the agency of the subject in trauma, its theorization is an expression of trauma envy. Given the link forged within liberalism between trauma and moral authority, the current preoccupation in and around psychoanalytical theory with things ethical should come as no surprise.[8] Thus, one might say, the quarrel with poststructuralism is a feint. The "real" enemies, as becomes clear in "Multiculturalism, or The Logic of Multinational Capitalism" (1997) and "A Leftist Plea for 'Eurocentrism'" (1998), are those partisans

---

8. I realize, of course, that here I appear to be treating ethics and morality as interchangeable. No less a figure than Lacan, in the opening of *Seminar VII*, might be invoked as my warrant, but since it is clear that I have a quarrel with the ethical turn, this is a gesture that would not ring true. In lexicographic practice a certain professional and secular orientation is used to separate out the properly ethical from the moral, and since Lacan was persistently contesting the grounds of his school's exclusion from the international psychoanalytical community, such a focus makes a considerable sense. However, Habermas, in Chapter 4 of *The Structural Transformation of the Public Sphere* (1961 and thus roughly contemporaneous with *Seminar VII*), provides one with the historical and perhaps even political means to distinguish the two. His discussion is far too rich to summarize in a note, but one of its conclusions is that ethics came to serve as the means by which—through the medium of the bourgeois public sphere—politics is brought under the sway of morality. Kant's discussion of pure practical reason figures prominently here as it does in Lacan. And while I realize that my concern about the displacement of politics would thus appear predicted in the very concept of ethics, what Habermas alerts us to is the more consequential matter of thinking about the university as an institution caught up in the structural transformation of the public sphere. Is an ethical stance sufficient to forestall the ruin of an institution whose ordinary routines and procedures are predicated on the maintenance of an ethical articulation of the relation between morality and politics? I have my doubts.

of identity politics who, by insisting upon the traumatic character of racism, colonialism, and the countless quotidian violations that maintain the cultural and political hegemony of the West, have called into question both the analytical integrity and the political efficacy of psychoanalysis. Their point is not the familiar rant against the "bourgeois" character of psychoanalysis, but rather such partisans seek to "smear" psychoanalysis with the charge of complicity, as if to say, "What adjustment must be made to the analysis of how to 'go on' *dans le merde*, when one indeed lives in shit?" Lest I be misunderstood, I am quite sympathetic to Žižek's attack, particularly on multiculturalism (indeed, his position shares much with Brown's), especially as he seeks to confront it with the task of reflecting upon its own relation to multinational or, as we now say, global capitalism. But when these critiques invoke "traumatic jouissance" to clinch their arguments (as, for example, occurs in "Multiculturalism"[9]), one cannot help but recognize a certain envy at work within them. It is as if psychoanalysis must be released from its guilt over the matter of its complicity in "real traumas," and to do so, it is bent to the task of discovering within its own conceptual resources the "mother of all traumas," the trauma that trumps the moral authority of all comers, the trauma that is the subject's relation to the Real itself. Armed with this strictly fetishistic concept, Žižek is in a position to undermine the credibility of all witnessing, arguing that Eurocentrism is not racist, it is the multiculturalists—precisely in their implied repudiation of the irreducible antagonism structuring the social order—who are the Real racists. As stunning and intellectually provocative as such reversals are, they appear driven by a politics of theory that, even as it insists upon the need to reflect upon the nature of "true politics," never quite manages to follow through.

When, at the commemorative conference that produced the volume *Michel Foucault: Philosopher* (1992), Jacques-Alain Miller identified the need for an "archaeology of psychoanalysis,"[10] he blazed a path that few others have taken. Žižek, who has discov-

---

9. Žižek 1997, p. 34.
10. Armstrong 1992, p. 64.

ered Lacan's teachings in every nook and cranny of the West's cultural storehouse, would appear to number among the few who have, and yet this is precisely what seems lacking in his approach to the Lacanian Real. The point is not that this Real must be subordinated to a realer real, for example, the one Sokal and Bricmont think that they are defending from poststructuralists and other science-phobes.[11] The point is rather to situate a concept so that its emergence can be projected across a complex graph that registers the intricate and uneven antagonisms that structure cultural politics. Doing so would render more conspicuous the appeal of trauma as a concept on which to prop up an account of the Real. To be sure, one would have to foreground here Žižek's desire, as a Slovenian public intellectual writing in the aftermath of 1989, to find the common ground on which to open a dialogue with potential interlocuters, but even so a certain vigilance remains necessary. Without it, the proximity between what Brown calls "wounded attachments" and the mantra "the wound is healed only by the spear that smote you" passes unremarked.

Some concluding thoughts then about envy. In my opening, envy is attached to the trauma of castration. I want now also to link it to the displacement of politics in the domain of theory. Within the corpus of psychoanalysis, envy is one of the more undertheorized concepts, despite the fact that it plays a decisive role in Freud's account of sexual difference. Freud himself had little more to say about it. Even in the 1920s when he returned to the problematic of the *Three Essays* and the concept of *Penisneid*, he tended to foreground the latter's relation to *Eifersucht*, or jealousy. And while Ernst Jones was among the very earliest to probe and ultimately contest the symmetry organizing Freud's account of sexual differentiation, it is

---

11. In *Fashionable Nonsense* (1998), Alan Sokal (best known for the hoax he perpetrated against the Left academic periodical, *Social Text*) and Jean Bricmont launch a full-scale attack on French poststructuralist philosophy, arguing that it is largely based on widespread and wanton misuse of scientific concepts. Motivating this misuse is, they allege, a repudiation of scientific realism that has its roots—and the nationalistic character of their rhetoric is unmistakable—in Cartesian rationalism. I have weighed in on this debate elsewhere. See Mowitt 1997.

Melanie Klein, in the pages of *Envy and Gratitude* (1957), who squarely confronts the task of thinking through the concept of envy. However, before turning to the details of her discussion and discerning there the "recipe" for a displacement of the political, a prior, albeit "contextual," observation is called for. One of the features of Freud's return to the *Three Essays*, for example, in "Some Psychological Consequences of the Anatomical Distinction between the Sexes" from 1925, is the prominence there of a distinctly antifeminist rhetoric. Nowadays, this hardly bears repeating. However, what I am concerned to stress is that woven tightly into the very theoretical articulation of envy is a struggle between psychoanalysis and an earlier avatar of what we would now characterize as one of the leading columns in the march of contemporary identity politics, namely, Western feminism. Thus in addition to tracking how envy serves to frame the "trauma" of sexual differentiation, it will be important to consider how this intellectual and ultimately political struggle remains indissociable from the frame. Part of why envy emerges here as the pivotal concept has to do with this very situation.

Klein, of course, inherits a vital legacy within the international emergence of psychoanalysis, a legacy that certainly reaches back to Jones and Karl Abraham (one of her own analysts), but even more immediately to Helene Deutsch and Karen Horney. Horney in particular is crucial, not only because Klein credits her with being the first to examine the link between Oedipus and the castration complex, but because in essays such as "On the Genesis of the Castration Complex in Women" (1922) and "The Flight from Womanhood" (1926), Horney lays the groundwork for the displacement of castration that Klein's own discussion of envy presupposes. Specifically, in "Womanhood," where Horney is concerned with reinstating the analytical centrality of maternity, she makes inspired use of Georg Simmel's *Philosophische Kultur* to argue that if Simmel is right—that "our whole civilization is a masculine civilization"—then wouldn't this apply to psychoanalysis in general and to Freud's account of female sexuality in particular? After thematizing the methodological problem mythically resolved through the figure of

Tiresias, she then proposes a critique of the masculinist character of Freud's account of castration, an account that centers on a clearly retroactive overinvestment in the penis. Ultimately, this leads Horney to split envy (between primary and secondary envy), thereby discovering in the greater guilt experienced by women the motor for Simmel's "masculine civilization" and the devaluation of maternity. This discovery is important for Klein's work because, although her "feminism" is less conspicuous, the notion that psychoanalysis might be caught up in the dynamic of cultural reproduction, and as such is a partisan enterprise, is fundamental to her treatment of envy. Because Simmel was part of the intellectual circle that informed Adorno's consciousness, surely it would be fair to say that this orientation might well be what is expressing itself in the latter's reading of Nietzsche. As I have argued, this reading recognizes without yet thematizing the dynamics of trauma envy.

The work that was to culminate in *Envy and Gratitude* began in 1955 with the presentation before the Nineteenth Congress of the International Psychoanalytic Association of a paper later titled "A Study of Envy and Gratitude." The key proposition of the later study was formulated here, namely, that envy is not first directed toward the penis, but toward the breast. Long regarded as psychoanalysis's quintessential "breast woman," Klein's position in this comparatively late text is far from surprising. However, certain of its details invite elaboration. First, of course, is the fact that in this construction, Klein is carrying forward Horney's insight about "masculine civilization." By subordinating the penis to the breast, she, in effect, recasts the trauma of castration as an echo of the more primordial trauma of nursing and ultimately weaning. Here, not only is the logic of sexual difference indexed to one's relation to the female and ultimately maternal body, but clearly the defining trauma of castration has been displaced by another trauma. Secondly, this displacement is lodged at the heart of a full-blown psychoanalytical account of envy. Though reluctant to characterize this in terms of necessity, a brief elaboration of Klein's account of envy will show why the displacement of the penis by the breast is not linked simply by accident to the theme of envy.

As though she had consulted either a dictionary or a commentary on the seven cardinal sins, Klein opens her discussion by attempting to isolate envy from jealousy and greed. She writes: "Envy is the angry feeling that another person possesses and enjoys something desirable—the envious impulse being to take it away or to spoil it."[12] This feeling arises in nursing because the breast, though a vital potential source of gratification, is also, for structural as well as physical reasons, fallible. Consequently, the "good feed," as Klein dubs it, is elusive. For this reason, the child (male or female) comes to divide the breasts along moral lines, that is, between the good and the bad, treating the breasts themselves as both the source of the child's enjoyment and the bane of its existence. The breast appears to withhold, almost sadistically, that which the child most enjoys, thereby stirring the envious impulse. It is crucial here that Klein characterizes one of the aims of this impulse in terms of a desire "to spoil" the breast and, by extension, the creativity of the maternal body. I stress this not simply because such a characterization underscores the extent to which the theory of castration fits within the movement of a certain analytical misogyny, but because it decisively complicates the concept of envy. How so?

When Klein writes "the envious impulse being to take it away or spoil it," she invites us to consider that the object of envy is susceptible to two sorts of action, one conspicuously more "virtual" than the other. "Spoiling" the breast involves (at least in English) the doting that parents often complain about in the parenting of others, yet it can also involve a strategy that, in reframing the breast's meaning, recasts the relation between the child and its mother so as to ruin the breast for her and, in effect, to deprive the mother of the breast symbolically. It is no longer what the mother values the breast as, but rather what the child's behavior implies about its value. If the breast thereby becomes a "gift that takes," then the child is positioned so as to proclaim, with all the ruthless precision of belatedness, its victimage. Envy, then, is not simply organized around an object; instead, it takes as its object a condi-

---

12. Klein 1986, p. 212.

tion of relating, indeed, the very condition where the guilt that might arise from an envious impulse can be causally attributed to and, in effect, be made the responsibility of another. Gratitude, of course, is the counterweight here. It is clear, however, that the gratification from which gratitude derives has been all but preempted by the constraints operating on the "good feed," obliging Klein to concede that its relevance arises primarily in the struggle to give shape, typically within analysis, to the psychic contents at play in belatedness. With regard to this last, Klein is no innovator. For her, as for Freud, belatedness designates the structural delay that organizes the link between meaning and experience. However, though both envy and gratitude are rooted in the vicissitudes of nursing, the significance of gratitude exhibits what might be called a belated belatedness. It comes later and is thus more accessible, in a certain sense, to the work of analysis. Precisely why this is so remains unclear in Klein, but her discussion prompts one to conclude that giving thanks is predicated on the perceived receipt of a "unique gift" that would thus appear to be as quixotic as grace itself. The step from the gift of gratitude to forgiveness is a short one, and once taken it is possible to discern Moses (the lawgiver) and Christ (the savior) in Klein's two breasts.

One provocative consequence of this treatment of envy is that in it, envy is made to share something essential with trauma. In Klein's formulations, this sharing expresses itself in the cause of envy, a cause that in depending for its legibility on its own effects remains indissociable from envy itself. When we recognize that this trauma is expressly designed to displace another (what Deutsch herself had called the "trauma of castration"), not only are we invited to regard Klein's account as envious, but we are positioned to recognize what constrains or otherwise limits cultural critique in the stealth pleonasm of trauma envy. What is at stake here is the political itself.[13]

---

13. Throughout *A Critique of Postcolonial Reason* (1999), Gayatri Chakravorty Spivak draws on Klein's treatment of envy as a way to problematize the status of the political within postcolonial discourse. Squaring off against her redoubtable

One need not turn to those passages in Klein where envy and resentment are aligned to discern the presence of *ressentiment* in her text. That it is there has less to do with her than with the psychoanalytical field itself at mid-century. The significance of its presence, as Brown acknowledges, has been forcefully articulated by Nietzsche, who spun out the concept of *ressentiment* as perhaps the red thread in the genealogy of morals. Since psychoanalysis preceded him, he was unlikely to have discerned the unconscious in what he called "willing against the will," but it is difficult to imagine that he would have failed to recognize the significance of the proximity between the past, present, and future illusions of Christianity and those of the heteronormative family. Of course, in *The Genealogy of Morals*, Nietzsche makes only passing reference to envy, but it is clear that his entire account of breeding "promise keepers" and the necessary link between memory and pain presupposes the importance, nay the centrality, of trauma. This is vital because it underscores the link between trauma and morality, not just in the sense that trauma might be construed as essential to the emergence of morality, but in the sense that morality is thus cast as the essential remedy for trauma, thereby vanishing into the chimera (or is that the kernel?) of the absent cause. Max Scheler, in his own study of *ressentiment*,[14] has drawn attention to the distinctive ways in which this construction of morality belongs to the political and cultural triumph of the bourgeoisie. While I remain unconvinced by his effort to separate Christian love from the genealogy of morals, the indisputable merit of his project lies in its clarification of the link between morality and capital, a link thema-

---

sparring partner, Benita Parry, Spivak uses Klein to legitimate the concept of a constitutive violence that founds the political, whether at the institutional or geopolitical level. Her expressed aim is to repudiate the claim—typically, in her mind, advanced by feminist scholars—that if approached with sufficient theoretical and practical care all geopolitical grievances can be redressed. While I share with Spivak a commitment to retreat and reiterate the political, especially once we have attempted to reckon with the concept of a constitutive violence, the preceding discussion of trauma implies that Klein's concept of envy may be, well, spoiled.

14. Scheler 1972.

tized in Nietzsche's discussion of *Schuld* (both guilt and debt) and remarked in Brown. The redemption of Christian love in Scheler is clearly motivated by Nietzsche's bad press, that is, the oft-repeated contention that any wholesale repudiation of morality leads implacably to fascism. This is, beyond question, a crucial problem. Indeed, I hope it is clear that my quarrel with the ethical is not about its necessity, but its sufficiency. However, if the rich and conflicted scholarship on the Holocaust of the last half-century has taught us anything, it is that what remains most difficult and urgent to discern about this catastrophe is not its moral significance or character, but how the conditions for it arose within a world that *remains* ours. True, these conditions include the status of the ethical, but it is nevertheless a remarkable feature of liberal discourse in the West that the Holocaust is the event that, in cleaving the moral universe from top to bottom, is regarded as providing humanity's moral compass with its poles. In relation to it, "we" know with a certain certainty where we stand. Indeed.

What troubles me here is not, however, this certainty, which is of course another matter altogether. Rather what troubles me is the way this casts the political in relation to the ethical. For me, the issue is not about priority, but about efficacy. When the political is conceived as a matter of taking sides, specifically sides separated along the fault between good and evil (whether banal or not), its link to the labor of "making" sides, of producing and advancing positions, is obscured. What is risked in this obscurity is not just the elaboration of the ethical as such (its production as "that which matters most"), but the importance of the political as the field within which groups struggle in and for power. Here, I would submit, the vital question is not "Whose trauma provides one with greater moral capital?" (as though the matter of efficacy could be exhausted in the "capture of speech"), but "What kinds of institutions, relations, practices need to be forged so that the trauma of capital accumulation can be abated?" Here I share Gutiérrez-Jones's impatience with the objective of inclusivity to the extent that the value of this principle is based on the presumption that it offers a moral remedy for a political problem. Obviously, the conditions analyzed in this paper require—given its deliberate aim of trauma-tizing trauma—that this characterization of capital accumulation be deemed, in turn, envious. I appreciate that, but insist, all the same, that the question of the political value of trauma and its theory still needs to be posed explicitly. What follows is up to those who hold themselves response-able to and for such an act. For my part, I suspect that regardless of the fate of Trauma Studies, my partial-ity for red over green will persist.

## REFERENCES

Adorno, T. (1974). *Minima Moralia: Reflections from Damaged Life*, trans. E. Jephcott. London: New Left Books.

Armstrong, T., ed. (1992). *Michel Foucault: Philosopher*. New York: Routledge.

Brown, W. (1995). *States of Injury*. Princeton, NJ: Princeton University Press.

Gordon, A. F., and Newfield, C. (1996). *Mapping Multiculturalism*. Min-neapolis: University of Minnesota Press.

Gutiérrez-Jones, C. (1998). Injury by design. *Cultural Critique* 40:73–102.

Habermas, J. (1961). *The Structural Transformation of the Public Sphere*, trans. T. Burger and F. Lawrence. Cambridge, MA: MIT Press, 1989.

Klein, M. (1986). *The Selected Melanie Klein*, ed. J. Mitchell. New York: Free Press.

Mowitt, J. (1992). *Text: The Genealogy of an Antidisciplinary Object*. Durham, NC: Duke University Press.

——— (1997). Survey and discipline: literary pedagogy in the context of cultural studies. In *Class Issues: Pedagogy, Cultural Studies, and the Public Sphere*, ed. A. Kumar. New York: New York University Press.

Ronell, A. (1994). Trauma TV. In *Finitude's Score: Essays for the End of the Millenium*. Lincoln: University of Nebraska Press.

Scheler, M. (1972). *Ressentiment*, trans. W. Holdheim. New York: Schocken.

Spivak, G. C. (1999). *A Critique of Postcolonial Reason*. Cambridge, MA: Harvard University Press.

Žižek, S. (1989). *The Sublime Object of Ideology*. London: Verso.

——— (1997). Multiculturalism, or the logic of multinational capitalism. *New Left Review* 225 (September–October):28–51.

# Index